Centralization and Autonomy

Centralization and Autonomy

A Study in Organization Behaviour

Michael Z. Brooke, MA, PhD

PRAEGER SPECIAL STUDIES • PRAEGER SCIENTIFIC

New York • Philadelphia • Eastbourne, UK
Toronto • Hong Kong • Tokyo • Sydney

Published in 1984 by Praeger Publishers
CBS Educational and Professional Publishing
A Division of CBS Inc.
521 Fifth Avenue, New York 10175, USA.

British Library Cataloguing in Publication Data

Brooke, Michael Z.
Centralization and autonomy.
1. Decentralization in management
I. Title
658.4'02   HD50

ISBN 0-03-068674-1

Library of Congress Catalog Card Number 84-060042

Typeset by Phoenix Photosetting, Chatham
Printed in Great Britain by Mackays of Chatham Ltd

Last digit is print no: 9 8 7 6 5 4 3 2 1

Contents

Preface

The author, in commending this book to his readers, wishes them a good voyage. The route along which he has attempted to escort them is the reverse of that which he has travelled himself. I began (some twenty years ago) by becoming curious about how the destinies of some large and extraordinarily complicated companies were in fact guided, if at all. The attempt to satisfy that curiosity has led me to study the organizations at close quarters; it has also led me to make enquiries around the numerous fields of thought where others have wrestled with similar problems.

The arrangement of chapters in parts I and II corresponds with the route in reverse, Chapter 2 reflecting investigations conducted after evidence used later in the book had been collected. The final part, of conclusion and comment, completes an arrangement which, it is hoped, will prove logical and digestible. For those readers who do not have the time to make the journey as planned, the book can also be used as a work of reference; the subject index is designed to suit this purpose. The outline and the aims are summarized in Chapter 1, where the title is defined and explained.

There are other personal statements to be made, including a mention of the dilemma that faces any author who dreads the accusation that he is repeating what he has written before, but is still more sensitive to the charge that he is assuming that his readers know his previous work. This dilemma applies to Chapters 11–17 which contain new material but rooted in a background of earlier publications. Cross-references to these publications are included only when essential to avoid long explanations of limited relevance.

The issues raised on these pages are topical for both theoretical and practical debates, and the author is glad to join in correspondence with any readers moved to write; especially welcome would be notes about control across the frontiers of organizations—an issue which crops up occasionally on these pages and is likely to be increasingly discussed at a time of hiving-off and management buy-outs. A companion volume on the topic is planned.

MICHAEL Z. BROOKE

Acknowledgements

Centralization and autonomy has been under way for many years and would never have come into existence without the help of the *Social Science Research Council* who made me a substantial research award in the 1970s and, more recently, a personal research grant to help complete the book. Much is also owed to my former colleagues, Chris Cragg and Michael Hurford, both of whom read the manuscript and whose contributions appear in almost every chapter. I also have to thank David Wilson (of the University of Bradford Management Centre) for many helpful suggestions. I have to thank three doyens of organization studies—Derek Pugh, John Child and David Hickson—who gave encouragement and advice at a critical time. Peter Jennergren, whose contributions to the subject are well known, has written part of Chapter 3 (3.4). Numerous others have given assistance including: the researchers who worked with me on both sides of the Atlantic especially (but not exclusively) Michael Dorrell, Mary Black and Paul Neville in Manchester and Susan Boucher and Peter Johnson in Kingston, Canada; Peter Smith and other colleagues who have discussed the subject with me in Britain as well as in the United States and in the eleven other countries where I have had the opportunity to lead seminars and join in dialogues; to the scholars in the various disciplines mentioned in Chapter 2 who have patiently explained their various approaches and to the officials of the organizations considered in Chapter 8; to my numerous friends in the field of international business, especially Lars-Gunnar Mattson and Dave Rutenberg who both organized well-timed seminars (one in Sweden and the other in Canada); to the many hundreds of executives in international companies who have endured my persistent questioning. Apart from this last group, most of whom prefer to remain anonymous, those who gave advice and assistance are thanked in notes attached to the relevant passages. The author is grateful to his innumerable advisers while disassociating them from any blame for what he has written. The responsibility for any shortcomings is, of course, mine.

Finally, I have to thank my family and friends for tolerating the intrusion of centralization and a lack of autonomy especially during the last months of the book's preparation, and to express my gratitude to my secretary, Elizabeth Hickson, who put up with countless changes and revisions to complete the final draft in an impossibly short time. I have no doubt that she would continue typing unperturbed while the *Titanic* was sinking, and only hope it did not feel as if that was exactly what she was doing.

Part I
Approaches to the Subject

After an introduction outlining the purpose of the book, this part contains six chapters which examine concepts relevant to the understanding of centralization and autonomy followed by one on non-commercial organizations, a discussion of methodology and a final chapter (10) summarizing the contents of a theory of centralization and autonomy.

1 Autonomy and Centralization: An Essay in Understanding

Organizations can be studied from three points of view—those of the fixer, the prophet and the bystander.[1]

The fixer likes his organization, admires its contribution to the good life, and feels at home in it. He launches investigations designed to correct both the master plan and the humble detail; he sets out to develop structures that are easy to live with and that cater for human rather than material needs. He sees himself as a useful citizen, destined to improve the world.

The prophet does not feel at home in an organization and looks for upheaval and radical change. He talks a questioning language of revolution and of the demands of existence. He sees himself as a liberator, destined to change the world.

The bystander lays claim to a neutral standpoint, as an objective collector of data who assembles hypotheses and takes a clinical look at the waywardness of society. He sees himself as a detached witness, uncontaminated by controversy.

This book is designed to contribute to all three interests—structuring, questioning and observing. In unravelling the much-pursued but always elusive processes that underlie centralization and autonomy, it pin-points a single issue with a double face, the where and how of decision-making.

The author's interest in the subject started with attempts to sketch out the forming and implementing of policies in the widely scattered units of an international firm. Intriguing folklore and legend confused an already complex system beset with assertion and counter-assertion about where authority lay. Much excitement, as well as intrigue in another sense, surrounded the struggle for supremacy and autonomy, and meetings summoned to unravel the topics were well supported. There had to be a way of sorting myth from reality, of staking out the landmarks whatever the starting-point. That was the idea behind this book: to tease out the meaning of the words, to construct a theory which would promote a closer understanding of the subject, and to make possible more accurate diagnosis and action. To put this idea into practice, a review was undertaken of relevant work in different disciplines and under different circumstances. The final purpose can be summarized in four propositions:

(1) that organizations waste resources (human and material) by adopting a

3

cycle of change between centralization and autonomy; good reasons are given for the changes when they occur, but the effect of the cycle is to cause a fatalistic attitude that the swings backwards and forwards are part of the natural order and cannot be broken;

(2) that the practical problem of breaking the cycle can only be cracked by an intellectual apparatus that penetrates the meaning of the processes at work;

(3) that the intellectual apparatus requires a contribution from many skills and disciplines which will lead to a body of theory sensitive to the dynamic and relative nature of the subject;

(4) that this body of theory can be stated in a series of propositions that apply to organizations under given circumstances and conditions rather than universally.

Attention is increasingly paid to the ability of formal organizations to match the need for coordination with demands for participation and democracy. The opportunities for central planning and disposal of resources are balanced against the advantages of delegation and the restrictions imposed by that planning. Centralization is supposed to help in allocating resources and in setting goals for the whole organization. It is also supposed to conflict with a desire for personal autonomy, satisfaction, quicker responses to external demands, and a need to ensure the loyalty of participants by giving them more responsibility. Centralization speaks the language of economies of scale, coherent goals and clear direction; decentralization fosters the idea of personal responsibility. The two opposing concepts seem to imply, in the ordinary use of the words, a conflict between the efficiency and size of the supermarket and the friendliness of the corner-shop. Both involve value-judgements.

Every organization encounters the conflict between centralization and autonomy as soon as it becomes large enough to have sub-units. That is the nature of growth. While much of this book concentrates on relationships within commercial organizations, the issue is just as alive in government, religious and voluntary bodies (although often with different consequences) and their position will also be considered. To centralize or to decentralize is a question every organization has to ask, and to keep asking.

The breadth of interest in the subject is attested by the literature quoted on these pages. Accountants, anthropologists, economists, historians, lawyers, philosophers, psychologists, sociologists and theologians as well as administrative, management and political scientists have been called as expert witnesses. They approach the subject in various ways and with different vocabularies, while the problem of determining where decisions are to be taken is never far from the mind of the organizer. Among the most ancient pieces of wisdom is to delegate, and there are no signs that the outpouring of such wisdom will lessen. Equally, the advice continues to pour because the pressures for centralization are ceaseless and strong, and these do not lie just in the personality of the decision-maker as some of the advice appears to assume. The knowledge available and the need to take an overall view press for decisions at a higher level and, whatever the reason, a discussion of centralization never lacks partakers.

It is less easy to be sure what is being discussed. Some readers will doubtless have a picture at the back of their minds of an ideal condition which is worth seeking after, a smooth-running organization in which all the participants plan their part in relative harmony and with minimum coordination. Other readers would think that such an organization confirmed their worst fears; but the ideal condition, however seen, provides a standard of judgement against which the cycle of centralization and autonomy operates, a cycle in which one gives place to the other in an endless sequence with little apparent reason behind it, giving rise to cynical comments like: 'this organization goes in for [needs] a shake-up every few years'.

The cycle can be compared to the solar system moving through space. The relative position of the satellites is constantly changing, but the whole system is also on the move; each unit is propelled in two directions at once. A simpler analogy, that of a measuring scale, is used on these pages; but the solar system illustrates the way an organization rotates between centralization and autonomy while simultaneously shifting the hub of the cycle in one direction or another. There are few fixed points and change is unceasing, but the process is not meaningless. It can be understood and thereby controlled; that is our theme. But there the parallel ends—there is no overarching generalization (like the law of gravity) to be found on these pages; rather the concern is with a process of stimulus and response.

Some readers will judge the cycle by views derived from their attitudes to organization; others will be biased by their experience. Those accustomed to personal or authoritarian institutions will see centralization as a natural state of affairs and find reasons for noticing – either with approval or regret – trends to greater autonomy. Their universe is moving in a direction different from those who uncover lures to centralization. One of the consequences, it is hoped, of the approach adopted in this book is to identify the conflicting pressures and to demonstrate that any attempt to understand the subject must do justice to the nature of the conflict and its results. Otherwise the responses that organizations make are, as some already claim, inexplicable. These responses lead to changes that become more rapid and more confusing as organizations grow larger, with the result that observers feel their fatalism or cynicism to be increasingly justified. These feelings make a thorough understanding of the concepts urgent—an urgency reinforced by the need to provide a systematic programme for thinking about the subject, for framing proposals designed to test the possibilities and consequences of different levels of centralization and autonomy, and for relating the results to the problems of living in an organization.

The book is divided into three parts, following a well-established arrangement[2] whereby part I provides the background, Part II draws on empirical studies to produce some illumination and modification of the conclusions of part I, and part III finalizes the discussion and offers comment. The general plan is outlined in Figure 1.1 and discussed in more detail in the following paragraphs.

Part I examines a number of approaches and relevant ideas in the light of underlying bodies of knowledge. This could have been carried out in much greater detail by arranging the chapters by discipline; however, the disciplinary

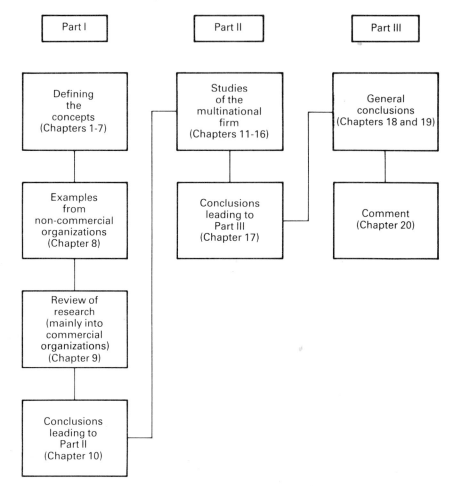

Figure 1.1 Centralization and autonomy: plan of the book

arrangement overshadowed interesting questions and provoked a barren discussion about differences of emphasis; hence, an arrangement by topic has been used in Chapters 3 to 7 which consider relevant aspects of decision-making, power, authority, communication, conflict and attitudes. The various approaches are summarized in Chapter 2. The rest of part I consists of a chapter (8) on non-commercial organizations, a review of methodology (9) and a conclusion (Chapter 10) which brings together the elements of a theory including criteria for assessing empirical data.

In executing our task, justice has to be done to the elements of paradox and contradiction which stand out in every approach—the losing your life to save it element. Attempts at decentralization are found to be self-defeating, while centralization chokes initiative.

Part II is to be regarded as a sustained case study. The insights worked out in part I are applied to one specific species of organization—the multinational firm.

With its worldwide network of units and sub-units, the multinational provides an ideal laboratory[3] for the study of a complex labyrinth in which autonomy for one unit equals centralization for another. In these chapters both are related to effectiveness, the time dimension, the type of organization, the size of the firm, nationality and other variables. A final chapter in this part looks at the present position of the multinationals and their future.

Part III assembles the strands to present an overall view of the subject and a summary of the significant indicators identified and tested in the preceding pages. There is a final chapter (20) which turns away from the mechanics of organization and looks briefly at the inhabitants. Living in organizations is easier for some than for others, as our opening paragraphs suggested, but there are problems for all. The final chapter re-examines arguments brought together throughout the book and discusses in more general terms the confrontation between the organizer and the participant.

The book is designed to be read as a whole. But it can also be used as a work of reference, and the subject index provides a guide to the principal concepts employed. This index is selective. The intention is that only subjects which are dealt with in more than a passing manner and only pages containing substantial references have been entered. The name index, by contrast, is more comprehensive on the grounds that readers may wish to track the authorities or organizations mentioned.

There is a widespread belief that, whatever the practice, centralization is a vice and autonomy a virtue. Since most people prefer to be regarded as anti-vice, honest discussion is inhibited while those who keep a firm grip on their own organization praise delegation most enthusiastically. In church and state, charity and business, centralizing tendencies can be detected. On these pages, the concepts are treated as neutral, objects of impartial investigation, and from this assertion of neutrality we turn to their definition.

Definitions

'Since this firm became decentralized, our performance has improved.' It was such statements that set the author puzzling over the meaning of the word 'decentralized' and how or whether it could be credited with improving performance. The puzzle was made no less interesting by the discovery that others in the same firm were saying that the improved performance had occurred in spite of increasing centralization. All were apparently agreed that decentralization was a good thing, but they held contradictory opinions about whether it was actually occurring. Clearly myths and legends had gathered around the words and a viable definition had to take account of the way opposite interpretations could be placed on the same facts.

A further difficulty is the relationship between the individual and the organization. The decentralization or autonomy discussed in this book is to a unit or sub-unit of an organization. Of course the particular unit may be staffed by one person, but it is the organization that is being considered, not the individual. Personal autonomy is, on principle, not the subject, in spite of some carefully signposted exceptions, mainly in the last chapter. The decision-making is under discussion rather than the management style or the subordinate response, although clear distinctions are not always possible, and organizations can be decentralizing in comparison with those they replace but still centralized in relation to the aspirations and expectations of their members. Any command structure, however relaxed, can be regarded as a centralized substitute for a collection of autonomous individuals. The converse is that some degree of centralized control is inherent in an organization and our aim is to clarify how this operates and the consequences for an organization's well-being.

As well as being useful across the artificial boundaries of the academic disciplines already listed, the concept of centralization can be attached to many questions from an application in terms of other concepts (the centralization of *authority* or *power*), to an application in terms of substantive matters (the centralization of *production*) and can even be used in an entirely different context of *geographical* space. In a given writing, the transition from one meaning to another can be rapid, as can the context. Anything that can be brought together can be centralized; anything that can be diffused can be decentralized. The concept stems from questions about power to questions of decision-making, from questions on participation and influence to questions on communications. It is possible to talk simultaneously about centralization of information and control, when one may be the necessary condition of the other, and then to try to divide them analytically. The multipurpose nature of the words under consideration, as well as their imprecision in normal usage, is a part of the background to the present study, while their definition is hampered by the fact that those who are the prime sources of information on the subject define centralization as one would a colour. They know it when they see it, and what they see is the view from wherever they happen to be in the institution under investigation. There are two further considerations. One is that centralization or decentralization implies a comparison. It is not possible to say that this company, or organization of whatever kind, is centralized. It has to be centralized in terms either of itself at an earlier date, or of another organization; that alone is enough to ensure that the concept implies a continuum—a list of points along a scale of relative centralization or decentralization determined by whatever criteria are being used. No interpretation of the subject can ignore this relativity, although the comparison may be with other organizations or an organization's own past. The second consideration is that centralization is a second order concept dependent upon others for its meaning. Take the statement—'This organization is decentralized'—the words are meaningless without the assessment of degree along a scale. They are also meaningless without some prior understanding of what precisely it is that is centralized. Even without the problem of defining centralization in terms of individual functions, it has to be made clear which aspect of those functions is centralized: decision-making, the power to make decisions, the influences on decisions and so on. The means of assessing centralization will be directly related to such a definition, and the questions asked be designed to estimate the first order concept on which the definition of centralization depends. It is no use defining centralization in terms of locus of decision-making and then using evidence of a company reporting system as representing it. What has been measured is the centralization of information, not that of decision-making; the two may be related, but they may actually be related in a negative way. Apart, then, from a general warning about the difficulties of definition and conceptualization, this section indicates how easily common assumptions about centralization can be reversed in social science usage.

At its simplest the word 'centralization' is used of an organization where the decision-making is biased towards the top, while 'autonomy' refers to one in which units and sub-units possess the ability to take decisions for themselves on issues which are reserved to a higher level in comparable organizations. This simple understanding, with its single dimension, will be modified and elaborated—especially in Chapter 9 in connection with the research implications—meanwhile the following list narrows the definitions in summarizing points already made.

Why centralization and autonomy?

On these pages autonomy equals decentralization; it is appreciated that many authorities distinguish between the two, but to do so here would involve a continual ugly repetition of centralization and decentralization. There are no other words,[4] and the difficulties caused by making autonomy identical with decentralization are overcome by distinguishing between different kinds and dimensions of autonomy. Delegation, devolution and discretion are sometimes used, but with care since they can carry a bias towards regarding autonomy as simply a favour from on high. Similarly, cohesion, concentration and integration are used for centralization but with caution on account of the danger of prejudging the issues to be discussed.

The relationship

The subject is about a relationship between two or more units of an organization. A centralized organization means, if anything, an organization in which the typical relationship is one where decision-making is reserved to a higher unit.

The comparison

The subject is also comparative. A relationship is centralized when a comparable relationship can be found in which the subordinate has more authority.

The measurement

The comparisons may be made by picturing a straight line stretching from centralization to autonomy, and placing a particular relationship along this line in a place that is suitable relative to others (the line is sketched out in later chapters where it is also shown that a multidimensional scheme is sometimes required). Even if not adequate for all purposes, the use of the measuring line does emphasize the fine gradations between complete centralization and total autonomy.

Absolutes
On principle, the items on comparison and relationship imply that a phrase like 'absolute centralization' is meaningless, but it can be used to fix a reference point, referring to a hypothetical organization or relationship which stands at either end of the line of measurement, the continuum.

Matrix
The word *matrix* conjures up another problem of definition. It may be that the complex organization does not have a decentralization to a rank or level, but a matrix of intersecting lines of authority. Certainly some business organizations have attempted to formalize such an arrangement. This formalization arises from the argument that the realities of the decision-making process form a matrix anyway. So the matrix organization is a recognition of an existing reality. The issue will be discussed in Chapter 15; meanwhile, a simpler definition will be assumed.

Related words
These are a number of words which linger on the periphery of the discussion but whose meaning is critical to the understanding of the main themes. Thus, *strategy* is used of what the organization is about and where it is going, while *policy* conjures up the main guidelines developed to facilitate decision-making, to determine satisfactory corporate behaviour and to ensure that strategy is translated into action. *Competition* is used of efforts to establish a relationship with other organizations having similar objectives whereby one may benefit at the expense of another. Competition may take many forms, all of which arise from the purposes the organization fulfils. In trying to increase its membership, for instance, a political party may regard itself as in competition with other parties. In practice, however, more serious competition may come from other leisure activities. The nature of the competition may make more centralization necessary, as quick reactions are required, or it may be a pressure for decentralization if it is at the lower levels of the organization that the main impact is felt. *Democracy* and *participation* are words that are related to decentralization, while *autocracy* and *oligarchy* point to centralization. But these relationships should be treated with caution. While there will be some links, common sense is not necessarily a guide. The autocrat may take more pains to delegate decisions than the democratic assembly, while the participation may be a technique or a passing fashion.

The final note in explaining the terms is to show that definitions of centralization and decentralization, because of their wide applications, need to clarify what is being centralized. They can range from *supra*-definitions in terms of concepts like authority and power, to *infra*-definitions which isolate a pair of levels in a structure. In the latter case decentralization at one level may preclude autonomy for decision-making at a lower level. Decentralization to a given unit does not necessarily mean decentralization within that unit. Thus, general statements about an organization are not necessarily valid.

With regard to the *supra*-definition, it is necessary to distinguish between the more general concepts used. For instance, Chapter 4 discusses the distinction between authority and power. In popular usage the latter word is most frequently employed. For present purposes, *power* will be understood as the underlying or ultimate attribute, whereas the ability to make a decision and cause an action to result is *authority*. Since all *authority* is delegated from power, and our subject is delegation, there is a special need to distinguish, otherwise the definition will determine the outcome. Hence, this book considers the *exercise of authority*. A problem that results from that view is that many of the authors discussed use the word *power*. In the text, attempts are made to clarify the way the words are used. By the definition employed here, the discussion is about the centralization and decentralization of authority not power.

In view of contemporary discussions about participation, it is well to bear this distinction in mind. Most recommendations using words like 'participation' or 'consultation', even those using the phrase 'power sharing', in fact refer to authority as here defined. There may be some sharing of the power, and a range of practical and moral undertones are certainly implied, but there is always a degree of participation in any organization. The absolute dictator does not take all the decisions himself and does involve others in the decision-making. The type of involvement varies between democracy and dictatorship, while in democracy the drive for participation is on behalf of a formal procedure. The informal exists anyway, and the procedures may be designed to preserve the power while sharing the decision-making.

This book attempts to take the reader on a guided tour of an area of knowledge which has been much explored, but where the directions are confused. Expressions as various as 'the suet pudding of politics' and the 'real life of democracy' are used in one article.[5] Some routes are staked out towards a systematic understanding designed to stimulate and guide informed investigations which add further knowledge. To this end the concepts have been refined so that a confident identification can be made of the elements of centralization and autonomy, their appropriateness in a given organization or set of circumstances, and the solution or containment of problems that arise. As a start the next chapter looks at the insights, the problems and the beliefs which underlie the subject and how these have been viewed through eyes focused by different disciplines.

2 The Background: Some Paradoxes

An early reference to the problem of centralization reads: 'And Moses' father-in-law said unto him, "The thing that thou doest is not good. Thou wilt surely wear away, both thou, and this people that is with thee; for the thing is too heavy for thee; thou art not able to perform it thyself alone".'[1] More dramatically, a later writer noted the drawbacks to decentralization when: '. . . every powerful man made his castles and held them against him: and they filled the land full of castles. They oppressed greatly the wretched men of the land with the making of castles; . . .' The two quotations neatly summarize the contradictory pressures urged upon the administrator—the accepted wisdom recommends delegation; the threat of disaster urges centralization. This chapter shows how such contradictions are characteristic of the subject.

2.1 THEORY, FOLKLORE AND FASHION: THE QUESTIONS TO BE ASKED

Advice to delegate can be heard in numerous phrases and in many languages. The character who ignores this advice is a figure of satire and ridicule. 'Our decision-making is too slow because the chief executive keeps everything to himself,' says the businessman. On the political level, local problems are blamed on the need for constant reference to central government. There are opposing voices as well which speak of the dangers of chaos, of the need to preserve the sacred truths and of irresponsibility among the governed. This chapter tracks back through deeply held and traditional beliefs on authority to examine the contradictions inherent in the folklore. The concepts, here called autonomy and centralization, are examined in the terms of the relevant disciplines and in various contexts. The same themes recur whether one listens to the politician on his country, the priest on his creed or the administrator on his organization. The logic of the organization and its objectives are held to point to the need for centralization, while people are believed to work less efficiently in a centralized system. Popular sayings support each side of the argument, but particularly favour 'leaving things to the man on the spot'. Another piece of folklore is the belief that policy issues are centralized while operational matters are decentralized. The distinction does not hold water—questions regarded as policies in one company are not in another—in fact, a company's definition of policy is a better (but still inadequate) guide to centralization than the distinction. Meanwhile, centralization is the option most frequently condemned, but its results are usually seen as irritating at worst and sometimes merely comic—'we're crowded with unwanted equipment because head office has fallen for some glib salesman.' The consequences of decentralization, on the other hand, can be disastrous; the people perish, the firm goes bankrupt. The fear of disaster holds back the grant of autonomy although its desirability may be universally recognized. The theme is a recurring one in a discussion that can be conducted at varying levels. In France *la Décentralisation*, the move to reduce the concentration of political power in Paris which became a major issue in the 1981 elections[2], has been the subject of controversy for centuries; but the emphasis increased when one party in the French revolution fought (unsuccessfully) for devolution, and a few years later Napoleon moved in the opposite direction. In countries with federal constitutions there are constant struggles between the authority of the federal government and that of the constituent provinces. These struggles sometimes lead to violence as in the civil wars fought in the United States and in Nigeria; more routinely, there is sensitivity over the symbols of local authority, and arguments over the levels of taxation. Usually, these arguments take the form of complaints about extortionate levies from the centre, but in Britain central government has taken to restricting local money-raising. This reduction in autonomy has been amplified by rule by circular—the sending of notices to regional and local authorities which are apparently advisory, but acquire a mandatory force when budgets are discussed. Sometimes the political resolution lies in an attempt at a precise definition of the powers of each element in the constitution.

Both the logic of an organization and its statement of objectives sometimes point towards centralization, while personal considerations lead to decentralization. In educational, business, charitable and other organizations there is tension between the desire for a strong centre, a desire which is not only expressed at the centre itself, and autonomy for the constituent units. Members of organizations are wont themselves to suggest that changes come about through factors they cannot influence, like leadership or the vagaries of fashion. This feeling of being at the mercy of forces that are hard to control may do less than justice to the insights possessed by members of the organization, although it is not hard to accept that a degree of determinism runs through the processes of change. The question to be addressed is how the beliefs and the folklore can be confronted by a body of theory with explanatory and predictive power.

The assumption from which the discussion starts is that there exist in an organization distinct units and that a number of factors can be identified in the authority relationship between these units – that it is meaningful to refer to a *more* or a *less* centralized relationship, and that such statements tell us something about how the organization works. The statements may be in quantitative and qualitative forms and can be expressed in a number of terms, such as:

The personal. Someone is determining the discretion of others because of his

temperament, outlook, strength, fears, ambitions, or other characteristics.
The social. Group relations or the logic of the situation determine the degree of centralization or autonomy.
Others. Other factors, such as the *accounting* or the *legal*, require consideration.

Naturally, these categories, like the personal and the social, are not mutually exclusive and the approaches do influence one another. Each can be more fully understood by reviewing the insights provided by a number of disciplines.

The philosophers, the theologians, the social scientists, the historians and many others have their various interests in how organizations work. Much of the interest stems from the legends and folklore which occur in some form wherever organizations exist. But the varying insights are seldom brought together face to face, as it were, to engage in a process of mutual assistance and conflict. Each system of thought, it should be added, contains similar contradictions—the pressures for centralization are constantly being opposed by beliefs in decentralization, while the changes may be ascribed to fashion or to causes which can be more readily analysed. This attempt to draw on the insights of different disciplines raises fundamental questions of understanding which cannot be fully explored here. Both author and reader, however, should be alert to the different types of activity that the different theories are interpreting; the borrowing from one approach to another often involves some sizeable leaps in one's thought processes. The present chapter selects and summarizes contributions from various disciplines that will be used later to interpret situations under discussion. Above all the contradictions and paradoxes of which any theory must take account are pin-pointed. Our starting point is the study of culture.

2.2   ACROSS CULTURES

The heading is a reminder of the influences across space and time that have provided content to the ideas of centralization and autonomy. Worries about the relationship between an organization and its component parts are a feature of modern discussion on administration, but can hardly have seemed pressing to the primitive tribe. Nevertheless, ideas and practices emerged early which illuminate later concerns. The issues over time, tracking back to the origins of the concepts, are examined under the heading of 'the antecedents', while the phrase 'comparing cultures' sums up a selection of the differences that occur in a variety of places at the same time. For the purposes of this section, work by social anthropologists on primitive culture is examined. Much of this is relevant to the study of the cultural context today as well.

The word 'culture' has been given many meanings, from a relatively narrow reference to the artistic side of life to a view of the distinguishing features of a society as a whole. This broader meaning is used in these pages where 'culture' includes all the activities and characteristics which distinguish a particular group, the patterns of behaviour that are normally taken for granted. There is a comparative element in this idea of culture, but of a different order from the comparative element in centralization. It is not possible, by the definition used here, to refer to a nation or organization as 'more cultured' than another. The comparison is of different attitudes towards issues like authority, kinship, work and so on. This subject is discussed later; meanwhile, the antecedents of the centralization discussion are well expressed in the following quotation.

The antecedents

'We cannot possibly interpret rituals concerning excreta, breast milk, saliva and the rest unless we are prepared to see in the body a symbol of society, and to see the powers and dangers credited to social structure reproduced in the human body.'[3] The author of that statement also describes how a sacrificial animal is used 'as a diagram of a social situation'. The quotations express four issues which concern us. The first is the view of *society as a body*, a view which later developed into a general use of biological analogies in the interpretation of social phenomena. This is likely to be a centralizing outlook—the body is dependent on the head. To expect any other would be to read back the thought of a much later age, but the idea does contain the germ of a debate on the role of the parts and how autonomously they can act. The head is supported by other members which must perform their tasks correctly if the whole body is to survive. The myths and rituals which represented society in bodily terms provided social cohesion, a cement to hold together the warring members. This aspect was further emphasized in the second issue, the *safeguarding* of the information required for the well-being of the organization. There may be some division of authority, but the ultimate power lies with the holder of the secrets, the ruler or the holy man who knows the ritual response appropriate to a particular set of circumstances. The 'powers and dangers' expressed in the ritual are also a part of the *instillation of loyalty*, the third issue which is closely related to the fourth—*the demarcation of the boundaries* of the organization. Participation in the ritual makes it clear who is regarded as a member and who is not, as well as how entry is effected. Loyalty is stimulated by rivalry towards the outsider, hence the boundaries need to be defined. The privileges of membership and the penalties of non-membership are also indicated.

Discussion of centralization becomes important, as in historical times, with the growth of numbers. As long as the boundaries of a village or tribe were limited to a group of hunters with a relatively egalitarian structure, the issue existed only as a possibility. The group was held together by its rituals and other activities practised in common, although the fear of rivals was also likely to be a force for cohesion. Further explanation was required when the attention of anthropologists turned from small bands to larger societies. Centralization ceased to be just a possibility when units and sub-units were identified within a common organizational framework as was found among primitive tribes in parts of Africa and the Middle East. The apparent decentralization of some African societies which yet accepted a common social order demonstrated the possibility of a relatively informal organization and the difficulty of understanding how that organization works. The study of 'tribes without rulers', as they have been called, starts from two factors—the existence of a network of interlocking kinship groups and the existence of individuals with special powers to mediate disputes.[4] However, later studies demonstrated that the kinship network was much influenced by a historical process, the assimilation of one tribe by another and the imposition of colonial rule. Through all the changes the mediators, whatever their status, had the ability to manipulate a number of levers of power of which the kinship network was only one. Another was the wealth they had accumulated as a result of the customary gifts to which they were entitled, and yet another was the religious veneration in which they were held. With these levers a political system developed with reasonably definable boundaries, but without any central authority.

The more centralized systems accompany urban civilizations, as in the Middle East and the Americas. This may only appear to be the case since more evidence has survived of such civilizations than of the rural; what is certain is that the technological changes required to produce urbanization are also related to the development of a centralized authority. In cultural studies a shadowy government, which is remote except in periods of emergency, is frequently seen to be accompanied by two units of authority in particular localities.[5] One is the village headman, who acquires his authority either by inheritance or conquest, and the other is the money-lender who possesses power rather than authority. He can influence rather than instruct, is often alien at least in origin, and may change over time into a landlord; the fact that he then succeeds in becoming a significant unit of local authority is not likely to give decentralization a favourable image, but helps to make the system economically workable.

Spatial decentralization, by locality, is not the only kind. One author[6] gives examples of functional decentralization among some of the indigenous tribes of British Columbia for whom 'every activity is segregated'. The rituals concerning puberty, the feasts and the dances, hunting, warfare and the other aspects of the life of the tribe are unrelated. Typically, where there is no functional decentralization, the rituals connected with each activity will support one another. One of the explanations suggested for the lack of integration is that a particular tribe has assimilated customs from different cultures. This can be seen as a precursor of the industrial age when the different functional services in a company develop their own cultures; but there is a danger in applying the findings of the anthropologists to modern society. However diverse or integrated a particular primitive culture, the participant has little choice but to conform, and there are powerful mechanisms safeguarding conformity—a warning to those who seek autonomy in its own right. Diversity, in other words, does not come as a result of a demand for personal freedom, but through the gradual absorption of the differing traditions by the tribe as a whole. In this way unity and cohesion can be safeguarded within relatively decentralized systems. A similar solution is sought in many ages and cultures, and this brief account of some of the concerns of the social anthropologist has provided clues about the roots of centralization and the possibility of autonomy within institutional boundaries. The ideas of culture differences over space as well as time follows to complete the discussion.

Comparing cultures

One approach to the comparison of cultures is by the investigation of attitudes across a continuum drawn between opposing concepts. This is a method frequently favoured in this book and has the advantage of simplicity, although as much complexity can be added as is required, and relative lack of bias—too often comparisons are biased towards an author's own view of cultural norms or theories of cultural change. The use of this method is not intended to suggest that a coherent profile of a culture can be readily drafted, but to identify characteristics relevant to the present discussion. Among the characteristics are the following.

Heredity and individualism

In some communities authority is derived from inheritance, in others from conquest, charisma or other individual quality or action. In neither case does the mode determine the degree of centralization, although the individual ruler may move nearer to a centralized system or the reverse; the hereditary ruler will retain elements of both. Other factors will be more influential, including the size and stability of the society and perhaps the self-confidence of the ruler.

Dependence on tradition and acceptance of change

The contrast might appear as an anachronism in the present context, but is in fact as valid in the understanding of modern as of primitive culture. A high degree of resistance to change in some societies compares with an ability to absorb alien influences in others.[7] Change frequently means centralization as the change agent comes to dominate a group, but the growth makes decentralization a possibility. A modern example of innovation having a similar consequence is the on-line computer link. Initially, the technology is seen to promote a high degree of centralization, speedier reactions from the centre are possible; later it is seen that local autonomy can also be enhanced with more complete information being made available more rapidly.

The roles of age and youth

Ceremonies described by a number of writers attest to different relationships between the generations. In some societies the vigour of youth is stressed; the old, particularly elderly rulers, may even be put to death. In others, especially those where tradition is emphasized, the wisdom of old age is valued and ceremonies are designed to keep the young in subordinate positions.

The words 'centralized' and 'decentralized' are rarely used by social anthropologists,[8] but when they are employed they describe a consequence of the growth of a society, rather than a technique or a motivating force. There are a number of options from totally decentralized tribes without rulers to highly autocratic empires. The appearance of a particular option arises as a result of factors which are conditioning a historical process including those already mentioned like the degree of tolerance for change or assimilation. The use of the word 'option' is not meant to imply a conscious choice, and the modern idea that decentralization strengthens motivation is an anachronism. It implies a process of devolution through constitution-making. Decentralization was present in primitive societies, but was not used as a stimulus, only accepted as a fact.

These notes from social anthropology demonstrate the diversity of approaches and their usefulness to the understanding of centralization. The development of the underlying ideas, but in even greater diversity, continues in the historical times reviewed in the next section.

2.3   THE HISTORICAL PERSPECTIVE

The words centralization and autonomy appear in the indexes of few history books, but the emergence of new styles of government and organization pose questions about relationships within a country or between units of an organization whatever the words used. Two historical processes are especially relevant to this study. One is the series of institutional changes in government, commerce and other similar activities. These changes produced new pressures, partly arising from new focuses of loyalty, to which fresh responses have emerged. The animal sacrifice becomes the bodily analogy which eventually develops into the corporate theory of the state, while opposing political views also come into existence.

The distinction between changing institutions and changing ideas is not a precise one, the two are inextricably mixed, but is useful in this context because of the paradox which underlies our interpretation of later events when a decentralizing ideology is seen to mask a centralizing reality. The second process was the other way round. The subordinate units—the barons and the boroughs—claimed an autonomy which central government was trying to take away; there was no contrast between the beliefs and the realities on either side. The upholders of Magna Carta practised autonomy their way, while supporters of government considered that centralization achieved 'the good peace which the King imposed on all'.[9]

Changing institutions

One of the historical processes was the changing scale of social institutions. Ancient Jerusalem, considered a mighty city by the writers of the Scriptures, is thought to have had a population of no more than 30000[10]—equivalent to a small suburb these days—and the building of an aqueduct to provide water for even that number was an occasion for rioting. In more modern times technical innovation made possible the supply of water and food to larger cities, while social and economic pressures led to growth. London reached a population of 250000 in the sixteenth century after many years of steady increase and was then the largest city in the world. European cities did not reach six figure populations until the nineteenth century. Meanwhile, other institutions—political, religious and commercial as well as civic—were beginning to grow, and the growth was to make centralization and autonomy important issues. In the case of the towns, some traditional independence was lost before more modern forms of local government began to emerge. So two relationships emerged: that within which the civic authorities were trying to establish rights and principles over against the government or the holders of traditional rights, and that within the city itself between the rising authority and the entrenched citizenry. The process was a slow one but illustrates an aspect of the subject which persists, that the body which is struggling towards a measure of autonomy (the city in this case) for itself is simultaneously trying to achieve greater centralization in relation to its subordinate units.

This principle works laterally as well as vertically. Some form of lateral specialization—organization into areas of expertise like the treasury or the judiciary—must have taken place at an early date to make the ancient empires workable. Doubtless the degree of delegation to the specialist functions was unclear, it can hardly be considered clear today, but the judges had achieved a certain autonomy in medieval Britain, and this autonomy spelt centralization for those they judged. The *King's peace* was a centrally determined system of justice mediated through travelling judges who placed their own interpretations on the laws. The state of communications made it impossible for them to consult before taking their decisions. Naturally, there were limitations on this autonomy—the judges had to return to court periodically to face accusations by those who considered them too harsh or too lenient—but the autonomy was real enough within the constraints. By the time more modern developments in transport and communications rendered centralization possible, the independence of the judiciary had been elevated to a principle. Figure 2.1 shows the processes in simplified form.

A word that was used of the conflict over the increasing powers of the state and its rival claimants to authority was *jurisdiction*, a concept with a number of overtones. The struggle between king, church and barons in the Middle Ages is part of a theme which continues in the struggles between governments and large corporations today. It can be said that anti-trust legislation in modern America is descended from the Constitutions of Clarendon of twelfth-century Britain and other similar attempts to assert the authority of central government against its rivals. In the twentieth century the sovereign power of government is unquestioned, though now partly subordinated to supranational bodies like the European Community, however much its intervention may be deplored. The medieval controversy was complicated by the fact that all the parties relied on traditional rights which were largely taken for granted. On the royal, imperial, side there were writers like the anonymous Norman (early twelfth century) who produced a theoretical justification for the lay case, while, on the papal side, there was a panoply of intellectual argument represented by Gratian's *Decretum* and many other writings.[11] The reaction of emperors and kings to popes and that of barons or burghers to their rulers was to claim rights handed down from time immemorial. This method of innovation by quoting precedent is less acceptable today, when it is regarded as a foible of the legal profession. In the Middle Ages, also, the struggle for jurisdiction between the national rulers, the

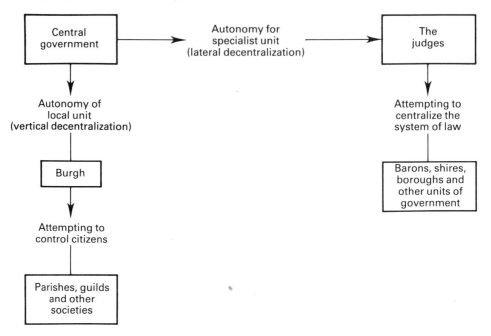

Figure 2.1   Vertical and lateral autonomy

clergy and the barons was not for exclusive authority; it was rather aimed at establishing acceptable boundaries. Each party accepted the role of the other, with reservations, and the struggle for exclusive jurisdiction is a part of a parallel theme—that of conquest and territorial boundaries. The way the three-sided struggle has been viewed since does, however, show some bias towards centralization. Contemporary records are usually generated by supporters of the church, less often by upholders of government, and least often by the barons. No wonder, then, that decentralization to these latter is seen as a prescription for disaster in the histories of King Stephen's reign as in the quotation from the Anglo-Saxon Chronicle with which this chapter began.

The emergence of the modern secular state was a victory for political centralization, but the process was slow and produced its own reaction as the terms of the argument over jurisdiction changed. Nevertheless, the outcome now seems inevitable; the powers of the church and the barons were reduced and to this end the ruler was able to call upon a number of aids. There was the powerful propaganda attached to his position, which itself had religious significance. The emperor was an anointed, holy man. There was the ruler's ability to maintain peace, at which his rivals were conspicuously less adept. There was, further, the development of the tools of centralized government, including a form of bureaucratic organization, the division of the apparatus of government into functionaries with duties separated into distinct decision-making areas, and the construction of a 'spider's web of patronage'.[12]

These tools have remained available throughout history, but the claim to custom and tradition has largely been replaced by a political process aimed at changes and counter-changes in support of which other criteria apply. The attempt to restrict the power of the commercial corporation, for instance, is conducted through legislation to enforce competition. The anti-trust laws in the United States, now over a hundred years old, have brought criminal penalties for economic offences. The most famous case under these laws led to the imprisonment of some senior executives in twenty-nine electrical components manufacturing companies.[13] In this instance an electricity supply company owned by the federal government, the Tennessee Valley Authority, announced that it was going abroad for its purchases because existing suppliers were agreeing prices to its disadvantage. The ensuing controversy brought to light evidence which enabled the attorney general's office to prosecute. The evidence demonstrated that the executives concerned knew that they were on dangerous ground; there were accounts of secret negotiations, codes and passwords; but a main plea was on the ambiguity of the law. The agreements, it was claimed, were designed to enable the smaller companies to remain in business. If they had been subjected to more severe competition, they would have been forced out altogether, in which case the same legislation might have been used to attack the larger companies, like General Electric and Westinghouse, on other grounds—the control of too large a share of the market. In the event the plea was not accepted and all the companies were penalized as well as individual executives. This case clearly illustrates the struggle for power between a government and its corporate citizens and it also shows how the latter are now without the defences used by their medieval precursors. The companies can, however, probe and discover the weak spots in the official system. A spokesman for the United States Treasury has referred to the difficulty the tax authorities have in keeping up-to-date with corporate financial expertise. In less-developed countries, where the bureaucratic apparatus is not yet developed, the control of the company is more difficult. Difficulties also arise where jurisdictions overlap. This permits, for instance, two views of the implications of the European Economic Community. The attempt to harmonize overlapping regulations can be seen as the final chapter in the march to fuller state control or, on the contrary, as a means of releasing the corporations from intervention as the authority of the member state is reduced.

The word 'decentralization', used in a different sense, has been a tenet of political movements in Europe. In France, for instance, la décentralisation has experienced an interesting history. Groups like the Girondins, advocated such a policy as part of the movement against the old regime and against their fellow revolutionaries. In the nineteenth century, the series of efforts to devolve authority from Paris to the provinces came from different parts of the political spectrum. The right-wing school of Le Play made this a principal issue in its programme from which many benefits were expected to flow.[14] In the twentieth century, political devolution has been more associated with the left. France was a relatively centralized country after the long years of Bourbon rule with a result that tight control from Paris has remained part of the status quo, and political initiatives are concerned with the case again. Other European countries, in particular Germany and Italy, were moving towards unity in the last century and centralization possessed the appeal of emerging nationhood. Political centralization affronts the rights of different groups of citizens. On the other side efficient government is brought into the argument, but is not the starting point as it is with commercial organizations.

Changing ideas

The body analogy, the corporate view of the state introduced earlier in this chapter, is concerned with delegation upwards rather than downwards. This accords with the struggle for power between units claiming a traditional autonomy. By historical times the units had become well-defined—church, state and barons for example. The concept itself is neutral, and all parts of the body are required for the satisfactory functioning of the whole, but the analogy is usually employed to stress the need for an authoritarian head. In the twelfth century John of Salisbury[15] extended the analogy by introducing an element of dualism. The king was seen as the head, but the clergy as the soul. Through the struggle for power between church and state, the concept had been refined. The germ of a debate between the bodily functions also emerged. Questions were being asked about what happened if the head turned out to be diseased and betrayed the other members.

Corporate theories of the state that have been emerging ever since, with or without answers to such questions, include those which provided a rationale for modern fascism; but the emphasis on delegation upwards appears in other doctrines including the many which concern elites. Writers like Locke and Burke[16] were in the tradition of those who maintained that an elite was justified in holding its power on the basis of some assumed tacit consent on the part of the majority of the population. In bridging the gap between autocracy and a modern view of democracy Burke maintained that 'virtue and wisdom' were required for government; Locke that 'when law ends, tyranny begins'. These virtues, in an appropriate form, were only to be found among those who were born and bred among the elite and, above all, owned property. Such ownership has been widely held as a qualification for government, but also for any political activity; the need for some property holding remained in the electoral laws of many countries, including Britain, well into this century. Burke, and those who thought like he did, at least considered that the governors had to respond to the governed and act in accordance with their supposed wishes. There were criteria, however vague, for determining the correctness of the upward delegation, the fitness of the rulers to rule. Earlier Locke[17] had affirmed that government existed for the benefit of the public and thus confirmed the main rival to the corporate state, a theme developed by Rousseau in *The Social Contract*. These writers and those who developed their opinions were concerned with authority; they were not much interested in the analysis of organization. It was Weber[18] who started the modern fashion of looking behind the leadership to investigate how the organization operated.

Another relevant historical concern was that with the separation of powers. This form of delegation within the elite ensured that there were checks and balances against the abuse of power and to provide justice for the people. To a certain extent this theory became enshrined in the United States Constitution and in those which imitated it. For present purposes the division of powers may be considered a form of decentralization based on principle rather than efficiency.

The idea of the division of powers was later expanded to give it a social as opposed to a purely constitutional significance, and there is a warning embedded in the history of political thought against too simple a contrast between autonomy and centralization. A more subtle distinction is between autonomy, heteronomy and tradition.[19] Autonomy starts from the self-regulatory community, while heteronomy is the control exercised from outside —from the greater society of which the community is part. Tradition stands between the two. Thinkers who span as many centuries as Plato, Rousseau and Fromm have recommended communities based on mutual under standing. This is a narrower view of autonomy than that employed here but it points to the search for more satisfactory institutions which is one element in decentralization. Heteronomy is regarded as the opposite extreme, but the degree of consent among the participants will help to determine how centralized any particular organization will seem. A contemporary word is 'pluralism',[20] —the view that society is made up of a number of groups with different outlooks and objectives held together in coalitions which may be tighter or looser according to circumstances. In pluralist analysis, interest is concentrated on the need for coordination and control rather than on the point of decision-making. The paradox of pluralism is that greater participation matches the sensitivities of a pluralist society, but the need for coordination is increased at the same time. This paradox is partly resolved by greater autonomy for social units, a fact which partly explains how decentralization becomes a norm of democratic societies.

Another dimension is added to the discussion by the dream of world government. This aim is sometimes promoted by the oppressor as the objective of his conquests and sometimes by the oppressed as a route to peace. The latter approach was stated in modern secular terms 200 years ago by Kant when he advocated and wrote a brief constitution for a world federation of free states.[21] It has reached a practical expression in the League of Nations, the United Nations and numerous movements towards some form of global authority. Writing in a period of history when nationalism is fashionable, such an idea appears centralizing, but that was not how Kant envisaged his federation.

2.4   CONTRIBUTIONS FROM PHILOSOPHY

'It is obvious that the sum of all the individuals in Zuñi make up a culture beyond and above what those individuals have willed and created.'[22] Most readers of this book will not find that statement 'obvious' at all. It is, on the contrary, an assumption of a *realist* philosophy—that institutions have existences which can be separated from those of their members—which is not widely accepted in the twentieth century. Some management and some Marxist theorists, to name just two groups not usually to be found in alliance, are inclined towards a nominalist view that arises from their common positivism[23]—that organizations and societies have no existence apart from the activities and outlooks of their members. Among sociologists this has been a subject of debate and scorn has been poured on those who reify an organization, crediting it with an independent existence of its own. Yet this form of *realism* is frequently assumed in general conversation as well as in law, where a corporation, for instance, is called a legal person implying that it has a life of its own and can be held responsible for its misdeeds before a court of law; it is further emphasized by writers like Durkheim who believed that a 'whole is not identical with the sum of its parts . . . By reason of this principle, society is not a mere sum of individuals. Rather, the system formed by their association represents a specific reality which has its own characteristics.'[24] The crowd and the mob, the supporters and the rioters, are among the many names used to suggest that a collectivity has an existence that can be understood separately from its participants. Statements of loyalty to a company or to a country, again, assume a different order of being. Indeed a patriotic affirmation like 'I vow to thee my country' (note that both pronouns are in the singular) sounds odd if for 'country' is substituted 'nominalist collectivity of Englishmen'. Instinctive realism presents some analytical difficulty when applied to generalized groups like the crowd or the country; even more difficulty exists when more clearly defined organizations are under discussion. What, for instance, is meant by a national policy? In this case the phrase is normally used of some guidelines for action decided by a cabinet or responsible minister; 'company policy' can be employed even more vaguely, sometimes of guidelines written into a manual or the minutes of a meeting. More often policy refers to the subjective view of a particular official as to what will be considered the correct response to a given set of circumstances. In a company with a strong personality as chief executive, the policies are likely to be associated with his or her opinions; but in many commercial and non-commercial organizations, customs, traditions and phrases that credit the company with an independent mind of its own are freely used. 'This firm consistently treats its employees well' is a statement that suggests a distinction between the organization and its members. The sentence can be translated into some circumlocution like 'The board of directors always agrees to adopt the most favourable known practices in dealing with employees', but more is implied by the original statement. The entity has established a policy that the individual officer has not determined and is unlikely to destroy. It has been suggested[25] that there may be psychological reasons causing managers to take a realistic approach to their organizations. Personal responsibility for disaster is limited if the firm is considered to have a life of its own—a parallel with blaming crop failure on the gods—and people are persuaded that they are working for a higher entity. The instillation of loyalty brings the instinctive realism of the primitive tribe, described as 'obvious' in the quotation at the head of this section, into the modern organization. The realist approach may be expected to make centralization more palatable. In the following chapters the words realism or semi-realism will be applied to outlooks on organizations which assume some characteristics above the sum total of individual decision-making.

The third approach, a half-way house between realism and nominalism, is conceptualism. Applied to corporate organization, this view affirms that company policy is an idea that certain individuals have about the way the company works. An organization is an abstraction that represents a reality. A framework for understanding decentralization is provided by this approach, which is better adapted than either of the other two to distinguish the units that make up the corporation as well as to do justice to the mutual interdependence of the individual and the institution. For the purpose of identifying explanations, realistic and nominalistic trends will be mentioned, but a generally conceptualist approach will be followed.

This discussion illustrates a philosophic contribution to the subject in improving our understanding of the relationship between units in an organization, to provide a perspective on the fundamental issues, to criticize concepts often employed all too glibly and to bring greater precision into the words used. In fact some human attributes will be willed onto the organization in the following discussion. For instance, self-confidence in an organization—the shared view that disaster is not lurking around the next corner—is undoubtedly a contributory factor to decentralization.

In examining the tools of the discussion, a number of difficulties have to be faced. The compass of relevant factors is broad, and the construction of a theory has to take account not only of the breadth but also of the paradoxical nature of these factors. Thus, centralization may be prescribed for the well-being of, for instance, a voluntary organization: 'when Mr Jones took over, the society was falling apart; there was anarchy. He pulled the whole thing together.' Or it may be denounced as the corruption of power: 'Mr Jones was a supreme egoist who did permanent damage to this society in his mania for power'. At the very least a theory of centralization has to cover the dangers of anarchy and the corruption of power. It also has to take account of the fact that different observers can see either of these contradictory phenomena in the same set of circumstances. Some of the contradictions will be verbal, the words being used loosely. Some will be due to faulty observation or the bias of the observer. But there are likely to be some paradoxes that cannot be explained away, and must be incorporated in the theory. Take another statement about a voluntary organization: 'if we leave our local branches to run their own affairs, we are told that the organization is losing its bearings; but when we attempted more central direction, we were charged with deflecting the society from its real purposes'. In the kind of debate that this statement presupposes it is easy to talk about arriving at a compromise; but this may be facile. The truth may lie in accepting the paradox. A relevant method of argument is by means of the supposition that the opposite might have happened.[26] Thus, to every assertion about centralization there is a counter-proposition. 'If Mr Jones had not imposed his lust for power on the society, it would have survived.' The examination of such statements may be expected to provide a list of the variables that need to be investigated. Another method is by the use of analogy.

Analogies are often employed to aid the description of organization concepts, but easily end by causing confusion. This subject is pursued in the next chapter, but the use of analogy can easily prejudge the argument about realism. When an organization is said to have the characteristics of a living being and be conditioned by predetermined rules of survival and reproduction, the actual pressures on the organization can be misunderstood. However useful, analogies frequently mislead. A relevant example is the use of the word 'systems', which is widely and loosely employed to identify a once-neglected truth that the interrelationships within an organization or its parts are a key factor in its understanding. The interrelationships can be identified without all the confusions caused by trying to shape the study of human organizations around the study of natural organisms.[27] It may be illuminating to compare the working of a social system, like a company, with a natural system like a human body, but the analogy misleads when it stimulates a search for the checks and controls in an organization parallel to those which keep an even temperature or fight disease in the body. Centralization, for instance, is not controlled by some homeostatic process. A correct, that is modest, use of analogy can illuminate concepts like those that are the subject of this book, but the upgrading of the body analogy by the use of technical terms is not helpful.

2.5   THEOLOGICAL CONTRIBUTIONS

'The New Being . . . is effective in the life of the community, and it is not even excluded from nature, as is indicated by the sacraments.'[28] The paradox which lies at the heart of this book is intensified when examined against the theological perspective. On the one hand the body of sacred truth, the knowledge of the ultimate which cannot safely be delegated, forms a centralizing pressure. On the other, a strong pull to autonomy exists in the inner voice, the higher loyalty and the conscience. The issues may vary according to the form of the religion, but the tension is inescapable. The vitality of the small community and of the individual believer has to coexist with a leadership whose prime task is supposed to be vigilance for the purity of the truth. 'The boundaries have to be monitored, there is too much at stake to allow diffusion.'[29]

The concept of the boundary, indeed, is one that is dramatized and invested with fresh meaning by the theological outlook. The frontiers between truth and falsehood, being and non-being, idealism and realism, imagination and reality are given special significance along with the boundaries within societies and organizations. The identification of the boundary is undertaken by a process that can be described as practical mysticism, choosing between straightforward options by criteria that are intangible and hard to express in words. The guidelines are provided by the infinite, but the guides are human. The holy man, the church leader, the imam and the religious community are examples of centralized repositories of information that are indispensable to the believer. Against the pronouncements of authority the individual or the subordinate unit is ill-advised to revolt. There is a strong possibility of perishing for all eternity, and there may be serious inconveniences in the here and now as well.

But obedience does not ensure nirvana, and the information contained in the religious systems includes yet another paradox. If you attempt too self-consciously to achieve the ultimate, you will fail. 'Hubris'—self-satisfaction at one's own endeavour—is a most damning sin in religions ancient and modern. This penetrating insight is not unknown in secular thought. Critical truths cannot be mechanistically internalized; the person who strives whole-heartedly after goodness is not usually regarded as the most attractive character. In business, to take a different kind of example, the single-minded pursuit of profit easily leads to bankruptcy. In many spheres it can be seen that he who seeks to save his life will lose it.

Autonomy is also a theological concept, and one much discussed by the theologian who is quoted at the head of this section; but Tillich uses the word autonomy of a personal ability to explore and to create.[30] It is not opposed to centralization, but to *heteronomy*—the rule of an alien law, the other directed as opposed to the self-directed—and to *theonomy*, the ultimate meaning or environment within which an autonomous culture has to exist. This is not autonomy in the organizational sense, but it is a driving force in that direction, a sense of tension which underlies even the clearest creedal statement. This sense of tension contains a principle of great significance for non-religious systems wrestling with apparently meaningless lurches of authority. A so-called organization design needs to hold together the rival pulls of self-direction and direction from other sources. The theologian sees that a group of individuals, who think themselves divinely guided towards similar objectives, can produce an institution for mutual support and for the influencing of others. This may well form a pressure for decentralization, but not necessarily. The group may, in fact, be brought together in revolt against reforming tendencies in the central authority which are considered too relaxed. Movements like the Catholic opposition to liturgical reform can be seen as pressures towards an inverted centralization where the rebels assert their autonomy only to argue for greater control from the top. The existence of pressure groups of this type suggests an organization with norms that are unfavourable to autonomy.

Assertions about mystical authority as well as about autonomy are matched by another emphasis, that on community. There is a social gospel, albeit frequently a subject of controversy, in many religions. The truth is of such a nature that it can be tested and refined in the experience of a dedicated community, and in the contribution the community makes to a wider society. 'The adjustment of the Christian message to the regeneration of the social order' is the description used by one authority[31] for an outlook which gives rise to yet another group of tensions—concerning the extent to which the religious community makes its impact through secular institutions. Is the local church, for instance, mandated to assist in the life of its neighbourhood through political or community institutions, or does it make its distinctive contribution in avoiding the compromises required by such involvement? The answer to this question is not simply a matter of tactics, as is often suggested, or of a view of the relationship between the church and the world, as is also argued. One contribution of theological thinking is to demonstrate that such distinctions are necessarily blurred. The tactics have to express beliefs which, in their turn, reflect the place of man and society within the context of a higher order. The implicit compromise between the secular and the sacred organizations will be watched by the higher authority in the light of the sacred truths—even though the authority may itself be compromised and prejudiced about the way the truth is interpreted, like an ecclesiastical authority who is also a land-owner.

At the level of organization some systems give rise to autonomy more naturally than others. Buddhism promotes decentralization more naturally than most forms of Christianity. Where there is decentralization this may relate to the faith itself—a belief in direct communion with God—or to matters peripheral to that faith; the centre does not trouble itself with local customs. On the other hand, there may be a relationship to the norms of the society in which the body operates. Whether a religion is seen to be shaping society, as a phrase like 'an Islamic state' suggests, or whether it is adopting a method of government that is socially acceptable ('the democratization of the church') will depend upon the viewpoint of the observer. Procedures normally have to be found which allow for some sharing of power between authorities sacred and secular without tampering with the core beliefs. Where this proves impossible, as with the anarchistic sect or the all-demanding state, there follows persecution or withdrawal—possibly both. Equally, there are few religions which do not have some procedures for ejecting those who compromise on vital issues of faith however rarely such procedures are used.

The safeguarding of the truth, then, is an important and usually centralizing, theological insight; the body analogy has a more ambiguous influence. The concept of the Christian Church as the body of Christ, for instance, reinforces the authority of the local community or that of the higher powers according to where the emphasis is placed. The same is true of the sacraments. In most forms of Christianity the sacrament of holy communion is not regarded as an analogy at all. It is a direct transaction with the Almighty which gives identity to the local community. The right to conduct the ceremony is usually derived from a higher authority and is mediated by phrases like 'with the authority committed to me . . .;' but that authority is exercised in a routine fashion and is seldom refused. The actual holding of the ceremony is an assertion of autonomy—the community has direct access to the Almighty—and an assertion of the reality of the participating group. The sacramental outlook takes seriously the existence of the faithful community and gives it meaning above that of the individuals that make it up. Philosophical realism, described earlier in this chapter as a centralizing force, is thus incorporated into the activity of religious worship where it asserts a measure of autonomy while defining the limits.

The theological concepts of truth, autonomy, the boundary and community are among those which have been seen to contribute to an understanding of the theme of this book, while the means adopted by religious bodies to organize themselves will be examined briefly in Chapter 8. Statements of faith come in two forms: the mystical, which contain dogmatic and visionary assertions about the nature of God and man as well as the relationships between the two, and the wisdom literature, which recommends moral and social codes appropriate to an adherent. The distinction is not always intended or clear. God is seen to speak as emphatically about the conduct of daily life as about the heavenly vision; both the Koran and the Bible hold the two elements together. The mystical writings may make centralizing assertions, but these are also used to underpin statements about when to delegate and when to exercise authority; and of course the believer always represents the other half of the equation in each statement. The tension between the centralizing truths, and the role of the believer and the local community to which he or she belongs is dramatically emphasized by the word and the sacraments.

2.6 THE SOCIAL SCIENCES

Centralization and autonomy have not often appeared as major items in either economic or behavioural theories; apart from a small number of scholars whose work is discussed in the following chapters, the concepts have usually been lurking in the wings, appearing on the stage only briefly as characters of controversy. For instance, in politics there is the constitutional issue between central and local government, in economics the question of optimization and in sociology and psychology that of motivation. It would be a caricature to say that decentralization is praised on the grounds that it increases the motivation of the small unit and the satisfaction of its members or that centralization is seen under all circumstances to result in a more effective use of physical resources. Nevertheless, statements are made that suggest just such caricatures. In the present study it is implied that all the factors, personal as well as physical, contribute to an understanding of the place of centralization and decentralization in a theory of organization. The route of such a theory lies through the consideration of the issues discussed in the next five chapters, including decision-making, structure, power, authority, control, conflict and alienation. These are the contributions of the social sciences, but closely related insights will be considered here—the unit of organization, the growth of the firm, rationality and the frame of reference.

The unit of organization

Discussion of decentralization is bedevilled by uncertainties about the unit of organization to which decisions are being delegated. This simple but neglected issue has already been illustrated and will recur on these pages. Too many generalizations fail to note the unit or sub-unit with sufficient precision. For instance devolution to one level can lead to less autonomy for those below that level. These latter find that they had more independence before the alleged decentralization, the immediate superior exercising more authority than the remote. A failure to understand this has led to generalizations which describe companies as decentralized when to most of their employees the opposite appears the case. Normally, the unit of autonomy will be a group in the hierarchy, those at some level in a chain. The 'group' may in fact be just one person but, in principle, this book is concerned with organizational rather than individual autonomy. There are other possibilities however, including units in a non-hierarchical arrangement or a lateral relationship between two groups on the same level. There are, too, the unofficial as well as the official units—interest groups or power centres like a number of employees of the same profession.

Another example of an unofficial unit is a group of managers of the same specialization or of the same nationality in an international firm who may influence the changing nature of the autonomy of the official groups to which they belong.

The growth of the firm

Theories of the growth of the firm consider many issues, among them: monopoly, oligopoly, maximization, managerial interests as against those of shareholders and the use of resources.[32] Consciously pursued policies of monopoly and oligopoly argue for a measure of centralization to mastermind the process. In the case of monopoly, the company as a whole may have to negotiate with government administrators and give undertakings binding on the whole concern. The firm in an oligopolistic situation will need to coordinate, at the least, its facilities to match its competitors. The requirements of maintaining a market position will lead to centralization unless it is seen that devolution will increase competitive efficiency. Maximizing policies are likely to have similar consequences, but under this heading the conflicts which have been identified will limit the centralizing effect. One theory upholds that it is the interests of managers that are being maximized, not the profits of the firm.[33] This is an illustration of an internal conflict—there are other possible priorities, from a concentration on shareholders' funds to that of market share—which restrains the centralizing tendencies. The deployment of surplus resources is another example. Where the resources are of central management expertise, the redeployment is likely to have a centralizing influence.[34] The effects and counter-effects of company policies will be observed in the following chapters, and especially those (11–17) which concern the multinational firm.

Rationality and a frame of reference

This problem of units and interest groups whose boundaries intermingle lies behind much of the discussion on rationality. The limits of rationality was a phrase that gained currency to explain why organizations settled for the second best—because what was best for the whole did not suit all the parts. Hence, there is a bargaining, lobbying process to secure consensus as far as possible. One authority expressed rationality in terms of the frame of reference of the participants and of the limits to their knowledge,[35] but the link is not essential. Both information and a specific frame of reference—a set of beliefs, expectations and objectives—do restrain members of an organization from a single-minded pursuit of its stated goals, but either by itself would do the same. Another contribution to the discussion of rationality is that which distinguishes between rational and natural systems.[36] Rational in this context refers to thought-out, predetermined arrangements which are in accordance with the objectives of the organization, while the natural system is the one that just develops. The two are not mutually exclusive, but when a lure towards centralization or a drift to autonomy is observed in an organization this represents a natural system, the pushes and pulls that are not immediately incorporated into the official structures. The rational system takes over when a change is proposed. Research into the subject is devoted to studying a current condition and a process of change, to discovering the forces that are at work beneath the surface, as it were, and propelling the organization towards greater centralization or the reverse. The drift is usually in the former direction; the lack of a policy of devolution leads to central decision-making. The process is sometimes reversed by thought-out moves towards autonomous units. Small firms may not have the resources for central decision-making, but may still only pay lip-service to delegation, a situation likely to cause considerable confusion.

Prediction is made easier, but not necessarily more accurate, where rational processes can be assumed. An illuminating example of the need to understand the less obviously rational as well comes from a new branch of the social sciences, the study of innovation. This study itself began with the premise that there existed an essentially rational subject, with clear objectives, and that the progress of discovery would be conditioned accordingly.[37] A whole system of innovation was mapped out, with its planning and its feedback, and the belief asserted that progress had become a matter of routine. The limitations that were noticed were capable of being overcome by more effective planning. A number of studies demonstrated that this view was altogether too optimistic and did not square with ascertainable facts. The uncertainties in the innovation process were much greater than could be handled by rational models. The organization, the individual aptitudes, the conflict of objectives, the cultural background and many other factors, called for attention. The conflict of the rational and the natural, as seen in such an example, will also be seen to have a considerable effect on the centralization or otherwise of the organization.

The distinction between rational and natural systems is illuminating up to a point, but it does not do justice to the conflicts that occur when participants have different frames of reference and perhaps contradictory objectives. More than one party may be pursuing a rational approach, acting in their own best interests but without achieving them. The lack of achievement does not necessarily mean that some natural system has taken over and pushed a group along other lines than rational considerations might indicate; it may simply mean that the conflict within the organization conditions the result, that the rational systems have been pursued but failure or compromise has resulted. The pressures for centralization increase where the conflict leads to frustration and opposition that threatens the existence of the autonomous unit.

Another approach related to natural systems is that of exchange theory.[38] This starts from the assumption that a group will expect to gain more than it gives out of a transaction in terms of its own values. The gains may be financial, social or related to some other interest, and will almost certainly be a combination of more than one kind of satisfaction. If the attempt is thwarted, then the probable reaction is to seek other and unofficial forms of reward. Over-centralization, like under-compensation, may lead to sabotage or to restrictions on work to make up for the denied discretion. This will produce reactions on the part of those in authority which sometimes lead to a continuing spiral of misunderstanding.[39]

2.7   THE CONCEPTS IN LAW

The legal approach differs from the perspectives examined so far in defining the subject more precisely. A relationship, often loosely stated, is replaced by an allocation of powers and responsibilities which can be upheld or denied in a court of law. The tighter definition, which also applies in accountancy, is still the subject of debate. The courts will scrutinize whether the powers are being used properly, in the way allocated by the legislature. The concept can be examined in the relations between central and local government, in the organization of the legal system itself and in the way the law influences the exercise of authority in commercial, social, political and other units of society.

In this country legal dealings between central and local government are not determined by ancient rights and privileges but by statute or delegation. The last-named is relatively uncontroversial. The local authority acts as agent for the central government, as in the case of a county council building a trunk road financed by the Ministry of Transport. Delegation, in this case, implies only a limited autonomy. One party possesses the authority and hives it off to another with restricted terms of reference—the engineering specifications of the road and probably its route have already been determined. The Ministry retains control of the operation whose conditions can vary but where there is always a 'revocable transfer of power'.[40] Limited autonomy, which can be terminated without much difficulty, is one type which will be considered later in Chapter 10. Substantial powers of decision-making may be transferred albeit for a limited period.

More controversial, and more difficult to alter in the short term, is the statutory allocation of responsibilities. In this case the law determines that certain powers are appropriately settled on local authorities, while others are retained by central government; some of the authority may still be retained at the centre, by means of financing or subsidy arrangements, but the local authority has powers that can only be changed by the legislature. Nevertheless, changes do occur and one cause of instability is that the legal principle is hard to define. Perceptions about a suitable division of the powers vary, so the assumption that some areas of decision-making are most suitably left to local authorities does not easily translate into a set of criteria. The other reason for instability arises where there is national debate on a subject, such as education, which has traditionally been a local responsibility. The fact that votes in local authority elections frequently represent reaction against the government in power rather than opinion on local issues increases differences of view as to how the issues should be handled. These differences are exacerbated still further by the fact that local decisions rely on the centre for part of their funding. Recent trends in this country have resulted in greater centralization; while in France, traditionally a more centralized country, there have been moves in the opposite direction. No doubt the changes partly reflect inherent problems, such as those already mentioned, and partly the difficulty of finding a suitable unit of local government for devolution—one that is not too small to be viable or too large to be acceptable. Nevertheless, the existing law clearly does provide for local authorities powers that they may, and often must, exercise; and these powers can only be removed by a change in the law. While the present legislation remains, and subject to the judgement of the courts, local autonomy on specified issues is absolute. This is more than can be said of subordinate units in other organizations and represents a level of decentralization which is guaranteed against arbitrary alteration. The guarantee is only limited by a means of change which is both predetermined and cannot be operated without due notice.

Another form of constitutional relationship is to be found in countries with a federal type of government. The United States is the archetype of constitutions that are found in Canada, Germany, Nigeria and other countries. In such cases there is a document, a written constitution, which sets out the relationships between the federal government and the states or provinces. There is also a court which adjudicates disputes. The guarantee of decentralization is, in this case, even stronger than with the unwritten constitution as there are likely to be provisions which make change difficult. The powers may be altered by unanticipated judgements of the court, but otherwise legal change is unlikely. Recent history in both North American countries has included controversy between the two tiers of government; but no attempts have been made to change the legal status by central government—nor by state or provincial governments, except for the referendum in Quebec in which the separatists were defeated. The pressures and counter-pressures have been economic and political. The legal system continues to protect a carefully defined separation of powers.

The two legal arrangements just described concern decentralization in constitutional law; in other branches of law there are circumstances where the powers of superior officers over their subordinates are restricted by the allocation of legal responsibilities. The Coal Mines Acts in Britain contain clauses making colliery managers responsible for the operation of the law in their pits, conforming to safety and other regulations. This is a legally enforced decentralization, identifying subordinate officers within an organization, and placing certain decisions out of bounds to their superiors. The Health and Safety at Work Act (1974) contains similar provisions whereby criminal actions can be brought both against the company, and against an individual who holds a position named in the Act as being responsible. Both the company and the named executives can be penalized, and their superior officers cannot instruct them to infringe the law. Legally, at least, certain decisions cannot be taken away from them. Yet another example is criminal libel, and the other laws which control publication. The editor of a newspaper is legally answerable, not the proprietor. In all such cases the law looks at the part of the organization which is most immediately concerned with safety or with the written word, or with whatever other issue is at stake, and not necessarily at the centre of authority in the organization.

Turning from the criminal law, legislation concerning principal and agent also affects the measure of centralization.[41] A subsidiary, for instance, is a company in its own right. In the case of a dispute that is unresolvable by other means, the parent company acts as owner through a shareholders' meeting which has powers to dismiss the board. A contractual relationship exists, although it may be difficult for subsidiary management to take advantage of this except in unusual circumstances. The position of the foreign subsidiary, discussed in detail in part II, may be different because in this case the two parties are subject to different legal systems. In some countries the law is more protective of the interests of national citizens than in others. For instance, the Fruehauf Corporation of Detroit has had troubles in recent years with its subsidiaries in both Britain and France, but with totally different consequences. In the case of France, the local management were given orders from Detroit which were contrary to their interests, as they saw them, and to French trading policies. The president of the subsidiary took the matter before a commercial court which agreed that a foreign company could not issue such instructions, a ruling that was upheld on appeal.[42]

That case occurred in the mid-1960s. Ten years later British directors resisted the purchase by the parent company of the outstanding shares in the local subsidiary. After the success of the bid, members of the British board were dismissed. These incidents bring up another relevant aspect of law, that only minimum standards are fixed; above these the law does not intervene. The difference between the French and the British cases was that one came above and the other below the line of intervention.

Despite the different circumstances and outcomes of these cases, the principle remains of a legal relationship which may be influenced by national legislation, but in which the shareholder and shareholding are important considerations. So is that of limited liability. This was brought out in the insolvency of the Belgian subsidiary of the Badger Corporation, an American firm of engineering consultants and itself a subsidiary of Raytheon, one of the world's largest companies.[43] The issue here was the payment of redundancy allowances to staff when the company went out of business. None of the parties to the protracted dispute doubted the legal position. The subsidiary had been declared bankrupt by a Belgian court and its shareholders were not under any obligation to pay; they were protected by the law of limited liability. The Badger Corporation was eventually induced to pay as a result of international agreements entered into by government, employers and trade unions in Belgium and America under the auspices of the Organization for Economic Cooperation and Development, but these were voluntary agreements and possessed no legal force in either country.

The parent–subsidiary relationship, then, concerns the allocation of powers in such a way that the subsidiary has certain legal rights and responsibilities. These may sometimes lead to dramatic assertions of independence, but more often produce statements designed to improve a bargaining position like the tax implications of certain policies in a given country. The parent company has the ultimate power of the shareholder, but also enjoys restrictions on its responsibility such as limited liability. The autonomy of the subsidiary is less easy to defend by resort to legal action than is the autonomy of a unit of local government, although the latter may be more circumscribed in practice. The legal concept is to point to defined issues on which authority is clearly stated. Other issues are determined by the processes of lobbying and control within the organization. A legal measure of decentralization may be narrow and have little influence on other relationships between the parties, but can also be the ultimate defence of autonomy. The law is usually invoked when there is a breakdown in relations, a time when it can be used to defend (or attack) the independence.

2.8   THE CONCEPTS IN ACCOUNTING

The profession of accountancy developed from the need to ensure that the income and the expenditure of an organization conformed to its rights and obligations. Thus, in the Middle Ages, the steward kept accounts to ensure that the money was collected and spent according to existing customs and agreements.[44] As organizations grew, two among the further demands placed upon the accountant were:

(a)   to ensure central control over the sources and uses of funds;
(b)   to facilitate administration by measuring the success or failure of a particular unit.

Under (a) the profession was asked to provide the tools for centralization, and under (b) appropriate measuring devices to enable decentralization to take place. Concepts were devised to form a theoretical framework for interpreting these processes. Centralization was explained in terms of the need for *optimization* and the fear of *sub-optimization*. The centre alone, in other words, could take a satisfactory overall view; the needs of the whole were regarded as different from those of the parts, and to leave individual units to make their own decisions produced waste. Ranged against the financial arguments for centralization are a number of arguments which suggest that greater autonomy for individual units reduces administrative expenses and delays, while improving motivation. The decentralizing demand is met in business organizations by *profit centres*, *cost centres* and other arrangements designed to allow the maximum decision-making within the particular unit subject to the overarching needs of the whole organization. The influence of the centre operates through the sanctioning of budgets, a word which forms the final link in the conceptual chain which produces a decentralized structure. Since the overseeing of administration has usually been among the duties undertaken by the finance function, the administrative bias towards decentralization is a counter-weight to the pressures in the opposite direction. The profit centre was one of the answers to the further debate as to how satisfactory loci of autonomy could be determined. It also provokes the decentralizing argument enshrined in sayings like: 'We make the money, while head office spends it.' If, however, the profit centre had control of its profits, the company would be prevented from embarking on new ventures. The ambiguous nature of moves which theoretically support decentralization, but can deny it, appears to be typical of the subject, and will reappear in that light.

   The development of accounting methods increased the visibility of the financial condition of an organization and further heightened the centralization debate. Once the ability existed to discern how individual segments were faring, growth in size led to a demand for autonomous units. More recently the development of management techniques, like standard costing, diminished discretion at lower levels; but at the same time limits within which other forms of discretion could be exercised. This development brought with it another of the paradoxes with which the subject is encompassed. The issuing of instructions restricting the subordinate levels, 'these methods must be followed', could lead to greater autonomy if followed by: 'You can spend your own money so long as the accounting forms are completed regularly.' This latter approach, in its turn, stimulated further developments which brought accounting theory face to face with the difficulty of producing a monitoring system which performs a number of functions simultaneously.

Among the functions are the effort to reduce the danger of sub-optimization by providing prompt and efficient messages to the centre about the state of each unit's performance, while at the same time the system provides incentives to the local authority or management to make decisions which will have a favourable effect on the well-being of the organization as a whole. The nature of the paradox is emphasized by the fact that more than accounting issues are at stake. The motivation of subordinate managers may be shattered if the calculations seem arbitrary and vital influences remain outside their control. In a business there is, for instance, the difficulty of allocating assets between different divisions with common services: 'There are four divisions using this site so who pays for the policing, the car-parking and the fence-repairing?' The implications of such a question lie at the root of much discussion on issues with deeper implications. Writers on business usually deal with the broader issue of allocation of head office overheads to divisions. Among the proposals made are the use of sampling techniques to relate, for instance, the corporate assets to the level of divisional activity, and the criterion of avoidable assets—those assets which would be rendered unnecessary if the division were abolished.[45] Another approach has been entitled the *contribution margin*, the revenue after deducting the cost of sales and the variable expenses. This concentrates attention on the factors that are subject to the manager's control. One criticism is that attention is directed away from all the fixed expenses, although some of them will be controllable, and this leads to another question: the relationship of decentralization to budgeting. The argument is that divisional managers have a greater or less influence on their fixed costs according to the part they play in formulating the capital budgets, and that to leave fixed costs out of the calculation is to relieve them of the responsibilities of decentralization, responsibilities which are inseparable from the motivation argument. The problem of identifying the controllable parts of a manager's contribution takes another form of a *return on investment* calculation as a means of identifying divisional performance.[46] While such a calculation is often regarded as the principal means of judging a manager—return on investment is what business is supposed to be about, while comparable measures are frequently sought for other types of organization—it has been argued that measurements based on this calculation encourage managers to take actions contrary to the interests of their company, like retiring assets prematurely to increase the nominal return shown by a particular division.[47] The upshot of the argument is to reveal that the decision-making is so complex that a single measure by itself cannot summarize the consequences.

A particular theme of discussion in the profession that will recur in this book is that of transfer-pricing—that is, the price which one unit pays for a product or service from another within the same organization. Clearly a small change in this price can make one unit appear successful while another seems to fail, and the mechanism for determining the price is all-important for any attempt at decentralization. There are likely to be two ingredients in the price when set: the rules, laid down centrally but perhaps after some consultation, and a process of bargaining. The rules presumably define the method by which the selling unit avoids a loss, but can only specify a market price if the product is not unique. If there is an acceptable market price, most writers recommend that it should be followed. The recommendation, in its turn, has some consequences. One is the need for provision for the special circumstances that apply within a particular company, another is that the purchasing unit may wish to go outside the company if more favourable terms can be obtained. There are always discretionary elements in a market price; if there were not presumably the same product would always cost the same and there would be no competition. Hence, a rule that stipulates adherence to the market price does not eliminate bargaining between the units concerned, but it does make the decision easier to interpret in theory. More difficult, in theory and in practice, is to determine the transfer price when the product is unique and there are no precedents. This is frequently the case when components are being sold within a company, and is even more frequent when services are being provided internally in any sort of organization.

A number of ways to determine a transfer price for the unique product of service have been proposed. All have their limitations, but are relevant to this discussion as elements in an attempt at decentralization. One is by *marginal cost pricing*[48] in which marginal manufacturing cost in the selling unit is related to net marginal revenue in the buying department. This method is designed to meet the problem of motivation; it gives both the units concerned an incentive to buy or sell at prices that are likely to be optimal for the company. The method has been criticized on the grounds that it may not give a clear reflection of the performance of the unit.[49] An alternative is to determine transfer prices by *mathematical programming*; but this has also been criticized on the grounds that the results provide a limited view of management performance, even if an optimal incentive scheme does exist. The administrative difficulties in practice also make it unlikely that this method will be used, even if some advantages can be demonstrated in theory. Game theory has also been suggested, but rejected on the same grounds. Studies have shown that market price is used as a yardstick for a transfer price whenever possible; where product uniqueness made this method inappropriate full cost is preferred as a basis for the rules rather than marginal cost.[50] It should be added that no rules or techniques have been devised which eliminate the bargaining process, even though it may be driven underground in an authoritarian organization. Bargaining power and the factors which influence it—importance to the organization, knowledge, personality and leadership among many others—will influence the result whatever the rules. The consequential need for a procedure for resolving disputes, normally devised at the centre, will constrain any measure of decentralization.

2.9   OVERVIEW

This chapter has brought out a mystery at the heart of the subject: the uncanny resemblances in the way that different disciplines, starting from different standpoints, identify and confront similar issues. The confrontation goes back to myths and legends which advocate both centralization and autonomy, while the former is preferred in harsh situations. The logic of pursuing objectives as diverse as those of the government, the business firm, the voluntary organization and the church lead to similar consequences. Normally, centralization is seen as a vice, but the same can be true of decentralization when it is regarded as a sign of weakness or indeed of irresponsibility. The following chapters, and in particular the case study that stands at the heart of this book, will explore this paradox further and examine concrete situations; local assertiveness brings pressure for greater autonomy, and danger or disaster lead to centralization. Meanwhile, a number of issues have been identified for further consideration, as diverse as:

(a)   the safeguarding of vital information;
(b)   the instillation of loyalty;
(c)   the defining of the boundaries of the organization and the unit of autonomy;
(d)   the practicalities of centralization;
(e)   the emergence of bureaucracy;
(f)   the division of powers;
(g)   the absorption of different and often conflicting traditions;
(h)   the bargaining process within an organization and with the environment;
(i)   the use of analogies drawn from the physical world.

These issues will haunt us throughout these pages as will the verbal pairs and the paradoxes that have also emerged, expressed in statements like: 'The approach can be realist, attributing to the organization characteristics which imply that it has a life of its own apart from its members, or nominalist, in which case it is seen as having no existence that is distinct from the sum of its parts. There is also the conceptualist view which stands between the two.'

Another pair of alternatives is the universalist, which assumes that a given prescription will apply to all organizations, and the contingent, in which prescriptions are only valid when related to particular sets of circumstances or conditions. This dichotomy has the added difficulty that a given set of contingent factors may then beget generalizations that are themselves treated as universal.

The list of contrasts and paradoxes—the realist and the nominalist, the universal and the contingent, the authoritarian and the participative, and the monitoring and the administrative and the rest—provides our point of entry. The distinctions are not necessarily alternatives; there is not always an either/or situation, although much discussion appears to assume that there is. The nature of the subject requires some exercise in synthesis, since both halves of each contrast contain some relevant truth. In the pages that follow, the distinctions will be further explained and used in interpretation while a fuller discussion of universalist and contingency theories will be found in the next chapter. In Chapters 9 and 10, as a prelude to part II, the distinctions are translated into a number of propositions.

3 Decision-Making and Theory

'No more distressing moment can ever face a British government than that which requires it to come to a hard and fast and specific decision.'[1] The quotation states a problem at the heart of the present discussion. The mythology of decisions that are taken is faced by the reality of decisions that just happen, and occasionally have to be made 'hard and fast'—a cautionary statement to introduce a review of decision-making, and a reminder that there is a process rather than an event under consideration. The process, however, is sometimes better understood by examining the result than the events which lead up to it. Without decision-making there is no centralization and this chapter selects some relevant aspects, some attempts to penetrate the meaning of decision. The review begins with a look at the words and analogies used in explanation and ends by sampling a mathematical approach.

3.1 THE LANGUAGE OF ORGANIZATION

The discussion of organization is couched in a language which can be traced to three sources. One is a group of words whose principal usage is for this subject; 'centralization' and 'decentralization' are two of them. Another source is the vocabulary of the social sciences from which are derived terms like 'roles', 'groups', 'authority' and 'socialization'. The third consists of terms introduced to the discussion by the use of analogy. These latter groups overlap to a certain extent. The word 'role', for instance, is derived from the theatre, but in this case the analogy is not obtrusive, it does not colour the argument as do words appropriated from the natural sciences like 'growth', 'evolution' and 'systems'. These are used to explain organization behaviour, but also confuse the explanations. Sometimes the boundary between analogy and reality is hard to detect. Social darwinism[2] is a historical example. The application of the theories of evolution and natural selection to the development of the social unit was intended to describe a process that was actually occurring; many exponents did not think they were talking in terms of analogy at all. As the factual basis for the theory disappeared, the language lingered on and lost some of its meaning. The word 'evolution' has come to mean little more than change, but still carries overtones of inevitability which are inappropriate to social organization. In any case natural evolution is too slow a process to be relevant to human history, and the idea of inevitability can be deeply misleading. When, for instance, a change in organization structures, undertaken by a number of companies at the same time, is described as 'evolutionary', there is a suggestion that other companies are advised to follow, but this is not so; the advisability depends on numerous circumstances unrelated to an evolutionary process.

Another use of natural analogy which can mislead is to be found in the phrase 'the corporate state'. As soon as the transfer to reality is made, the phrase acquires emotive power unrelated to the truth or falsity of the comparison. A similar criticism applies to the idea of age. An organization does not suffer an unavoidable loss of vitality such as accompanies human ageing. It is not young or old; it is new or old. It does not suffer hardening of the arteries, although some organizations are all too likely to experience resistance to change; but the changes can occur or be resisted at any time in its history. Yet another word used in misleading ways is 'growth'. An organization grows incrementally, by adding fresh business in the case of a commercial concern. The growth may be in large or small increments, and it may be by the expansion of existing business or by the purchase of other companies; in no cases does the process resemble the growth of cells in a natural organism, and phrases like 'organic development' produce a distorted view.

'Homeostasis' is a distinctively biological term that has been applied to organizations to make a parallel with the steady state observed in nature; its use is often accompanied by another analogy—the survival of the fittest. Both concepts are plausible, although the meaning of the word fittest has to be extended to make it so.[3] One trouble with such analogies is that they often appear to support the status quo or at least a restricted view of possible developments. If the health of the organization is felt to depend on the present balance of forces, planned change is seen as unhelpful. This is a dangerous view at a time when innovation may be essential to commercial survival. A further misleading use of analogy is when a rival power centre within an organization is called a 'parasite', obscuring its necessary function.

Nevertheless, there are occasions when a word from natural science like 'equilibrium' can be used of observable facts. In part II of this book, for instance, the concept of the normal line is an example. This simply indicates that there are strong pressures preventing most companies from becoming too centralized or too decentralized, between them producing a normal level of centralization around which changes occur. But these limited observations do not suggest complex and universal forces like those that maintain the body temperature in a mammal. Nor, above all, is there any inevitability. On the contrary, the pressures operate independently of conscious planning and there is no principle which begins to resemble a natural law, although there is support for predictions whose force will vary according to the type of organization. In the case of commercial bodies the degree of centralization will vary, for instance, according to the nature of the business, but there is usually a lure to centralization; in the case of voluntary and charitable organizations, there is frequently a drift in the opposite direction.

The ultimate use of biological analogies arrived with the systems approach.[4] Inasmuch as this phrase is used to emphasize that organizations are indivisible and that changes in one part will affect the whole, the approach is no more than a much-needed corrective to generalizations that ignored such considerations. But if presented as an elaborate scheme, full of biological jargon like 'homeostasis', it fails to assist in the understanding of how organizations work. On the contrary, the statement of the theory prejudices the understanding and prejudges relationships in favour of centralization. Taken to biological and physical extremes, systems theory becomes a sophisticated restatement of the body analogy discussed in the last chapter and found to be a view with a centralizing bias.

This discussion illuminates the need to distinguish between analogies which are used to express a single point, and can be a considerable aid to explanation, and those which represent a total transfer of an analytical framework and frequently prejudge and confuse issues which demand further examination.

Other relevant entries in the vocabulary of organization are considered in the pages that follow. Here it remains to discuss the process whereby a person enters an organization and adapts to it, the general initiation procedures and absorption of standards and customs collectively known as 'socialization'. The conditioning process, during which the outlooks of new participants change, takes place gradually and with differing degrees of completeness, while there is a dual relationship with centralization. The formal processes, those that are planned and programmed, are usually framed towards the acceptance of the norms and outlooks of the central authority. The military recruit swears allegiance to the sovereign, not to the regiment, the converts are baptized into a church that is wider than the congregation that accepts them, and the new entrant to the large company goes through a course that is likely to have been designed at head office. Indeed those businesses which run on more centralized systems also develop more elaborate measures of socialization. This is part of the general care of the organization which is a feature of some centralizing companies, but is not the whole story; a high level of unity and unanimity produced by thorough initiation courses can also make delegation easier. The conditions under which this is likely to happen—like a military unit on operations or, more ambiguously, the foreign subsidiary of a multinational company—will be specified later, but they are exceptional and normally a high level of formal socialization is linked to centralization.[5] A notable exception to this is to be found in some voluntary organizations where decentralization is the norm but is coupled with elaborate and selective socialization procedures. This feature of such organizations has been noted by a number of authors.

The informal processes, on the other hand, are usually seen as decentralizing—the absorption of the ideas and aims of the peer group which clash with those of the organization as a whole. In fact this is the point at which resistance to the central authority is built up and aspirations for local autonomy arise. Many factors will influence the intensity of loyalty that develops around the subordinate unit, but the strength of feeling will be affected by a divergence of interest from the centre. Thus, the prison will have the greatest difference between the official socialization—to keep the inmates confined and to reform them—and the unofficial which develops standards of resistance to authority and skills in evading recapture. The company in which all the benefits go to the centre is likely to develop resistance in the subsidiaries. Informal socialization is one of the checks and balances in the system.

Another useful contrast is contained in the words 'instrumental' and 'expressive'. First used to differentiate between the requirements of an organization for the instrumental needs of inputs and allocations and the expressive needs of social and moral qualities, the words are drawn from the distinction between training and education. More recently, the phrase 'instrumental activities' has been used of calculative involvement in an organization (working for reward) in contrast to expressive (voluntary).[6] This use is readily transferable to decentralization. 'Expressive' means decentralization for its own sake, as an appropriate method of structuring an organization. 'Instrumental', on the other hand, is the use of decentralization as a technique, an effective way of ensuring that centralizing objectives are attained by granting an appearance of autonomy which is revocable.

3.2   THE UNIVERSAL AND THE PARTICULAR

The distinction between universal prescriptions and those that are closely related to particular circumstances is inescapable but hard to define. Here is one of the essential dichotomies at the heart of the subject, where definition is made difficult because few would be willing to be placed on either side, and those who place others often argue loosely from a limited universality. To say that 'decentralization is to be preferred under all circumstances' is certainly to make a universalist statement; it is also unlikely to be said. To say that 'centralization is to be preferred for an organization which has logistic problems in the constant movement of objects from one unit to another' specifies a particular condition, but is still universalist compared to more detailed statements bringing in an array of conditions. It can be said that a truly universal approach, which states that a certain prescription will prove correct under all circumstances, is rare. Some writers on motivation appear to take such an approach, although most would admit that their evidence has been collected in one culture or under limited circumstances. One, known as the 'personnel development series', is a management technique which, it is claimed, has been tested in different cultures,[7] and can be applied, with adaptions, under all conditions that a company is likely to encounter. There have been a number of such prescriptions for management style. Normally, they show weaknesses when elevated to a general theory. For instance, they apply to certain cultures, certain types of organizations or to commercial concerns in certain industry sectors. A series of proposals have attracted attention in the last thirty years. Some have distinguished between different kinds of needs—named by one authority as a hierarchy of needs and by another as hygiene factors and motivators.[8] Other writers differentiated between styles—by means of the managerial grid, theory X and theory Y or by distinguishing managerial styles.[9] Each of these theories has its own strengths. All identify human needs and responses to work; they remove the argument from narrowly interpreted incentives and responses on the one hand, or impersonal forces on the other, to concentrate on the actor. The distinction between hygiene factors, those which have to be put right first like money and physical conditions, and motivators (the opportunities for more interesting and challenging work), appeals to common sense. Many puzzling features of responses to changes in working conditions are illuminated by these propositions.

Problems arise with these universal views partly because they appear to assume what they need to prove, and only to be supportable within narrow frames of reference. If a person shares the values proposed, then the system works. Given a different view of life, a different social standpoint or a different work ethic, other prescriptions may be required. The values and their ranking often seem to be arbitrarily selected in spite of claims that they are research-based. Any failure to respond to universal approaches is regarded as deviance, or misfortune, rather than as evidence that personal objectives differ; but a major weakness of universal approaches is their inability to explain cultural differences. One example is the present fascination in the United States and in Europe with the Japanese style of management. Bewilderment as to what are the differences from Western methods, partly caused by the difficulty of distinguishing between the appearance and the reality in both West and East, illustrates the problem of assessing the force of cultural differences. Nevertheless, the first attack on universalism came not from the standpoint of culture but from that of technology.

Early management theorists were usually universalist, indeed the view that management principles would apply anywhere was a cardinal tenet – principles like unity of command and span of control were considered paramount. The attack came with the discovery that the span of control actually existing in an industrial organization depended on the technology in use rather than on opinions about management principles.[10] The average number of workers controlled by the first line supervisor, for instance, varied from 14 for plants which manufactured to the customer's specific requirements to 56 for mass production factories, and the variations, at least at the lower levels of management, were convincingly shown to be related to the technology.

For over twenty years authors on both sides of the Atlantic have been identifying specific factors which appear to influence organizations in spite of beliefs about what ought to happen;[11] the results have been systematized into contingency theories, as the statements are now called.[12] Technology, size, nationality, industry sector and many other factors have been held to influence organization variables. Among the studies that extended contingency theory to non-industrial concerns was one that examined mental hospitals, rehabilitation centres, family agencies and schools.[13] This affirmed that the more routine the organization, the more centralized the decision-making. The policies were also more likely to be stated in a manual of rules backed by precise job specifications. When organizations operate with routine technologies, staff tend to report more managerial emphasis on efficiency and quantity than on quality of service and morale. These are the kind of results which could be expected to vary by culture, but an example of another specific influence is this effect of routine tasks on the degree of centralization.

The present study is much influenced by the contingency approach in a general sense, which may not coincide in detail with the view of any particular supporter or opponent about contingency theory. It is also recognized that many authorities are sub-universalist; they look for one level of contingent factors rather than facing the complexity of multiple variables. It is easy to become, as it were, hooked on a particular variable, like the routine nature of the task just mentioned, and stress this to the exclusion of other influences. This sub-universalist view may sometimes be justified, but the assumption in the present study is that a complex variety of pressures combine to influence the degree of autonomy that a unit has and that the process can only be understood by identifying the variety.

The approach can also be called semi-deterministic—where certain factors arise, then certain conditions are likely to follow. This corresponds with the results of the present writer's investigations into centralization as recorded below in part II, where a lure to centralization is identified; this sets up problems and leads, in its turn, to pressures for more autonomy in the units. The strengths of the lures and pressures are much influenced by a number of factors, like industry sector, and can be offset by planning; semi-determinism implies that certain results will follow unless a sustained effort is made to move in a different direction. There is assumed to be a range of variables which affect the degree of centralization. While it is denied that there is any universal principle to indicate what that degree should be, there is a need to identify the factors which will influence the organization and the conditions under which any particular factor will operate. The results, then, lead to statements about the optimum conditions under different sets of circumstances. Meanwhile, we turn to the language of decision-making to explain how centralization and autonomy arise.

3.3   THE LANGUAGE OF DECISION-MAKING

'The very complexity that has made a theory of the decision-making process essential has made its construction exceedingly difficult.'[14] In the language of decision-making the word 'process' holds an important place. A continuous stream of activity and of interactions between groups and individuals who are privy to the decision, is understood. The style of the activity may vary from the absolutely dictatorial to the fully participative, running through many degrees of sharing in between. But the distinctions are formal, based on the way a particular organization determines its style, the actual position is less clear. The dictator's discretion is constrained by the information supplied to him or her. Dictators are at the mercy of their advisers just because they take so many decisions themselves; their knowledge of the background to any particular decision is limited by the sheer range of choices. They sit, as it were, at the apex of a biased filtering system the effects of which they only partially overcome by their selection of the advisers. Naturally, they will have been chosen because their prejudices are similar to those of their leader; but total centralization remains a myth, as does total participation. The latter would only exist if all the characters concerned were of equal strength, or weakness. Total participation would produce infinite decentralization, and centralization would stand at infinity if the reverse occurred. Neither of the two extremes exists, but it is useful to picture them in order to focus on the oscillations that occur in between.

The shared nature of decision-making is an insight necessary to a discussion of the measurement of centralization. If the decisions are shared, then a straightforward measure of where they have been taken is unlikely to be accurate. Contemporary theories of decision-making stress the amount of participation. Words like 'bargaining'[15] and 'arena'[16] are being used to suggest a virile exchange rather than a simple identification of where a decision is taken.

Identifying a decision

There are a number of ways of examining decisions for the purpose of measuring the degree of centralization. The most straightforward and the most common is by determining the *locus* of the decision-making,[17] that is, the position in the organization at which the decision is normally taken. Questions can be asked about who is known to decide on a particular issue; by comparing the results in one organization with those in another, a measure of centralization can be established. The difficulty about this method is, as already suggested, that most important decisions are not taken by one person; an idea works its way around the organization until the final result emerges. If the decision is negative, then it may be possible to determine who finally said no; it can be much more difficult to make sure who said yes. Was it the person who made the proposal, or someone who collected the evidence, or an official who agreed to the idea going ahead, or another who had the right of veto if he had cared to exercise it, or who? Is a decision made by a consulter or by a person consulted? The possibilities are endless. Apparently straightforward questions about who actually decided can lead to blurred answers if asked of a number of different people. Sometimes it seems as if the answer has more to do with the personalities involved than with any actual situation. There are those who answer 'I do' to any question posed in the form: 'who takes this decision?' There are those of a different temperament who claim to delegate, and yet others who defer to higher authority. Each type can produce contradictory opinions about the locus of decision-making, especially if the people concerned are widely scattered in the organization.

The theoretical argument is reinforced by examining actual decisions. Heathrow airport exists, so a decision was made to bring it into existence; but this decision defies identification. A small landing strip used for test purposes was converted into a military base in the middle of World War II. It was recognized that this could be upgraded to a civilian airport later; it was also understood that there were severe disadvantages to doing so. Nevertheless, Heathrow emerged stage by stage. The third London airport does not exist at the time of writing, at least not officially, in spite of many decisions taken over a period of twenty years. Maybe it also is emerging by stages, and the effective decision was taken many years ago as is feared by some and hoped by others.[18]

In spite of these problems, the locus of decision-making is frequently used in measuring centralization as will be seen in later chapters. One reply to the objections is that decisions about building a new airport are not useful indicators of centralization. It is taken for granted that such a project can only be decided at the highest level; if a parish council embarked on its own on the development of a major international airport that would indeed be a sign of autonomy. The decisions that interest the investigator of centralization are those that can be taken at more than one level of the organization. These can still be very complex. A local authority decision which depends on government financing is an example. There may not be any overt government interference, but the proposal has been framed to avoid such interference. There is an unseen hand at work in the decision-making, and few would doubt that the autonomy is limited. Some variation of this unseen hand can be detected in many types of organization, and it may be that there are two types of strategic decision at work—the first all-embracing and a second, though also allocating substantial resources, which is virtually made inevitable by the first. Government funding to a local authority is one example, when a proposal is implemented because the finance is available rather than because a pressing need is felt. An example occurs in business where executives in charge of operating units prepare capital budgets in the light of their knowledge of corporate policies and priorities rather than in line with the principles of budgeting and optimization as they see them. The nature of the super-decisions and the unseen hand are currently under investigation.[19]

The other principal approach to measurement is to investigate the degree of influence that is brought to bear on a decision. This depends upon asking a number of subjective questions about a person's view of the respective amounts of influence which went into making the particular choice. There are no convincing objective measures that can be applied generally, and identifying a locus of decision-making is also subjective but to a smaller degree. The locus approach at least poses questions that are easier to answer, and therefore more likely to produce objective responses.

Exponents of the degree of influence view either look at the general effect of one group upon another or examine the influence exercised by the various participants on the determination of particular issues. In either case questions are asked of those taking part about their perceptions of how much influence is brought to bear either in general or on the named decisions. Both methods produce a bias towards centralization when the questions asked evoke responses which exaggerate and suggest, perhaps, a greater influence than is the case. This can be a problem with the locus method, but in this case it is usually possible to probe into a wider range of decisions.

The argument over which approach more accurately reflects the decision-making, sometimes conducted with passion, is not just about methodology or degrees of subjectivity, it is over defining the concept. Those who adopt the degree of influence approach regard the locus of decision-making as an unrealistic and misconceived indicator, but they may be attempting the impossible—to measure the exercise of power rather than that of authority.[20] An advantage claimed for studying influence rather than locus is the possibility of a multi-dimensional measure. Whereas the locus only identifies vertical relationships, the degree of authority exercised over one unit by another where one is subordinate and the other superior, measures of influence also take account of horizontal relationships between units of the same level. If two local councils, for instance, share the running of a transport system both have equal status but one may be a dominant partner in practice. This is an important point which will be considered later along with other dimensions of autonomy, but can hardly be taken account in measuring the degree of centralization.

The word 'locus' must, of course, be stretched to include split locations. The decision can be made at more than one level at the same time and the fact represented in empirical studies by the use of fractions. If one unit is dominant then the autonomy of the other is *de facto* restricted, and the locus of decision-making a relevant issue.

Centralization and its consequences are not only of interest in hierarchical structures. An unofficial hierarchy has its decision-making locations as much as an official one, although they may be harder to identify. There is another reason for preferring the locus of decision-making—the implication that an exercise of authority is envisaged. This subject is the theme of the next chapter, but any concept which belittles the role of authority is outside the centralization discussion. A decision naturally has many and varied inputs, but centralization is studied for the purpose of determining the effects on behaviour and well-being of the exercise of authority; those effects are assumed to bear a relationship to the degree of autonomy permitted, whether by regulation or in practice. For these purposes locus is a more satisfactory concept than influence, but reservations must accompany this statement and be taken into account in considering a methodology, if only, as already suggested, by splitting the locus into fractions. It may also be necessary to look at the unofficial as well as the official position and to take account of the unseen hand.

Explaining a decision

To penetrate the measuring of a decision is to reconsider some of the issues already raised like realism and nominalism. Profit-maximizing, for example, is a realist concept; there is an assumption of underlying and impersonal forces which condition organization choice. A meeting of minds between economists and psychologists in the 1950s produced the view that a commercial organization did not normally maximize its objectives, but rather was content with acceptable results, a performance that satisfied. This was seen to be a consequence of the emergence of professional managers who had the knowledge required for profit-maximization, but were looking to other objectives like growth and the containment of problems which would improve their reputation and career prospects. So long as adequate profits and adequate market share were achieved, commercial organizations did not usually demand more.[21]

An argument against the view that corporate objectives are maximized is that different groups and individuals within an organization possess different aims. Decisions are reached through disagreements between the individuals and pressure groups which participate in the organization. The outcomes are new situations in which the controversies and divisions of interest appear in a new form. A single-minded pursuit of official objectives is rare even when those objectives are sufficiently clearly expressed. This situation applies at the top of an organization as well as among the other ranks. Especially at the top, it might be argued, because the length of tenure of the most senior positions is usually limited and the holder may well wish to indulge personal ambitions while he or she can. Of course in the long term an organization may be forced into certain actions in order to survive and survival may override, at least temporarily, all personal considerations. A company which is in the intensive care of a bank will be restricted in its choice of policies.

Arguments such as these have been rehearsed before, they are repeated here because the explanation of the decision-making provides a perspective for determining the degree of centralization. Well-established theories explain both the lure to centralization and the vagaries often detected in an organization's response. These vagaries are illustrated by sayings such as: 'This company used to be highly centralized but, after the appointment of Mr X as chief executive, a measure of devolution has been achieved with responsibilities firmly fixed at operating level.' Such statements are often accompanied by others like: 'We have experienced four changes in the system during my time with the company.' This characteristic is illuminated by the concept of organization learning, the means by which social units adapt to experience—investigations and resulting actions are largely oriented to problems, which are the key factor in the learning process. One consequence is that an effect may be attributed to a cause which is assumed but not proved. If a period of low profitability occurs at a time when the operating units are enjoying a high degree of autonomy, greater centralization—described in some such words as 'a tightening-up of our control procedures'—is likely to follow and may be credited with improving the performance; but the low profitability could have resulted from a change in the market, and a high level of centralization at the time would have been equally blamed. Nevertheless, the particular identification (decentralization equals low profitability) has become firmly established in the traditions of the company. Examples occur frequently of unwritten statements of policy which influence policies long after the reasons have been forgotten. An example from international trade is of a company which suffered severe damage at the hands of a foreign agent who was also working for a competitor and the decision was taken never again to use agents. For many years after the original problem had been forgotten because of staff changes, any proposal to operate in a new market through agents was ruled out. It was only when a rival gained a considerable advantage in a particular market where one of the other options was being used that the assumptions on which the policy on agents was based were questioned. The historical reasons for the policy were then painstakingly pieced together and future decisions considered on more relevant grounds.

If problem-centred learning accounts for swings between centralization and autonomy, uncertainty avoidance is a concept which helps to account for the lure to centralization. The lengths to which companies will go to reduce uncertainty have been vividly illustrated in many examples of actions against the restraint of competition. There is evidence to suggest that such restraint is a more marked feature of corporate life than is usually allowed for in decision theory. Legal actions against cartels or for the promotion of competition arise because agreements with competitors are used to overcome a main source of uncertainty. The executives who were imprisoned for price-fixing knew that they were risking severe penalties in the way they attempted to overcome uncertainty, yet the limitation of uncertainty was considered to be worth the price. In general, greater autonomy for an affiliated unit increases uncertainty and the reverse is frequently considered to be worth some cost in operating efficiency.

The use of phrases like 'organization learning' and 'uncertainty avoidance' recalls the discussion in the last chapter on nominalism and realism. An assumption is being made that an organization's memory is in some way different from the memories of its members, and that an adjustment to changing circumstances is taking place in a way that is not necessarily willed by the decision-makers. The adjustment is likely to be in the direction of greater autonomy if the problems have come at a time of intense centralization, or vice versa. As already shown it is also likely to continue beyond the memories of those involved. The 'realist' element in the argument is inescapable and helps to explain some of the bewilderment felt in organizations at apparently haphazard changes. This is another example of an unseen hand at work that links with the distinction between rational and natural systems. The control of corporate behaviour is never entirely divorced from the will of individual members in that their will can always be reasserted, but this can be more difficult in practice than appears when the options are under discussion.

The discussion so far has followed a semi-determinist and semi-realist route. There is a possibility that decisions may be largely random or nominalist or both. An article with the title of 'A garbage can model of organizational choice'[22] suggested that an attempt to find a rational explanation of decision-making might be doomed, at least where the decisions involved unclear goals, unclear technology and frequently changing participants. A model is designed to reduce the uncertainty in spite of the lack of clarity about the goals. This particular article is about a university organization where decentralization is a strongly-held norm. The fulfilment of this norm in universities varies from country to country but nowhere does the decentralization resemble the one-time model of the independent scholar. It is significant to the present argument, nevertheless, that the holding of such a norm goes with a nominalist outlook.

The wholly nominalist view of decision-making maintains that individuals add a contribution to the decision uninfluenced by the organization as an entity. Of course they will not be uninfluenced by the opinions of their colleagues and the traditions of their company or society, but the assumption is that the decision-maker is less affected by impersonal forces. This assumption emphasizes the element of conflict in decision-making, a subject that is discussed in Chapter 6 and is seen as one of the decentralizing influences, the obverse of the realist approach. The assumption is that a decision is reached through the cut and thrust of debate, in which the struggle for greater independence of the various units of the organization is relatively unhindered by considerations which transcend the individual participants who are therefore free to strive for their own objectives or opinions. The realist approach concentrates attention on the integration of the organization, which usually means central authority, whereas the nominalist view focuses on the fragmentation.

Theories of decision-making have been either semi-realist organization theories, which look to a bargaining process between the groups and sub-groups which make up the whole, or a nominalist conflict theory. An ingenious restatement of the semi-realist theories is provided by a group of scholars[23] who suggest that the shortcomings in earlier statements partly derive from a failure to specify clearly the elements of the decision-making process. Figure 3.1 shows the attempt to separate out the five elements as this group sees them. Each of the five contains a number of variables which can be researched. Thus, 'complexity' includes the rarity and the predictability of the subject of the decision. 'Cleavage' in particular covers the differing objectives of the participants, but also the influences that are being brought to bear on the decision-makers. These variables, which contain much of the content of earlier studies, are seen as manipulators of the process rather than as the process itself. This is to be found in the variables that fit into the other three boxes on the chart and which are collectively regarded as a kind of arena of sub-decisions which go to make up the whole process. 'Activities' comprises the review, the bargaining and routinization. 'Involvement' is the box which includes the degree of centrality of the decision. Finally, the outcomes are seen in psychological terms. They are identified along a number of continuous lines such as fast to slow or bold to timorous or optimal to acceptable.

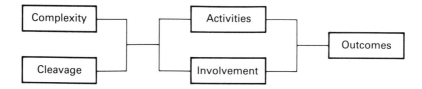

Adapted, by permission, from Astley and others 1982[16]

Figure 3.1   An outline of the decision-making process

The story could be taken a stage further. The link between a decision and a sub-decision is complex and sometimes reciprocal. Thus, a business decision to establish a new product line in a foreign country will include a sub-decision about how closely the new operation will be supervised; equally, a decision to decentralize the foreign subsidiaries will include a sub-decision on the new product line. A hypothesis to be considered is that the choice between centralization and autonomy does not normally lead to more autonomy if it is a sub-decision. This observation explains why the phrase 'lure to centralization' is so often repeated.

This discussion is followed by one which considers decision-mechanisms in mathematical terms and produces models that are semi-deterministic in the sense that they take mathematical values from a given set of circumstances, usually expressed in money, and lay out the patterns of options that assume a distinct set of goals. In this the models derive from the ability of commercial organizations to identify their goals with some precision, but are less useful where the goals have to be blurred. This approach to decision-making is included to complete and emphasize a picture of a many-sided subject.

3.4   DECENTRALIZED DECISION MECHANISMS: A MATHEMATICAL INTERPRETATION

The firm's overall decision problem and a related resource-allocation problem

Decentralized decision mechanisms are an important topic in management science, and a great deal has been written about the design of such mechanisms. This subsection will summarize some of the main ideas in these writings.

Consider a business firm with a head office on the first level of the organization chart and n divisions on the second. Head office is responsible for the performance of the firm as a whole. The firm has to draw up a production plan for, say, the next month. Suppose the *firm's overall decision problem*, for example production planning, can be written as the following linear program P:

$$\text{Maximize } c_1 x_1 + c_2 x_2 + \ldots + c_n x_n$$
$$\text{s.t. } A_1 x_1 + A_2 x_2 + \ldots + A_n x_n \leq a$$
$$B_1 x_1 \qquad\qquad\qquad\qquad \leq b_1$$
$$B_2 x_2 \qquad\qquad\qquad \leq b_2$$
$$\cdot$$
$$\cdot$$
$$\cdot$$
$$+ B_n x_n \leq b_n$$
$$x_j \geq 0 \ (j = 1, 2 \ldots n)$$

In P, a is an m-vector. The c_j and b_j are constant vectors, and the A_j and B_j constant matrices of suitable dimensions. x_j is a variable vector, representing the levels of some divisional activities, such as production and sales, pertaining to division j ($j = 1, 2 \ldots n$). $c_j x_j$ is the divisional contribution to overall profit associated with the divisional activity levels given by x_j; the individual components of c_j express the net contributions of the individual divisional activities. The restriction $A_1 x_1 + A_2 x_2 + \ldots + A_n x_n \leq a$ expresses the fact that the n divisions jointly utilize m resources, of which limited supplies are available. Those limited supplies are given by the m-vector a. Each restriction $B_j x_j \leq b_j$ ($j = 1, 2 \ldots n$) defines the local production and sales possibilities of division j, as given by the plant and other local conditions. The interpretation of P is thus that the firm is seeking a production and sales plan maximizing total contribution to profit, while being feasible for each individual division and also not utilizing more of the m common resources than is available. If it were not for the common resource constraint $A_1 x_1 + A_2 x_2 + \ldots + A_n x_n \leq a$, each division could plan its own activities independently of the rest of the firm; the inclusion of that constraint means, in the terminology of Thompson (1967), that there is pooled interdependence between divisions.

Problem formulations like P arise often, and naturally, in connection with planning in business firms. The joint resources could include machine-group capacities (Ljung and Selmer (1979)) or steam from a central boiler house in a chemical plant (Abrams (1971)). If head office had complete information about the overall decision problem P, it could solve P directly, as an ordinary linear programming problem, and then issue production orders to divisions. This would be centralized decision-making.

Suppose, however, that the information necessary to formulate P is dispersed in the organization, meaning, in particular, that division j knows A_j, B_j, and b_j (with head office or division j knowing c_j). Suppose, moreover, that this information cannot easily be transmitted in explicit matrix or vector form from divisions to head office (for instance because divisions are unwilling to cooperate in such a transmittal). In this situation, head office may have to utilize a *decentralized decision mechanism*:[25] head office will first allocate a share of the common resource availability vector to each division. Formally, each such share is an m-vector a_j, with $a_1 + a_2 + \ldots + a_n \leqslant a$. Given that share, division j will then select activity levels, by constructing and solving the following divisional sub-problem $S_j(a_j)$, which is denoted in that fashion to indicate that it is parameterized by a_j:

$$\text{Maximize } c_j x_j$$
$$\text{s.t. } A_j x_j \leqslant a_j,\ B_j x_j \leqslant b_j,\ x_j \geqslant 0$$

Having solved $S_j(a_j)$, division j will then implement the solution as an actual production and sales plan for the next month.

From head office's point of view, the original production-planning problem P gets replaced by a resource-allocation problem, denoted R:

$$\text{Maximize } v_1(a_1) + v_2(a_2) + \ldots + v_n(a_n)$$
$$\text{s.t. } a_1 + a_2 + \ldots + a_n \leqslant a$$

The function $v_j(a_j)$ is defined as the maximal value of $S_j(a_j)$, for a given vector a_j. If $S_j(a_j)$ is not feasible, given that particular allocation vector a_j, then $v_j(a_j)$ may be defined as $-\infty$.

It could, for instance, be that division j has already contracted with outside customers to deliver certain minimal quantities, in which case the allocation vector a_j must be sufficiently large to accommodate that commitment. The resulting decision mechanism, whereby head office first decides on the a_j, and each division j then decides on x_j, taking the allocated a_j into account, is obviously decentralized, at least in comparison to a mechanism where head office solves P outright and then issues production orders to divisions.

Price and resource directive decision mechanisms

From head office's point of view, a certain simplification of the task immediately at hand has been achieved, in that R is normally a simpler problem than P, at least conceptually. However, not having precise information about the total planning situation, head office will not be able to solve R right away either. Rather, it has to ask divisions for information which will enable it eventually to solve R and allocate the common resources. Based on ideas from decomposition in mathematical programming, this information gathering can be done in the form of an iterative dialogue, where in each iteration a message—actually, a question—is transmitted by head office, to which divisions respond. Since decomposition methods are commonly classified as price or resource directive, the resulting decision mechanisms are labelled accordingly. After a certain number of iterations, the dialogue comes to an end, when an optimality test is passed, meaning that head office knows that it has gathered sufficient information to make an optimal allocation decision a_1^o, a_2^o . . . a_n^o (and once that decision has been made and announced, each division determines its own production and sales activities, by solving the divisional sub-problem $S_j(a_j^o)$).[26] This means that the decision mechanism includes an *adjustment phase* and an *execution phase*. The adjustment phase consists of the iterative dialogue, and the execution phase is where the actual and definitive decisions—on allocations and production plans—are made and implemented.[27] A reward phase at the end of the planning period, after the production decisions have been implemented, may also be included in the decision mechanism; in that phase divisional performance is evaluated and divisions correspondingly rewarded. The reward phase is discussed in the next subsection; the focus here is on the adjustment phase.

As already indicated, two major groups of decision mechanisms may be distinguished: *price directive* and *resource directive*. The distinction has to do with the nature of the information exchange in the adjustment phase. Under a price directive mechanism, the information going from head office to divisions in each iteration consists of prices for the common resources, and divisions are asked how much of the resources they would acquire, if they could purchase them without rationing at the prices announced. The information going back from divisions to head office includes resource demand vectors. In the following iteration, new tentative prices are announced by head office, and divisions respond with new resource demands. Obviously, divisions must undertake certain calculations in order to respond correctly; head office must also perform some calculations in order to revise the price vector from one iteration to the next. Precisely how these calculations are to be performed depends on the particular mechanism. Different price directive decomposition methods can be used as models, and the resulting decision mechanisms will then have the same algorithmic properties as the underlying decomposition methods. This means, in particular, that a decision mechanism will eventually enable head office to obtain an optimal solution to the resource-allocation problem R, to allocate the common resources among divisions in an optimal manner. The number of iterations required for that can usually, but not always, be shown to be finite.

Resource-directive decision mechanisms formalize the idea from economic theory that a resource should be allocated among competing usages—here, divisions—in such a manner that its marginal benefit in each usage is the same. In each iteration of the adjustment phase, head office announces tentative allocation vectors. The divisional responses include information about how their profit contributions would change, if the tentative allocation vectors were varied slightly. The precise specification of the adjustment phase depends on which particular resource-directive decomposition method is taken as a model, but again the decision mechanism will provide head office with sufficient information, usually in a finite number of iterations, to enable it to calculate an optimal solution to the resource-allocation problem R.

The design of incentives[28]

Suppose a decision mechanism for the firm's overall decision problem P has been designed in so far as an adjustment phase and an execution phase have been specified. The mechanism is then well defined. It is known how the iterative information exchange in the adjustment phase should be carried out, and how the final decision should be made and implemented in the execution phase.[29] It then remains to ensure that divisions will cooperate with the rules of the mechanism, and transmit 'honest' information in the adjustment phase and make a correct decision in the execution phase. Failure to cooperate honestly in either phase has been called divisional *cheating*.

In order to induce divisions not to cheat, one may reward them in relation to some evaluation measures (one for each division). This means that another phase is added to the decision mechanism: the *reward phase*. It takes place at the end of the planning period, after the actual decisions have been made and implemented. Head office then checks the actual values of the divisional evaluation measures and distributes rewards accordingly, perhaps as bonuses to the divisional heads. The relevant question is now: how should the evaluation measures be constructed in order (a) to induce divisions to transmit truthful information in each iteration of the adjustment phase; and (b) to induce divisions to pick optimal solutions to their sub-problems $S_j(a_j^o)$ in the execution phase?[30]

In investigating cheating possibilities under different evaluation measures, only cheating that cannot be detected by head office need be considered. The reason is obviously that cheating which can be detected can be correspondingly punished, thus making it unattractive. The capability of head office to detect whether or not cheating is going on depends on the information it has available at the end of the planning period, after divisional decisions x_j^o ($j = 1, 2 \ldots n$) have been made and implemented. That information defines head office's *monitoring capacity*. It is assumed that head office's monitoring capacity is such that it then knows the actually realized divisional profit contributions $c_j x_j^o$ ($j = 1, 2 \ldots n$) plus, of course, any information obtained in the adjustment phase. The evaluation measures can then depend only on these items of information.

The assumed monitoring capacity imposes certain limits on the possibilities for cheating: if the adjustment phase is carried out until the optimality test is met and not truncated after some smaller number of iterations, head office can compare $c_j x_j^o$ with its expectation of what the divisional profit contribution should be, namely $\tilde{v}_j(a_j^o)$. $a_1^o, a_2^o \ldots a_n^o$ are allocation vectors decided on by head office in the execution phase, and the tilde in $\tilde{v}_j(a_j^o)$ denotes head office's approximation of the $\tilde{v}_j$-function, which may differ from the true function if cheating by division j has taken place. Actually, any discrepancy between $c_j x_j^o$ and $\tilde{v}_j(a_j^o)$ would in a deterministic planning situation, like the one considered here, be due to cheating.

A number of different divisional evaluation measures have been proposed, but it turns out that several of them do not work.[31] One that does not work is, for instance, the following. For division j ($j = 1, 2 \ldots n$):

$$A\bar{v}_j(a_j^o) + B_1(c_j x_j^o - \bar{v}_j(a_j^o)) \quad \text{if } c_j x_j^o \geqslant \bar{v}_j(a_j^o)$$
$$A\bar{v}_j(a_j^o) - B_2(\bar{v}_j(a_j^o) - c_j x_j^o) \quad \text{if } \bar{v}_j(a_j^o) > c_j x_j^o$$

where A, B_1, and B_2 are constants such that $0 < B_1 < A < B_2$. This evaluation measure is actually the new Soviet incentive scheme applied to the situation at hand, a scheme which has attracted a great deal of attention.[32] It is easy to see that a division may obtain a higher evaluation measure value through cheating than through honest cooperation, if the Soviet incentive scheme is used.

Other, more satisfactory measures exist. One is profit sharing. Each division is evaluated on the basis of $\sum_{j=1}^{n} c_j x_j^o$. Another one is $c_j x_j^o + \sum_{k \neq j}^{n} \bar{v}_k(a_k^o)$ for each division $j = 1, 2 \ldots n$. This latter measure is a special case of a general class proposed by Groves[33]. Both evaluation measures are satisfactory in the following sense: if the adjustment phase is not truncated, if it is continued until the optimality test is passed, and if all other divisions are cooperating honestly, then each division j will maximize its own evaluation measure value by cooperating honestly too. That is, honest participation constitutes a so-called Nash equilibrium.

The design of incentives in decision mechanisms is a fairly recent research area, and so far only partial results have been obtained. In particular, the situation where the adjustment phase is truncated prior to passing the optimality test is a more complex one for the design of incentives and hence has not been much investigated. This is regrettable, since it is realistic to imagine that the adjustment phase gets truncated after some small number of iterations of information exchange.

Conclusion: on the usefulness of decentralized decision mechanisms

The previous three subsections have outlined some main ideas underlying decentralized decision mechanisms founded on decomposition in mathematical programming. Before attempting to pass judgement on their usefulness, it is worth noting that the relevant literature is large. This is evidenced by the fact that several surveys have been written.[34] In fact, not only management scientists have written on this topic, but also economists concerned with national and regional planning. The overall decision problem P can easily be reinterpreted to relate to n industrial firms and a planning commission in a centrally planned economy. The relevant economics literature is also large.[35] It may also be mentioned that decision mechanisms based on decomposition methods are particularly important among Soviet economists, some of whom apparently envision that national economic planning, or at least planning of substantial sectors of the national economy, will eventually be accomplished using decision mechanisms of the type discussed here; this has also been noted by Western observers of Soviet mathematical economics.[36]

Considering the volume of relevant writings, it is ironic that well-documented implementations in business firms of decision mechanisms like the ones discussed here are not known. However, a couple of simulation studies of the performance of such decision mechanisms in real-world planning situations have been undertaken.[37] In these studies two real-world decision problems were used, taken from a slaughterhouse and a paper-board factory, and it was investigated by means of computer simulations what kind of plans the firms would have ended up with, if certain decision mechanisms had actually been used. In particular, it was investigated how good the plans would have been, if the iterative information exchange in the adjustment phase had been stopped after, say, two to four iterations. This is obviously relevant, since only a very small number of iterations would normally be undertaken in a real-world situation, as mentioned earlier. The results of these two simulation studies are mixed. In the paper-board factory very good plans could be obtained, and it is not entirely unrealistic to imagine that the particular decision mechanism simulated (which was based on the Dantzig-Wolfe decomposition method) could be implemented in that firm with beneficial results. In the slaughterhouse it was not possible, or at least very difficult, to obtain usable plans by means of the decision mechanisms simulated.[38]

The issue of usefulness for real-world firms of decentralized decision mechanisms of the kind discussed here is hence not yet settled. However, quite apart from any practical usefulness which they may or may not have, these mechanisms are also of *theoretical* interest: by providing precise models of decision situations, they enable a sharply focused discussion and conceptual clarification of many issues related to decentralization, cheating and monitoring capacity. They represent an interesting research direction.

3.5   THE CONTINGENT FACTORS

A chapter which opened with some reservations about analogies from the natural sciences can itself be summarized with an analogy from biological research. A number of specimens—concepts and organization variables—have, as it were, been selected from relevant studies. These specimen concepts have revealed under inspection the paradoxical nature of the process. This finding was not unexpected but it confirms that any theory must do justice to the operation of opposing forces. The forces begin to take effect when the individual is initiated into the operation. The informal processes of adaptation and socialization are usually decentralizing pressures—the emphasis is on the peer group, loyalty at the grass roots, at a sub-organization level. Official introductory courses and teachings for the beginner, on the other hand, are normally designed to emphasize the central authority and its role as the source of wisdom and knowledge. Many an induction course was started in order to counteract the informal decentralizing pressures and to develop loyalty to the organization, while stressing the need for integration. This view is expressed in phrases like: 'Where we fail in this company is in getting across our standpoint, as managers, to the new recruits, who never come to see themselves as part of the organization as a whole.' In general, then, there is a contradiction between the official and the unofficial procedures, but there are some exceptions.

Professional outlooks may be centralizing and informal; the expert looks to the centre of expertise, and some courses may emphasize the need for local initiative, but in both official and unofficial activities the reverse is more common. An example of the contradiction in its normal operation but its most sophisticated form is provided by the ceremony of baptism. In those churches where this ceremony exists, there is normally a dual content: a central authority or body of truth and a local congregation. The dual emphasis is always there although within different frameworks in, for instance, a Roman Catholic or a Baptist church.

The need to examine the influences for and against centralization in contingent rather than universal terms was the second element in this chapter, with some of the opinions about how decisions are reached as the third. From the discussions arise a number of points which will be reconsidered later. One of these is described as the unseen hand, the influence that cannot readily be identified but helps to determine the decision-making at subordinate levels and thus the degree of centralization. Other issues discussed can be summarized by cautious-sounding phrases like semi-determinism and semi-realism. Although giving expression to different areas of thought, the two are related. The view that organizations do have characteristics of their own that transcend the aspirations of their participants does stimulate the search for the consequences of such activities as organization learning. These are then seen to include effects, like greater centralization, that have not been specifically willed by individual decision-makers. This review continues in the next chapter under the general heading of 'authority'.

4 *Power and Authority*

Crucial to the understanding of centralization is the unravelling of the distinction between power and authority. Power, as defined in Chapter 1, refers to the attributes or resources which enable the authority to be exercised, but the distinction is sometimes ignored and is frequently difficult to maintain. There are three reasons for the difficulty. One is the existence of a grey area in which power and authority overlap, another is the mutual dependence of the exercise of each on the other, and the third relates to the use of different conventions in the way the underlying disciplines are accustomed to use the words.

4.1 POWER, AUTHORITY AND LEGITIMACY

Power is broad in its scope. It does not require any formal arrangements nor acceptance on the part of its subjects. The wind has power over the trees, but presumably no authority. A newspaper has power over its readers, but again no authority; equally that exercise of power has no relevance to centralization. A similar relationship exists between blackmailers and their victims. Authority, on the other hand, requires a structure and an acceptance. The structure may vary, as may the reasons for the acceptance, which requires some form of legitimation in terms of the values of the subject. The exercise of authority may be enthusiastically obeyed, passively tolerated, or received with any other degree of submission or acquiescence. The amount of centralization is likely to be a subtle blend of enforcement and acceptance.

A person can speak with authority on account of knowledge or skill, and can exercise that authority as a result of his or her appointment or election; but without the legitimation the authority disappears. This is the point at which the distinction with power becomes difficult to make precise. No one doubts that trade union officials have power, but they only have authority over their own members and that is restricted. If a member chooses to ignore an instruction, penalties, such as expulsion or a fine, can be used to enforce its acceptance. The sanctions can be serious, a job may be at stake, but they are frequently ignored. The authority is constrained by contingent conditions, like the value of a particular job, which are not in the possession of the trade union officials but which they can sometimes manipulate. Power, then, is an attribute that enables or restrains authority. The link between the two is provided by the concept of legitimation, the means by which the exercise of authority is made acceptable to the object of power. The acceptance may be voluntary or reluctant, permitted or enforced, but without it the authority collapses. In the smallest unit, the family, legitimation is a complex mixture of affection and self-interest. In a major aggregation of power, like a nation, the mixture is very complicated indeed. As Blau has said: 'Legitimating values expand the scope of centralized control far beyond the reach of personal influence, as exemplified by the authority of a legitimate government'.[1] Another author, Gross, suggests that 'administrative authority' is 'like a hunting licence; it legitimates and limits an administrator's search for power, but it does not guarantee that he will find it.' Compliance, a subject which is discussed below, is achieved through the process of establishing a right to rule, but this may be by force as well as by consent.

In a business concern, there is greater clarity in the distinction between power and authority than in some kinds of organization. The shareholders possess the power—so long as the company remains solvent their votes are absolute—but their authority is limited. Unless shareholders are also managers, they have virtually no authority, only votes limited to the number of their shares at a meeting summoned in accordance with the articles of association. Ownership in the modern joint stock company provides power without authority but, to repeat, legitimation is the link. The power does carry the right to legitimize or to disqualify the exercise of authority.

It has been suggested that a problem in making the distinction between power and authority lies in the different conventions of the underlying disciplines. Sociologists have usually distinguished between power and authority, and equated power with influence, a word which is more important for the vocabulary of the psychologist in whose writings influence comes closer to that of authority. The use of the word 'influence' in this latter sense emphasizes the unreality of assuming that a specific decision locus can be identified. The two views are brought together in these pages where it is assumed that justice must be done both to the reality of authority and to the error of insisting that a decision can always be clearly ascribed to an individual or group. Any measurement of centralization must do justice to the tension between these conflicting views, but there is no need for the conflict to be exacerbated by an inability to comprehend that different definitions are being employed. In discussing the different approaches to research in Chapter 9, the link between power and influence will be assumed but generalizations about authority will be criticized if they appear to over-simplify the nature of decisions.

To be transmitted into authority, power requires its own legitimation and the means for this are limited. A government exercises its authority because it possesses power, but the acceptability of the power will affect the exercise of authority. Thus, a dictatorship may only retain power by its control of the military and the secret police; the acceptability depends upon fear, an example of the mutual dependence of power and authority. An unpopular regime which is yet unwilling to abdicate may be driven to more and more violent and forceful measures. The fact that both the power and authority will disappear at the same time if a revolution occurs does not make the distinction between the two unreal. After their exercise of power has destroyed existing authority and its legitimation, the revolutionaries will build up their own sources of legitimacy through persuasion, slogans, hope, fear and other means. The new exercise of power is eventually legitimized, unless a counter-revolution intervenes, and becomes authority. The mutual dependence is further demonstrated by the centres of power in an organization which are in conflict with the main lines of authority. Trade unions have authority over some participants in an organization and may exercise that authority in direct contradiction to the decisions of the employer, or the rival centres of power may be more intangible as in a profession. Excluding the influence of any professional body, the sense of professionalism itself may influence members against the authority of their employer.

The existence of several centres of power is a source of problems in many organizations, and studies of professionalism have demonstrated the difficulty of the dual loyalty.[2] An example occurs where a person belongs to a powerful body—like the British Medical Association, the Law Society, or the Institute of Chartered Accountants—and is an employee of a business organization at the same time. The dual loyalty is regarded as a threat to authority, but the consequences for decision-making are not automatic. Only when the threat becomes a reality is the degree of centralization changed. It is the authority that directly affects the decision-making, not the power centre.

One issue that arises from this discussion is that the greater the difficulty in legitimating the authority, the greater the likelihood that the decision-making will be centralized. The reverse is not necessarily true because other factors may influence the decision-making process in a popular regime, but if the authority rests on force and has few allies the scope for devolution is limited—and limited where it might become useful, when a wider distribution of the decision-making could be a means to widen the basis of acceptance. This is a kind of opportunity that often passes unnoticed, and in situations where legitimacy is a problem it must also be considered as part of the lure to centralization.

4.2 POWER AND COMPLIANCE

Power, then, is understood to be an attribute or relationship,[3] with a potential for a stronger or a weaker influence on the decision-making according to the circumstances. The translation of that power into actual decisions is the exercise of authority. A highly relevant work, but one that uses different definitions, is that of Etzioni;[4] in this 'power' is understood in terms of compliance and authority is narrowly defined as voluntary acceptability. Etzioni's approach provides a framework for the comparative study of all types of organization. Empirical investigations have examined the theory in the working of voluntary organizations, hospitals, trade unions, prisons, churches, professional associations and numerous other bodies.

Etzioni starts from a typology which is used as a means of analysing a series of concepts relating to organization and beginning with compliance, involvement and power. Compliance is achieved by the congruence between the kind of power exercised over the lower participants and their response, described as the kind of involvement. The kinds of power are coercive, remunerative and normative, while the responses are labelled alienative, calculative and moral. The basic hypothesis is that organizations tend to move towards the so-called congruent relationships—coercive-alienative, remunerative-calculative and normative-moral—and to be unstable when there is a lack of congruence. Thus, the charitable organizations normally possess a normative-moral compliance structure, and attempts to move towards a remunerative one are resisted and regarded as bribery. The cause is degraded if payment is made other than to full-time officers and administrators. At the other end of the spectrum, prisons find it difficult to move towards liberal regimes based on business principles. The compliance structure provides an analytical scheme to aid the understanding of the pressures and counter-pressures that build up in an organization.

There are two possible disadvantages of the scheme. One is that a unitary view seems to be implied. The existence of rival power centres within an organization is not provided for and this is no doubt why such a limited view of authority is suggested. The present study sees authority in its unofficial as well as its official relationships—the actual consequences of the exercise of authority for decision-making. The other possible disadvantage of the Etzioni scheme is that the bases of power are limited to three. Other authorities have suggested adding knowledge and charisma;[5] these do not appear to fit easily, although a refinement of the types of organization might produce a compliance structure in relation to knowledge and expertise, at least.

The Etzioni scheme does, however, allow of mixed compliance organizations where there are, for instance, both coercive and moral issues involved, as in armies fighting for a cause. A mixture of remunerative and moral involvement may be seen in the case of the manager striving for the well-being of his company beyond the immediate call of duty. It is always hard to assess exactly what a person is being paid for, and where that person's activities exceed the expected response to the payment, but the use of phrases like dedication to the job imply that financial calculation is not regarded as the whole story.[6] A different kind of example will be found in Chapter 12 where 'inverted centralization' is discussed.

The relevance of the compliance structure theory to the present study can be seen in two formulae which assist the analysis of centralization. One is that the resources of power which help to determine the exercise of authority lie somewhere in the achieving of a satisfactory relationship between the means of involvement and the achievement of compliance. An incongruent relationship, the administration of a prison with highly alienated inmates by normative means for instance, can be expected to diminish the resources and lead to demands for greater centralization. On the other hand a congruent relationship, which may be hard to achieve because of a mixed compliance system, can produce a self-confidence in the organization leading to the possibility of greater decentralization.

Figures 4.1 and 4.2 summarize the argument so far. The two diagrams are meant to be read side by side since they are intended to show how weaknesses, and by the same token also strengths, in the power base or resources eventually influence the degree of centralization. The difference between the base and the resources is not great; a congruent compliance structure is a resource, whereas the conviction of the participants may be both. This may be clear to the insider on occasions when the outsider finds it hard to conceive how the structure is really working. Thus, a religious body is sometimes accused of bringing more than moral pressure on its members to ensure their loyalty. This can be a misunderstanding—the critic from the outside sometimes fails to grasp what moves the insider—although the relationship between religious, national, political and general social factors is always many-sided.

A compliance structure is a relationship between a kind of power and a kind of involvement; the normal (congruent) structures are:

coercive ————————➤ alienative
remunerative ————➤ calculative
normative ——————➤ moral

To these may be added:

(1) Other relationships

Knowledge/expertise ➤ contractual
(as in rather loose-knit commercial or advisory organizations)

(2) Dual structures

coercive ⟵——➤ alienative
                  ➤ moral

remunerative ⟵——➤ calculative
                         ➤ moral

(based on Etzioni 1975, p.12, with additions)

Figure 4.1   Compliance structure

Both figures suggest some hypotheses for further consideration. A case in point is the weakening of power resources and its consequences for centralization. These consequences will vary with different sets of factors; a government within a democratic tradition will react differently from a dictatorship, but the nature of the changes will also be significant, whether they are intentional or unintentional; the word 'unintentional' suggests a *drift* towards a non-congruent relationship. The resultant problems may then lead to a demand for centralization, or vice versa. Hence, the process of change is partly dependent on the power-compliance structure. In general the present analysis sees drift as a common route of change, as common as the reactions against it

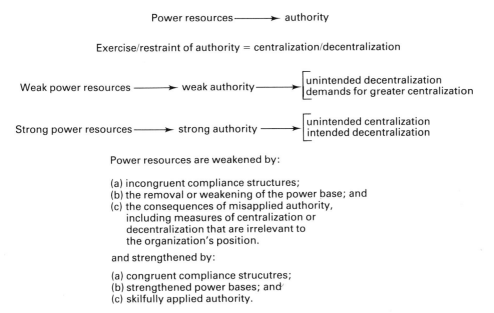

Figure 4.2 The relationship of power to authority and centralization

which lead to planned alterations. Unless an organization disintegrates, it will be brought back to its perceived purposes when the drift appears to have gone too far.

4.3 THE MEASUREMENT OF POWER AND INFLUENCE

'Give me where to stand and I will move the earth' is a statement ascribed to a pioneer writer on power.[7] The fact that the concept has gathered to itself such a large body of quotable sayings makes clarification harder, but the assertion that power is less readily definable than authority does not make it unmeasurable. Numerous efforts have been made to measure power in degrees of influence and at various levels of sophistication. Some have asserted that this is the nearest approach that is possible to a measure of centralization. Three groups of writers have approached the measurement of influence: political scientists, organizational psychologists and management scientists. The first group includes those who attempted to apply game-theory criteria to the measurement of power. For instance, it was suggested that in a committee, where decisions are taken by voting according to predetermined rules, 'the power of an individual member depends on the chance he has of being critical to the success of the winning coalition.'[8] This approach produced a number of insights, but is limited in its usefulness to one specialized arena and does not apply where the elements of group decision-making are lacking.

A more elaborate proposal distinguishes seven constituents of the power relation:

1. The *base* of power. The economic assets, constitutional prerogatives, military force, popular support and other resources that A can use to influence B's behaviour.
2. The *means* of power. The promises, threats, appeals and other actions by which A can use the resources to influence B's behaviour.
3. The *scope* of power. The obedience to instructions and other responses that B will perform as a result of A's use of the means of power.
4. The *amount* of power. The increase in probability that B will respond in a particular way as a result of A using a specific means of power.
5. The *extension* of power. The set of individuals over whom A is exercising power.
6. The *costs* of the exercise of power. The opportunity costs to A of acquiring and using his power over B.
7. The *strength* of power. The opportunity costs to B of yielding to A's exercise of power or of resisting it.[9]

One problem in using these constituents for measurement purposes is that of comparison. Indeed their nature emphasizes how easy it is to slip into a concept of measurement which is misleading for just this reason. Naturally, comparisons between organizations are not the only ones that can be considered, comparisons between different time periods in the same organization are possible, as are comparisons with some accepted and predetermined amount of power.[10] The difficulty with this latter, normative, measurement is to find relevant criteria for fixing the norms in the first place and for working out consequential hypotheses.

The organizational psychologists have attempted direct measures of influence by questionnaires in which the respondents are asked to rate the amount of power in a system. This has been called 'direct measurement', as opposed to the indirect proposed by the political scientists, and can itself be subdivided into three categories:

Measures of attributed influence
These are used when 'the members of the group under examination [are asked] to rank each other according to influence, either over the individual respondent or over the group as a whole (*re* a particular situation).'[11] March has claimed that the advantages of this method are that it is simple and taps unexpressed feelings and the implications of facts that have not been understood. However, distortion is difficult to cope with, the enquiries are necessarily subjective, and comparisons are as difficult as they were with the political scientists.[12]

The use of measures of attributed influence has been closely connected with the work of Tannenbaum, who uses the word 'control', but asserts that this is synonymous with power. There is conceived to be a 'process in which a person or group of persons or organization of persons determines, that is, intentionally affects, the behaviour of another person, group, or organization.'[13] Underlying this is an assumption, made explicit in an earlier writing, that control is a capacity to manipulate and this is an ingredient in Tannenbaum's approach to measurement. In his supervisory studies, like his earlier studies of power within trade unions, he plots control or influence graphs to represent the amount of power in the system. The respondents were asked to rate the influence by level of management in terms ranging from 'little or no' to 'a very great deal'.[14] From this, hypotheses relating effectiveness to the 'total amount of control' in the system, that is a reflection of the degree of participation, are held to fit the evidence gained from these researches. The exact relationship between participation and manipulation is, however, never fully explained. The measure is of a shared authority, partly designed to achieve the objectives of the higher authority, not of independence. There is also a problem of distinguishing the power of an organization and the power *within* it. The chief executive of a large decentralized company has more power than the manager of a centralized small business. The other difficulty of this approach concerns the reliability of the measurement as a comparative tool even within the limitations described. The concept of the 'amount of power' is a difficult one to pin down, and the results of evidence collected on the basis of this imprecise idea are unlikely to be reliable.

Measures of opinion change
In this measure the investigator plays a greater role than in the measure of attributed influence, where respondents are asked to identify the position as they see it along a predetermined scale and an average is then taken. In this latter case, an attitude is defined, an interaction is observed, and a shift of outlook is identified. This provides a measure of influence,[15] but its reliability depends on the investigator having some control over the situation.

Influence attempts and the hierarchical structure
Among indirect measures, March has developed one of *influence attempts* for which he makes only modest claims and which does not appear to provide a useful basis for understanding the amount of power in a system. Another attempt at indirect measurement is provided by various methods of assessing the *hierarchical structure*. This is based on an assumption that the power of a person or a group is related to the structure of the organization. One exponent[16] distinguishes three dimensions in the hierarchy of an industrial concern: that of skills, of rewards and of authority. In this case the word 'authority' is used of allotted responsibilities. These, it is argued, can be assessed on the basis of objectively verifiable criteria and do not depend entirely on perception. Thus the skills can be measured by the time spent in relatively formal training and the acquiring of necessary experience, although the relationship between this and the exercise of power may not appear close. The same reservation applies to the hierarchy of rewards. A high salary does not necessarily go with the ability to exercise power in the organization. On the contrary, the authority as well as the salary may depend upon success and profitability. The illusion of power is removed not only by dismissal but by being 'kicked upstairs' as the saying goes. Yet another indirect method uses the word 'authority', but regards the hierarchical allocation of levels of authority as a proxy for power. A number of indices are proposed, including the span of control, the number of levels, the

ratio of administrative to production employees, the time span of control and the limits to discretion. The difficulty of producing a measure from such indices is discussed later.

The proposals considered on these pages for measuring the power relationship surmount some problems; they exclude a simplistic assumption that centralization can be viewed in terms of the power accruing to a specific office. No satisfactory solution of the problem of measuring such an imprecise concept as power exists, but some of the elements considered here will be carried over into the discussion of centralization and authority, to illuminate issues that would otherwise be more difficult to analyse.

4.4 AUTHORITY AND BUREAUCRACY

The definition of power adopted for this study has already been extended, but the word also has a legal meaning—the powers allocated to a person or to an office under a given set of rules. This allocation of responsibility and accountability according to predetermined procedures is a hallmark of bureaucracy.[17] There is an ambiguous relationship between this mode of organization and centralization. The process of change from the individual rule of the charismatic character to a more predictable system of division into offices and career structures gives meaning to the word 'autonomy'. The autocratic ruler may delegate, either by design or by neglect, but the delegation is instrumental; it depends on whim or favour and can easily be retracted. Once a formal allotment of duties and appointments is introduced, decentralization becomes a relevant issue; the delegation to units in a formal organization enables efficient government to be exercised over scattered territories and allows large organizations to come into existence. This development is accompanied by attempts to ensure that the behaviour of the units is predictable and that relatively inflexible rules assist the predictability. Nowadays, it has been pointed out,[18] this traditional strength is a liability; the tendency to adhere rigidly to the rules blocks the introduction of new methods and organizations that are called upon to innovate rather than to coordinate require flexibility and individual responsibility. This consideration is likely to underwrite deeply held beliefs as well as practical difficulties to counteract the lure to centralization.

A division of labour, then, is one sign of bureaucracy with special implications for the centralization discussion. Another is the pressure to impersonality. Crozier[19] makes the point that the principle of impersonality ensures that decisions are made away from the point where they will be carried out. This, in its turn, produces a situation in which downward communication is strong and upward communication weak. A consequence of the weak upward communication is that messages are distorted, failures in the system are inadequately explained and the decision-makers have inaccurate information on which to revise their policies. A 'vicious circle'[20] is produced which ensures that the decisions become increasingly irrelevant to the problems and the subordinates take more steps to protect themselves against the whims of the decision-makers. The circle, or spiral, then operates in a centralizing sense; the decision-makers find themselves less able to delegate, for reasons which are all the more powerful if they are unexplained. A further twist is given to the circle when subordinates avoid all decision-making and thus increase the overload of work at the higher levels.

The practical consequences of this circle will be traced in later chapters. The origins are to be found in an inherent contradiction in a bureaucratic system whose logic is towards decentralization despite lures in the opposite direction. An ideology has stemmed from this logic which adds a moral dimension expressed in such phrases as: 'Set up an operating unit and leave the local management to their own devices; people work best when left to run their own show.' In many non-commercial organizations, rights are established to which subordinate groups cling tenaciously. The set of beliefs that favour autonomy is reinforced by the opinion that centralized decision-making produces waste and inefficiency but has also produced counter-balancing pressures. One example is the vicious circle, while another is the threat of disaster. Suppose those responsible for the subordinate units do prove incompetent or unable to safeguard the vital truths? The risks of decentralization must often seem to outweigh the benefits of greater autonomy. Facts and figures in commercial and governmental institutions, at least, can more often be produced to support centralization than the reverse. The belief that autonomy is less wasteful depends upon long-term assumptions that are hard to quantify; short-term measures often point the other way. Allied to such measures are more personal factors like ambition and trust, or the lack of it. Since the more powerful personalities are likely to rise to the top, they are also likely to be less respectful of subordinates. The larger the organization, the tougher the rise to the top, and the greater the probability that personal influences will press towards centralized decision-making.

There are circumstances, as Dahrendorf has pointed out,[21] when personal influences can press for greater autonomy. If the pressure to impersonality leads to centralization, the availability of people to staff the hierarchy may produce a contrary effect, at least where there is a shortage of professional or trained staff and a competition for scarce skills. Professionalism has already been suggested as an influence, as is specialization. The old-established professions possess powerful norms asserting freedom from interference. These norms, it should be noted, do not inhibit teamwork when required. To a less extent members of the teaching profession hold to similar precepts. Evocative phrases like 'academic freedom' express a belief in decentralization.

In government it is the rise of the professional and the middle classes in general that make bureaucracy possible; hence Dahrendorf's assertion that this form of organization requires autonomy, but the form of the autonomy depends upon the viewpoint from which the organization is observed. The autonomy may be within a particular projection—the different offices of either central or local government, for instance, rather than between the two. Another influence detected in organization is that of the number of levels in a hierarchy, combined with the shape or configuration of the structure. There was an assumption among the classical organization theorists that closeness between superior and subordinate was essential to good communication, and that this was achieved by limiting the span of control to about six and not worrying how many levels this produced.[22] Indeed, it was assumed, the ability to add levels was the key to enabling the large organization to operate efficiently.

Research during the Second World War and after cast doubt upon this assumption and turned up evidence to show that organizations which reduced the number of levels, even at the expense of widening the average span, achieved improved communication.[23] This discussion was carried into a different context when it was shown that the shape of a hierarchy in a manufacturing organization was related to the technology in which it was operating,[24] that this appeared to happen because a particular configuration proved more suitable to a particular business sector and that the suitability in its turn was related to the special requirements of the decision-making. Mass production required only a limited number of decisions to be taken, but these were of great importance. Hence, fewer levels and wider spans of control developed. Unit and small batch production needed more decisions, but the consequences were less critical and more of them were short-term. Process production also demanded fewer critical decisions but frequent problem-solving which had to be coordinated when there was a crisis. The general move towards fewer levels in a hierarchy favours decentralization: more authority is concentrated at each position, while the reverse usually means less autonomy. The process technologies, where routine decisions are taken at a large number of different points in the hierarchy, is also usually centralized for policy-forming purposes.

Another concept used in the discussion of bureaucracy is routinization, simplifying the decision-making and introducing an element of impersonality which forms a major element in the move from the relatively freakish decisions of the charismatic character (the absolute ruler or the entrepreneur) into a predictable system.[25] Perfect routinization means total centralization, since no decisions have to be taken. Of course the central authority is limited by the fact that each level of the organization is working within a framework, but that is always the case. Absolute dictators operate within a framework of national sovereignty; they do not have authority outside their own country while political and military conditions remain static. Against the capricious decisions of a less formal system, the predictability of bureaucracy leads to decentralization. The process of change is usually gradual and neither extreme (of total predictability or total capriciousness) is ever reached, so the checks and balances are always evident, hence the lures towards and away from autonomy noted in these pages and set out in a paradigm in Chapter 10.

One restriction on the operation of these lures is the resistance to change and emphasis on stability in the bureaucratic organization.[26] Since organizations tend to change through solutions that apply to the whole and not just the parts in which the problems have been diagnosed, the effects of responses thought to be trivial by the decision-makers can appear drastic to those affected. This builds up further resistance and makes the centralization cycle less drastic until stimulated by a crisis.

Within the cycle, autonomy can be regarded both as an outcome and as a bargaining counter. The compromises involved in the assertion of authority lead to specific grants of independence.[27] The limits to control are set by the need for the decision-making to match the objectives of the organization and its participants. Too great a mismatch threatens stability which is itself among the objectives. In this section some of the concepts employed in studies of bureaucracy have been considered and their relationship to the centralization issue appraised. The lures and counter-pressures operate through communications and weaknesses in the communication system, through personalities and through the process of routinization.

The acceptability of bureaucracy is a large question. Its characteristics have been modified since they were expounded by Weber.[28] The present author has identified the *repersonalized* bureaucracy which some companies have developed. This means the switch in emphasis from the office, the appointment with its job specification and inflexible rules, to the individual as the basic unit of the organization. Outward signs include the personal signing of letters and the inclusion of names on the organization chart; the inward change is less easy to identify just because the process has been continuous, not dramatic. This process is away from the object of a totally impersonal, machine-like system but not necessarily towards one that provides more autonomy. The aim is to find means of greater motivation for those who are restricted in their decision-making to bridge the gap between a liberal political system and a harsher work environment.

The political system in the industrial democracies is undoubtedly less centralized than in most dictatorship countries where there is central control of resources, but the power, the ability to achieve this central control, may not be so different. It is the legitimation of its use that alters. This subject is discussed in the last chapter; meanwhile the problem of the extent of authority has to be addressed—how are the limits prescribed?

4.5   AUTHORITY ON THE BOUNDARY

'Students of organizations must often make decisions about the boundaries of the unit they are studying: who is a participant and who an outsider.'[29] For the present study such decisions are especially important; a decentralized organization may appear centralized and vice versa by redefining its boundaries. For many purposes a simple statement about the units under investigation is sufficient, but when the locus of decision-making is around or across the limits of an organization there is a problem. Studies of boundaries have been mainly concerned with distinguishing between internal and environmental influences on a unit's behaviour; there has been little study of the exercise of authority. Of the many attempts to mark out the boundaries, Etzioni has proposed four criteria which appear to be the most satisfactory obtainable:
(1)   Persons who rate high on involvement.
(2)   Persons who rate high on subordination.
(3)   Persons who rate high on performance.
(4)   (Amplifying the other three) persons linked to the organization in routine, patterned exchanges of rewards for contributions.

Other definitions involve recognition of a domain by outsiders[30] and an all-inclusive view which (for the business organization) includes investors, suppliers, distributors and consumers as well as employees.[31] This may seem unduly comprehensive for most purposes, but it carries a gesture towards the discussion of a possible lack of autonomy across boundaries by pointing towards a distinction between the legal and the actual (not illegal—that is a subset of the actual) boundaries. The distinction between formal and informal has been worried to death, but the legal boundary can be drawn at a number of different places, and where it is drawn will partly decide whether the organization is considered centralized or not. The contract of a customer or supplier is different from that of an employee, but there are situations where some influence on the decision-making is implied. Incorrect use by a customer of a supplier's trade marks or processes may result in legal actions which effectively reserve some decisions to the supplier. The reverse may be true where a small firm is under permanent contract to a larger one—the lorry owner, for instance, under permanent contract to one customer.

The actual position may be even more constrained than the legal. A company may effectively manage a subcontractor in the same way as another unit. Paradoxically, the only real independence may be through other legal features, such as arm's-length dealing for tax purposes and the identifying of various forms of liability. In Japan (with six million businesses, well over six times the number in Britain) the blurred organization boundary is a normal feature of business life. Most small companies are separate but highly dependent, while it is 'sometimes difficult to perceive whether a concern is an independent subcontractor or a subsidiary'.[32]

A trend towards more companies with a high degree of actual, if not legal, dependence giving them a low level of autonomy has long been noted in the West as well. World slump has accelerated the process whereby companies prefer to employ outside rather than internal services. External suppliers provide greater flexibility in two ways. One is that of wider choices and the possibility of greater quality control. Inside suppliers are part of the corporate politics and can defend themselves on more subjective grounds than the outsider whose services can more readily be terminated. The other form of flexibility is that external supplies, of both services and goods, can be turned on and off more readily according to variations in demand. The result of these insights is a greater interest in the discussion of authority and control across boundaries which will recur in a different context in part II; there the issue of joint ventures between domestic and foreign companies is one in which boundaries are seen to be even more blurred.

4.6   MANAGEMENT STYLE AND CONCLUSIONS

There are two difficulties endemic in the discussions reviewed in this chapter. The first is the elusive distinction between power, the ability to influence a situation, and the formal and legitimate authority to make decisions. Without the background of power, the authority would be an illusion; but hypotheses that derive from an understanding of centralization, and its consequences for an organization's well-being, assume an exercise of authority as defined in these pages. This is re-emphasized in the discussion on organization boundaries. No one doubts that one social unit has power over another; what is doubted is the authority to make decisions on behalf of a legally independent unit. The suggestion is that this happens at least between business firms, and that the exercise of control and authority can be separated from that of power. There are, in effect, two forms of centralization. One is a relationship between the centre and a subordinate unit whereby more autonomy is permitted than is usual with that particular relationship. The other is the existence of a tenuous, but actual, relationship between the centre and a unit on the boundary of an organization.

The second difficulty that arises in discussing power and authority is between delegation as a result of belief in sharing or as a means of manipulation. Is decentralization the most appropriate long-term prescription for certain situations, or is it a handy tip for overcoming a temporary problem? Writers on style of management sometimes seem to wander between these two standpoints. One authority, Likert, identifies four principal styles: exploitative authoritative, benevolent authoritative, consultative and participative.[33] Each of these produces a distinctive effect on centralization, such as the authoritarian styles which allow a smaller number of options. The systems that result are usually sustained by strong, centralized decision-making, although it may lurch to a more decentralized but controlled arrangement. The participative styles, on the other hand, are also less rigid and can move more freely between degrees of centralization as circumstances change. Of course complete participation is incompatible with total centralization, but most systems find at least some measure of delegation to be workable and necessary.

One of the extra options available to the participative organization is that of varying the style between different units. International companies, for instance, have been observed with high levels of participation in the home country, while appearing authoritarian in nature and centralized to the foreign subsidiary. Indeed, as is noted in part II, a degree of autonomy among domestic units frequently accompanies centralization internationally. Every organization has a repertoire of tools for the establishment of authority, including the compliance structures. The emergence of a means for making the exercise of authority appear legitimate to the participants in a particular organization can be understood in terms of the relevant means of compliance, but there are other means of persuasion, coercion or manipulation. Some of these are discussed more fully in the chapter on conflict (Chapter 6).

The pressures and counter-pressures involved in the possession of power and in the exercise of authority, lead to upheavals in organizations. The diagnosis of such problems is aided by an understanding of how these pressures affect the unstable equilibrium between centralization and autonomy. This chapter has concentrated on the distinction between power and authority, a distinction described as crucial to the understanding of centralization. Some forms of power may increase the pressure towards the central authority, but power itself is neutral, providing the decision-maker with the means to assert his or her will or to delegate; it is when the authority is exercised, is translated into decisions, that centralization or autonomy arises. As far as definition can resolve the difference of opinion, power will be equated with influence and the locus of decision-making with authority. The one is then required to legitimate the other, and the closer the relationship between the two, the more effective the organization is expected to be. This leaves a number of problems unresolved which will be considered later; meanwhile, the exercise of authority has to be monitored and the monitoring, control, will be the subject of the next chapter.

5 Control, Communication and Planning

'And things are not what they seem' (Longfellow). This quotation can hardly be used more aptly than in a discussion on control and centralization. The claims recorded below, for control systems increasing autonomy, for profit centres providing independence and for both as integral to decentralized organizations, can truly be said to require examination. Many of the myths and legends that surround the subject become explicit in statements that an organization is finding a new course through a control system which is described as decentralizing, a description whose truth is frequently more evident to the staff or consultants who introduced the system than to those who have to operate it. This chapter examines these and other statements about control, as well as the related issues of planning and communication.

5.1 THE MEANING OF CONTROL

The use of the word *control* in management thinking can be traced to efforts to acquire more accurate and rapid information about performance in the subordinate units of a business. One of the purposes of developing more elaborate control systems was to make greater devolution possible, to free senior executives of expanding businesses from considerations of detail by instituting, as it were, trip-wires to warn them of trouble. Managers were encouraged to accept a more intensive reporting system in return for greater responsibility. The monitoring would reveal the emergence of problems in any part of the business. The origins of modern control systems have been well documented, not least by the articulate executive who developed them in General Motors,[1] and claimed that the combination of decentralization and tighter control rescued the company from the brink of bankruptcy. Whatever degree of acceptance or doubt greets such claims, a study of centralization must consider the concept of control.

The word is used here in the specialized sense of a means of determining whether objectives, translated into figures, are being adhered to. This sense is different from its common meaning of the ability to give instructions. The title

73

controller is used in business of an official who does not give instructions personally—apart from 'fill in these forms'—but verifies that other people's instructions are being kept. The contents of the forms vary, but include at least a profit and loss account together with some details of sources and uses of funds. The amount of detail in either the capital or the revenue accounts varies, some companies including information not required by the unit for running its own operation but perhaps needed for corporate planning purposes. Variances from the budget, an essential part of the control system, and operating ratios are normally required, but other reports—market growth, market share, production figures, stoppages and labour statistics among them—usually form an integral part of the system. In fact management information systems outside the accounting function have been noted as a current trend.[2] In spite of these developments, the problem still remains that the control system too easily ignores objectives that cannot readily be quantified—phrases like 'market image', 'first class product', 'worthwhile career' or 'satisfactory human relations' express purposes that are often omitted from the controls. The fascination of numbers can easily lead to the neglect of objectives that would otherwise have priority.

Control systems have acquired a bundle of techniques since they were first introduced and a body of wisdom which defines their usefulness. This wisdom can be encapsulated in a number of assertions which are commonly made, although usually with qualifications. The assertions are that an adequate control system:

(1) enables responsibility to be delegated;
(2) makes it possible to identify the success or failure of individual units;
(3) makes it possible to judge the performance of individual managers as well as units;
(4) also provides greater job satisfaction for managers by letting them know where they stand;
(5) provides the necessary information for effective planning at all levels;
(6) provides education and training for subordinate managers;
(7) stimulates the development and use of new techniques;
(8) directs top management attention to areas of need;
(9) is nevertheless no substitute for clear direction or sense of purpose; firms with an apparently adequate control system can still fail;
(10) can be dangerous if given an incorrect orientation.

Each of these assertions will be considered further.

Delegation
There is little doubt that control systems have brought benefits, indeed this is widely believed outside business where other organizations have tried to adapt management controls to their purposes. Voluntary, educational and religious bodies, for instance, usually prefer not to use the word because it has overtones which conflict with their norms. Nevertheless, some have used the services of control experts in an attempt to improve their own performance. Phrases like 'the introduction of business methods' into bodies such as the civil service usually refer to control in the sense used here. The general support for control

systems leaves, however, a number of problems which can be exposed by examining alleged advantages like the assertion that the control system makes possible greater delegation. The organization, so the argument runs, is able to relax its scrutiny of subordinate decision-making because information on the progress of any particular unit can be monitored. If that were true fifty years ago, how much more valid is the argument today when control measures can be observed on a visual display unit. There are, however, a number of limitations. One is that the nightmare of an autonomous unit seriously damaging the organization is never completely exorcized, and the control system must be one among the many factors that together determine the relationship. If a particular unit is able to cause harm (because it is either large in relation to the whole or in a position of especial visibility through being the subject of publicity for political or other reasons) then the effectiveness of the control system is likely to be reduced. A countervailing factor is the confidence in the leadership of the unit. Autonomy is likely to be a vote for competence or discretion rather than for the control system.

Another limitation on effectiveness is that the information is inevitably out of date. Most systems are insufficiently sensitive to change, and may fail to signal a reversal of fortune before incorrect action has been taken on the strength of previous signals. In theory such clumsiness could be avoided; the technology is available to provide reports on a daily basis with the overall picture always available. Many organizations, like the Stock Exchange, are accustomed to having indices on display which are continuously updated. For the average business, however, this would be impossibly expensive and the efficiency of a control system is always related to its cost. Calculations are required to balance the dangers of ignorance, in this case infrequent reports, against the costs of knowledge.

A well-known problem of a control system is the number of items that are out of the 'control', in the more general sense of the word, of the unit being monitored. If many policy decisions are taken in other parts of the organization, to what extent does the reporting really demonstrate management effectiveness? The question presupposes a double-edged argument, a control that is intended to promote greater autonomy and responsibility is thereby intended to stimulate independence and an ability to fight for one's interests.[3] In practice the delegation is also meant to ensure that a range of opinions are represented in policy-forming, but the ill-effects of the control system are more wasteful when it comes to niggling over shared services. The arguments may be wasteful, without necessarily reducing independence. Equally, the control system may produce priorities that demonstrate the effectiveness of management in reporting back rather than in managing. The system may be so demanding that it determines the whole direction of a unit rather than leaving room for individual (and idiosyncratic) decision-making. The greater the level of control data required, over and above cash flow and profit statements, the less decentralization actually exists, whatever the original intention when the system was established.

A control system does limit independence when it dictates the line of action to be followed, either because the intentions are misunderstood or because of an inflexible interpretation. The extent of the misunderstandings that can arise has been documented in a number of studies. One example showed widespread misunderstandings of the purposes of the control system in a group of manufacturing companies studied.[4] The managers found much of the information generated to be unusable on a number of grounds, including: the fact that the subjects covered were outside their control, the material arrived too late to influence action, and insufficient and inaccurate detail was provided, some of it in a form that was not understood.

The complaint about inflexibility is heard when form-filling dominates a manager's life. The small unit in the large organization may find its structure strained and distorted by the demands of the reporting system. Staff may be hired whose qualifications and qualities are more relevant to the reporting than to the unit's business, while too much attention is concentrated on the measurable activities rather than the less quantifiable. This aspect of the problem is not confined to small units. A company, with its sights fixed on a quality market, may find itself gradually shifting to a different sector because short-term measures like market share proved to be more potent than objectives like quality and market segment. It thus proves all too easy for the imaginative and independent approach which formal controls are meant to encourage to be lost. This does not mean that the intention of control as a decentralizing force is a failure, but that without some vigilance the intention is not only frustrated but actually reversed in practice.

Appraisal of units—the profit centre

The control system is intended to help identify the contribution that any particular unit makes to the well-being of the organization, to show where the profits and where the losses occur. In the process a new art form has come into existence—the allocation of costs across unit boundaries—and the phrase 'profit centre' has entered the vocabulary. The intention of the profit centre is to provide a convincing unit of decentralization, and thus to achieve the alleged benefits in greater personal responsibility. The profit centre managers are supposed to be running their own business; the drawbacks to this supposition have already been suggested. The pricing of goods transferred from one unit to another, services rendered or facilities shared are subjects that rise high on the agenda once serious attempts are made to allocate costs. Complaints are heard in the form of: 'There are four divisions operating on this complex, and we spend half our lives arguing over payments for the security services.' The bargaining process to which that complaint points does, however, suggest a measure of decentralization—the decision is in the hands of the local managers even if they make heavy weather of deciding. A sign of autonomy is the power to negotiate untrammelled by rulebooks and standing orders. In this case the centre is an arbiter to be appealed to, not an instructor.

In fact the profit centre concept encapsulates the problems of decentralization in a commercial organization, the degree of interdependence. In a conglomerate, a holding company with a number of independent businesses held together by a common shareholding, there is a reasonable chance that the profit centre managers may be able to control their own destiny sufficiently to provide a convincing example of the merits of independence. Even so, there is evidence that the more successful conglomerate has a more directive head office.[5] The more usual type of profit centre is a product division or operating unit within a company to which are attributed its own costs and proceeds. It serves the three main purposes already mentioned of judging performance on acceptable criteria, of providing valid information on the basis of which the profit centre management can reshape the unit's strategy and tactics, of enabling head office (as the group's bankers) to reinforce success or penalize failure, by allocating or withholding investment funds, and of encouraging entrepreneurial flair. Indeed, the purpose of the exercise is to turn the bureaucrat into a thrusting businessman working within a system of positive commercial accountability.

The attraction of the idea is that straightforward questions about success or failure, and the need for expansion or contraction, can apparently be answered in the unequivocal terms of comparative or absolute profitability. The hope is that the profitability yardstick will encourage the entrepreneurial approach. However, the profit centre manager never has the same relationship with the parent company board as does the chief executive of an independent company with shareholders and bankers. The manager in charge of the profit centre, it could be argued, takes greater personal risks than the entrepreneur. The ultimate penalty for the latter is bankruptcy, but there are many manoeuvres and appeals possible between setback and disaster. The manager's reward for failure is dismissal, against which there may be few safeguards. The risks to the company exist too. Designating a profit centre in no way ensures profitability, as many companies have discovered when a serious failure in one division has pulled down the rest. With all these reservations, however, the profit centre does delineate a part of the business which is of particular concern to management and on which regular information is required. This discussion of the subject is justified on the grounds that the concept is an attempt to combine control with decentralization. As so often with such attempts, the control works more obviously than the decentralization, and the working does not always support the declared objectives.

Appraisal of individual

Normally, the appraisal of the unit and that of the individual will go together, although a unit that is not worth retaining may still be well managed. But the consequences of the appraisals may be contradictory when, for instance, the process is adequate for resolving disputes between units but less satisfactory in determining the excellence of an individual contribution. A more impressionistic method, one that takes into account the less tangible personal qualities, may produce more acceptable results, yet by its nature it will also be more centralized, to take account of a wider knowledge of individual attributes.

Job satisfaction

The control system, it is claimed, can increase job satisfaction among managers by providing them with a picture of their performance which they regard as fair and objective. This statement is often made but can only be true when a number of conditions are met. One is that the managers have confidence in the system, that they understand it and that the feedback from the centre is adequate. Another condition is psychological, that the manager is disposed to regard the system as fair and objective.

Planning
Another advantage of the control system is that it enables systematic planning techniques to be used. The complex relationship between planning and centralization is considered in more detail later.

Education
The control system, it is claimed, serves an educational function. The insistence on the regular monitoring of predetermined activities ensures that these duties are impressed on the manager's mind. The production of regular accounts, inventories and other listings ensures that all managers are working to similar standards. This educational aspect may have been an afterthought to those who originally had the task of framing control systems, but it can be said to have contributed to making decentralization possible. The mutual understanding and conformity to which the education leads provides a framework within which greater discretion is possible.

Stimulus
The cumulative effect of these benefits is expected to provide a stimulus towards improved performance supported by the competitive effects of circulating control figures. The stimulus is increased by relating performance to pay, either through payment by results on the shop floor or through an executive bonus scheme for the manager. The possibility of relating pay to performance has been much criticized. Bonus schemes, it is discovered, soon turn into fixed salaries since the schemes are manipulated to ensure a regular income. At higher levels arrangements which add a small highly taxed portion to already large incomes can hardly be a convincing incentive and at lower levels efforts are made to frustrate any inequalities that arise. Such statements are supported by impressive evidence, but there are some facts to the contrary as well. The abolition of bonus schemes has frequently led to setbacks and it would seem that there are other factors beside the financial reward, like the power to bargain, which the scheme provides.

Directs top management attention to areas of need
Subject to the potential drawbacks already mentioned, like setting its own priorities, the control system can concentrate attention on the weaknesses in the sub-unit and avoid energy being diffused on those that are working well.

The system and the sense of direction

It has been argued that the atmosphere in which the control system operates is as important as the control system itself, both in producing the intended results and in determining the related degree of autonomy. This atmosphere is compounded of a number of factors that it is hard to quantify but which include a sense of direction and commitment on the part of top management together with a clear understanding of the firm's opportunities, purposes and constraints. Within this the unit manager who has to respond to and operate the system requires:

(a) a statement of the policies, strategies and constraints within which he or she has to work;

(b) a statement of the main purpose of the unit and how it relates to other departments within the company;

(c) a statement of the limits to his or her authority, preferably designed to delineate an autonomy subject to named exceptions;

(d) a statement of priorities for the unit;

(e) a statement of how judgements about success or failure will be made;

(f) a statement of the guidelines for what is acceptable and what unacceptable in the style of management.

The manager also requires periodical confirmation of these statements and regular agreement, or the recognition of lack of agreement, about the strategies and tactics within which he or she is operating. Within the small organization, much of the information and understanding will, no doubt, pass informally. In the larger companies formal procedures and communications experts are usually considered to be necessary, although there are many different ways of arranging the procedures and incorporating the expertise. The provisions made are likely to be on a narrower basis than those implied in the above list which needs, in any case, to be balanced by provision for the executive's response. The key to the effect of the system may well be in the unit manager's appreciation of what is expected and of his or her capacity to achieve it, of the additional resources required, of the constraints and how they can be coped with, of the priorities, the underlying assumptions, and of the validity of the measures in force.

Dangers in the control system

The need for control systems is nowadays taken for granted and the debate is on how to reduce the problems which are treated as side-effects. Indeed many a company in trouble has been turned round by the conscientious introduction of adequate controls and little else. At the same time there has always been resistance to activities that take a manager's attention away from other activities which he or she considers more congenial and productive. There is also the chilling principle, proposed by Simon, that programmed activity tends to drive out the unprogrammed; this makes it necessary to ensure that the control system does not leave out some element that is critical to the organization's well-being. One research into a government department in the United States showed how the supervisors appraised their subordinates on the number of interviews undertaken. As a result important tasks, and difficult clients, were avoided because they reduced the number of interviews that could be undertaken in the time available.[6]

A psychologist writing on the subject has pointed to the need for a match between the reward system and the structure of the organization, the expectations generated and the technology employed. Table 5.1 presents an outline of his findings which relate the human relations climate, the production type and the degree of centralization to the controls and rewards. In general, it is asserted that the control system measures only a limited part of a person's objectives, not always the most appropriate, that the standards are often unrealistic and that the assessment is distorted when the assessor has the power of reward. Where the match does not exist there is a likelihood of centralization and other unexpected by-products. This proposition emphasizes the theme that the control system may be a force either for centralization or autonomy—a finding confirmed by empirical research[7]—and that the way the force will operate in any given set of circumstances depends on the operation of other aspects of the relationship between a centre and its units, a theme to which we shall return later. During this discussion on control, the profit centre idea has been mentioned. This and other means of identifying a unit of control are considered next.

Table 5.1   The match between organization and control

Characteristic	Variable	Control
Human relations climate	Authoritarian	Hard data arising from predetermined list
	Democratic	Hard data arising from participative goal-setting
Production type	Mass and unit	Hard criteria rewards on individual and small group basis
	Process	Individual performance not measurable
	Professional	Individual criteria
Size	Large	No organization—wide rewards except at top
	Small	Organization—wide rewards
Degree of centralization	Centralized	Sub-unit controls a problem
	Decentralized	Sub-unit controls practicable

Adapted from Lawler (1971)

5.2   THE UNIT OF CONTROL

The large organization normally has two kinds of unit which may be called the *sectional* and the *local*. The former is a cross-section of the whole, relatively self-contained and with its own sub-units, and includes top executives. In the civil service, for instance, a ministry is a *sectional* unit, while its regional office is a *local*. The latter is comprehended in the former, while the sectional includes at least one officer who is senior to any of those in the local. In the business organization the sectional unit normally includes all those executives and operators specifically charged with responsibility for a particular line of products, but may cover other groupings of business activities, like a geographical area. Names like 'division', 'subsidiary' or 'business' may be applied—some of them, including 'subsidiary', also having legal connotations. The local units will be called 'branches', 'plants', 'sales offices' or other similar titles.

The 'formation of divisions', a term borrowed from the military where it refers to a group with sufficient resources and skills to undertake an action on its own, is often hailed as decentralization in a company. But the corporate division is normally a less autonomous unit than the military and, in any case, the nature of the exercise depends on the standpoint of the observer. A reorganization which appears to be a delegation of authority at the top, may well appear lower down to be nothing more than a reshuffle of offices at headquarters. The consequences may seem more centralizing to the subordinate units, including those abroad. The sharing of responsibilities around a slightly larger group may reduce the authority available lower down.

This is not to belittle a number of conscious efforts that have been made to provide a wider devolution, but to stress that the standpoint is all-important. Indeed some of the efforts mean a redistribution of activities to enable a wider responsibility within existing constraints. At operator level the arrangements that have come to be known as work structuring or job enrichment[8] represent a form of increased autonomy without necessarily much delegation of authority. The operator is working within defined and understood limits, but with more discretion than is usually attached to a comparable job. The same can be said of flexitime where employees are given more control over their hours of work. Some activities are autonomous by their nature. The airline pilot and the train driver are examples of positions where there is a necessary element of independence, but where technological aids are reducing the amount of discretion. Mechanical devices replace human supervision to reduce the scope for error.[9]

Whatever may be the unit to which responsibility is devolved, and whatever the consequences of the devolution, any position from which facts are fed into the control system is a unit of control. Appraisal and accountability are possibilities wherever the facts are being collected; but a greater level of accountability is expected at a point where they are being consolidated. The profit centre, cost centre if located in a supportive function, may be in a *sectional* or a *local* unit. If the latter, then the company may be said to be decentralized and an operational definition of an autonomous organization might well be one in which the accounts are made up in a number of local units and not just in the sectional. The types of centralized-autonomous relationship will be formulated later by considering the unit of control more closely; meanwhile, control in a particular political system will be examined.

5.3 CONTROL IN A SOCIALIST SYSTEM

Twenty years ago a controversy was launched in the Soviet Union as a result of a scheme designed to overcome the deficiencies of the manufacturing system. The scheme resembled a Western-style control system, although it was presented as a theoretical approach designed to overcome notorious bottlenecks in supply. Also proposed was a measure of decentralization—independence within the national planning framework. The package was held together by an emphasis on consumption rather than supply and this made other changes necessary. The suggestions were highly controversial and led to a considerable debate in the Soviet Union, a debate which was widely reported in the West. Whatever may be the merits of demerits of the rival systems into which the industrial world is divided, the debate illustrated two points. One is the essential similarity between control systems, whatever the differences of political regime, and the other is that the differences are determined partly by the relationship between the control system and other business relationships—that with the consumer, the supplier, the shareholder, the planner and so on. A kind of *cui bono* principle applies; the system aims to satisfy the agency regarded as the most influential under a given set of circumstances.

The Russian proposal was not a total change of outlook but a substitution of one set of indices for another. The resultant problems demonstrated clearly the difficulties of such an exercise. One case study, of a clothing company,[10] illustrates the attempt to correct distortions and how established methods reassert themselves. The problem was a rise in inventories at a time when sales and savings were increasing (between 1950 and 1963 retail sales increased by 132 per cent, soft goods sales by 247 per cent, inventories by 509 per cent and personal savings by 737 per cent). The imbalance led the authorities to develop an experiment, at first in one enterprise only, to try to produce an organization which was more interested in consumption than in supply. By 1963 the principal controls were two indices: the gross output and the relation of planned to actual costs. Executive appraisal was largely based on performance on these two figures as was the fixing of the annual bonus (which could be up to 40 per cent of basic salary). Like payments by results systems in the West, the effect of these bonuses was more apparent than real. Targets were regularly exceeded by an amount sufficient to provide some extra money, but not too much for fear that the norms might be increased. To outward appearance there is a minimal difference between such a bonus scheme and a fixed income; the reality may be that the effects are not as similar as the appearance.

The change in the control system was accompanied by organization changes as well. The factory was brought nearer to the consumer by selling direct to retail stores with more rapid information about sales trends becoming available. To achieve the objects of the experiment several measures of decentralization were introduced.

The management team was strengthened and planning controls were relaxed, together with some centrally imposed regulations. But basic price lists, wage rates and capital investment decisions were reserved for a higher authority. As the consequences of the experiment were evaluated the following problems, familiar enough to Western observers, came to light.

(1)   The disappearance of traditional and well-understood incentives.
(2)   The new incentives did not always prove compatible with greater sensitivity to the consumer. The control indicators showed worse results when the changing demand produced shorter runs in the factory and

increased costs. Pleasing the customer meant working hard to retain the bonus.

(3)   The continued existence of so many factors that were outside the control of the unit management as to make the appraisal system unreal. In particular, prices and wages were still fixed by established methods and were not responsive to market forces.

(4)   Well-known guidelines were swept away but continued to influence procedures. In particular the consequences of the controls in enhanced salaries were largely negatived. Work was arranged so that existing bonus levels continued.

(5)   In general, the selected indicators did not achieve the desired aims; on the contrary, they penalized those who moved towards those aims.

(6)   Weaknesses in the infrastructure reduced still further the managers' ability to perform.

(7)   The attitudes of the people concerned and their cultural backgrounds were inimical to the experiment.

The changing control system at first produced decentralization, but was eventually declared unworkable and the experiment was not much imitated in the Soviet Union itself. It has been alleged that such experiments 'failed to take account of the bureaucracy's in-built conservatism and the fact that most of the country's managers, although qualified by Soviet standards, were of peasant stock.'[11] The writer of this passage links the failure of experiments, which have been more successful in other socialist countries like Hungary, to the cultural background of Soviet management. He also assumes that the size of the country has some connection with its inability to experiment, although he does not explain why. A more cogent explanation may be that such experiments cannot succeed in isolation. A market orientation in a supply-based economy is frustrated by the suppliers. Whatever weight may be given to the various reasons for the rise and fall of Soviet experiments in Western-style controls, the case illustrates the difficulty of ensuring that control techniques do motivate in the required direction. The incentives were damaged, so the controls proved counter-productive.

5.4   CORPORATE PLANNING

Corporate planning is a word that calls forth a variety of responses both of support and of scepticism. The practice of planning enjoyed a vogue in the late 1960s when it was seen that a competitive advantage could be gained, but a set-back followed when so many organizations learned that their planners had not provided for direction-changing events like the oil crisis or the revolution in Iran, although both had been widely forecast. Since then the methods have been revised and refined and their place in business decision-making is accepted. Corporate planning is the process of identifying the options open to the company in responding to opportunities and problems as they arise, and of recommending which is the most viable. This process can be conducted at a number of levels and within various time horizons. At each level of the organization the practice can vary in sophistication from the use of a considerable apparatus of data and techniques to the drafting of simple predictions and guidelines. The whole process can be understood in three phases[12]—strategic, tactical and operational. At each phase, criteria are produced to guide the policy-forming process.

Strategic planning is used to describe a general review of the possibilities of the organization and to provide a sense of direction. This is sometimes called long-term planning, but the actual time horizon varies according to the nature of the business. The phrase 'long term' means something quite different for the mining, shipbuilding or pharmaceutical businesses than it does for clothing, food and other consumer industries. The essence of strategic planning is to work out the options available and the contingencies that may arise within a horizon that is relevant to the particular sector, covering at least the period that must follow between the mooting of a new idea and the day when it begins to earn revenue. This may vary from two years to thirty according to the industry. The minimum has been increased both by legislative action on the part of governments which turns prospecting for minerals and seeking permission to build facilities into a long-term exercise; it has also been stretched by technology. As the level of technology in an industry rises, the time span of decisions grows longer. In the energy industry, for instance, long-term planning may focus on nuclear energy. When the plans are implemented in, say, ten to twelve years' time other fuels like coal may be cheaper; but the decision will already have been taken at the top and other options will be closed to those lower down. In this sense capital-intensive technology with long lead times (including planning inquiries as well as development) is a centralizing force. Much strategic planning is relatively timeless, developing a general review of the company's outlook which can be used as a yardstick against which specific proposals can be assessed.

The second phase is the tactical in which the longer-term plans are translated into actual programmes with lead times attached. During this phase the various departments, divisions and subsidiaries become committed to outlines which specify their roles in implementing the plans. The final, operational, phase turns the results of what has gone before into budgets and other detailed arrangements. Within each of these progressive stages there are other dimensions and levels of activity, like the international which is considered in Chapter 14. Corporate planning can also be regarded as a part-time function in which line managers play a leading part, and this can be its sole place in a small company if it is formally recognized at all—there will always be some degree of informal planning, like the business idea which is fixed in the entrepreneur's head even if he never articulates it or commits it to paper. In the larger concern, corporate planning may be given a more specialized place which varies from a one-person unit, mainly responsible for exploring opportunities for diversification, to a highly professional department with its own sub-departments responsible for country studies, industry investigations, appraisals of competitors, forecasting and other specializations.

The rise of corporate planning is frequently described as part of a trend to centralization. Those who oppose such a trend are found to oppose the introduction of formal planning methods, alleging that they lead to the concentration of too much power at the centre. A further allegation is that the costs of such a concentration outweigh the benefits. In fact the relationship between planning and centralization is more complex. The pressure towards a central review of resources may also cause a loss of autonomy, but, even where there is a lure to centralization in the system, the planner can still identify areas where responsibility can be more efficiently delegated. This might well be regarded as part of the function of corporate planning. The consequences in any given set of circumstances are likely to be related to the type of business, whether or not an all-embracing view of the corporate prospects makes sense for instance. Finally, the relationship of planning to centralization can be said to start at both ends of the planning cycle.

At the beginning

At the beginning, in the initiation of the planning, a subject for debate is whether the role of the centre is to initiate or to respond. Are the strategies a summary of the proposals of the operating units consolidated and coordinated at the centre, or are they formulated at head office for the company as a whole and then parcelled up into appropriate packages for each of the subordinate parts? The question is not necessarily of an either/or variety but is apt to be answered that way in practice. The growth of central expertise will frequently lead to top-down rather than bottom-up procedures.

At the end

At the end, in the influencing of results, the ability to affect the outcomes is a form of inverted autonomy (inverted centralization is discussed in Chapter 12). This means that the planner has to take account of the implementer, the human and organization resources that can be brought to bear. The consequences of diplomacy and bargaining between the staff planners and the line managers may well be to transform the original intentions. The centralizing aims of the strategic plans have been turned upside down before they are put into practice.

At each stage

At each stage, there are constraints on the planning process. Modern corporate planning is most concerned with the staking out of the objectives and the proposing of routes, with provision for contingencies. There are limits to the amount of guidance that can be given on significant decisions; hence, the centralizing effect may be more apparent than real. In addition, the corporate planner relies on line management for information and the corporate plans can be seen as rationalizing a multitude of projected futures; in this sense the plans, like the control system, can be seen as a stimulant. The unit manager has a greater chance of becoming more involved in planning the future than the day-to-day business usually permits.

Techniques employed

In relation to the techniques employed, the authority of the planner, as with other managers, will partly be related to the expertise deployed. A highly expert department will be able to exert more muscle within the company, but may also have an outlook which sees its role as purely advisory. Professionals will not be so quick to see themselves usurping the functions of others.

The general view that the establishment of a corporate planning department leads to centralization is not entirely supported. The last paragraph, which detected a relationship between professionalism in planning and a sensitivity to local autonomy expresses a contrary point of view along with the suggestion that planning is a stimulant to the line manager to look beyond his day-to-day concerns. Nevertheless, the ability to take a global outlook on corporate resources frequently makes autonomy undesirable. The whole is seen to be greater than the sum of the parts, and the distribution of funds between competing units is a centralizing exercise. In the case of the foreign subsidiary there may be the opportunity to generate its own finances, but even so the intervention of central planning in their use is probable. In the domestic units the funds will be normally allocated from the centre, and this may extend to considerable detail. The author once met the director of a substantial plant who had only recently been granted the right to sign his own cheques.

5.5   THE COMMUNICATION OF CONTROL

Control and communication are inseparable, the one mediating the other. This self-evident fact is frequently overlooked when examining the problems of control, which include all the problems of communication along with those of monitoring the results, and the transmission of the data as well as their selection and collection. At issue are misunderstandings at any point along the communication chain as well as deliberate changes made for reasons like self-interest. Such problems have already been mentioned, as has the vicious circle in which the decisions at the top become steadily less related to the realities they are meant to influence owing to a breakdown of upward communication. This occurs where there is an excess of downward communication over upward, especially where those at the top have lost the art of listening. An excess of upward communication can also lead to problems such as indecisiveness in the face of a threat to the organization's existence, even a failure to recognize the threat. Other influences have been recognized such as the number of levels in a hierarchy.

These and similar factors affect the good working of the communications and therefore of the monitoring. The control staff are manoeuvring for their reports within a broader system which is carrying messages for a number of other purposes. The exercise of authority, but also the practice of friendship, together with the seeking and giving of advice, admonishment and even encouragement, all these and many more have to share the communication system. The emphasis on each will influence every other and form a context in which the same amount and frequency of monitoring appears to the units as either centralizing or decentralizing, according to the effect on the decision-making.

It is likely that the most formal and impersonal of the messages passed will be the monthly reports keyed into the head office computer, and efforts are frequently made to mitigate or reinforce the effects by personal visits or casual phone calls. The consequences are sometimes different from those expected. Just because of its formality, the control system does not pose an immediate threat, however much of a nuisance it may be. The informal approach, although intended to humanize the system—'to take the nonsense out of centralization', as one executive expressed it—brings a greater pressure to central decision-making, unless used sensitively and purposefully in the opposite sense.

The communication of control, then, is directly related to centralization when its operation increases or reduces the pressure to central decision-making. But the indirect effects are widespread, partly depending on the contents of the other communications. This subject is discussed more fully in Chapter 15, but the effectiveness of the system together with the confidence it produces is likely to have consequences for the decision-making. The reverse is also true. A centralized system has its own characteristic problems of over-active downward communications, while a decentralized system can result in indecisiveness, even a lack of recognition when the organization is under threat.

5.6   CONTROL, PERFORMANCE AND A SENSE OF DIRECTION

One of the objects of control is to direct the attention of those being monitored to the main influences on the performance of the organization. In section 5.3 it was observed how experiments in control were initiated in the Soviet Union with this aim in mind. That example illustrated attempts that are continually being made to influence a course of events through the control system. The purpose of the reports is first to assure head office that all is well, but also to provide a measure of performance. The relationship of this measure to centralization is debatable.

The argument for greater autonomy is usually linked to some belief about motivation, an assumption that independence stimulates effort. This is a specialized, although common, use of 'motivation', a word which is also applied to fear of consequences, like loss of employment—the stick as well as the carrot. The evidence for the belief that motivation can be equated with independence can only be described as elusive and complex, more convincing in the negative sense that lack of discretion reduces motivation than in the positive. There is, in any case, a limit to the possibilities of autonomy at any given level. Some decisions in a business must be taken at the top. An operating unit cannot declare the corporate dividend (although a loss-making department can sabotage it) nor appoint a chief executive (although such a unit can provide an environment in which the next chief can make his or her reputation). The parentheses demonstrate two of the restraints on centralization, and the motivation argument leads to an emphasis on identifying the appropriate level for any particular decision. When this level is the lowest possible in each case, the organization is certainly decentralized. There are, however, two riders to add to that statement.

One is that some convincing way of relating the degree of decentralization to the measure of performance found in the control system is required. The argument can easily become circular. A relaxed, decentralized system is regarded as a successful outcome for decentralization, while the profit and loss figures are excused away on the grounds that too much is beyond the individual manager's control. The argument for decentralization cannot permanently rest on motivation; this has to be translated into accounting figures, however unsatisfactory, if it is to carry conviction.

The other corollary to the observation about decentralization is that of identifying the unit discussed above in 5.2. The debate on what actually happens, as opposed to the claims, depends partly on the viewpoint from which the generalizations are made. Divisionalization is an example. Viewed from the top this appears as decentralization. Indeed the current fashion for organizing companies along product group lines has led some authors to furnish evidence for a supposed relationship between growth and autonomy. Extravagant claims are made for divisionalization which include the reduction of overload in the communications system. More rapid decision-making is also said to be possible along with the use of the talents of a wider range of executives. Against this are ranged the dangers of sub-optimal behaviour and of a shortage of executives suitable for running divisions. The difficulty is to find any evidence of the benefits, or even how to identify relevant evidence. One study, for example, showed that there was little connection between divisionalization and share price.[13] The money markets evidently are not convinced that such reorganization produces automatic benefits. In fact even the ambiguous figures recorded were influenced by a company whose price had been steadily increasing before divisions were introduced. From the point of view of subordinate units divisionalization is often seen as a reduction in autonomy. To them the reorganization appears in the light of a reshuffle of posts at head office after which they find their discretion more restricted than it was before. Hence, generalizations which cast doubt on the success of decentralization as a policy must be interpreted in the light of the unit of centralization, and measurements must take account of this.

One line of research that did find a connection between the grouping of a company's basic activities into divisions and improved performance also found nine other influences on achievement, including greater formality and integration.[14] This finding emphasizes that performance derives from a range of measures and that the forming of divisions can accompany greater centralization, as can any change that involves the appointment of new managers. Also emphasized in the research is the chain of complicated relationships that this chapter has already exposed.

In contrast, a simple model consists of such statements as: 'Controls designed to promote autonomy produce local optimization but risk global suboptimizing.'

By 'optimization' in the above paragraph is meant the ability to make use of the resources available to the company which is not most in line with its overall objectives, like profit or growth. Sub-optimization, then, is a failure to make such use due to consideration to the demands of sub-units or other sectional interests. Naturally, this statement begs the question as to who is judging the degree of optimization and how; it emphasizes the more important point that even if the judgement is accepted, there are other factors which determine the result.

The proposition can only be upheld or denied on the strength of a number of other insights which include the actual consequences as well as the design, the various measures of performance, the operation of the communications system, the interpretation placed upon the controls, and above all upon the position of the unit being controlled. Amid complacent claims for the operation of monitoring systems are warnings that these are widely misunderstood.[15] So the model has to be elaborated to: 'Controls that are interpreted as promoting autonomy can, under certain conditions, produce local optimization; the conditions include the state of the communications as well as the type of business and a number of other factors; on the operation of these factors will also depend whether or not global suboptimization follows.'

The final formula will need to include a number of considerations balancing assumptions like the motivating effects of autonomy against the speed and effectiveness of the controls. As with every human activity, success in business is a mixture of perspiration and inspiration. The control system represents the perspiration without which the inspiration is easily dissipated. The balance of forces in any particular organization at a given moment of time depends less on a deliberate exercise of judgement than on a process of bargaining. The next chapter examines this process in terms of the conflicts which condition it.

6 *Conflict and Cooperation*

The principle that 'good news is not news' means that discussions of organization emphasize the element of conflict rather than that of cooperation. In contrast, it could be said that, as organizations grow, the most impressive characteristic is not the symptoms of stress or strain, but the massive amount of cooperation required to make the venture viable. The forces that are pulling the organization together are usually more powerful, even if less regarded, than those that are pulling it apart. Necessarily so, but such a statement can still contain the seeds of a fallacy—that peace is a sign of a healthy organization and lack of peace the reverse. On the contrary the absence of conflict may represent a condition where points of view that are vital to a group's well-being are suppressed or unrepresented. The corpse, it has been well said, is the archetype of the peaceful organization.

This chapter concerns the issues that cause disturbance and those that produce cohesion, with the implications of both for our central theme. Various words are used for the disturbance: bargaining, negotiating, disruption, turbulence. The word used can sometimes tell more about the user than about the phenomenon; 'conflict' is preferred here although this term is used in a broad sense. It refers to an underlying condition which may remain latent or may produce a range of symptoms which vary from a relatively mild disagreement to a serious disruption; from a discussion to a war.[1] The aim is to consider the types of conflict that occur and how the degree of centralization and decentralization is likely to be affected; these types will be grouped under four headings: internal conflicts about means, internal conflicts about ends, conflicts with other organizations and a brief consideration of the occurrence of any of the four on the boundaries of an organization. The chapter will close with a look at cooperation and cohesion—terms which are not necessarily to be regarded as the other side of the coin.

All conflict can be either destructive or constructive in the life of an organization, more usually a mixture of the two; a more subtle distinction is between a conflict of opinion, where the desired upshot is mutually understood, and a conflict of interest, a built-in conflict which may properly be described as inevitable. Any discussion of the subject which ignores this reasoning is prone

90

to a faulty diagnosis, and both distinctions, along with that between ends and means, are considered in the following pages.

6.1 INTERNAL CONFLICT OVER MEANS

Members and groups within an organization may have conflicts and disagreements either about the objectives to be achieved or the means pursued in realizing those objectives. The conflict over means can itself be subdivided into two: a basic and unavoidable disagreement that is inherent in the decision-making process and a dissension about the way to achieve the common purpose. The latter is straightforward enough. The only effect of such dissension on centralization depends on the stability or otherwise of the organization and the methods by which the opposing views are expressed. In organizations that exist primarily to further a cause, like churches and political parties, these expressions are likely to have a more profound effect on the structure than in others. In such bodies there is usually a general agreement about aims, and the discord is likely to be concentrated on the means. While controversy of this kind is still unlikely to affect the degree of centralization, if the dissensions become too acute then the autonomy of subordinate units is called in question.[2]

The other form of conflict over means, the disagreement that is inherent in the decision-making process, is here called built-in conflict; it was intended to be present when the formal structure was designed.

Planned or built-in conflict takes a number of forms. One is the arrangement of appointments around functions which are intended to counterbalance one another. A well-known example of this is cabinet government where the spending ministries—defence, education and transport among others—are intended to fight for the available resources, while the treasury is intended to curb spending in the interests of the taxpayer. This planned conflict with ministers appointed to champion their departments, and often judged by their success in doing so, is considered to make for efficient government. It ensures that the various rival interests which necessarily exist in the decision-making, such as the provision of services against the need for financial restraint, are represented by strong establishments and highly placed individuals. The departments of a company fulfil a similar function. Production, marketing, finance, personnel and the more specialist units are set up to ensure that no vital requirement is overlooked. Indeed the discovery that some aspect of the decision-making is being neglected is frequently regarded as a signal that a new appointment or a new department is required.

The conflict is not, of course, as straightforward as the last paragraph might suggest, nor as planned or creative—the parts are meant to be subordinate to the well-being of the whole in government and in business—but the principle remains that without the built-in disagreements important elements of the decision system would be neglected. To this extent the conflict is necessary and constructive, but there are factors that damage the organization as well. The necessary trend to greater specialization to match the needs of a growing company in keeping abreast of an expanding body of knowledge and techniques, both commercial and technical, increases the problems of communication. The resulting disputes between line and staff, between the departments directly concerned with the company's main products or services and those whose role is intended to be advisory, have been analysed in the context of a theory of conflict.[3] The analysis uses a model which contains four influences (the authors call them 'mechanisms')—that staff and line have differing perceptions of their role descriptions, that staff behaviour is influenced by factors other than the role description, that line expectations are influenced by factors other than the role description and that there are different perceptions of role behaviour. These influences produce harmful effects on a relationship which, as the authors make clear, is not precise. The difference between a position that entails direct authority and one that is of an advisory nature is frequently blurred in practice. Staff managers have a power of veto, like personnel officers who control recruiting, and a strong influence over other activities. Production levels and standards are partly determined by marketing staff, for instance. The consequences for centralization are in this case clearer and are reminiscent of the unit of control discussion in the previous chapter. The position can be stated in a simple proposition: 'The more autonomy that is vested in specialist functional departments, the greater their ability to interfere with direct line managers; hence, less autonomy will remain to the operating units.'

This is matched in non-commercial organizations by the relationship between administrative and other departments.

There is a natural tendency for line managers to exaggerate the authority of their staff colleagues, but the latter do exercise considerable influence. That is the nature of a system in which authority is increasingly based on expertise. In government another example of the same trend is the setting-up of regional organizations which reduce the scope of local authorities. In both cases departmentalization provides the opportunity to manipulate particular units, and to restrict powers that would otherwise produce autonomy.

6.2   INTERNAL CONFLICT OVER ENDS

Voluntary organizations, it has been pointed out, are prone to conflict over means. There is usually a general agreement about ends, even if hedged around by misunderstandings and ambiguities. It may be, for instance, that a particular person joins a church for social or other motives unrelated to the promotion of religion, but the discord does not arise from ambiguous motives as much as from disagreements about how the official purposes are to be furthered. In commercial and governmental organizations, on the other hand, substantial differences about aims are endemic.

Part of the skill of a manager is to use manpower more efficiently. Under some circumstances this means to use fewer people—the current word is 'redundancy'—which conjures up an inevitable conflict of aims. The personal objectives of those being made redundant are presumably opposed to the objectives (both corporate and personal) of those who decided to dismiss them. The phrase 'voluntary redundancy' witnesses to this by identifying exceptions.

Redundancy provides a stark example of a normal situation. In a commercial organization there is a network of groups, some official and some unofficial, with varying aims, which frequently confront one another. There is a general assumption that personal objectives coincide more closely with those of the organization at the more senior levels, but the rise of the professional manager has produced a division of interest between the executive director and the shareholder. The official aim of the company may be to earn an adequate return on the shareholder's equity, but the purposes of top management are likely to be more diffuse. Reputation for themselves and for the firm, the standing of the company in the outside world and the harmony inside, victories over competitors and predators, and the performance of a professional job of management will all be among the objectives. Any or all of these may also contribute to profits, but that is not the only concern. The very development of a profession of management implies a difference of purpose between that profession and the owners.

In considering this issue, the time factor is also significant. The horizon of the shareholders varies with their objectives. For some income is required, for others capital gains. Where the holding is widely spread, both will exist and their interests may appear to cancel one another out. Where there is a single owner or a more homogeneous group, the aim will be clearer. The manager's time horizon will also vary, but according to different criteria. There will be the demands of the technology or other factors which determine the gap between the decision to launch a new project and the receipt of income from that project. This may vary from a few months in the case of some simple consumer goods to over twenty years if a mine has to be sunk. The owner will, of course, understand that some industry sectors cannot produce quick returns, but in all industries the professional is likely to emphasize the longer-term opportunity against the quick profit. In fact the most public confrontations between ownership and management—the takeover battle, particularly where asset-stripping is involved—demonstrate most clearly the conflict over time horizons. The manager is conserving assets, sometimes including long-term research, against their possible future usefulness, while the owner is seeking to find a more profitable use for them in the present. Under such circumstances conflict is probable, and it may be over opinion or interest. The manager may conserve fruitlessly or the owner may destroy wantonly.

Differing perceptions as well as rival objectives lie behind the conflict, but the implications are clear. A conflict exists even at the top level of an organization. Other factors may also be involved at this level. Age and ambition are among the personal influences. A group of executive directors who see their entire future with the company are likely to identify with its interests more closely than those who are using it to further careers which will continue in some other organization. Such conflicts, between personal and organizational objectives at the top, are likely to occur more strongly elsewhere. The personal objective of security and continuity of employment, with which this discussion started, will be strongest among those employees who have little opportunity of other work, and is unlikely to be found at all among the objectives of the owners—although there may be a statement about 'providing continuous and worthwhile employment' in the official aims of those companies which possess a policy manual. There will be other group objectives, like the struggle for recognition or upgrading, among various classes of employees from professional engineers through foremen to skilled craftsmen. For all groups, competition for higher wages will be an important objective in itself, and for some greater opportunities for leisure will be more important than any conditions of work.

The argument, then, points to the underlying conflicts of interest between groups of participants in commercial, governmental and other organizations. The existence of the dissensions has been identified here in relatively humdrum terms; there has been no attempt to relate them to historical forces, or long-term trends, simply to acknowledge their existence in order to examine the implications for centralization.[4] It should also be emphasized that the existence of a potential disagreement does not produce an actual dispute. In a company the quarrels may remain latent until some issue or personality emerges around which the diverging interests collect. The condition of the business, the state of the morale, the skill of the management and the other options available to the participants are among the factors which will determine whether and when the latent conflict becomes overt.

When this does happen, and an open dispute is in progress, there are many different ways in which it will be waged. The shareholders, for instance, may resolve a dispute with top management rapidly by removing the chief executive. Where the shareholding is diffuse, this implies a widespread agreement and may not remove the causes of the trouble; at the least an open quarrel has now become latent again. In terms of the concept of quasi-resolution of conflict,[5] the problem is now off the agenda even if the divisive forces continue to operate below the surface. The use of a sanction like dismissal is, then, one way of resolving a conflict; another is the process of bargaining and negotiating or the use of conciliation procedures. The profession of industrial relations has developed around efforts to resolve disagreements between managers and other groups of employees with the minimum of damage to the organization. Whether the agreements are taken as symptoms of an underlying disorder or whether they are dismissed as misunderstandings, patient effort has been put into the building-up of procedures for avoiding and settling disputes. In the end there may be confrontation, and the belief does exist that some confrontations are helpful in creating a new situation which would have proved unobtainable by any other means. The popular saying that 'a row clears the air' bears witness to this belief, and certainly needs to be taken seriously when analysing the consequences of conflict. The difficulty about taking the saying seriously is the common difficulty about translating an individual characteristic to a group, the issue of realism that forms one of the themes of this study.

Confrontation may have a constructive effect for individuals and indeed small groups. It may be that there is some cathartic consequence in a factory walk-out for instance. If both sides are now prepared for an arrangement which neither would accept before, this is so. But it is hard to believe that such a principle can be applied to a larger group such as an industry sector, and much harder to believe that it can apply to an international dispute. There may well be some creative consequences of military conflict, although it is hard to believe that the causal sequence is direct or that the benefits are in any way related to the costs; in this context too there are popular sayings which are relevant. Phrases like 'making a fresh start', and 'post-war reconstruction' attest to beliefs that 'good can come out of evil', while the words 'they did not die in vain' do not only refer to a negative achievement—the end of the threat the war was fought to overcome.

War is, of course, not regarded as an internal conflict unless the boundaries of an organization are extended to continental or global proportions, although civil war and urban violence have not been unfashionable in recent years. The reference to war illustrates extremes among the methods of waging conflict and their consequences. Whatever the methods used, the light in which they are viewed will be the factor that influences the degree of centralization. If the conflict is internal and about objectives, like most industrial disputes, then the discussion about centralization and autonomy may be seen as part of the cure. Normally a conflict of interest that is perceived as such will lead to greater centralization, where a more optimistic view supports a local resolution. The pressure for plant bargaining comes from those who see the problems in less dramatic terms, while the arguments for central bargaining are upheld by those who are dissatisfied with tinkering with symptoms. Perceptions about relative advantage in the power struggle also apply. In fact the means used to resolve conflicts are an important indicator of centralization. The overriding of local negotiations by management can occur either because the handling is considered too severe or too lenient, while local managers have more authority where the issues are unusual or outside the experience of their seniors. The issue appears in a different light to the unions (as to the employers' federations) where centralization can either refer to bargaining with the head office of a company or with an industry sector. On the whole unions, while themselves decentralized, prefer industry-wide bargaining, which they think favours their interests. The balance of power changes, however, when the company goes international.[6]

6.3   EXTERNAL CONFLICT AND DISPUTES ON THE BOUNDARY

The difference between internal and external conflict is determined by the drawing of boundaries. If the whole human race is the unit under examination, then all social conflict is internal. An industrial dispute is internal to the company concerned and external to affected customers; there is also a mixed category where a strike, for instance, is both internal to the company and to an industry sector as well. These differences are obvious enough, but the fact that a redrawing of the boundaries changes the nature of the dispute is relevant to the study of centralization. The principle, as already suggested, is that a crisis constitutes a pressure towards central authority, but the effects are more ambiguous when the pressure comes from outside. The sense of unity in an organization under threat can lead to a relaxing of the authority, together with a more ready acceptance of the degree of centralization considered necessary. On the other hand the mixed category carries a more definite impetus to centralization. External conflict can also be expected to establish some limits to the bargaining process, the 'arena' as it has been called.

One study which examined the effects of external disputes, generalized that 'managers who encounter turbulent and threatening business environments will react by "pulling in the reins", resorting to a mechanistic structure in order to gain a sense of control over the situation rather than to face the perceived risks inherent in delegation . . .' and conversely: 'a more stable and supportive environment would result in a manager's "loosening up" into a more organic style.'[7] The authors tested another hypothesis—that, given a stable environment which becomes turbulent, decision-makers will shift from the organic to the mechanistic. This hypothesis was not supported by the evidence which suggests that some caution should be exercised in assuming direct links, but support for the previous proposition emphasizes the connection between uncertainty and centralization. This also applies to uncertainties caused by intense competition.

An interesting further question concerns the situation on the boundary of an organization. The exercise of authority does not necessarily end with its formal limits—as defined in a company, for instance, by those who are actually employed—and attempts are often made to control related organizations. This subject is most relevant to international companies with agents, licensees and other foreign partners and is considered in more detail in Chapter 16, but numerous cases arise of companies on the perimeter whose independence reduces the need for capital but increases the uncertainties. At a time of management buy-outs and demergers, more problems can be expected between companies with commercial links but no common ownership; internal conflict will become external.

6.4   COOPERATION AND COHESION

The relation between conflict and centralization is enshrined in the simple maxim that a rising level of conflict leads to a greater exercise of central authority. This applies whether the conflict is internal or external, although in different ways. A lessening of conflict, a sense of security and a greater predictability can be expected to lead to decentralization. The search for social order produces centralization, its achievement decentralization. Examples of this were mentioned in Chapter 2 where the coming of social stability was seen to lead to autonomy, and any set-backs which threatened anarchy to the reverse.

A number of theories have attempted to explain how the cohesive forces of society work. Cotta, for instance, has developed a theory of teams to explain cooperation.[8] This emphasizes the communications system and the interpretation of messages in the system. Where there is acceptability and credibility the system works well and decentralized decision-making follows. The emphasis is on the costs and benefits to the participants rather than on the constraints. A more substantial, and more optimistic, statement comes in a paper entitled *Toward a Sociological Theory of Peace*.[9] Starting from the view that war makes a contribution to society, the question posed is whether that contribution is essential. A social order without violence is declared to demand five conditions: a commonly accepted set of values which are stronger than the values which divide, social controls to reinforce the values, acceptable means to arbitrate differences and to mollify the losers, measures to adapt to change and adequate force to subdue those who refuse to accept the consensus. In that last condition, this 'theory of peace' assumes some central power than can enforce the condition if required. Although the paper goes on to discuss pluralism, the author does not believe that social atomization is the way to end conflict.

There have, of course, been many exponents of the alternative view, that total decentralization is a viable route for the human race. There is a sturdy tradition that is anti-authoritarian and anti-organization exemplified, for instance, by Kropotkin's *Paroles d'un Révolté* (1885) and numerous other writings ancient and modern. More of this tradition in Chapter 20, but set against it is the chilling quotation from one of history's most famous centralizers: 'Anarchy is the stepping stone to absolute power.'[10] Empirical studies have demonstrated the unsurprising result that cohesiveness and conformity go together.[11] Such studies emphasize that the connection between centralization and cooperation has its roots in the very processes of group formation.

7 *Motivation and Alienation*

An account of the attitudes which provide the personal influences for and against centralization rounds off this series of five chapters on related concepts. The human element is placed against the systems, the pressures and, to use a term normally avoided on these pages, the mechanisms implicit in words like 'power', 'authority', 'control' and 'planning'. To emphasize the individual aspect as against that of the social system, motivation and alienation are accorded a separate chapter from conflict and cooperation. The considerations are similar, so this is a short chapter, although the order is reversed with the more positive concept placed first—'more' positive because a simple antithesis between motivation and alienation is not assumed any more than it was between conflict and cooperation. The healthy organization often has to recognize and contain deep-set antagonisms rather than to manipulate them out of sight. Deviance as such is not the issue on these pages; it is recognized that hostile (alienated) attitudes can be criminal while they can also be creative—a necessary antidote to apathy, for instance. It is also recognized that a criminal can be as highly motivated as an advocate of good causes. The former is motivated *towards* crime and *against* society; the prepositions are important. Within the normal functioning of society, however, both positive and hostile attitudes exert long-term influences on decision-making.

7.1 MOTIVATION

The consequences of motivation, or the lack of it, are plain enough; the content is difficult to define. One approach frequently adopted is to distinguish between the preconditions and the motivation itself. The preconditions may be described in two-tier terms (as with Herzberg—the hygiene factors which must be satisfied first and the motivators which must operate only after the satisfaction has occurred) or in hierarchical categories (as with Maslow), the assumption being that certain requirements have to be fulfilled before a positive motivation begins to operate.[1] The distinction certainly sheds light on some puzzling facts. Why, for example, a workforce which has been materially satisfied can still be rebellious, or why liberalization measures in a country do not prevent revolution. The answer may not be complete—the hygiene factors may be met and the motivators still not work—although this criticism can be met by the search for further factors. A more stubborn criticism is that the distinction between preconditions and motivators rests on another assumption—that there is a unity of purpose which will produce results if only the appropriate measures are taken, the correct buttons pushed. If an underlying unity of purpose does not exist, the critic may well argue, there will be disenchantment with any efforts at motivation however well-intentioned. The workforce that is set on revolution, or the army on rebellion, will not be diverted from their ways by improved job satisfaction—measures to this end may, indeed, facilitate the revolt. The effect on the individual may be even more perverse. His motivation depends on personal, idiosyncratic considerations.

Another criticism of the universalist approach to motivation is that the lists of factors are culturally determined; they will work in some countries, or among some classes or occupational groups, but not others. Consultation, for instance, increases motivation in one country but destroys it in another. This criticism suggests that motivation is so closely related to aspirations which vary to such an extent that no general considerations are possible. There is also an objection of a different order altogether which suggests that the link between attitudes and conditions is over-simplified and that personality differences are more significant than social conflicts.[2] This, in its turn, can be matched by an objection on opposite grounds—that social attitudes cannot be explained in psychological categories at all.[3]

None of these objections necessarily invalidates the distinction between preconditions and motivators; their acceptance leads rather to a refinement of the distinction which sees that its meaning depends on a number of contingent factors. The extent of the divisions in society, the cultural outlooks and the personal influences are among these factors. This interpretation is sketched diagrammatically in Figure 7.1 where the intensity of motivation is plotted against the social tensions in a notional curve designed to demonstrate the implications of distinguishing between preconditions and motivators. The distinction, thus refined, is relevant to the theme of this book in that it illuminates the expressive and the instrumental approaches introduced in Chapter 3. The expressive aspect means that an organization in which the level of motivation is high will have an appropriate level of decentralization. Local units can be trusted to make their own decisions. There is also the instrumental aspect that decentralization can itself be regarded as a motivator, a technique for improving the level of activity. Both the instrumental and the expressive facets are clarified by the distinction after taking account of other contingent factors.

7.2   ALIENATION

'The miner, like other wage-earners, works at the ultimate direction of people he never sees.'[4] At least, one could add, he does see the fruits of his labour and know its uses. There are process workers in a chemical plant, for example, who

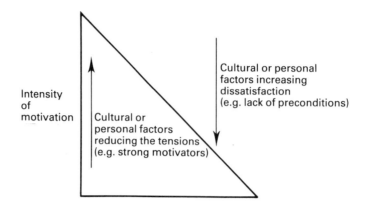

The arrows represent forces expected to distort the curve by
increasing or reducing the intensity.

Figure 7.1　A notional curve showing the intensity of motivation against the tensions
within an organization

never even see the product—unless there is a disaster—while those who work in
electronics factories are often given only the haziest idea of the purpose of their
output and no control over the results of the work. Such sources of alienation in
an industrial society arise from the normal operation of social forces. Romantic
notions apart, similar degrees of alienation arise in rural communities, but in a
different context—usually the disruption of an accepted order. There is a theory,
stemming from social anthropology, which explains this contrast and provides a
link to the subject of centralization.[5] Briefly, this theory refers to the *density of role
texture* which is high in a rural community and becomes lower as society
becomes more urbanized. The density is measured in terms of the number of
different relationships between the same people, and the number of different
contexts in which they encounter one another. In the city relationships are
usually at their most specialized—people mingle with different groups at work
from those they mix with at leisure or in the home or in any other activities in
which they take part. The looser and more specific relationships of the city
produce problems of social cohesion and delinquency, but promote
decentralized institutions partly to meet those problems. If this is accepted, a
contradictory circumstance becomes evident.

The centralized institutions of an industrial society have been blamed directly
for social problems by others than the author of the quotation at the beginning of
the last paragraph. Child, for instance, has written that the 'centralized source of
authority tends to create a generalized sense of individual powerlessness and
dissatisfaction.'[6]

Alienation in any form of society is differently regarded by those who, like
Sartre and his followers, regard it as a product of lack of freedom in a more
general sense.[7] The historical process is said to be working towards 'a truly
human order—that is, free relations among men'. Sartre takes a universal view

in the sense that the concept of alienation is placed in a cross-cultural context. It is not just regarded as an attribute of industrial society.

The seriousness with which the forces of alienation are regarded can vary considerably. A study of communities in Britain employed three contrasting approaches in discussing the observations recorded. One approach considered the increasing sense of deprivation as forecast by Marx in his earlier writings; another noted the lack of spontaneity which was seen by Durkheim as resulting from the division of labour; while the third looked at the gap between aspirations and opportunities according to the analysis of functionalists like Merton.[8] A society where alienation, in the sense of estrangement, is deeply rooted is unlikely to throw up decentralized institutions. So there would seem to be a contradiction between the decentralizing effects of the loose role relationships of urban society and the centralizing consequences of the alienation that results. The contradiction becomes less apparent if a less dramatic view is taken of the alienated attitudes, but to remove the contradiction altogether is to remove one of the explanations for two trends already noted: the propensity of organizations most subject to industrial, and especially commercial, pressures to swing between centralized and decentralized conditions along with the instinct to use decentralization as a means of improving (not just delegating) the exercise of authority. Decentralization as a technique, be it said, can hardly be expected to operate under conditions of extreme confrontation, and its successful use may be a symptom that the depth of alienation should not be exaggerated. Nevertheless, hostile attitudes are influencing the degree of autonomy.

The discussion is further related to the issue of law and order. For example, in a highly alienated society law and order will of necessity be stricter and at least appear more unjust. The harshness of the law will then produce even more alienation and may ultimately defeat its own purposes. The process is likely to be mirrored in the degree of centralization which will increase and thus create fresh problems as it temporarily overcomes existing ones—another version of the vicious circle which appears frequently on these pages.[9]

7.3   THE PERSONALITY AND THE SYSTEM

A champion of the individual against the organization once wrote of the intolerable human situation in an over-centralized society.[10] Decentralization is usually advocated on the grounds that an organization is deprived of skills it could well use if the decision-making is reserved to the top. At the same time failures in an autonomous unit can result from inadequate personalities and attempts have been made to sketch character profiles which match the requirements of the organization. The literature on leadership is relevant to this subject.[11] The leader of the autonomous unit requires initiative and the ability to feed information and ideas upwards.

One study that found a relationship between the degree of certainty in the external environment and the unit's performance also found that some personal characteristics influenced that performance but not others.[12] Those working in an uncertain (decentralized) environment showed a high tolerance for ambiguity, an ability to handle complex problems of integration, a preference for freedom and autonomy as well as for working alone—in contrast with those working in less autonomous units—although the difference between the successful and the unsuccessful was also related to other characteristics. The high performers showed a higher sense of competence, a longer-term orientation and a stronger scientific goal orientation as well as: low formality of structure and a low level of coordination, perceptions of participatory supervision and a confrontation method of resolving conflicts. Another investigation referred to the transition in unit management according to the 'company's life cycle.'[13] The entrepreneurial type is needed to boost sales and then to be replaced by the cutter of costs and the increaser of productivity.

These examples are culled from a body of literature which provides cumulative evidence that organization design is fruitless if entirely divorced from considerations of personality. A further step is also implicit: the relationship between character traits and attitudes.[14] For every centralized system that is frustrated because able managers are not recruited or retained, there is a decentralized system that is failing because the persons appointed have not the dispositions needed by such a system.

7.4   CONCLUSION

This chapter has reviewed the divisive *attitudes* as a supplement to the divisive *activities*, the conflicts, which were the subject of the last chapter. In general, the greater the divisions, the more the organization turns to centralized authority, but the exacting demands of autonomous leadership must also be taken into account. Where these are met, autonomy becomes a possibility. The demands, and the means of fulfilling them, will be related to cultural as well as personal factors, as is the relationship between motivation and divisiveness. The social conditioning that produces alienation, as well as the personalities which increase or mitigate it, play their part in determining the pressures towards centralization or decentralization.

8 *Centralization in Non-commercial Organizations*[1]

The pressures for and against centralization have been examined mainly, but by no means entirely, for their relevance to commercial organizations. Among them are the possession of a distinctive body of knowledge, the existence of beliefs that favour autonomy, the threat of disaster, the location of expertise, the financial situation, personal abilities and the allocation of scarce resources. Many distinctive features of non-commercial organizations have already been mentioned, but are reconsidered in this chapter in order to explore their implications for understanding the subject. Nine types of institution have been selected: social and charitable, educational, governmental, health, military, penitentiary, religious, trade union and professional. Each is considered in general, usually with one or two examples, and some relevant issues are identified. The examples are of organizations which illustrate the issues especially clearly; for readers unfamiliar with the selected organizations the details required to understand the issues are included but are kept to the bare minimum so as not to distract other readers unduly. The examples must be considered illustrative rather than typical, especially in the first category: the voluntary bodies designed for social or charitable purposes.

8.1 SOCIAL AND CHARITABLE ORGANIZATIONS

A large, amorphous group of institutions exists for the purpose of channeling effort into causes that are supported, sometimes with enthusiasm and sometimes with passion, by various sectors of the community. The variety of the causes is enormous. Some are entirely local, and the issue of autonomy from a national head office does not arise (although independence from other bodies may be jealously guarded and may be one of the objects of the exercise); these include parent-teacher associations, friends of a local theatre, hospital or museum, supporters of a football club or restorers of some amenity. Others are national bodies, some with large memberships and local branches. Organizations exist for such diverse purposes as the relief of poverty and distress, at home and abroad and among various groups like children and old people, for research into long-term disabilities and dangerous illnesses and the support of sufferers, for upholding a point of view on matters of government and social concern, for promoting and enjoying numerous sports and hobbies, for support and development of the arts and for the promotion of ideas and beliefs.

Many countries have laws which encourage some of these activities by granting tax or other concessions, but these laws usually attempt to define the causes for which the benefits are available. In Britain, for instance, political parties and bodies that promote what are considered to be political causes are excluded. This causes problems to those that are on the borderline, and is itself a pressure for centralization where there exists a fear that an enthusiastic branch might overstep the limits. The tax concessions apply both to the organizations and to the donors.

The word 'donor' identifies a person who gives financial support but is not necessarily a member (and may indeed be dead—bequests are the largest donations that some charities receive), and is a reminder that the boundaries of these organizations are not clear-cut. Unlike the shareholder in business, who is a member of the organization but may have little influence, the donor does not have to be a member to exert authority by a threat to withdraw funds. No one supposes, for instance, that a research council is a member of a university to which it allocates grants. An item frequently to be found on the agenda of charitable bodies is how to retain independence in, for example, adopting a new approach to the cause without alienating financial supporters. The pressure from donors, usually exercised in support of the status quo, is matched by that of the registering authority which confers the right to the tax and other concessions. In Britain this is the Charity Commission which interprets a law that limits not only the purposes of the organization seeking charitable status but also its methods of raising and holding funds. The charity's trustees must ensure that the ground rules laid down by the commissioners are observed in order to retain its status. Legally, a registered charity can be said to be answerable to the commissioners, not to its beneficiaries, but the commissioners interfere very little once they have accepted an organization. It is the acceptance which is the principal hurdle, but many voluntary bodies (including Amnesty International, one of those discussed below) do not have charitable status and operate successfully without it. The special expertise required to deal with donors and the authorities ranks as a centralizing body of knowledge.

Another constraint on the activities of the charity is its constitution, whose observance will also be supervised by the registering body and enforced by law if necessary. The older organizations, those founded more than fifty years ago, are likely to have constitutions which do not provide for devolution. There are exceptions and the dating is arbitrary, but the emphasis on strong local branches is comparatively recent. The older norm was to establish a body which would campaign on behalf of its members rather than with them. Hence, the idea of identifying a special role for the branches was not provided for, although the difficulty of identifying such a role is not confined to long-established institutions. A review of the magazines and newsletters of a number of organizations shows that 'news from the branches' is a common feature, but that the items are of a subordinate nature, mostly fund-raising, and do not indicate that the branches are playing an important role in the decision-making.

A complicating factor in some voluntary organizations is that there is an alternative unit of autonomy to the branch in the local office. The distinction between the role of the full-time officer and that of the branch member or branch committee is frequently blurred except that one is employed by the organization and one is not. Yet an organization can describe itself as decentralized, meaning that the decision-making is devolved to local offices rather than to local branches.

Another pressure for centralization is expense. In the commercial organization, centralization is expensive, requiring central staff to process the decisions. In the voluntary body decentralization is expensive, requiring communication with members and the sustaining of local units. The servicing of local decision-making also distracts the attention of the staff from other tasks in upholding the cause. As labour costs have risen, even some institutions which did emphasize the role of the local organizations have had to reduce their support. For the charity, poverty is a great centralizer which is easy to defend. Members wish their money to be spent on the declared objectives of the society and are sensitive about administrative costs, however strongly they may argue for a greater influence on policy.

Against all these centralizing pressures, many organizations have norms and traditions which favour autonomy, and make centralization a grievance. This characteristic has some similarity to that of commercial firms where business logic supports central authority, but deeply held views and personal considerations operate in a contrary sense. For many voluntary bodies the direct route to the objective seems to be through retaining authority at the centre, but the route itself is human and becomes impossible if the personal factor is overlooked. Active participation by the members is required to create a favourable climate of opinion and to raise funds. This poses a dilemma for those bodies which grew up in times when paternalism was more acceptable and thus have centralizing constitutions. Sometimes the membership is satisfied if the branches are mainly occupied with fund-raising; the argument that participation is costly carries weight with fund-raisers. Where voluntary bodies differ from commercial bodies is that the controversies concern means rather than ends. Where there is agreement about objectives, debate about how those objectives are to be achieved can become bitter.

Voluntary bodies are both numerous and individual. It is not possible to write about a typical institution, only about the characteristics that any one illustrates. In order to show some relevant issues, three organizations have been selected, all interested in promoting their aims and in fund-raising and each having its own administrative problems, but untypical in many ways: the National Trust, War on Want and Amnesty International.

The National Trust

Founded in 1894 to preserve 'places of historic interest or natural beauty', the National Trust is an organization for the holding of properties for permanent preservation and public enjoyment. The Trust holds this purpose in common with many preservation societies but, unlike some, it concentrates on direct preservation work rather than promoting a point of view. Propaganda has not been one of the activities for many years and was relegated to a minor place in a report of 1968, but the preservation and accompanying activities like facilitating public access have to be conducted in a way that reflects and promotes a body of opinion. This is partly expressed by the means used to run the properties, the methods of farming permitted on the Trust's estates for instance. The body of opinion is the Trust's equivalent to the centralizing knowledge which has to be safeguarded, the beliefs that could be compromised by ill-judged projects. The stress on preservation has partly resulted from the fact that the beliefs are taken for granted, partly from growth and partly from the organization's legal status. The growth has been rapid and testing by the standards of any organization, membership rising from 200 to 8000 in the first 46 years of its existence and then to over a million in 1982 after another 37 years. The legal status, first provided in an Act of 1907 and subsequently redefined, provides for permanent succession as a charitable body and for the right to declare property inalienable. This means that it cannot be disposed of, although it can be let, and no authority except Parliament can change the status of any property once declared inalienable.

The Trust is subject, like other such bodies, to the Charity Commissioners with whom its officers are in regular contact; it also feels constrained to use its powers, especially that of declaring land inalienable, with discretion so as not to lose its credibility. Within these limits and the publicity given to some of its activities the Trust is relatively free from outside interference. The question of centralization and autonomy was not, of course, on the mind of the founders; nor was the later development of a wide spread of properties and members. The country's richest charity and third largest property owner has been faced with the need to examine the costs and benefits of centralization and this subject has been considered by inquiries in 1956 (the Nichols report), 1968 (the Benson report) and 1983 (the Arkell report).[2] These reports encapsulate aspects of the controversies over centralization which affect successful charities and throw light on a number of issues, including the problem (shown in Figure 8.1) of the unit of decentralization, the membership branches or the local offices. As is normal with organizations, of any type, the inquiries that led to these reports were set up in response to a problem, but the findings went well beyond the implications of the problem. The Nichols committee appears to have been most concerned with efficiency and professionalism and reduced the part of the members while encouraging a limited amount of devolution.

The Benson committee produced detailed proposals, including 21 appendices, one of which proposed a new form for presenting the accounts. This did not suggest a regional breakdown, although there was considerable emphasis on decentralizing the organization. This was proposed where economies could be made and the issues to be reserved to head office and those to be devolved were listed. There was no proposal for greater involvement of the members who already had the right to elect half the council (the other half being nominated by outside bodies). The regional committees and subcommittees were to be appointed, not elected; while in spite of a reference to the 'need to be aware of local feelings and to adapt the Trust's administration accordingly' (para. 234), the report reaffirmed that 'the task of running the Trust must necessarily devolve on the Council. The members are entitled to make their views known and it is most unlikely that a view which clearly represents the opinion of a majority of members will be disregarded' (para. 121). The assumption was that the members were made aware through some undefined method of communication about any proposition on which they might legitimately have strong feelings. As a result of the Benson report, considerable responsibilities were allocated to the regions and an assumption of decentralization was made. In fact this devolution was later blamed for the long time taken to uncover some dishonest officers; it was asserted that 'detecting accounting deficiencies took longer than in a centralized organization',[3] an unusual defence of centralization. The decentralization in this case was to fourteen regions and covered what was assumed to be day-to-day management. Retained to the centre were financial control (the region must adhere to agreed budgets and cannot spend more without permission), acquisitions and the number of staff. The membership organization, including the National Trust centres, remained on the periphery with no place in the management structure.

The Arkell report (1983) reaffirmed preservation as the first priority, but criticized the lack of communication with members. In particular, the regional committees were described as appearing 'too remote' and 'too narrowly based' (para. 41). However, it was made clear that the Trust is responsible to the nation and not exclusively to its members, an emphasis which has always made it difficult to identify the proper role of the members who only bring a quarter of the income, a proportion that is not likely to increase (26.7 per cent in 1982). The rest of the money comes from admission fees (8.1 per cent), investments (13.2 per cent), grants (such as those available for historic buildings, 12.0 per cent), rents (15.6 per cent), gifts and legacies (17.7 per cent) and other sources (6.8 per cent). The responsibility to the nation arises from the legal position whereby the Trust holds its properties for the enjoyment of the nation. The members do not own the organization—ownership or its equivalent is a common problem of charitable bodies—and only have limited voting rights. However, the report advocates a greater role (para. 36) and proposes how this can be realized at small additional expense (para. 172), in effect adding 10 per cent to the existing costs of servicing membership or 1.8 per cent to all costs apart from the upkeep of properties, plus an initial cost of about £56000. This suggested that the participation of members could be increased at a reasonable price, but not in a decentralized form. Election to regional committees was not included, only the broadening of the basis of their appointment. The emphasis was mainly on communications and it was not suggested that the membership centres ought to have any greater part to play except that their chairmen and secretaries should have annual meetings with regional officers.

The results of this report convey that a charity with a professional staff and national responsibilities confirms a policy of decentralizing administration while centralizing membership participation (the election of half the council together with communication to and from the centre including the overseeing of members and mailings to them). The regions are given information and limited liaison relationships with local members, but there is much contact especially through the centres. The Trust is an example of centralization mitigated by increasing attempts at contact. The position is not, of course, static but represents some of the pressures illustrated in Figure 8.1. The figure shows the two units of decentralization that are possible and the influences that are usually noted by voluntary societies. The separate square on the left of the diagram emphasizes the centralizing effect of two powerful pressures that are external to the organization. In most charities, but not in education (see below), the external influences have a centralizing force.

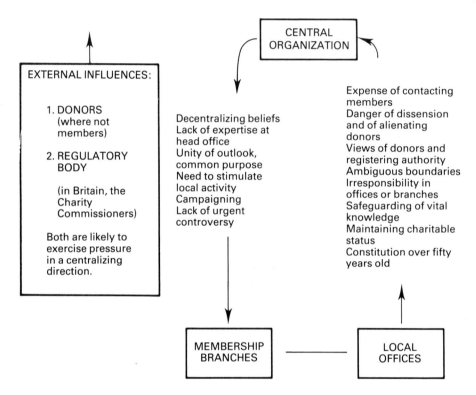

Figure 8.1 Pressures to centralization and autonomy in voluntary societies

On the question of the two lines of authority, it is by no means unusual for voluntary organizations to operate a dual system whereby regional officers are accountable both to head office and to local membership committees. Such a system, like a matrix organization of multiple responsibility in companies, has been shown to work successfully; some safeguards are needed, as with any system, to provide ultimate authority for the centre where a dispute cannot be resolved in any other way. The Ramblers Association[4] and the Youth Hostels Association in Britain both have dual responsibilities as do trade unions and employers' organizations in many countries.

War on Want

An organization which attempts a greater involvement of its membership than the National Trust, but finds expense an inhibiting factor, is War on Want, a body that exists, as its name implies, to fight deprivation, but the objectives are drawn broadly and its concerns include world peace and reconstruction, food production, community health, the role of women, unemployment and refugees. Campaigning and fund-raising are more evenly balanced in this organization, and there are other differences. The National Trust faces a more fragmented competition for its funds and has the ability, in common with other societies whose objectives are national rather than international, of providing tangible benefits to members, like free access to sites. It is also arguable that other organizations do the Trust's campaigning for it such as those invited to nominate to its council (which include societies for the conservation of nature, the preservation of footpaths and the protection of ancient buildings), but they are invited because of their relevant expertise, not because of their campaigning fervour.

War on Want, on the other hand, is concerned to build up a climate of opinion on a number of causes related to poverty and suffering throughout the world. The aim is that members shall belong to local groups which are represented on regional committees as well as representatives of affiliated bodies. This aim has had to be modified in practice because of expense, but the intention is to implement it when the income is sufficient. The regional committees are represented on the general council and are intended to operate in liaison with a full-time regional officer who is also a channel of communication with head office. The structure is designed to develop campaigners in the regions whose motivation is expected to increase as a result of their part in the decision-making. This development has brought to light a problem that is common to many such organizations, the relation between the active members and the less active who can always command a majority on a controversial issue, which suggests that the choice of units for decentralization is even more complex than suggested in Figure 8.1. It could be that there is a third type of unit for possible decentralization, by dividing the membership into the two groups of active and non-active, militant or non-militant. Few organizations are anxious to accept the distinction, if only because it is not unknown for the non-active to vote in ways more congenial to head office than the active. For this reason attempts to build the distinction into a constitution—by, for instance, providing for two grades, members and subscribers, with voting rights confined to the former—are not usually successful.

A price for decentralization, in addition to the administrative cost, is the possibility of confusing potential members and the general public by uncoordinated campaigns. Local groups are asked to support head office initiatives; but the more enthusiastic are likely to want to mount campaigns of their own. The local groups will also wish to develop liaison with like-minded bodies in their areas, and the definition of 'like-minded' may vary considerably between groups and with head office. In general, it seems that a body which places propaganda on a similar level to fund-raising will be subject to decentralizing pressures, but these will be modified by the problems caused by divisions inside the membership. Most organizations have experienced attempts by special interest groups to sway policies; but major changes, even if proposed by branches, are implemented at the centre. War on Want, like other organizations including the Royal Society for the Prevention of Cruelty to Animals, has experienced changes of emphasis in recent years as a result of a changing membership of its governing body. Such changes in voluntary bodies are represented as a reinterpretation (or correct interpretation) of the purposes of the organization by their supporters or entryism by their opponents; they are examples of centralization even when their aim is to produce a more decentralized structure.

Amnesty International

An organization that exists to campaign on behalf of people imprisoned for their opinions is Amnesty International.[5] This has a more specialized aim than the National Trust or War on Want, and implies a more complex relationship between the centre and the membership. The credibility of this organization depends on its reputation for independence, universality and impartiality. Subject to that, its controversies are of a different order from those of the other organizations mentioned. There is no equivalent to the would-be developer of a holiday complex looking askance at declarations of inalienability placed on a desirable coastline, although there may be disagreement about the means of registering dissent. Amnesty International is careful to avoid condoning violence while supporting the right of the accused to a fair trial and opposing the use of torture. The dividing line is also a narrow one when the prisoners are to be found in countries of many different political opinions.

These considerations combine with the delicate position of the people the organization exists to help to make necessary a tight control on reports and public statements. Even the use of words is carefully vetted to ensure that those which might appear to violate impartiality are not used. The impartiality is carried further by allocating the work for individual prisoners to local groups on the basis that each supports prisoners from different kinds of national regime (like one in a Soviet jail and one in a South American). This tight control on the central body of knowledge and expertise has to be balanced by the need for enthusiasm and initiative on the part of members. The problem is solved, in this as in similar organizations, by providing the maximum involvement of the membership groups in the policy formation, subject to the minimum discretion in applying policies once determined—open decision-making with central enforcement.

Conclusion

These examples have been used to illustrate the relevance of our subject to voluntary organizations. They were not selected for being typical—there is no institution that could be called a typical charity—but for representing issues relevant to the centralization–autonomy debate. All these organizations, it should be noted, are self-critical and publish discussion material on their own problems; the National Trust has committed considerable resources to the reports mentioned earlier. What none of the documentation shows in these, or other charities not named here, is much awareness of how other organizations have addressed the same problems. The reviews have been conducted internally and there appears to be an assumption of uniqueness. At least comparative material is seldom quoted. This is in comparison with commercial organizations each of which is similarly regarded as unique by its members, but where numerous comparative studies demonstrate that the problems, together with the options for solving them, are much more common than the insider imagines.

Each of the organizations possesses its body of knowledge and expertise which has to be safeguarded. Each also has a need, albeit in varying degrees, to involve its membership. It has been shown how voluntary bodies acquire two lines of authority, and perhaps three under certain conditions. There is no parallel to this in commercial organizations, but there is a similar ambivalence in attempting to fix the unit of decentralization. Other organizations possess a similar ambiguity, including the educational organizations which are considered next.

8.2 EDUCATION

The debate on centralization relates to that on education in a number of different ways. The demand for autonomy and its practicality, for instance, depend partly on the ability to behave autonomously and to find leadership for decentralized units. Education provides a basis for self-government and an impatience with control. At the same time the institutions of education have developed a rigidity that is frustrating to reformers, including those who wish to emphasize that education is a life-long activity, and one element in this rigidity is a different level of tolerance for centralization at different stages in the system. Educational institutions have developed from a number of starting-points, usually the provision began by being decentralized but sometimes the process has been reorganized under central control as with the reforms of the Napoleonic era in France.[6] The British system has been as decentralized as any and has consisted in the past of autonomous institutions which claim extensive powers over their members as exemplified by phrases like *in statu pupillari* and terms and conditions of attendance at schools as well as the wearing of uniform. By contrast, in Japan the wearing of a uniform is a sign of centralization in that every boys' secondary school wears the same. Other elements in the discussion are dual (or multiple) sources of authority related to different units of autonomy. The present discussion illustrates the issues mentioned in this paragraph by looking briefly at two of the many systems which together make up formal education in Britain: primary schools and universities. Both started as independent units and have proved more or less resistant to subsequent attempts at centralization.

Primary schools

Most primary schools before 1870 were religious foundations, owned and managed by churches, chapels or other religious foundations. In that year legal provision was made for secular schools to be established by locally elected school boards. The ultimate result was a structure with a number of tiers and considerable doubt about the powers available at each level. Figure 8.2 shows the units of authority, but it is not to be regarded as a hierarchy in the way that is familiar to other kinds of organization; the exercise of authority varies from area to area and institution to institution. One difference from other hierarchies is that the educational system has grown upwards; the top, the government department, came into existence last. Pressure towards centralization comes mostly from within the department, and those concerned with it, on the grounds of the centre as a repository of knowledge and the provider of funds.[7] 'Value for money' and the 'maintenance of standards' are the two phrases used to support centralizing pressures. The word 'standards' is used to summarize the vital knowledge in the educational system and, like all such words, it is hard to interpret. The difficulty is increased by the fact that the abstraction refers to

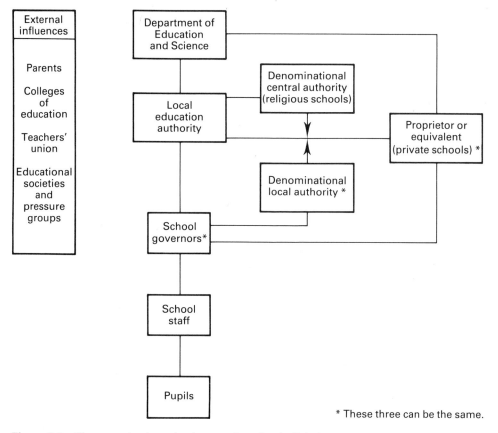

* These three can be the same.

Figure 8.2　The organization of primary education in Britain

widely differing, sometimes irreconcilable, conditions ranging from the most rigorous following of a disciplined routine to the most free self-expression. The pressures for decentralization include strongly-held beliefs based, in this case, on tradition and supported by most of the external influences. Some are parents, pressure groups, and other interested parties, including those in government and Parliament as well as those directly concerned with the Department of Education and Science, who favour greater centralization; but most uphold decentralizing outlooks which are also, in the main, inculcated in the colleges of education and universities from which the teachers come. The decentralizing pressures have been further strengthened by the abolition of the external exam which used to mark the end of the primary school career.

The most tangible elements of centralization are the necessity to obtain funds, together with some control of appointments, and the employment of inspectors and advisers. The effects have been reduced, rather than increased as in some organizations, by a change in the unit of decentralization—a weakening of the power of the governors. There was a time, it would seem, when the proprietors or governors were all-important. The days when most of the teachers were senior pupils or unqualified persons of a minimal education as described in many nineteenth-century tracts, as well as novels like *Jane Eyre*, were days of little autonomy for the school as such; even from those days the characters that are remembered are the reforming headmasters who asserted their own personal rule, rather than the advocates of educational change from outside the schools. The governors possess a constitutional authority derived from articles of school government (including control over the curriculum); but the authority is seldom used except in the event of a dispute, and the governors are not usually regarded as a unit of decentralization; the schools themselves are that. In the state sector, at least, the governors are more likely to be regarded as cushions between the schools and the local education authorities who, in their turn, limit the influence of the Department of Education and Science. It is true that there has been no trial of strength between the various units as has been associated with the switch to comprehensive education in the secondary schools, and the lack of such an issue must itself be regarded as an extra reason for decentralization. As a result of the various beliefs and pressures, the typical primary school is an example of considerable decentralization with the various authorities having the duty of ensuring that it exists and that certain minimal standards are maintained. The expertise used in maintaining those standards is partly, although by no means entirely, derived from the schools themselves and disseminated through courses, meetings, inspectors, advisers and other means, including a number of authoritative reports.

If the local education authority rather than the school is taken as the unit of autonomy, it has to be said that the legislation has a centralizing intention. The modern system has been built around the 1944 Act and subsequent measures although, again, their main effect has been on the secondary sector. The Act greatly strengthened the powers of the government department, but the effect has contributed to the weakening of the intervening levels, the local education authority and the school governors or managers, who can be overruled if the minister thinks they are acting unreasonably in relation to a particular school.

The Act also retained and revised the relationships of religious and other influences within the schools, emphasizing in many instances a dual authority which would not normally weaken the autonomy of the schools themselves—asserting, for instance, that teachers could not be penalized for their religious views. The autonomy within the primary education system is effectively greater than in most others in spite of central control of income and largely of expenditure, through negotiations on teachers' salaries. The official system resembles that in the health service (see below) but the actual autonomy appears to be greater. The curriculum, the most important decision once a school has been willed into existence, is largely under the control of the school itself.

Dramatic evidence for this autonomy was provided in the case of the William Tyndale School in 1975.[8] This school, within the area of the Inner London Education Authority, became the subject of public debate as a result of a controversy over experiments in which some of the teachers were giving the pupils, all under the age of eleven, wide discretion to decide what they wished to learn and how to learn it. The experiments, although considered by some observers to be no more radical than those going on elsewhere at the time, caused great divisions, including serious conflict between the headmaster and the governors, between members of staff, and between members of staff and parents. Complaints were made at the level of the school and at that of the local education authority and there was a debate in Parliament. Accusations and counter-accusations, disputes on the nature of educational philosophy and practice and complaints of political interference came to a climax in a full-scale inquiry. The barrister who conducted this inquiry expressed incredulity that no one appeared certain about where authority did lie in the primary school system; the uncertainty was compounded because control of the curriculum, the most ambiguous issue of all, was at stake. In the Parliamentary debate, a speaker emphasized that the House of Commons had never determined the position at which the curriculum was decided and the decision was normally left to the head teacher and staff. The debate confirmed the autonomy of the primary school and the uncertain nature of the decision-making. Apart from unusual incidents, like the Tyndale case, the primary receives less publicity than the later stages in the educational system, in spite of medical and psychological evidence about the importance of formative influences on this age group. The lack of public attention, which also helps to leave the authority blurred, can itself be considered yet another decentralizing influence.

The universities

The universities have an even stronger tradition of autonomy than the primary schools. They are widely believed to have begun in Europe as groups of independent scholars with their bands of pupils, although the monastic connection will have imposed some hierarchy.[9] They also, nowadays, are mainly dependent on central administrations for their income and for important decisions about their expenditure such as staff salaries. After noting these resemblances, the position of the universities becomes more complicated. They are, of course, larger and the equivalent of a primary school is a department rather than a university; each has its own individual constitution (its charter, laboriously drafted and redrafted). The universities have also developed their own hierarchies, in spite of articulate criticism of such growth. Nevertheless, the reality of their independence is attested by the growth of other systems of tertiary education, colleges and polytechnics; institutions, which would have university status in some countries, have been brought into existence partly as a result of a wish to produce facilities for higher education that are more amenable to public policy.

If the autonomy of the universities is undoubted, the nature of the influences both inside and outside are harder to identify with confidence. There is a continuing struggle on at least two issues. One is the independence of the university itself. It is part of a vague, amorphous entity known as 'the educational system'. One of the features of this system is that the organizational boundaries are unclear. Maybe the whole system should be regarded as an organization; Figure 8.2 (primary education) might appear to make such an assumption. A similar diagram for the university would include the University Grants Committee; this body provides a majority of the funding of all British universities, and virtually all the funding of most. It is more nearly a part of the universities themselves than are other funding bodies with their clients. The Arts Council, for instance, funds a smaller proportion of the income of the opera, ballet and theatre companies it supports, although their existence depends on this source of funds. Further, many members of the University Grants Committee are academics, and the committee has gradually increased its powers of influencing the activities of its clients. Nevertheless, the universities are separate organizations by any normal definition and are likely to remain so. Proposals for change are usually more concerned with internal organization than with a wider integration.[10] Within the universities, the autonomy of the faculty or department is safeguarded both by strong beliefs and by the fact that the special knowledge is contained at that level, a reversal of the centralizing influence that exists in most organizations. At the same time there have been efforts to bring university organization more closely into conformity with established principles of administration, and there has been little sign of the experimentation which has become a feature of multinational companies. Two developments may, however, be seen as signs of change relevant to the present discussion. One is the increasing emphasis on the department in the oldest universities and the other is the increasing representativeness of the decision-making bodies in the newer universities. The nineteenth-century foundations, on the other hand, with their attempt at a division of powers between administrative and academic decision-making, produced a result which may appear more decentralized than the intention. The future, as with other organizations, could turn out to be closer to either extreme on the centralization–autonomy spectrum. The more centralized situation is likely to occur as a result of the move of the specialized knowledge back to the centre through more representative institutions, the move the other way through a reversion to the ancient ideas of the scholar and his pupils. Current pressures for less specialization militate against this and greater centralization seems more probable. If this occurs, some mitigating measures will be required to maintain the avenues of original thought and discovery.

Conclusion

Educational organizations, then, produce a different perspective on the subject. Their demand for funds, a demand which has perhaps been under-emphasized in this discussion, leads to the establishment of central institutions, but these institutions are regarded as having the relationship of a client, rather than an authoritarian relationship, with the teaching units. The seeds of centralization lie in the desire for value for money and for greater responsiveness to political or other policies; against this powerful traditions press for decentralization in establishments where the unit of autonomy is in any case far from clear. The brief discussion of education emphasizes the need for complementary studies on the boundaries of organization.

8.3   GOVERNMENT AND LOCAL GOVERNMENT

Writers on government are prone to issue warnings like: 'Every time the government attempts to handle our affairs, it costs more and the results are worse than if we had handled them ourselves', or: 'Every central government worships uniformity: uniformity relieves it from inquiry into an infinity of details, which must be attended to if rules have to be adapted to different men, instead of indiscriminately subjecting all men to the same rule.' Both these quotations are translated from French writers of the early nineteenth-century;[11] they are not obviously time bound, but both use the word 'every', a dangerous word in a discussion on government. The issue of centralization can be discussed in terms of conformity, but other words like 'efficiency' and 'responsibility' conjure up different images. Although government is the most all-embracing of organizations, claiming an authority which includes the power of life and death over those within its jurisdiction, it shares with other non-commercial organizations the difficulty of identifying a suitable locus of decentralization. There are several possible units each of which raises different issues. There is, for instance, delegation within central governments to the major departments of state and beneath them to more specialized units and sub-units; there is also geographical delegation. Many government departments have their regional organizations including customs and excise, employment, energy, health and social security, industry and trade, inland revenue, the property services agency, the stationery office and transport. There is also the relationship between central and local government and that within local government. As with other forms of organization, decentralization to one unit can mean centralization for another. In particular the regional departments of ministries reduce the powers of local authorities. Some of the boundaries seem to be especially designed to reduce local powers. The Department of Health and

Social Security has three regional organizations each with different sets of boundaries. One set would presumably increase the powers of the regional authorities who would be able to work together within each region. In most countries there exists some form of local government which has responsibilities separate from those of central government and the boundaries vary considerably. In France decentralization has long been a political issue with senior administrators in the local Departments directly appointed by the state and many activities, like education, coming under central control. One political irony is that left-wing parties, who usually favour government activity more than right-wing parties, have become in, for example, both France and Britain the champions of local against central authority. There may be pragmatic political reasons for this, but support for local government—firmly entrenched in right-wing Switzerland—is an issue which cuts across other beliefs. In federal constitutions, like Switzerland and the United States, there is an additional level of local government, but this does not necessarily mean greater centralization for subordinate authorities. In the United States it is still possible for a group of citizens to form a new local authority, like a town council, with powers that would be considered wide in many countries, while in Canada a small town owns its own police force.

One symptom of autonomy on the part of a local authority is its ability to go bankrupt. In some countries this is virtually impossible, but in others it is a threat even if usually overcome. In Belgium both Liège and Brussels have recently been saved from bankruptcy by special loans from the central government, and drastic measures have had to be taken in some American cities. This ability to go bankrupt is a sign of autonomy, but the threat that it will actually occur leads to a reduced independence. In Belgium a recent law[12] imposed a number of conditions on authorities that are unable to balance their budgets, but it also increased the tax-raising powers of local government in a country where 117 different methods of raising local finance exist. This suggests a more decentralized system than that in Britain where the government has reacted to escalating spending by restraining local money-raising and where there is one uniform method of raising money locally, but there is disagreement on the relation of income to local autonomy. The disagreement arises from the fact that the local council has two sources of authority, one delegated by the centre and the other acquired directly from its electorate, and central government funding acts as a cushion enabling the councils to spend money without a backlash from citizens who can either change their vote or move to a less highly-taxed area. The latter is an option frequently used in densely populated regions.

The common experience that local elections, especially in populated franchise areas, reflect national rather than local politics weakens the claim to autonomy at local level; this is emphasized in countries like France, the United States and Britain where local elections frequently represent a protest vote against the government in power. Such a tendency reduces the credibility of the local authority when it claims to represent local opinion and has combined with financial stringency, central expertise and low voting figures to form a considerable centralizing pressure; the support for autonomy, however, has proved tenacious in the face of these pressures.

Local government in Britain

Studies of local government in this country frequently present a picture of increasing centralization, said to go back to the 1920s and emphasized by the abolition of small local authorities in 1974.[13] The evidence is not so clear-cut as some of these statements suggest. Central government has taken over functions previously undertaken by *some* local authorities, varying from hospital management to the provision of public utilities like gas, electricity and water, but this has been during a period of expansion of all government activities including those of local authorities whose freedom of manoeuvre is frequently greater than it looks on paper. This freedom of manoeuvre is partly due to the increased skill and consciousness of local politicians, who can often use their representatives in Parliament to good effect in the single member per constituency system.[14] The freedom is also supported by a belief in local authorities as partners with central government, a partnership in which both are seen as having their own sources of authority in their electorates. This view contrasts with the centralizing opinion that local government is an agency for the central; a review of the legislation gives support to both the centralizing and the decentralizing standpoints. The legislation on which local authority powers are based is of three types. There is the mandatory legislation with standards attached like health, including such issues as pollution, and policing. The rules still leave a margin for discretion. The second type of law includes the mandatory provision of services, like education and housing, with wide discretion as to how the provision is made. The bulk of local education authority spending is of this type (about 65 per cent) which can be held to support either the centralized or the decentralized view. The third type of legislation is enabling, providing the power to act if the local authority wishes, and covers leisure and some social services.

In times of prosperity the devolution will be emphasized and the need to cut back reduces the discretionary spending as a proportion of the whole. The irony is that it is just at a time of reduced spending that greater discretion is needed in order to be able to switch scarce resources more rapidly from one purpose to another. There are innumerable problems that come into a broader discussion, such as the size of the authority and the extent of public involvement, but a conflict of objectives exacerbates the problem just outlined. It is difficult for a non-commercial organization to define its objectives in a sense which facilitates the allocation of scarce resources. A company in difficulties can abandon one product line in order to concentrate on another; local government cannot abandon education to improve the fire service or vice versa, and even if it could, the subtle relation between the different activities—for instance, between the provision of leisure activities and the need for policing—would make it difficult. The necessary lack of clarity in objectives is bound to place a limit on the amount of devolution that is possible.

8.4   THE HEALTH SERVICE

Health services to all citizens according to need is an accepted principle in industrial countries. In the richer nations the principle is taken for granted; the differences are over how the services are to be provided and how the bills are to be paid. Any lack of provision is the cause of a controversy or a scandal. The poorer countries are compelled to regard a comprehensive health service as, at the best, an ideal to be aimed at in the process of development. In any country the distribution of large resources in peculiarly difficult circumstances makes health administration a case for special provision and one that has been widely studied. The problem of distributing these resources produces a number of issues that hinge on centralization or autonomy. One of these is the desire of funding bodies, whether public or private, to ensure value for their money. Another is the fact that some of the institutions, the hospitals, grew up with local and voluntary support to become part of the local patriotism. Costs as well as technical developments have drastically reduced the number entirely supported by the township or benefactor which built them, and the voluntary support is often confined to peripheral amenities; but the memory of and the wish for local participation lingers. Many features of health care are universal, but the funding and administrative arrangements vary considerably. The particular problems of the British health service will be considered here.

The British health service[15]

Most of the funding of the health service in Britain is from taxation (87 per cent) with small amounts coming from social security payments and charges to patients; since 1980 the health authorities have power to raise funds from voluntary sources. The whole population is permitted to enrol on the list of a medical practitioner, the normal means of joining the service, and less than 3 per cent do not do so, although the number opting out for specific services (like hospital or dental treatment) is larger. The expenses of medical innovation, an ageing population and a labour-intensive operation make the containment of costs a critical issue and one which, given the central funding, causes severe difficulties for decentralization in spite of a belief in local participation.

The service came into being in 1948 and is presided over by a government department, known as the Department of Health and Social Security since 1968, for which central health administration is one function along with running the social security system and providing or supporting personal social services. The constitutional, formal autonomy has been increased by legislation, although not necessarily the informal, that is, the way the service operates in practice. One issue illustrated by the record of the health service is the difficulty of finding suitable administrative units, a subject for controversy since the service began. The original controversy at its founding was between existing local authorities and newly formed regional authorities. The latter were chosen for a number of reasons, including the preferences of doctors and other employees, but against protests that well-established local links would be broken. In the event local authorities were represented on the new governing bodies, but some links were broken; the hospitals were no longer managed by the county councils. In 1974 changes were made as a result of a management consultant's report and a chain was set up running from the Department of Health and Social Security through the Regional Health Authority to the Area Health Authority to the District Health Authority. The scheme was never completely implemented, but each unit had its administrative and financial arrangements and its professional services.

In 1980 a Royal Commission investigated the working of the service[16] and, following the recommendations of this commission, the government produced a report entitled *Patients First*, since when most area authorities have been abolished. The commission's report emphasized decentralization. There was a need, it stated, for sensitive attention without 'endangering the quality of local responsibility and flexibility to local circumstances which is fundamental to these services'. At the same time a reason for centralization was underlined when the great differences in health provision that existed in different parts of the country—a legacy from the arrangements before the health service started over 30 years before—were noted. In keeping with other findings on organization, the reduction in the number of levels would be expected to improve communications and furnish the lower levels with more responsibility. Whether this has actually happened it is too soon to know. But the area authority had its supporters; those who argued that it was especially suitable for tackling two problems of health administration: relations with local authorities and between professions—the former because area boundaries were conterminous with those of local government, the latter because this level provided a convenient size for bringing together medical and nursing and other relevant units.

These two problems which the area authority was supposed to tackle illustrate a characteristic of many organizations which is particularly evident in the health service; it could be called the *leakage* of authority. This refers to situations where the scope for centralizing or decentralizing is limited because there exist rival centres of power which restrict the authority inherent in the organization itself. Expertise represents centralization in most organizations, but the opposite in the health service. The medical and the nursing professions are highly organized and articulate and require arrangements that suit their traditions and status. There are also a number of new and growing professions involved, like physiotherapists, radiographers and dieticians. Some instructions are not acceptable except from a fellow professional, especially in the more established occupations which possess strong bargaining powers.

There are a number of limits to the power of the professions, including the influence of official bodies and the rights (legal or otherwise) of patients, but the principal limit is cash. In a public health service the efforts of the professionals do not produce funds directly and these are provided centrally, although, on principle, decentralization is written into the method of funding. The money made available by the government is allocated to the fourteen regional health authorities on the basis of population broken down into categories according to their need for medical services. The Department of Health and Social Security has established a Resource Allocation Working Party (RAWP) to produce a viable formula. This working party is also attempting to level out the disparity of resources in the regions. Percentage increases and decreases would leave some districts permanently worse off.

The discretion on spending by the regions is also limited, since salaries are negotiated nationally, and form 70 per cent of the expenditure, with drug prices also under central control, fixed by central bargaining with the manufacturers and absorbing another considerable proportion of the budget. The resource allocation is a central function along with other advisory services including medical and nursing. There is also a construction department which designs model hospitals; the regional authorities do not have to use its services but if a proposed budget could have been cut by using the service, it is likely to be questioned. For the lower tier, the district health authority, the chairman is appointed by the Secretary of State, the other members partly by the regional authority and partly by the local authority, while most members of the regional authorities are appointed by the minister, which limits local discretion on appointments but enables greater autonomy on other decisions. Meanwhile some of the regional authorities are attempting to establish schemes for allocating funds to the districts on similar lines to their own allocation—population structure and need. The system appears to allow a high degree of autonomy, but there are a number of limitations.

One is that the Secretary of State is accountable to Parliament for the working of the whole service. This does not appear to mean that serious maladministration in one hospital could cause the Secretary to resign, but questions can be asked about the details of the system in a way which is not acceptable for questions about the nationalized industries, for instance. Another limit to autonomy is the location of expertise at the centre. There would appear to be less convincing ways for this central expertise to be forced on the regional and local units than is the case in international companies, made less convincing still by the problems of appraisal of performance. The 1980 report described the monitoring as 'inadequate' and this was a reason for placing responsibility more clearly with the regional authorities, who were also to be the main planning units. Nevertheless, a pressure to the centre does exist and efforts are being made to produce standards for measuring the effectiveness of the units and sub-units. In the United States a series of hospital studies used measures of costs per patient and anticipated recovery rates. It was shown that performance on those measurements was improved where publicity was given to the figures themselves.[17]

The pressure to centralization, such as they are, are reinforced by the visibility of the health service. Since any alleged error or any fresh development is likely to receive publicity and perhaps become the object of a campaign, either local or national, the government is usually blamed and those within the service regard this as a safeguard. The internal response to external pressure groups brings greater centralization and makes it more acceptable. On paper the health service appears to be a highly decentralized institution, with its financial arrangements and other safeguards to the local units, but the form of decentralization carries with it a number of tensions, and the reality differs from the appearance when

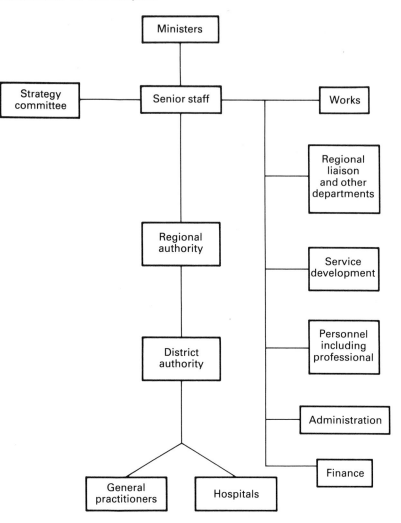

Figure 8.3   The organization of the British health service

so many decisions are restricted for one reason or another. The regional and district health authorities are constrained both by the pressure of central expertise and by the influence of professional bodies; the skills, knowledge and other factors are universal not only within a country but also internationally. While the facilities vary from district to district, methods of treatment, which become known internationally as soon as established, are similar and the resemblances are often more obvious than the differences.

The structure of the service is shown in Figure 8.3 and the pressures for and against centralization in Figure 8.4. The belief that the decentralized system is the most suitable is hard to assess in view of the lack of a clear method of appraisal and the central control of finance which provides an alibi for any shortcomings in the local provision. The particular mixture of safeguards, tensions and visibility produces an example of confined decentralization which carries down to the smallest of local units—a local practice or an operating team in a hospital.[18] At this level there is a limited decentralization with a greater autonomy than is usual in such circumstances. Subject to limited exceptions, like current proposals for compulsory retirement for general practitioners, the autonomy is mainly bounded by financial and professional standards. At this level there are few suggestions that reducing the autonomy would increase the effectiveness.

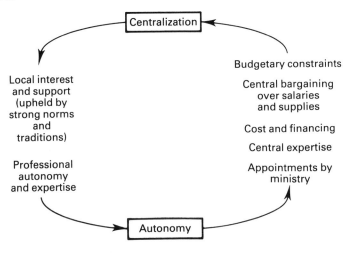

Figure 8.4   Influences for centralization and autonomy in the British health service

8.5   MILITARY ORGANIZATIONS

'Chance selected this field out of so many, that low wall, this gentle slope of grass, a windmill, a farm or straggling hedge, to turn the tide of war and decide the fate of nations and of creeds.'[19] Few readers of this book would agree with that statement; most would rate leadership, military organization, logistical skills (including feeding), training, equipment, discipline, recruiting and a number of other factors above 'chance'; the order in which the factors are placed depends on the point of view. Historians tend to dwell on the importance of leadership, whereas strategists naturally concentrate on the skills involved, although being quick to emphasize that the knowledge required is only a part of the gifts of the commander, who also needs the more indefinable elements of character and personality. Among the skills that have long been identified is that of devising the particular mixture of centralization and local autonomy required by an army in the field.

This skill becomes necessary as soon as an army takes on a representative character, when it is fighting on behalf of an interest wider than that of the unit itself. Warfare in earlier and in pre-industrial societies is not always like this, the central authority being contained within the army itself; the same is true of the small guerrilla band, a source of problems for a regular military organization. The need for the organizing skill emerges when the scale of the operation grows and there is a controlling unit, whether a civilian head office or a military headquarters or both, separate from the troops on operations.

In fact the problem of centralization recurs in a number of circumstances. For present purposes the relationship between a national government and its military forces, a comparatively straightforward example of centralization and decentralization, will be ignored; the problem of military authority will be the focal point. This involves the need to develop an organization with units that can react quickly in the field, and must therefore possess a high degree of independence, but must equally be under strict control since too much independence can lead to disaster. The military illustrates, in its clearest form, the type of autonomy which is total during limited periods of time and within a limited range of discretion. Total, that is, for a clearly defined purpose.

The problem has long been understood, indeed the success of the Roman armies 2000 years ago has been ascribed to just this organizing ability,[20] a greater understanding of how to decentralize. It can be said that the relationship between Rome and its commanders in the field is a sustained study in devolution. In Rome itself, in the two centuries before Christ, the most important body was the Senate. All military commanders were drawn from the membership of that body and gaining a command required political wheeling and dealing. However, commanders, once appointed, appear to have been virtually free of centralized constraints. If there were constraints they existed in the arrangements that had been made during the period when a man was seeking command but, once appointed, he carried with him the authority of the Senate. As most of the wheeling and dealing was concerned with subordinate appointments and preferences there were problems of split loyalties; but once the commander had left for his theatre of operations and as long as he was achieving his targets, he was to a great extent able to ignore Rome.

There were two good reasons for this. First, the problems of communication over vast distances meant that actions were complete before Rome found out what was happening. Even in Spain a commander could wait several weeks for communications to arrive from Rome, yet the Romans believed that they had revolutionized the speed and effectiveness of the communications systems. The second reason lay in the military understanding of the elite who made up the Senate. As many of them had experienced military command, at one level or another, it was widely appreciated that a commander could not expect to gather the necessary military intelligence upon which to base his campaign until he arrived in his theatre of action.

The act of putting together an army was a further example of why autonomy worked. Until Marius (died 86 BC) the Roman army was largely composed of non-professional troops. While they had experienced soldiers at their disposal, most commanders relied upon being able to raise their armies from local tribesmen. Other troops might well be drawn from distant parts of the empire. Whatever these armies were they only existed in a particular theatre of war. Thus, the Roman military commander, while out of Rome, experienced the ultimate in devolved power. If he won, he and his army earned itself a triumph: if he lost he earned disgrace and frequently death. Decentralization was backed by drastic penalties.

The field organization, developed during the Punic Wars, led to the creation of a structure that will be familiar to students of bureaucracy. The basic units were the centuries, two of which made a cohort. Although numbers varied it was not uncommon to find that six cohorts made a maniple and then a number of maniples made up a legion. From time to time these numbers were varied, depending upon the size of the legion, but somewhere around 120 BC trial and error seems to have led the Romans to believe that six hundred men, three cohorts, was the ideal size for a basic unit. When the whole legion took the field commanders would be faced with the problem with their subordinates that Rome had with them. The subordinates would go off on their own campaigns and retain the most tenuous communications. Once a force was split it was necessary to devolve power and, of course, trust. As simultaneous actions could yet be days apart this was inevitable. From time to time there were major modifications of the military system, but throughout the period the hierarchy established by this type of organization survived. An army in the field was expected to live off the land. Nearly 150 years later Caesar recorded how, while on campaign, he sequestered granaries, and the practice deprived the enemy of their supplies. If the same high-handed action is maintained in times of peace, endless problems ensue and, by 150 BC, the Roman Senate was embarrassed by the steady stream of complaints that were flowing in about corruption and maladministration. Although the complaints would be lodged against a particular commander, it is probable that the villains were his legates. As a result of the complaints, the Senate finally instigated a practice of arraigning offenders, but was unable to bring itself to impose punishments. If a military commander accepted his command, the principle of devolution and the communications difficulties demanded that he be assessed at the end of his term of office by his ends, not his means. This is the difference between military objectives and military strategy. While it is reasonable for the central power to have a major part in the selection and negotiation of objectives, it is hard to formulate a strategy when it does not have the essential information that can only be found in the theatre of action.

In more modern times, the implications of devolution have been examined in detail, and successes are credited to the recognition of these implications more often than failures are credited to the failure to recognize them. For instance, it has become customary for a number of armies, including the British, to train their officers (commissioned and non-commissioned) one level above their current appointment. This enables them to take command more readily when isolated and with greater understanding of how to exercise their new responsibilities. It also makes the survival of an embattled unit or headquarters more likely. Even in the most limited war and with all the benefits of modern communications technology, a unit can be out of touch with its command for long periods, and independence has to be accepted. A further importance of the training for one level up has been found in guerrilla warfare, especially against urban guerrillas, where the army normally needs to operate in very small units indeed. These units must therefore be entrusted to a leader at a level designed for minor responsibilities (like a corporal in command of a section in the British Army), although the military infrastructure provides quick support, advice and direction where necessary.[21] The devolution increases the danger of blunders in a situation where publicity and propaganda, with their effects on public opinion, are especially important.

In peacetime armies may be called upon to carry out a variety of civil activities from earthquake relief to road-building together with duties that border more closely on the military, like reinforcing the police or other services; but their main peacetime activity is training, much of it directed towards enabling units to act more independently. The training is also designed to inculcate strong feelings of loyalty and other attitudes designed to prevent abuse of the independence. Both the loyalty and the independence are supported by a system which demands adherence to predetermined lines of communication—the chain of command. This chain has, of course, to accommodate other requirements including the need to control operational duties, to provide an authority structure and a career and to supply skills and expertise where they are required.

Many features of the traditional business organization were, indeed, pioneered by the military, notably the ability to cope with a wide range of specializations within a unified command. The so-called line–staff relationship whereby the direct operational command (the line) is supported by a number of specialist services (the staff), is usually a centralizing force. The staff are not supposed to have direct authority, except over their own specialist teams, but the officers involved are devising policies and strategies which limit the autonomy of the line commanders. In the army the problems that arise from line–staff relationships are met in a number of ways. Some units—the support arms—are integrated directly into operating units. These include the artillery, armoured and engineering supporting arms. Others, known as the services, set up their own systems of supply and distribution.

The British Army

There are two chains of command in the British Army. First, the static chain provides the normal routine through which the Army Board exercises command in peacetime. Second, there is the operational chain in which overall command is exercised by the Chief of the Defence Staff who uses the central staffs of the Ministry of Defence for planning and coordination and the Army Department for execution. Command of the various elements of the British Army is vested in operational commanders as follows.

(1)   In the United Kingdom, the Commander in Chief (United Kingdom Land Forces) is responsible for the defence of the United Kingdom.

(2)   In the British Army of the Rhine (BAOR) national command continues to be exercised by the Commander in Chief BAOR. On the appropriate North Atlantic Treaty Organization (NATO) alert measure, operational command of I British Corps will pass to a NATO headquarters.

(3)   For overseas operations outside NATO or BAOR, forces from the United Kingdom will be placed under an existing commander, or a joint force commander specially appointed for the operation and directly responsible to the Chief of the Defence Staff.

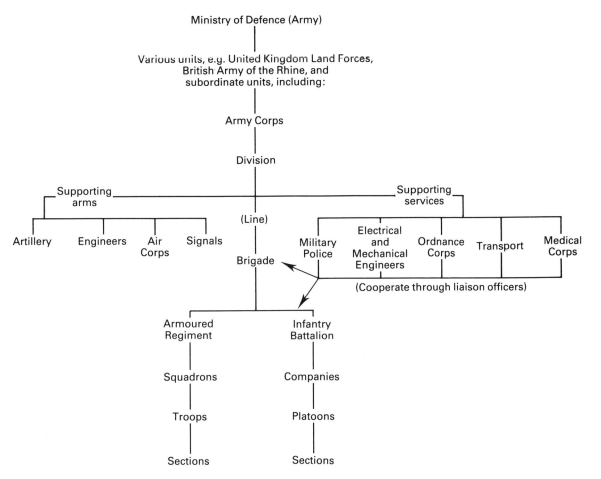

Figure 8.5   The static chain of command in the British Army

The two chains of command are shown diagrammatically in Figures 8.5 and 8.6. The main difference is that in the operational chain the conduct is vested in a commander in the theatre of operations. This permits the local commander greater autonomy in his own area. Prior to hostilities starting all headquarters will move to another location to prevent detection and possible destruction. In BAOR, for example, all headquarters become mobile and leave their peacetime locations, and all units deploy tactically into their field locations. BAOR, therefore, reverts from being a force using static headquarters buildings and barracks into one tactically deployed in preparation for hostilities.

Planning and control is normally exercised one level up, although there are exceptions and each commander is free to deploy his subordinate units as he thinks fit subject to overall directives and policies, but including the ability to select their own locations within a predetermined area. If instructions are being passed to a subordinate unit they will always follow the chain of command which is not short-circuited. Each major unit has its own planning and

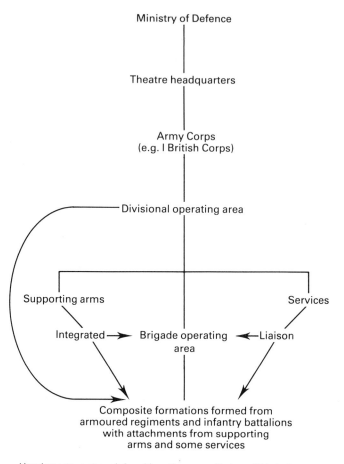

Ministry of Defence

Theatre headquarters

Army Corps
(e.g. I British Corps)

Divisional operating area

Supporting arms   Services

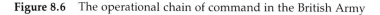

Integrated ⟶ Brigade operating ◀—Liaison
area

Composite formations formed from
armoured regiments and infantry battalions
with attachments from supporting
arms and some services

Headquarters at each level has the capacity to split into two to prevent
total destruction of the headquarters.

Figure 8.6   The operational chain of command in the British Army

command staff, intelligence, surveillance, fire support, logistics and other
functions as required. A headquarters unit, down to brigade level, has the
further ability of splitting into two so as to prevent its total destruction by enemy
action. In addition, each headquarters has the ability to delegate its functions
one level down.

The reporting system varies according to the conditions. In peacetime
information is passed upwards as it occurs, if of an urgent or non-routine
nature, otherwise monthly. The monthly reports cover all matters that affect the
efficient operation of the unit—personnel, training, financial, technical and
others. Information is passed back through electronic and mechanical means,
regular briefings and visits. During operations, information is passed as it is
received and additional reports are put together daily. Briefing of commanders is
also conducted twice daily or once every one or two days according to the nature
of the operations; for example, there are twice daily briefings at BAOR and
Corps level.

The army requires that each unit is well commanded and regularly exercised, and that officers and soldiers are masters of their jobs. In fact most officers and soldiers are trained in at least two jobs, thus giving extra flexibility and the greater possibility of independent action; there is the additional principle that training in a particular skill comes second to training as a soldier. Normally, the structure of commands provides for three operational units at each level with up to three support units. Through all this structure, great emphasis is placed on the personal links. At each level there is a thorough selection and there are regular personal reports which comment on all aspects of an individual's performance. A bad report is a bar to further promotion and in some cases to further employment and training. A corollary of the autonomy of the unit is that the greatest possible predictability has been ensured, although slightly varied standing operating procedures may exist within similarly structured organizations, dependent on the personal inclination of commanders.

The high degree of training and versatility makes it possible to detach a particular unit, a brigade for instance (see Figure 8.5), and to use it in a separate operation. The independence will be limited to the extent that it may not be possible to provide every form of expertise required; the brigade will depend on the division for some services, but this may not be a severe constraint and the unit may be expected to carry out a complete operation on its own for a short period of time within an overall strategy. The constraints of autonomy are: the strategy, indicated by the operating procedures, the requirement to report developments and the lack of specialist support and advice available to a particular unit. Over and above these limitations there is complete freedom of manoeuvre reinforced by the knowledge that a superior will at the time support the action of a subordinate as the best possible decision under the circumstances, although a later enquiry may establish that a mistake was made. The process has been described as a four-fold one: the circumstances of each decision are *unique*, to be considered in the light of the training of the person having to make the decision; the result will be *respected* right up to the top level, subject to the law of the land, and the *responsibility* recognized; subsequently, a justification may be required if the decision is questioned.

The degree of autonomy granted to a military unit has many dangers. A disloyal commander can wreck a campaign. To safeguard against disastrous consequences, the system tries to ensure that the way an individual will react is as predictable as possible in any circumstances without restricting initiative. There are four principal ways of ensuring this predictability.

(1) A selection system designed to uncover elusive qualities of character: temperament, attitude, frame of mind.

(2) A training system geared towards inculcating loyalty and obedience to superior officers, to the system and to the unit. An officer with ten years' service may have spent up to seven years on formal courses, particularly those in specialist services.

(3) An organization geared towards identifying with a particular unit—a battalion, a regiment or a service corps, for instance. Every possible activity is designed to promote the identification and the achievement of unit objectives.

(4) An appraisal system designed to promote those who demonstrate that they possess the qualities required and filter out those who do not. The formal appraisal system operates only one way—that of regular personal reports—but any subordinate can use the redress grievance system to question the actions or reports of an officer considered to be unjust. The officer's instruction has to be obeyed, but can be criticized afterwards when an explanation or justification is required.

The army is a close-knit group and every member knows the capabilities and responsibilities of his colleagues. This provides an example of the exercise of a large measure of autonomy within narrowly defined boundaries, an autonomy that is made possible by a number of safeguards but that also depends upon a system in which personality and close relationships play an important part. Also apparent is an intensive socialization system (items (1) to (3) above) which minimizes the risks of decentralization.

8.6 PRISONS[22]

Prison organization in the United Kingdom is a centralized and hierarchical system. Parliament is ultimately responsible for all aspects of the service and discharges its administrative responsibilities through the Home Office, for England and Wales, and through the Scottish Office. The Prisons Board for England and Wales is chaired by a director general and includes amongst its membership controllers of planning development. Its remit covers policy on the treatment of inmates, administration (which includes casework with prisoners) and operations, which embraces staff management, security and control. The Prisons Board also includes the directors of the four regions into which the country is divided, each being responsible for the management of prisons, remand centres and other penal establishments. Each region is expected to carry out national policy in its penal establishments, which are under the immediate control of a governor.

The governor and the staff are required to implement decisions and policies that are disseminated from the centre. The service is uniformed, discipline-based and might well be described as verging on the paramilitary. However, the prison service has found itself in a difficult situation that has been developing for several years and has now reached the point at which observers are referring to a crisis which consists of four interrelated problems. First, there is not enough prison space to accommodate the increasing numbers consigned by the courts. Second, much of the space that exists is archaic, having been built over a century ago in an age when prisons were more avowedly punitive. Third, there is a lack of finance to expand through the construction of new prisons and the improvement of facilities in old ones. Fourth, there is considerable unrest among prison staffs as a result of what they see as a deterioration in their conditions and the ambiguity of their position.

The effects of these problems have thrown into sharp contrast what the prison system claims to do for prisoners and what is now happening. Prison rules call for the training and treatment of convicted prisoners to encourage them to lead a good and useful life on discharge. The pressures within the system, however, have generated an overriding emphasis upon security and control. This means that the nature of the system at present is not conducive to variation or experimentation and is characterized by strict adherence to hierarchical rules, where autonomy is likely to be limited. The intractable nature of the problems tends to produce tensions within the system between central administrators, local governors and prison officers. The discontent of the latter is compounded, or aggravated, by dissatisfaction with pay, overtime arrangements, gradings and promotion opportunities. There is also evidence that the severe criticism aimed at welfare professionals by the officers is rooted in a concern that such professionals are eroding their position. Furthermore, it is also possible to detect a sense of grievance against various authorities, academics, social workers and media commentators, all of whom appear, to prison staff, to be leaning too heavily in favour of the prisoner without giving sufficient attention to the problems faced by the staff.

Prisoners too can hardly be blamed if they see prison, under present conditions, to be nothing more than a punitive system. Prisoners have their own organization, Preservation of the Rights of Prisoners (PROP), formed in 1972 to fight for the protection of such residual rights as the prison population has. As far as the prison officers are concerned PROP has been little more than an irritant. Far more serious has been the recent development, particularly over the past decade, of unruly behaviour, protest, demonstration and riot by prisoners at several establishments. It is ironical that the conditions that have done so much to make the prison officer's job unpleasant, and indeed against which they have protested loudly and publicly, also spark off protest and violent behaviour by the inmates. These outbursts of violence have, in some cases, led to a few prison officers being accused of reacting with a violence that is illegal and contrary to central policy. In 1976 Hull prison suffered a riot as a result of which some of the prison officers were eventually charged and convicted of conspiring to assault and beat prisoners who had taken part in the roof-top protest. There are other problems that beset the system, not the least being the prison officers' view of the central administration. Although reorganized in 1963, with some commitment to greater flexibility, it is seen by officers as being both centralized and remote. Centralization is seen as compounding the other problems in the prison service.

The picture is one of a formally constituted centralized system in which the inherent problems have led to the development of a policy contrary to the declared aims of the prison service, one in which containment has to be achieved through coercive means. This policy, whether official or not, is leading, in its turn, to various manifestations. Power struggles break out between the various parties in which, for example, prison officers may take unilateral action against the prisoners through unofficial punishments, or against the system by working to rule. In addition to this prison officers have a further level with which to reduce the oppressiveness of their management system through the use and development of unofficial and informal relationships between themselves and a few influential inmates. These relationships may well be employed by officers to defuse dangerous situations through direct negotiations, an activity that is probably not part of central policy. There are at least two interpretations of such behaviour. The first, and perhaps most obvious, is that such short-circuits make life more tolerable for both officers and inmates. A second lies in the possibility that the relationships allow the officers to feel some sense of personal autonomy from the management system that controls them as well as the prisoners.

Etzioni classifies prisons as coercive and alienative organizations and compares them with institutions such as armies.[23] If this is true then it is worth considering who is actually alienated. While prisoners are subjected to a rigid system of control, it is apparent that so too are prison officers. It should not be forgotten that these officers are uniformed, which not only allows them to be distinguished from other members of their community but also carries with it the psychological controls of a military type of organization. These controls are not imposed upon the prisoners but upon the officers. If we accept the arguments put forward by Kaufmann, the officers are likely to become as alienated as the prisoners.[24] The term 'total institutions' has been coined to describe prisons or any institutions that exist to cut people off from the outside world. Other examples would be closed wards in psychiatric hospitals and reformatories for young delinquents. Various studies have shown that a common factor may be found in all such institutions in the existence of a set of complex relationships and factors that come into play in order to achieve control and accomplish the aims of central authority. This, however, leads us to note the double standards or self-delusions that are alleged to operate within the system. There is an assumption of a pattern of discipline imposed by the officers upon the inmates. As long as nothing disturbs that view then authority is being served. Any observation of the setting will expose the fact that there exist unofficial social systems among prisoners and officers. It is through the interaction of these unofficial systems with the official system that it becomes possible to manage such institutions. Formal centralization is mitigated by informal autonomy.

Various concessions may be made by the staff that can go so far as to include connivance at minor infringements of rules on a regular basis. In return for this staff will expect to receive, at a minimum, a more cooperative response to their demands. The degree to which this happens and indeed its strength within the system may be judged from the converse situation when the withdrawal of customary privileges, that may well include institutionalized connivance at rule-breaking, can set off prison riots. It is also likely that, within closed institutions, a social system may develop among prisoners, which has sufficient cohesiveness and strength that staff come to rely on it in times of threatened trouble. When trouble occurs it is frequently those individuals and groups who have attained key positions and influence in this sub-system who are able to exercise a degree of control which authority is not able to match, an informal delegation.

In a North American study of an authoritarian prison regime the author described how the authorities attempted to exercise authority largely through the retention of tight control over the communications system.[25] Paradoxically, the outcome of this lack of information was to increase the dependence of the prisoners upon the few who really knew the ropes. The author also produced a finding of importance in the understanding of prisons when he noted that inmate culture was, on the whole, supportive of custodial values, partly through the emphasis on conformity and doing one's time without fear or complaint, and partly on avoiding behaviour that would 'bring on the head' (his phrase). In the same situation it was also noted that the social system of the inmates had its own system of sanctions for non-compliance and these were more severe than those available to the prison staff. By virtue of this the inmate leaders were able, in alliance with the authorities, to secure the goals of reasonable orderliness and the avoidance of conflict. The comment was made that 'in some respects it could be said that the inmates ran the authoritarian prison'. Senior prisoners were in regular contact with the authorities and had influence in the decisions about the placement of men and the distribution of privileges. These leaders were further able to develop their power to the point at which they were able to negotiate a degree of rule evasion for their fellow prisoners. Just as the authorities were able to use their control of information to sustain their own power, some of the inmates, being the only ones allowed to communicate with authority, were able to use their knowledge to maintain their position.

This particular prison subsequently experienced a programme of liberalization, as a result of which there was a period of instability marked by outbursts of violence and an increase in the number of escapes. McCleery recognized that the old order which had benefits for both staff and some prisoners was severely disrupted by an opening-up of the system of communication. It was countered by the prison officers disregarding the instructions, and ignoring new policies of treatment and therapy; this was paralleled by similar problems within the social sub-system of the prisoners. Eventually, steps were taken to make the liberalization regime work. Prisoners were allowed to enrol voluntarily in a range of rehabilitation activities and were allowed opportunities for the expression of opinion and participation on an Inmates' Council. It was through these devices that a different pattern of communication was developed which gradually earned recognition as a more viable approach to the maintenance of stable government. In the process prisoners were able to achieve a greater sense of personal autonomy in so far as opportunities for contacts between themselves and officers were freer. There was also a general belief that inmates were part of some consultative process concerned with the administration of their social system.

Such experiments are constantly being repeated, and many of the lessons described were in fact learned during the 1930s when Moreno conducted his famous social experiments inside an adolescent reformatory.[26] Moreno's experiment has been widely misunderstood and used to justify other less plausible experiments. He was enabled to establish a new social system within a closed institution, and his central thesis was that rigidly authoritarian regimes teach people little that they can use when they leave the institution; if penal policy had any purpose it had to do with rehabilitation. He managed to persuade the authorities to move themselves into the background of the reformatory and to allow the inmates to create and develop their own social system. Under Moreno's guidance the prisoners created their own leadership and sanction system which, as McCleery discovered, was much more punitive of offenders than anything authority would normally allow. He was also able to show that, even within a system based upon authority and power, inmates can be allowed sufficient autonomy to discover patterns of behaviour that are useful outside. His real problems were not with the prisoners but with the staff who felt that their role and status as well as their power had been taken away from them. After Moreno had left, the institution returned to a more authoritarian stance, but he had made his point.

The conclusion to be drawn from the studies is that the most strongly centralized type of institution develops informal systems which produce a measure of autonomy. The unit of autonomy is itself an unofficial unit of prisoners or prisoners and members of staff. A measure of recognition can be accorded to the informal system, but there are dangers as well as pressures against doing so. The threat of disaster, a pressure against decentralization in other institutions, prevents turning the unofficial system into an official one.

8.7 RELIGIOUS ORGANIZATIONS

'Most of us have very quaint ways as Christians and some of our rituals are really quite ridiculous but it is unlikely that we shall be reasoned out of them.'[27] That statement underlines the difficulty of discussing centralization in the context of religious organizations. The two paradoxes at the heart of religion—that between the institution as a repository of the faith and the individual access to the Almighty, and that between gaining eternal life and losing it through awareness of the gain—are reflected in the institutions. It is possible to visit a mosque, a temple, a shrine, a synagogue or a church and find an authoritative, closely guarded and usually centralized care for the truth; the centralization can be so close as to include death for heretics like the Baha'i in modern Iran,[28] and many Christians in the past.

Part of the appeal of places of worship is their numinous effect and all make exhortations to personal prayers and rituals, exhortations which are no less powerful where vicarious petitions to the Almighty or the heavenly powers are also on offer. There is the risk that this direct access might lead to the exposing of officialdom, and some of the most memorable names in religious history, whether Buddhist, Christian or Moslem, have been of people who did just that. Other figures have not exposed the existing authorities directly, but rather by implication. Bernardette of Lourdes was as powerful a figure in her time as almost any member of the official hierarchy of her church; but she did not translate that power into authority and not the least interesting elements in her story were the measures taken to ensure that she did not. The measures included incorporating her insights into the mainstream of Roman Catholic practice and this ability to incorporate the charismatic figure must surely be relevant to a study of centralization in religious bodies.

In other contexts, conformity has been taken as a symptom of centralization; but, to the outsider at least, the Roman Catholic Church appears to have the highest degree of centralization with the lowest degree of conformity of any Christian body. To travel around Europe, and to observe and to listen, is to acquire evidence of the diversity; but this increases greatly outside Europe, where Catholic churches have absorbed the local cultures more rapidly and with less apparent pain than some Christian sects. Such observations raise questions about the relationships between hierarchy and centralization, for the appearance of centralization arises from the hierarchy itself which contains a dual authority; it has been described as a matrix in which there exist lines which cross one another in the clerical ranks as between the secular clergy and the monastic orders as well as other bodies to which special powers have been entrusted. While the safeguarding of the truth is highly centralized, it would appear that a great many important decisions are diffused.

This general discussion poses a number of interrelated problems concerning the identification of centralization and autonomy in diverse organizations which have centres of authority centrally and locally along with unpredictable centres of power. The fortuitous appearances of such centres are matched by the apparently freakish treatment of the people who form them—the decision as to whether they are treated as saints or heretics.[29] Clearly, any leakage of authority in religious organizations is related to fundamental beliefs, and cannot be discussed in terms of benefit to the organization: rather the reverse, the organization may need to be judged in accordance with its ability to cope with the distributing effects of direct access to the supernatural.

Centralization and autonomy in some British churches

The contrasts brought out in the discussion so far are reflected in the bodies that together make up the British Council of Churches. The Church of England has, along with the Methodists, the most apparently centralized structure but the most local diversity. Poverty increases centralization at least to the extent that closures, and new developments, are difficult to determine locally unless outside funding is withdrawn. In the Baptist Church, for instance, the local church is an autonomous body in a voluntary association with the centre. The theory has been expressed in a convoluted statement that 'the Church is to be understood theologically as both universal and local, that the Church universal is not an aggregate of local churches, that there is one universal Church which "in locality" finds visible concretion.'[30] Organizationally, each church is separate, but a large number seek the security of holding their property on the *Model Trust* which imposes the condition that they do belong to the Baptist Union.

Like other voluntary bodies, the churches have two possible routes of decentralization, a third if the keen adherents are distinguished from the nominal; although the clergy identify with the enthusiastic members, there is still a career structure for them which there is not for the laity unless full-time employees. A chart of centralization and autonomy in the Church of England is shown in Figure 8.7. For greater realism a particular denomination has been selected. In this case the career structure is distinguished from the participative structure, and all the lines are broken to indicate the ambiguity of the authority. Against every statement of obedience (whether in the ordination or the marriage service) there is a reservation in favour of some higher authority.

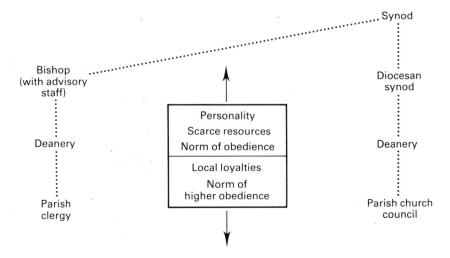

Figure 8.7 Centralization and autonomy in the Church of England

A document produced by the British Council of Churches has proposed an integrated hierarchy for its member churches. The suggested boundaries were to coincide with those of local authorities on the grounds that the churches should 'take seriously the secular structures'. It is admitted that these boundaries, which are called levels, cut across the existing arrangements of all the denominations, but this is described as an advantage. A chart shows how the integration would proceed at each level from (1) the neighbourhood, to (2) the town or suburb, to (3) the district, city or borough, to (4) the county to (5) the region and finally to the nation.

One obvious question such a proposal poses is how the churches keep pace with local authority reorganizations and which of the numerous regional boundaries they adapt to. This question is not just flippant; the timelessness of religion is not a feature to be treated lightly. Another objection is that such an arrangement may impose a degree of centralization which even the most hierarchical churches do not have. To underline this objection, the proposed chain is longer than exists in member churches. The centralizing implications are drawn out in another document prepared with Roman Catholic participation. This states that it 'is obligatory that any document should state clearly the status accorded to it; e.g. "approved by the Assembly," . . ., "a discussion paper prepared by a working party on . . ."' An even more substantial objection to efforts at imposing new boundaries is that decentralizing norms are stronger in churches than in any of the other voluntary organizations examined and the benefits of centralization less clear. Even the cause of unity, the object of the exercise mentioned, is usually frustrated by codes administered from the centre rather than problems at the grassroots, where the objections are more in terms of local loyalties and traditions (including prejudices) than in theoretical obstacles.

The local loyalties which cause the exercise of central authority to be disliked in the churches, are combined with an acceptance that definitions of faith and morals come from the centre. The British Council of Churches and its constituent members frequently issue documents about belief, but these are understood to interpret and initiate further discussion on articles of faith the member churches are assumed to be safeguarding. A *modus vivendi* is possibly a more accurate description of relations between the centre and the local units than centralization or autonomy, a *modus vivendi* the disturbance of which is instinctively avoided.

Conclusion

Organization for the purposes of religion provides an example of strong reasons for centralization, the safeguarding of the truth and the continuity of a timeless institution, with strong pressures to decentralization caused by local loyalties and personal access to the source of truth. Religious organizations are faced with the problems of coping with the charismatic individuals or groups who challenge the existing institution but are also an accepted avenue of change. There is no evidence that decentralized bodies show greater flexibility towards heretics than centralized bodies.

8.8   TRADE UNIONS

'The decentralization of the trade union movement mandated by the new laws has resulted in a much weaker union movement since most labour contracts must now be negotiated on a factory-to-factory basis without the strength of numbers that unions traditionally need to represent their constituencies effectively.'[31] The quotation, about industrial relations legislation in Malaysia, illustrates the view that the trade unions are stronger when dealing with employers centrally. This opinion is by no means universal; the reverse view, that an individual employer finds it hard to resist union pressure when concentrated against his or her firm while leaving competition to operate freely, is also widely held. Where national bargaining does occur, the unions can expect to be more centralized and the leadership to be in a position to exert considerable authority; if plant bargaining is normal, the leadership acquires a more advisory role supporting the branch officers. The desire to mobilize their full strength in any major encounter is a reason for favouring national bargaining, along with the supposed weaknesses in employers' organizations, a supposition which rests on two assumptions. The individual company can be expected to fight more resolutely for its own interests, while the able trade unionist seeks promotion nationally and the able manager remains within company management and does not usually seek a national post in an employers' federation.

In spite of the preference for national bargaining, unions in the main regard their constitutions as decentralizing—'the power is in the branches'—and have little other incentive for centralization. The labour equivalent of special knowledge is to be found in the enthusiasm of the members as much as in the negotiating powers of the officers, and most negotiations are local, while the central bargaining reaches broad agreements and contractual conditions. It is alleged that a combination of apathy at local level and outstanding personalities at national level stands to reverse the decentralizing emphasis of the constitution, but the apathy is often exaggerated by outsiders and the most outstanding leaders are sometimes repudiated by their membership, while there are few centralizing tools in the hands of the leaders. If the officials are appointed, then their career structure is linked to the centre, but where the officials are elected, their careers may be assisted by opposition to the centre in winning votes from the rank and file. The unions, then, contain evidence of decentralization in both the official and the membership organization, and the two resemble one another more closely than in the voluntary organizations considered earlier.

The other relevant feature of the trade unions is that they form rival centres of power within their members' companies; as such they constrain the centralizing tendencies within companies. This feature, which is also the case with professional organizations, provides another form of the leakage of authority. It also reinforces unit management. In a local conflict, the union officers and the managers may be ranged against one another, but the unit's autonomy against head office is often strengthened by its own internal conflict. Head office policies have to be reframed to permit local settlements. The special case of trade union activity in one country will put these considerations into a more realistic perspective.

The trade union movement in Canada[32]

The Canadian scene provides a number of special characteristics of trade unionism which yet illustrate general principles. The country has a liberal regime and a generally favourable attitude to trade unionism, but overall membership is not high (at about 30 per cent of the labour force), and there have been some exceptions to the liberal laws. For instance, the province of Nova Scotia legislated a measure against union activity in plants belonging to the Michelin tyre company as part of the deal which brought Michelin investment to the province. The country also has one of the highest strike rates in the world (at 0.81 days lost per employee during 1981—the equivalent figures for the United Kingdom were 0.2 and for Germany 0.02; see the *Statistical Yearbook* of the International Labour Organization). Trade union decentralization, we have seen, can have three different meanings: autonomy in organization, autonomy in bargaining and an influence on the autonomy of the members' workplace. In Canada, decentralization also means independence from North American unions based in the United States. This produces a reaction of a kind so commonly observed when there are moves to decentralization. On the one hand the pressure to greater independence in a situation where industries are closely integrated (over half of Canadian industrial investment is United States owned) is leading to autonomous rather than separate institutions, although the different political outlooks between the two countries had already produced tensions. On the other hand the desire to strengthen the union movement in

Canada is leading to greater centralization within the country. This cuts across the jealously guarded rights of the locales (branches).

Two hypotheses have been framed from Canadian studies which also apply in other countries. One is that the union is more centralized where the full-time officials are appointed rather than elected and the other that the union structure grows to match that of the corporation or industry with which it is associated. Fragmented industries, like textiles and shoe-making, produce a more decentralized system. The local differences make central bargaining less viable and the small employers are weak beside the union locales. Other unions, for instance in the utilities and public services, are more centralized at least by the province if not by the country. The central federation of trade unions (the Canadian Labour Congress, CLC) does not have a high profile, but the present leadership is attempting to develop its strength.

The United States influence has given the word 'decentralization' a special interest to Canadian labour which reinforces the norms of local authority in other ways. An articulate membership which expects results and is quick to criticize the consequences of new agreements brings pressure for results on the central officers. The consequences of collective agreements and grievance handling measures are subjected to close scrutiny, and the officials are closely watched but not provided with great authority. The white-collar unions have further demonstrated that a more articulate membership is unsympathetic to central authority.

Conclusion

The decentralization issue is often confused with that of democratization, the provision of more power to the union member. The strengthening of members' rights and voting powers has been the subject of legislation in some countries (for instance the Landum-Griffith Act of 1959 in the United States) and is currently under discussion in Britain. This raises a general issue of leadership—the consequences of consulting participants on specific issues when opinions may be biased by extraneous questions.[33] Forcing the unions to ballot their members on significant issues can have unsought consequences, like making it more difficult for the officials to negotiate a complex agreement. Central authority is also likely to be strengthened where members are invited to vote individually over the heads of the local organization. Whether this is a gain or a loss to the effectiveness of the unions themselves depends on views about their role, but they do provide an example of an organization where local branches can (and do for sometimes unpredictable reasons) reject all pressures from the centre, while upholding centralized bargaining.

In general, the trade union experience illustrates three issues relevant to the subject of this book. One is the decentralizing nature of an institution where promotion of a cause has priority. Another is the need, which may override the decentralizing nature, to engage in bargaining at the point where maximum pressure can be exerted. The final issue is that of rival centres of power within an organization when the same participants are members of both the organization itself and the rival centre. This is an instrument of decentralization.

8.9 THE PROFESSIONS

The professional institutes are more centralized than the trade unions. Their work is legalistic, involving the protection of members and the guaranteeing of standards, rather than bargaining or opinion-forming. This is not to belittle the necessity of establishing an image of the membership, especially in the case of the more recently established professions, but the priorities are protective rather than aggressive. The centre determines and promotes the policies, although a representative constitution is also safeguarded. On principle the institutes uphold defined rights; they do not bargain for them. This may be modified in practice but, however centralized the institutes themselves, they exist to promote the autonomy of their members inside their employing organizations. In a sense professional standards are not negotiable, although this statement may be modified in practice and the standards themselves change and have to be adapted to changing circumstances.

Professionalism is more relevant to individual autonomy than that of the group. Nevertheless, the issues raised are common to other organizations and provide fresh insights which apply whether the professional is an isolated member of an organization or one of a group. The relevance of the subject is well illustrated by a list of the attributes of professionalism which contains many of the factors seen to influence centralization and autonomy. This list includes the following traits.[34]

(1) A *systematic* theory and body of specialized knowledge not generally possessed by users of the profession's services.
(2) *Authority* in the eyes of clients, including autonomy in the professional's decision on behalf of the client.
(3) *Community sanction* whereby society recognizes and respects the profession for a variety of reasons, including the possession of esoteric knowledge and the fact that the profession can be trusted with guilty secrets or sensitive information about individual clients which is divulged to the professional to enable him or her to deal with the client's affairs (for instance, crimes revealed in the confessional to a priest, embarrassing diseases revealed to a doctor and evidence of guilt revealed to a defending counsel).
(4) *Ethical codes* which arise because the esoteric knowledge and techniques used by the profession make it difficult for clients or outside bodies to regulate the behaviour of members without at least the participation of the profession itself.
(5) *Culture*, including rules governing behaviour, a set of opinions and information generally adopted within the profession and symbols marking someone out as a member of the profession.
(6) A *disaster* criterion which means that the intervention of the professional must occur in situations where serious adverse effects could arise for the client through inexpert advice or treatment.

The guilty secrets, along with most of the other implications of points (1) and (5), and the disaster criterion of (6), resemble issues that feature widely on these pages but as centralizing factors. In the case of the professional, as opposed to the institute to which he or she belongs, they become pressures to autonomy.

The importance of professionalism is that it reverses the usual trends and provides a degree of autonomy within an organization which may be otherwise highly centralized. Many businesses find the accommodation of employees who belong to professional institutes, the biggest source of tension they experience; even the military, it would appear, modify the principle of soldiers first and other considerations second when it comes to the employment of doctors, dentists, chaplains and other professionals.

The professional institute exercises discipline over its members and sets minimum standards for training. Their autonomy is preserved by the skill and expertise of the members and the way in which they uphold the reputation of the profession. The upholding of the reputation may be more related to other traits than the specific body of knowledge. Skills in human relations, the bedside manner of the doctor or the synthesising ability of the lawyer, are as significant as the knowledge of medicine or law, but the knowledge is regarded as so specialized that it can only be judged and its use controlled by fellow professionals. Certain types of professional, such as accountants, chartered engineers and managers, are to a large extent operating as employees within private companies or public organizations. A tension can then be set up. The professional desires to attain standards of expertise, to have freedom to pursue professional objectives and to influence decisions based on the validity of the professional analysis rather than on the status of the individual professional inside the firm. The bureaucratic organization may seek to emphasize conformity to procedures and the restriction of expenditure within budgets in such a way as to stifle the innovative effort of its engineers. Whilst it has little option but to accept the legal requirements pointed out by its accountants, there are many areas in which it may seek to lean on the professional opinion for commercial or political reasons.

A conscious effort to unify and strengthen the engineering profession by increasing the standing of engineers in the community and their influence on the industries in which they work was made through the Finniston committee.[35] The problem is partly caused by the dual approach of engineers—unlike lawyers and doctors, for them management is often as important to their careers as engineering. They are more likely to be drawn into commercial problems and projects where autonomy is circumscribed and a main area for the exercise of discretion lies outside that of their professional expertise. In many firms the experts propose but top management decides. The engineer may indicate that the performance to be expected from a product lies within a certain range and because of the economies of prolonged test programmes to establish basic data there is an element of estimation. It then falls to the marketing staff to assess the position of rival products and the probable reaction of competitors to the publication of particular performance figures. The final decision may be reserved for general management and in this process pressure may be applied to the professional to change his estimate if the organization considers this expedient. He may be more concerned about his career prospects than about rigid adherence to his original estimates and so be willing to sacrifice his autonomy. After allowing for these and other constraints, the professional does establish a degree of autonomy—another example of the leakage of authority and a rival centre of power which is different from that of the trade unions who, on principle, seek to represent all employees.

8.10 CONCLUSION: THE TRANSFERABILITY OF MANAGEMENT SKILLS

This review of centralization and autonomy in non-commercial organizations contains some warnings about the use of the same concepts in different contexts. The resemblances found in the underlying disciplines hide some contrasts in practice. For instance, costs normally support decentralization in business but centralization in charities, while vital knowledge is usually centralizing in religion but supports autonomy in the professions. External influences have also been seen to operate in opposite directions. Another difference is in identifying the unit of decentralization. The identification is often ambiguous, we have noted, in commercial organizations, but there is no resemblance to the parallel lines of authority between paid staffs and voluntary adherents that religious, political and many charitable societies encounter. An examination of the various kinds of organization aids the understanding of the concepts, but warns against facile assumptions about the universality of management skills. It is fashionable to assume that experience in business can easily be put to use in these other bodies and governments, churches and charities are eager to enlist the aid of business experts. It happens that most of those consulted in the preparation of this chapter were sceptical about that trend, but it continues nonetheless. The main reason given for the scepticism is not one of those listed above but the problem of clarifying objectives. The reorganization of a business is conducted after a restatement of simplified objectives. Other institutions do not have the same ability to limit their objectives, to axe an uneconomic part of their activities.

The whole is a more complex sum of interrelated parts. A problem that arises from the multiplicity of objectives is the difficulty of monitoring performance. Commercial control systems depend on clear and limited aims and, in any case, can easily become so expensive to operate that the costs outweigh the benefits. Both the aims and the costs make difficulties for other kinds of organization—increasing the fear of autonomy, but not necessarily the reality of centralization. A body of knowledge on this is coming into existence, but is difficult to implement.

The differences, then, between the commercial and the non-commercial should not be underestimated, while there are also many resemblances. The fundamental clash between decentralizing beliefs, reinforced by education, and the centralizing lures of material considerations applies to most organizations even if the form varies. The beliefs also colour perceptions and make the gaps between the different units greater and more prone to misunderstanding. The centralizing effect of funding, and the desire to ensure that value is received for funds provided, also applies. Another, more subtle, resemblance is the need for mitigation where centralization is found to be inevitable. This is met in different ways in, for instance, an international company or a group that exists to promote humanitarian aims like Amnesty International; but both are picking their way among sensitive political issues.

For all the resemblances and the differences there is a common thread. The tensions between the centre and the units may be more pressing, and more frequently examined in their own right, in companies but these tensions are part of the functioning of an organization; an attempt to determine some measure of centralization against a suitable standard of comparison is relevant to any institution and will be examined in the next chapter.

9 Empirical Research on Centralization and Autonomy

To produce a method of research which matches the complexity of the subject is not easy, and some attempts have not unnaturally been oversimplified. To reduce the issues to ones that can be answered by a straightforward scoring of questions about the degree of centralization cannot provide a satisfactory analysis of its effects. More detailed questioning, however, can produce more biased results; the researcher is likely to become involved with the organization under observation. This chapter will not concern itself with debating objectivity, but will assume a reasonable detachment and honesty. In this context words like the *skill* of researchers or their *integrity* are used to indicate that any process of measuring centralization is a process of honest recording and informed judgement. The counting and the calculating are subsidiary to this. A convincing measure, furthermore, requires the use of more than one method at the same time so that there is a built-in means of verification even if this does involve some compromise in the scoring. Thus, the two units concerned in a particular relationship may provide different answers, and there may be a similar contrast between written and oral evidence. The judgement of the researcher is then required to reconcile the contradictory information before making the calculations.

The correctness of this statement is underlined by the choice that so frequently faces the researcher between performing complex calculations on the basis of simple questions, where the reliability of the answers is in no way guaranteed, and asking more sophisticated questions where the answers are not amenable to statistical treatment. The questions are normally designed to determine the degree of centralization that exists in one organization relative to others, and the consequences that a high or low level have for other characteristics of the organization. Whatever the method of measurement used, it needs authenticating by another.

Most of the questioning is concerned with ascertaining whether decisions are taken in or influenced by subordinate units, although some are more indirect in asking about general perceptions of centralization; other subjects of enquiry are also undertaken. The checking of the answers requires taking the views of more than one person and perhaps at more than one time. At the end of an interview, when a respondent has gained confidence in his questioner, a different answer may be given than at the beginning. Checking and cross-checking are essential to verify the answers.

The following discussion picks up on issues already raised in theory (in Chapters 1 and 4) and considers how they apply to methods in current use, beginning with the relationship of definition to research method.

9.1   RESEARCHABLE CONCEPTS

'An administrative organization is centralized to the extent that decisions are made at relatively high levels in the organization, and decentralized to the extent that discretion and authority to make important decisions are delegated by top management to other levels of executive authority.'[1] This definition is used as the basis of most empirical work on the subject; it relies on the notion of a locus of decision-making, although this reliance is made viable by the word 'discretion'. Challenges to this notion, already examined in Chapter 4, are recorded in more detail below. One piece of research that is based on the locus approach, clarifies the meaning of the phrase and expands the need to discover precisely where a particular activity occurs in the following words:

> 'Centralization has to do with the locus of authority to make decisions affecting the organization. Authority to make decisions was ascertained by asking: Who was the last person whose assent must be obtained before legitimate action is taken—even if others have subsequently confirmed the decision?'[2]

Two points arise out of that definition and subsequent research questions. Unlike Simon, for whom the relationship between authority to make decisions and where the decisions are actually made was implicit, for Pugh this was the case by definition—the assumption being that the point in the hierarchy where decisions are made is the point where real authority to do so exists despite subsequent confirmation. Secondly, the fact that others have to confirm the decision, while acceptable if they do so, raises problems about where the decisions are made if they do not confirm them. Presumably, the right to confirm implies the right to reject. The precise location of any particular decision has always puzzled those adopting the locus of decision-making approach. There are other possibilities: some definitions embrace power and authority as well as decision location. Some definitions, on the other hand, confine themselves to the question of power, and leave it at that, producing a simple definition which while easily comprehensible is less useful for research purposes. For example: 'Centralization is . . . the degree to which power is concentrated in a social system.'[3]

The problem of these elementary definitions of centralization and decentralization in terms of locus of decision-making, power and authority or indeed of all three, is that there is an implicit assumption that all the concepts mix sufficiently easily as to be interchangeable; but Jennergren has pointed out that this is not the case. There is a fundamental difference in the implications of different definitions along the following lines, he suggests.

(1) Decentralization of authority implies participation in decision-making, which links up with the concept of democracy and non-hierarchical decision-making.

(2) Decentralization in terms of power connotes an ability to distinguish between power and legitimate authority and may well imply that the question of what level the decisions are taken at is less important than the range of choices available to the decision-takers.

(3) Centralization of power may imply centralization of decision-taking at a certain level in the hierarchy, but decentralization of power does not necessarily imply the reverse: decisions may be taken centrally but choices for those decisions may be very few.

(4) Defining centralization in terms of locus of decision-making tends to obscure the issues of power, authority and participation by defining locus in such a way as to eliminate considerations of influence on the decisions, and, as already shown, takes no account of the degree of necessary further agreement after the decision is made, or for that matter the real width of choice available to the decision-taker.

Centralization can refer to the 'hierarchical level in the organization at which decisions are made or, more generally, to the relative decision-making influence of different hierarchical level'. Centralization can also mean 'the degree of participativeness in decision-making, but without reference to hierarchical levels.'[4]

This dichotomy is implicit in a great deal of the literature. Writers are continually being pulled between participatory notions of centralization and decentralization, and a hierarchical analysis. Frequently, centralization is seen in locus of decision-making terms, specifying a particular type of hierarchical structure with decision-making at the top, and decentralization is seen as increasing participation with all the alleged benefits of a democratically organized company. In fact, these two are not opposites but different interpretations of the same concept. Decentralization in locus of decision-making terms may not imply any increase in participation at all. One can illustrate the difficulty by saying that it is theoretically possible to have a company that is both centralized and decentralized simultaneously if both definitions are used at the same time.

(1) A decentralized (centralized) company is one in which the major decisions are actually taken at a high level by the chairman or chief executive but only after he or she has solicited the views of everybody remotely concerned and discussed the problem with them. The chairman takes the decision. They influence it.

(2) A centralized (decentralized) company is one in which the major decisions are taken throughout the company, some at low levels, but with little consultation and discussion between middle managers and those above and below them. The decisions are taken by a wide variety of autonomous individuals throughout the company.

Neither of these patterns of decision-making have much reality but they do illustrate the inherent conflict between seeing centralization as a level of decision-making phenomenon and as a participatory one: a distinction between the management sciences' use of the terms and that used in studies of public administration.

The two distinct and contradictory notions of decentralization and centralization will be labelled for convenience 'horizontal' and 'vertical'.

Putting these two together it is at once obvious that certain types of centralized systems are really decentralized in other senses (Table 9.1). In this connection two points should be noted. The first is a minor distinction between *making* (through consultation) a decision and *taking* it; the latter implies a degree of autonomy. The second is that power and its centralization is not equivalent to either vertical or horizontal centralization, but runs diagonally across both. The important point about this understanding of centralization is to emphasize that describing a company as decentralized in the vertical sense, in accordance with locus of decision analysis, does not imply that it is decentralized in terms of either power, authority or participation. To say that a firm is decentralized because its subsidiary managers are autonomous may well imply that the management hierarchy of that subsidiary is highly centralized. Decentralization to a particular level may imply centralization from that level downwards: one person's autonomy precluding that of his or her subordinates.

Table 9.1 The horizontal and vertical dimensions

Horizontal	Decentralization	Centralization
	Wide participation at all levels, group decision-making, consultation.	Autonomy of decision-taking, individual decision-taking, direction.
Vertical	Decentralization.	Centralization.
	Decisions taken at all levels in the group, coordination.	Decisions taken at a high level, control.

While it is true that to some extent decentralization in a vertical sense may imply greater participation, this is not necessarily so. Indeed, the lower down the hierarchy the authority to make decisions goes, the more jealously that authority may be guarded. The sergeant-major may be less willing to accept advice from those below him than the brigadier, and the analogy holds equally for the shop-floor supervisor and the director of finance.

A problem with both definitions is that they have to apply a comparison and thus some idea of a continuum. As Simon puts it: 'centralization and decentralization are not genuine alternatives for organizing. The question is not whether we shall decentralize, but how far we shall centralize. What we seek again is a golden mean: we want to find the proper level in the organizational hierarchy—neither too high nor too low—for each important class of decisions'.[5] The concept of the *normal line*, which expresses the finding that there are pressures operating against moves to either end of the spectrum from complete centralization to the reverse, has encapsulated this notion of the mean for research into multinationals between head office and the subsidiary, but the notion also applies within any type of organization; as Fayol pointed out: 'the degree of centralization or decentralization may itself vary constantly . . . It arises not only in the case of higher authority, but for *Supervisors at all levels*, and there is not one but can extend or contract to some extent his subordinates' initiatives.'[6]

An empirical research into the subject has to take this continuum approach into account. A researcher is saying that X is more decentralized than Y, not that it is decentralized in any absolute sense, where X and Y are two separate companies, two separate sets of relationships within one company or two different dates in the history of one company. On the other hand the pursuit of empirical data must have some means of distinguishing the one position from the other in order to measure it. On a pure continuum basis there can be no degrees of centralization since each position on the scale fades imperceptibly into the other. Any researcher attempting to create a system for measuring centralization has to have a definition which acknowledges the comparative basis of the concept and yet produces recognizable degrees. This is a problem in discussing a continuum for centralization for a whole organization.[7] To complicate the problem further, there has to be a recognition of the fact that a constant movement is likely, corresponding to the short-term shifts around the normal line, along the continuum and over time, in any organization. A measure of centralization, however defined, has to take this into account since the measurement of centralization within an organization will only apply precisely at the time of the research. This brings up problems about the relationship of centralization to other organizational characteristics. There is also a danger caused by ambiguities inherent in seeing centralization either as a management technique or as a structural variable. The connotations of centralization and decentralization are summarized from a number of empirical studies in Figure 9.1.

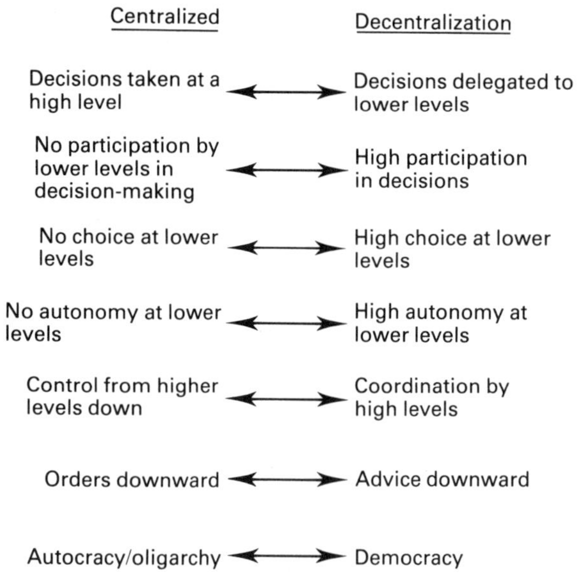

Centralized — Decentralization

Decisions taken at a high level ⟷ Decisions delegated to lower levels

No participation by lower levels in decision-making ⟷ High participation in decisions

No choice at lower levels ⟶ High choice at lower levels

No autonomy at lower levels ⟶ High autonomy at lower levels

Control from higher levels down ⟷ Coordination by high levels

Orders downward ⟷ Advice downward

Autocracy/oligarchy ⟷ Democracy

Figure 9.1 Connotations of centralization–decentralization

The implications of comparing the degree of centralization over time should be considered separately from comparisons between companies or within a company at any one time; the reason is that another source of possible inaccuracy is introduced—that of memory. It is hard enough to identify where the decision was taken yesterday; it is much harder to be confident about statements on where the decision was taken five years ago. But this is often the question which needs answering to check statements in the form of: 'this company is more successful now that it is more centralized'. Once again verification over as many respondents as possible is needed.

In the light of the responses to these preliminary considerations the reliability of research will be verified by cross-checking to arrive at a measure of centralization which allows other generalizations to be tested. The research that has been conducted can be classified under a number of headings which form the next section.

9.2 TYPES OF RESEARCH USING THE CONCEPTS

The variety of types of research that use the concepts of centralization and decentralization itself bears witness to their rich and complex content. Among them are the following.

Management theory analysis
This sees the problem of centralization and decentralization as solvable by management techniques, seeking a midpoint between the two which combines the advantages of both. Essentially, the function of this type of research is to identify the organizational structure *best* suited to the aims of the company by increasing management motivation and yet avoiding the problems associated with lack of coordination.

Organization theory
Organization theory in contrast sees centralization as a variable among other variables; the organization being a matrix of structural traits bound together and essentially interdependent. Analysis of this type attempts to discover the relationship between the size, standardization and specialization variables of an organization; that is to say, a particular size and type of organization will inevitably be centralized to a certain degree.

Quantitative approaches
These involve the construction of theoretical mathematical models of decision-making choices with a set number of hierarchical levels. Normally concerned with resource allocation, the analysis looks at the means of satisfying the aims of the individual level and the different resource allocations required to do so. Systems satisfying the aims of the lower levels of production units are

decentralized and those that satisfy the top level are centralized. Quantitative methods imply the use of the logic of mathematics and thus explore the formal possibilities of a set number of hierarchical levels. As such they provide the limits to a certain type of centralization or decentralization but lack any descriptive element about the way the term is used in general discussion. (For an example of this approach see Chapter 3.4.)

Political economy approaches
These measure aspects of control and participation to determine the relative strengths of the various elements within societies and their component institutions, including the commercial. One advantage of these approaches is their focus on underlying conflicts. Exponents use the language of power rather than that of authority, especially when they focus on rival power-centres like the trade unions, but they also examine the locus of decision-making. One author, employing a political economy approach to examine industrial democracy, concludes that there is a cyclical process in the rise and decline of worker participation schemes.[8] This finding bears some resemblance to the view put forward in part II of the present study on decentralization in international companies.

Accounting approaches
These are primarily designed to analyse a single question: How do you produce adequate accounting and reporting systems for large companies? As such they are more closely related to the management theorists' view of centralization and decentralization, and indeed provide techniques aimed at solving the practical dilemma between coordination and over-control. Since accounting methods aimed at promoting the best compromise between centralization and decentralization have been produced, the method used by an individual company can offer considerable evidence for stating that a particular company is more centralized than another. One researcher has shown how the method of accounting used before the consolidation of accounts, the units from which the information is assembled, can be of use in analysing the degree of centralization in multinational companies. Even taking account of the national rules and conventions in the light of which subsidiaries have to present their accounts and parent companies to consolidate them, there is a wide variety of methods of collecting, assembling and forwarding the figures. This research demonstrated that more variety existed than the usual instruction to submit accounts on the head office form according to head office convention suggests.

Within these four modes of analysis, a bewildering selection of variables relevant to the study of centralization has been proposed. Some of these variables will now be examined.

9.3 THE RELEVANT VARIABLES

Given the wider variety of meanings implied by centralization and decentralization it is necessary to recognize the distinction between the structural and contextual variables adopted by the organizational theorists and the indications or symptoms recognized by management scientists as evidence of degrees of centralization.

Centralization within the context of organization theory is regarded as a *structural* variable—a means of contrasting different structures together with standardization, formalization and configuration.[9] By means of multivariate regression analysis the relative presence of each structural variable, measured against the similar set of contextual variables such as size and history, is shown through the correlation between the incidence of each kind of variable. At this level of abstraction the effective operational definition of centralization is given by weighting the answers to the question: 'Who is the last person whose assent must be obtained before legitimate action can be taken?' The definition is founded upon a locus of decision-making analysis. Broadly, such studies are trying to find a decision model which allows prediction to be made of an organization's structural characteristics including centralization from a knowledge of its contextual features. Direct causal influences were not established.

The subsequent extensions and replications established important difficulties in connection with centralization, particularly in its relationship with standardization. Standardization, in this context, refers to both procedures (the form-filling) and roles (the job specifications), following Weber's original distinction between bureaucratic and other types of organization. The original studies by Pugh and his colleagues produced a low negative correlation between centralization and standardization; that is, they confirmed the view that standard reporting procedures went along with decentralization. An even clearer relationship was subsequently established in a national sample.[10] However, another study showed the opposite, that high standardization and high centralization could also go together in some circumstances.[11]

The difference between the two correlations was thought to be the result of the heterogeneity of Pugh's sample, which included a higher number of branch offices than the national sample, but such a view was called in question by Donaldson's rerun of the original sample without the branches. There is a continuing debate on the problem of the status of branches and subsidiaries within this type of locus of decision-making analysis, while other contingent factors remain to be identified. An analysis of centralization requires consistency across different organizations if each level is to be weighted correctly in the subsequent statistical analysis. A level in X Company, given a specific weighting, must be parallel to the level in Y Company given the identical weighting. This is more difficult if one of the companies is a subsidiary and one is not, for the organization theorist assumes that it is *the degree of centralization* which changes rather than the *importance of each level* within the company hierarchy. The manager of a subsidiary may appear to take a larger proportion of important decisions than the manager of an operating unit when both companies have the same degree of decentralization to middle-management. The chief executive of the subsidiary is of higher rank, but not necessarily of greater importance.

In dealing with the question of the negative correlation between centralization and standardization found in the Pugh and the national surveys, the implication is that the greater the degree of decentralization within an organization, the greater will be the degree of standardization of its roles and procedures. This corresponds with the intention of divisionalization (explained in section 5.2) and provides a contrast between the opposing notions of participatory decentralization and level of hierarchy.

Mansfield has explained the views of the organizational theorists thus: 'it would seem that increasing size forces organizational managers to create rules to govern behaviour and hence reduce the range of possible day-to-day problems which confront them. This increase in rules and paper work allows them to delegate the right to make decisions without losing their overall control as those delegated are made within guidelines designated by the rules. If this is the case the decentralization of decision-making does not necessarily carry with it any delegation of discretion or weakening of the power of the highest ranks in the organizational hierarchy.'[12] In effect he is saying that decentralization on a decision locus analysis does not imply decentralization on a power basis. On the Pugh model, with a negative correlation between centralization and standardization, the notion of decentralization implies a limitation of the possible freedom of action of the subordinate in contrast to earlier participatory notions such as that of Fayol: 'Everything that goes to increase the importance of the subordinate's role is decentralization, everything that goes to reduce it is centralization.'[13] Both use the concept, but with different implications.

The major problem with the organization theory framework is that it has concentrated on the level at which decisions are taken to the exclusion of how important the decisions actually are, and the degree of choice and discretion involved. There is clearly no relationship between centralization according to the organization theorists, and the decentralization perceived by the managers of subsidiaries when they complain of increasing paper work, if the former is negatively correlated with standardization. Nor indeed does the 'compensatory relationship between greater delegation of decision-making and greater structuring of bureaucratic control', to use Donaldson's phrase, sound like the public expectation inherent in demands for decentralized local government.[14] In this connection the understanding of centralization has to take notice of the degree of choice attached to individual decisions. It should follow that the narrower the limits of choice given to subordinates, as implied by the greater structuring of bureaucratic control, the less actual power of decision they have and, by implication, the smaller the degree of job satisfaction and incentive. Not that any necessary connection between a greater power of decision and greater job satisfaction has been proved, but Pugh's use of the word 'decentralization' implies no devolution of authority or of discretion if bureaucratic control is increased by greater standardization. There is an apparent paradox in the implication of the link between decentralization and standardization. This indicates once again the difficulty of using a locus of decision-making basis for centralization and then attempting to draw conclusions about it in terms of concepts like power and authority. As Vickers pointed out, there is more to decision-making than who takes the decisions.[15] The Japanese emperor, for example, always had the last nod of the head when a matter of new law was to be decided. His advisers always reached unanimity before giving him advice, and the emperor always agreed. Did he make a decision?

Whatever the conclusion in terms of discretion and authority demonstrated by the negative correlation between centralization and standardization, the organization theorists have imposed a sense of order into the debate regarding centralization by rigidly defining the concepts in viable research terms, and by elaborating and refining the techniques used to find interrelationships between them. A consequence of the refinement is to produce a formula (standardization equals decentralization) which contradicts the normal understanding of the words—a common occurrence when the social scientists refine their concepts, but one which calls for a reconsideration of the data on which the conclusion is based. At least it would be rash to assume that the amount of routine report writing and paper work reflecting the degree of restriction on the discretion of the subordinate cannot be used as evidence of centralization.

The problem arises in part from the attempt to pursue decentralization down to the lowest level of an organization at which specific decisions are taken 'even if this remained subject to routine confirmation later.'[16]

Management theorists, in contrast, have usually chosen to avoid pursuing the decentralization down to the lowest levels, concentrating their attention on the distribution of decision-making authority at the top of the corporation. Centralization and decentralization are seen as aspects of management, their manipulation a trait inherent in an organization with a particular nexus of structural and contextual traits. There is a realization that centralization will vary with technology, ownership, size and dependence and indeed will affect standardization, specialization and the other structural variables. But the aim is not to establish the relationship between these variables but to find the most effective organization structure either for efficiency or for control.

In consequence, the concept of centralization is looser and the variety of indicators pointing to a centralized or decentralized position are broader. Perhaps the frequent implication that decentralization is a means of distributing authority, influence and power is often at odds with the equally frequent implication that it is about maintaining control over a large and diverse organization. Management theorists see the degrees of centralization as being changeable within a set framework of other variables by management decision alone—thus the concept is loosely seen as part of the style of individual company managements. As a practising manager put it: 'good management rests on a reconciliation of centralization and decentralization or decentralization with coordinated control.'[17] As with the organization theorists, this notion of decentralization is in conflict with the political notion of a distribution of power. In a coordinated company, power has not been diluted and remains identically placed in a decentralized as well as a centralized system. Blau has expressed one view on this in the words: 'Managerial decisions in organizations are either significant in which case they are not delegated; or delegated in which case they are not significant.'[18]

Frequently, the notion of centralization and decentralization is seen in management theory to reflect a means of maintaining control under a rhetoric of lowering the point of more mundane decisions. As Stopford and Wells hypothesize, the rapidly changing company structures of multinational companies during the 1960s along product group lines were, in general, an attempt to form a system of control adequate to widening product lines and geographical dispersion. Control was increased by 'decentralization' rather than relaxed.[19]

This view has been expanded to create a picture of changing company structures which relates to size. As a firm grows, in management theory, moving from owner-operator to complex worldwide structures, it goes through a series of decentralization measures, in the process of which the relative importance of decisions is redefined. Some will never be delegated; others will normally be left to subsidiary units. This interpretation can look remarkably like a simple notion founded upon size: that the greater the size, the greater the number of decisions to be made and the greater the number of people to make them, the more decentralized the company will be. Decentralization in this context will be a means to maintain control and a concept primarily concerned with company structures in relation to their size.

Management theory thus pursues its evidence in terms of the structure of company reporting to determine which approximate type of management system produces the best result given the product diversification and the company size. By implication the theorists are in pursuit of systems which recognize the impossibility of maintaining the total decision-making authority at the highest level in the organization, due to pressures on executive time, and the need for a trade-off between allowing decisions to be taken lower down and retaining control. One authority[20] has made the distinction between indirect, where limits are imposed by monitoring procedures and records, and direct control which formally retains decisions to senior levels in a hierarchy. Centralization in this context may be an indicator of the degree of autonomy each managerial member possesses. Similarly, in the relationship between the subsidiaries and the headquarters of a multinational company, the general evidence provided by managers suggests a marked conflict in viewpoint as to how far their company is decentralized. It could be suggested that this conflict arises out of the different conceptions of decentralization. The head office sees the process of decentralization as producing strategies of control which involve reporting and limiting mechanisms antipathetic to the subsidiary's conception of decentralization as productive of greater autonomy and decision-making authority.

The differences in approach between organization and management theorists rest on the purposes of the research rather than the view taken of what decentralization actually means in practice. The delegation of decisions to lower levels coupled with a rapid increase in checks and reporting, limitations on freedom of action and choice, and a more rigidly structured hierarchy may well leave the actual power and authority position identical, and provide little information about the degree of participation in decision-making.

9.4   THE MEASUREMENT

Two approaches to the measurement of centralization have been proposed—the locus of decision-making, estimated at a certain point in a hierarchy, and the proportionate amount of influence attributed to groups or individuals. Both organization and management theorists use each method. Those who use the influence approach are more inclined to justify their usage; those who employ the locus approach more frequently take the correctness of their method for granted. Despite the theoretical issues, already discussed, no convincing evidence has been produced to show how the results differ. The influence approach might be expected to reveal a bias towards decentralization, but the results of both methods depend upon the integrity of the researcher and his or her skill in limiting the bias among the respondents.

The locus of decision-making

The advantage of this approach is that it is more relevant to the questions that the measurement is expected to answer, such as:
(1)   Is an organization decentralized or not?
(2)   If so to what units, and what are the consequences?
(3)   What are the differences between perception and reality, and how can the reality be improved?
The disadvantage is the problem of determining where the decision is taken. A number of proposals have been made, all of which have some disadvantages.

Pugh and his colleagues asked for the level of decision-taking from 37 recurrent decisions, scoring each level from 0 to 5, with 0 for the lowest level. These individual scores were then averaged for each organization giving an overall score for the average decisions. The actual question asked in regard to individual recurrent decision was: 'who is the last person whose assent must be obtained before legitimate action is taken, even if others have subsequently confirmed the decision?'[21] Khandwalla asked chief executives to score the extent to which they delegated decision-making authority in nine important areas, thus getting a senior viewpoint on a smaller range of decision areas rather than specific decisions, an approach which can be expected to increase the subjectivity of the response.[22]

While these two approaches differ marginally as to the means of discovering the locus, both are open to criticism. The Pugh approach fails to deal with the question of where the decision was made if the review does not confirm it, and Khandwalla's decision area depends upon the view of the chief executive as to what delegation actually means.

In the latter case both groups average out the scores for each individual decision into one overall score; they cannot then distinguish financial decision centralization from any other and their average decision may be the product of what the individual company actually makes or does, rather than of the other relevant structural or contextual variables.

This problem is tackled by Blau and Schoenherr and Meyer and Abell. They reject the notion of an overall average decision and leave the centralization scores unaveraged in specific functions like finance, personnel and goal-setting, finding in the process that there seemed to be very little correlation between them.[23] This brings up again the problem of either seeing centralization as an overall continuum or of dividing up the concept according to functions and abandoning the simplicity of an overall measure. It should be noted that the fact that managers in a particular function have more discretion than those in others does not invalidate the overall measure, since the purpose of the measure is to distinguish between organizations. A range of different measures doubtless exists in different functions but the measurement of the relationship, if any, between functions is a separate problem.

In general, the problems of measuring centralization, after an interview in which the responses are scored, falls under four headings:

(1) Are the decisions chosen comparable across organizations?
(2) What questions are appropriate to discover precisely where those decisions are taken?
(3) How can the locus of decision-making for each of those decisions be averaged to give an overall measure of centralization for a particular organization?
(4) How does one weigh the importance of the decisions?

It is in the case of (2) that management theorists have had their greatest difficulties, as a result of which some have adopted an approach which has emphasized the influence attributed to a particular group or person.

Attributed to influence

It has been argued that the notion of a specific decision locus was naive and that each decision goes through three phases: definition of the choice, impetus towards a particular choice, and authorization of that choice. The two former stages were generally placed at a lower level in the hierarchy than the latter.[24] While this brings a certain degree of reality into the analysis of how decisions are made in large organizations, it runs into the danger of viewing decision-making as a continuous flow of suggestions and actions, the precise responsibility for which is blurred. The result would be the complete abandonment of the locus of decision-making concept. Even with Ackerman's concept of the three parts of a decision—definition, impetus and authorization—the problem of weighing the relative importance of each part in a measurement system across different companies would be enormous. And since the suggestion was a solution to the problem of understanding the decision-making, the question has to be asked—would the impetus and authorization be any easier to discover than the locus? To say the least the answer is doubtful, for three complex concepts have been substituted for a simple one..

The most notable exponent of measurement of influence is Tannenbaum. His view, which has already been discussed in Chapter 4, is that since the answer to the question about who makes the decision is likely to be subjective anyway, why not abandon the locus of decision concept with its spurious precision and replace it with the more subjective but more realistic notion of influence—the approach from power rather than from authority? People may not know the precise location of a decision-making authority, but they will all have opinions as to the hierarchical levels which influence it most. The way of measuring this influence was to ask those in different levels of the organization to assess their own and other people's influence on the most senior group and plot the results on a graph. The method is illustrated in Figure 9.2.

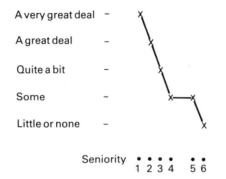

Seniority · · · · · ·
1 2 3 4 5 6

Adapted from Tannenbaum (1966) p.97

Figure 9.2   A measure of influence

The results taken from each group's assessment of itself and of the influence of other groups are averaged and the slope of the graph constitutes the measure of centralization; the steeper the graph, the greater the degree of centralization.[25] An objection to this method of questioning is that the respondents are not offered a standard of comparison. Their point of reference, on which their answers will depend, will vary enormously—from the one-company people who can only compare with previous conditions in their company, to the people who have changed jobs frequently and whose answer will depend on experience in their former companies. The appropriate allowance for consultation is also a problem. A system of industrial democracy in which, in fact, little notice was taken of the works councils could rate a greater influence than was in fact the case.

A solution to the debate between the locus of decision-making approach and that of influence turns out to be much more elusive than the protagonists suggest. Sometimes there seems to be an element of a trick picture, that is, one in which there are two objects portrayed but the viewer can only see one at a time. Perhaps it is necessary to try to keep both pictures—centralization in terms of locus of decision-making and in terms of influence—at the same time. To do this is to admit that both are worth measuring, useful data can be collected in both cases, and both have conceptual drawbacks; the influence approach has the most operational difficulties.

There has been a simultaneous search for hard data to establish a degree of centralization that is not dependent upon the subjective assessment by individuals of where decisions are actually made or the degree of influence certain levels may have on this. This has led to proposals for measurement by executive span of control, time span of discretion, the analysis of the payment structure, or the analysis of communications within and between companies. The span of control approach, arising out of the work of the classical organization theorists, affirms that a wide span of control—numerous subordinates reporting to one supervisor—allows little time to take decisions and this represents a symptom of decentralization of decision-making. A small span of control at the top and a wide span at the bottom is the pattern for a centralized organizational structure. Thus, all that is required to measure centralization on this basis is to measure the span of control for each hierarchical level.[26] The problem of this is that the style of supervision may well differ at each level of the hierarchy and its immediate relevance to the decision-making of top executives, rather than middle-management is slighter, the distinction between staff and line is ignored, and the problem of subsidiary as against headquarters group relations cannot be easily analysed, since they are two organizations, not one.

The time span of control measurement, which originated with Brown and Jaques as a method for determining salaries, is a technique for discovering the maximum period of time a manager will expect and allow subordinates to work without reviewing the results.[27] The greater the time span of discretion, the greater the responsibility and thus, if the hierarchy is analysed as a whole, the greater the degree of decentralization within it. Like other measures designed to analyse work close to the shop-floor, time span as a measure between organizations or sub-units of one large organization is more subjective than may, at first, appear. A lengthy time span between a subsidiary and its head office could be the result of a breakdown in communications and is, in any case, remarkably difficult to assess adequately at the top of the hierarchy.

Whisler devised a system for measuring centralization through the payment system of an organization, proposing that the money paid to say two per cent of the highest paid employees as a fraction of the total wages and salaries bill would give some indication of the degree of centralization since the larger the fraction, the larger the responsibility taken on by these individuals at the top.[28] The argument against this is simply that the salary structure might be inequitable. Finally, there are studies of the communications system. One such formed part of the research on which part II is based and is described in Chapter 11.[29] Another is that of Chorafas who examined the blocks in the communication system of international companies, although the assumed connection between communication problems and centralization goes back to Katz and Kahn. Chorafas is concerned with the physical and personal issues which block rather than the organizational.

One body of research which attempted to bring together some objective and subjective measures was a study of centralization among banks which used three measures of centralization: lending limits, hierarchy of authority and participation. The results showed that there were a number of dimensions to both centralization and formalization, and thus provided a possible reason why the correlations between these two characteristics vary in different studies. For instance, a relationship between hierarchy and lending limits was found in some banks but not in others. At the same time, formalization produced different scores when work roles or job specifications were under consideration.[30]

Thus, there are many techniques for the measurement of centralization, but there is doubt concerning how far they measure the same thing. Despite the fairly high congruence noted by Whisler and others between their control graph, average span of control and payment system measures of centralization in a study of insurance companies,[31] there is a sense in which all these methods measure those aspects of centralization which are easily definable in figures. Locus of decision-making indices depend upon a subjective self-assessment of the precise location of a decision, and the centralization measure depends basically upon that which may differ according to the functional area of the decision. Another approach rests on an equally self-assessed notion of influence. Payments systems as pictures of centralization portray the centralization of reward—not necessarily that of authority. It can be argued that the subjective measure, so-called, is the only valid one. Since the generalizations to be drawn concern the effects of centralization or decentralization on motivation and responsibility and such effects can only result from a perceived situation, the need of research is to make the subjective more accurate. This study shows a preference for the locus approach because it stems from the more readily definable concept of authority, but the critics' implications are incorporated to allow the need for taking a number of views before determining the locus and if necessary producing a measurement in fractions. This is not easy and the measurement becomes an aid to judgement rather than a substitute for it.

9.5   THE CULTURAL CONTENT OF THE CONCEPTS

Most empirical studies of centralization ignore the cultural content; the mode of questioning assumes some background of beliefs and motivation, but seldom are questions asked about the influence of assumed patterns of thought on the answers. Where evidence has been collected across national frontiers, the results have provided ample reason for emphasizing that cultural differences are important in spite of resemblances. In fact, the resemblances may be more superficial than the casual observer realizes, and this may be the case within a country as well as across frontiers. Regional, racial or social backgrounds may be expected to influence answers which imply perceptions about control and influence.

It is tempting to assume that the political system will be a main source of difference, that an authoritarian culture is also one where decisions are centralized. But this may be facile. A conscious effort at decentralization is not incompatible with dictatorship while, as is shown on these pages, there is a strong lure to centralization in democratic societies. Indeed the pressure to greater efficiency is often a centralizing one—'we must be efficient to survive' can mean 'we must accept greater central control'—and arguably it is more acceptable in a democracy than in a dictatorship where every available local privilege will be grasped tenaciously.

Attempts to measure cultural differences do not usually look at centralization directly, but the concepts used are closely related. One such attempt uses a *hierarchical power distance* measure,[32] designed to answer three questions: the views of subordinates about whether their boss is autocratic or paternalistic, the degree to which subordinates are afraid to disagree and whether or not they prefer an autocratic boss. The index thus compiled is used to provide the basis for a comparison of management in different cultures, both national and occupational. The results show a link between the autocratic cultures of southern Europe and the centralized businesses in that area, and the more participative cultures of northern Europe with more autonomous styles of management. The calculations may be open to question but the method avoids a common assumption that one culture, probably that of the particular author, provides a norm against which others are to be tested. Hofstede's approach was supported by a study of management in Iran.[33] This investigation into a specific organization in that country made effective use of a *power distance index* which recorded high autocracy accompanied by a high level of centralization. Even if the political position is more complicated, the business situation does seem to demonstrate this relationship.

A series of comparative studies carried out simultaneously and in a coordinated manner have been reported by Heller.[34] These throw doubt on Hofstede's research in that French as well as Swedish managers employed decentralized styles. Apart from this exception to the contrast between northern and southern Europe, the studies did confirm national differences in management style. They also introduced an important new element into the discussion—the phases of the decision-making process. Thus, Heller finds that the participation of workers and supervisors is high at the initiation and development phases as is that of representative and external bodies, while the influence of middle and top managers is higher in the finalization and implementation phases. The problem for the present study is that Heller appears to be using yet another definition of centralization—he is thinking of the place of individuals in the organization rather than sub-units. His focus of interest is participation and this also means a concentration on power and influence. Indeed the measure used is called a 'power influence continuum' and demonstrates how employees at different levels in an organization perceive their influence on different kinds of decision.

Another authority, Weinshall, has studied the differences in attitude that influence communications and therefore centralization as shown both in management education and in the management of international companies.[35] Those nationalities which practised the most verbal communications were also more likely to develop decentralized structures. Weinshall is especially important methodologically as a representative of the advocates of action research—the method by which those involved in an organization conduct investigations into their own or a related institution, or researchers become part of the organization which they are studying. This method has not been widely used for studies of centralization as such. Some of the researches might have produced more plausible results if they had, although there are dangers of bias and over-identification with the object of study. Some maintain that these are not dangers but advantages, and the demands on the investigator's honesty are no higher in this than any other method. Without doubt action research is particularly relevant to the study of culture where so many of the variables are hard to define.

For all the differences of approach and definition, there is accumulating evidence that culture is an important influence on the degree of centralization. Incidental to that evidence is the further finding of a relationship between high centralization and an authoritarian society which has been regarded as an open question on these pages.

One consequence of this is that comparisons within a country must be regarded as operating within limits set in that country; a further implication is that the search for correlates to centralization or autonomy must take account of cultural differences. A certain degree of decentralization should not be considered a universal norm, nor should the same effects be anticipated in different countries. Job satisfaction and high performance, among others, can be expected to relate to autonomy in some cultures and autocracy in others.

9.6   INVESTIGATING CENTRALIZATION

A representative selection out of a broad array of research effort has been reviewed in this chapter. No formula has come to light which is beyond criticism, and the task is to outline a method of investigation which takes account of the problems and incorporates the essential factors. This involves a number of compromises, but it also involves maintaining a clear view of the meaning of centralization and autonomy as well as the questions that any investigation is designed to answer. The subject can be summarized in a list of stages in each of which there is a compromise but there is also a feasible element in a research programme. The following list is summarized in Table 9.2.

Identify the basis of comparison
The concepts of centralization and autonomy are meaningless without a comparative element, but this element can vary. Already proposed are comparisons within an organization between different units or different dates as well as comparisons between organizations. Also possible is a comparison with some theoretical standard or model which the investigator has derived from other sources, such as personal experience, the scanning of the literature or the questioning of experts. The standard list of items can be further refined by the use of some Delphic-style enquiry in which the experts are asked to reconsider their statements in the light of further evidence. This list then becomes a predicted profile against which any actual profile can be checked. The compromise in these proposals is between an objective which requires the greatest possible degree of comparability and the reality that such an aim must be modified in the interests of depth. Determining the degree of centralization in any given instance involves questioning and cross-questioning as well as the examination of documentary and other evidence.

Table 9.2 Investigating the degree of centralization and decentralization: a summary

Action	Qualification
(1) Identify the basis of comparison	The concepts only have meaning in a comparative context but there is a choice of standards of comparison: (a) between organizations; (b) between units of the same organization; (c) between units of the same organization at different dates; (d) as against a theoretical profile. *Need* to balance search for comparative evidence against search for depth.
(2) Identify the units	The investigator must decide which decisions or indicators are to be compared
(3) Identify the issues	between organizations. A compromise may be necessary where the organizations
(4) Examine specific relationships	rate differently or use different indicators, and where decisions have to be split into fractions. Place relationship along an assumed line running from centralized to decentralized. An overall measure, if any, must be estimated from the sum of specific relationships.
(5) Identify the exercise of authority	Look for a point of decision-making while allowing for the bargaining process. Prepare a list of decisions, submit it to analysis to identify issues and compute weightings.
(6) Reconsider the personal position of the investigator	The investigator must filter the information but needs to ensure the maximum objectivity without making false claims.
(7) Employ a variety of approaches, by examining for example: (a) the significant issues; (b) the actions or arrangements; (c) the communications; (d) the perceptions at head office level; (e) the perceptions at unit level; (f) the judgement of the investigator.	Limitations of resource, including time, will restrict the ability to cross-check thoroughly, but at least two approaches form a desirable minimum.

Identify the units

Identify the units between which centralization and autonomy are to be measured. Naturally, a unit may be represented by an individual, but the study is between units not between individuals—although the edges may be blurred, a distinction is being made between the autonomy of a unit and the participation of individuals. The choice of unit can bias the study and a decision has to be made as to whether a particular relationship or an overall measure is the aim. The distinction is particularly marked in non-commercial organizations.

Identify the issues

Normally, questions are asked about specific decisions, whether the locus or the influence approach is adopted. The choice of the type of decision, or decision-making area, or other indicators will bring out the multi-dimensional nature of the subject and allow more precise relationships with other variables to be established. The assertion that some functions, for example, are more centralized does not invalidate the overall comparison, since the aim is to compare organizations, and to compare individual functions against one another is not comparing like with like.

Examine specific relationships

Attempts to produce an overall measure of centralization for an organization produce a number of problems, including the following: standardized questioning is not always appropriate over more than one level; different levels may have different degrees of autonomy; the exercise of authority may not follow the official rules. It would seem, therefore, more satisfactory to measure specific relationships and to infer from the results a measure for the whole organization. This does not guarantee total accuracy, but it does produce a more reliable reflection of the facts than is otherwise obtainable and a result that is sufficiently accurate to test generalizations and to diagnose organizational problems in most circumstances. Frequently, indeed, the individual relationships will be compatible, *for purposes of comparison*, but problems arise when they are contradictory. In this case a compromise measure is needed.

Identify the exercise of authority in the decision-making

This includes the share normally exercised by a given unit. The identification requires questions about where the decision was last taken and what were the shares of the different participants. The compromise on this issue is between an unrealistic search for a decision point and the more vague examination of influence, which is more suitable to a study of individual participation. The identification must, however, do justice to the element of bargaining in the system, and needs itself to be carried through a number of stages.

To prepare a list of decisions. Like the basis of comparison, this will be confirmed or modified by a number of experts (a scheme used for international studies is described in Chapter 11). At various stages during the research the decisions will be modified by using factoral analysis and other techniques. The original selection will be partly determined by the nature of the comparisons to be made and this statement introduces another compromise—between the decisions specific to an order or even a sub-order of organizations. On principle the more specific the questions the more convincing the results. Decisions, for instance, which attempt to compare a commercial organization with a charity may have to be so general that they omit the main indicators of centralization. Comparisons between different companies in the same industry, or different parts of the same company, can include decisions that are more specific. A possible means of enabling the broader questions to be asked is by introducing one or two decisions which can be considered as touchstones—decisions which are known on other grounds to be satisfactory indicators of centralization in particular organizations. These can vary from organization to organization. The objections to this are that like is not being compared with like and that the introduction of weightings is difficult under the circumstances. Nevertheless, the results may be sufficiently illuminating to compensate for the reduced accuracy.

Feed in data. The results of the questioning are filtered by the investigator and then prepared for the further analysis suggested above, not forgetting that bias can be introduced by the way the filtering is conducted.

Reduce issues and compute weightings. The analysis will reduce and group the number of decisions being examined and suggest weightings for each to be used in later analysis.

Feed in fresh or revised data.

Compute a measure of centralization, for the relationships under examination.

Reconsider the personal position of the investigator

Appraisal of the data is required in as objective a manner as possible without pretending either that straightforward scoring can be accomplished or that all bias can be eliminated. The replication and reworking of data in some studies has already shown some of the ways in which results can be distorted and no scheme is entitled to profess to reduce the distortions without referring to the personal skills and attitudes of the investigator. Naturally, this statement does not overlook the statistical apparatus along with the checks and cross-referencing in the system which will eliminate personal prejudices and misreading of the situation as far as possible. All of this has to be achieved at the same time as a relationship is established with the organization. There is almost certain to be a bias in the relationship. At one extreme the researcher may wish to aid the institution under investigation to greater success and at the other its abolition may be sought; the attitude is unlikely, however, to be as simple as either of those and the very lack of simplicity may take the elimination of bias harder.

Employ a variety of approaches

Since every approach has both theoretical and practical difficulties, the ability to match one against another is an asset in producing a convincing measurement. The methods that can be used include:

(a) the identification of significant issues and the framing of a measure based on the unit of the organization whose management last took (or had the highest share in) a decision on each issue;

(b) the identification of actions or arrangements held to be suitable proxies for centralization or autonomy in the organizations being observed;

(c) studying the contents of communications between units;

(d) collecting the perceptions of head office staff;

(e) collecting the perceptions of unit staff;

(f) the judgement of the investigator.

The object of the exercise is to place the relationship along a scale ranging from centralization to decentralization which can produce a standard of comparison for the purpose of reviewing generalizations about the consequences of the degree of centralization or the reverse. Some of the theoretical statements that can be tested by such a measurement are examined in the next chapter.

10   *Raw Materials for a Theory*

'What may be called the classic businessman's view is to be so impressed with the complexity of coordination that great stress is placed on the need for central control.'[1] To this the 'classic' answer can be presented in another quotation:'centralization or decentralization is a simple question of proportion, it is a matter of finding the optimum degree for a particular concern.' The present study has set out to demonstrate that there are other options for dealing with the problems of coordination and that the questions raised are not simple. Indeed, no answers are valid that do not face adequately the contradictions and paradoxes inherent in the subject. Decentralization, for instance, has been blamed for such occurrences as corporate disaster and national anarchy. So has centralization. The contradiction does not make the subject irrelevant, but points towards a more detailed analysis of the forces and factors which increase or reduce the autonomy of the various units and sub-units within an organization. These forces relate to the purposes of the organization, the culture in which it is set and the criteria by which its success or failure is judged. Some are impersonal, like the possession of special knowledge or the threat of war or disaster; others are personal like motivation. As a general rule (there are exceptions) the impersonal forces indicate centralization and the personal ones indicate autonomy. Any theoretical statement has to take account of this conflict. For present purposes the theory needs to be of the middle range—not attempting to cover a major area of knowledge, nor issues that are just mundane, but providing a scheme or model for interpreting relevant phenomena.

The first step towards understanding how the pressures operate has been to focus on the meaning of centralization and autonomy and their relationship to other characteristics like authority and alienation. In different states of society (from the rural to the industrial) and in institutions designed for religious, political, commercial, charitable and other purposes, there are problems of relating the units to the centre. The problem exists as soon as the organization begins to grow. Two people experience difficulties in communication, but the difficulties increase by geometrical progression as more participants are added. This occurs in all types of organization, whatever the purpose, although the issues which collect around the centralization and autonomy contrast vary with the type.

The unravelling of the elements that give meaning to the subject has demonstrated a number of ambiguities which must influence any theoretical statement. One is the difficulty of specifying the unit of decentralization. The lack of specification calls in question generalizations about the benefits of autonomy that are sometimes made, while each specification produces its own characteristic consequences. For instance, a reshuffle of responsibilities at the top of a company, perhaps only making official a degree of delegation that already existed informally, does not automatically create a decentralized organization; on the contrary, a consequence may be less autonomy for units at a lower level. Decentralization means a significant sharing of authority with units away from the centre, a point which comes out clearly in part II when attention is concentrated on the foreign subsidiaries of international companies. Another ambiguity concerns the nature of the decentralizing exercise. If it is considered as a technique for ensuring greater loyalty and effectiveness among subordinates (instrumental decentralization), then it is of a different order from the expressive decentralization in its own right. Yet another source of ambiguity lies in the relationship of the individual to the organization, the equating of the leaders with the units which they lead. To observe that personality is only one of the influences is not to belittle its importance but to indicate how frequently this influence is exaggerated. The ambiguity is both reflected and sustained by the use of biological analogies; but even for the leader, let alone the followers, the interests of the individual will often conflict with those of the unit he or she controls. The argument for or against autonomy may hinge on the organization's power of survival; whereas the individual may be more interested in his ability to stay or to leave even if the organization does survive.[2]

Other propositions relevant to the understanding of centralization and autonomy include the degree of universality and the relationship between power and authority. The breadth of application of any of the propositions is a subject which will be latent, retained as it were, throughout this chapter. An assumption is being made that, as the various contributions to a theory are assembled, the more the particular and contingent factors become evident. Decentralization in a military unit, for example, has been seen to be related to training, confidence, communications and attitudes as well as the necessities of war to which the whole effort is supposed to be directed. Take out any of those items and even a limited decentralization can lead to disaster. This is why there can never be a straightforward connection between decentralization and effectiveness; there are too many variables. However, a valid prediction (a 'what if?' kind of forecast) can be made once the variables have been recognized.

The connection between centralization and authority is more straightforward, so long as the distinction between the expressive and the instrumental is kept in view. Power makes possible the use of authority, but its exercise is often in abeyance, latent. The most convincing measure of centralization is the one that assesses the exercise of authority. Such a measure also has the advantage of indicating answers to most of the questions a study might be set up to answer—questions about the relationship between the degree of autonomy and the effective working of the organization. A scheme of the relationship of power, authority and centralization has been sketched (in Figure 4.2). The scheme asserts that a strong power base will ultimately produce a centralized organization unless conscious efforts are made in a contrary direction, or there are effective countervailing forces, and that the reverse will occur where the power base is weak. A strong base is derived from a compliance structure in which the elements match—a business firm, for instance, is able to use convincing economic motives to achieve its objectives—and authority is skilfully applied. However, normative influences are more usual among higher participants in any organization. The contrasts come among the lower participants, and that is one of the weaknesses encountered in using compliance theory: the higher and lower echelons are not sufficiently distinct. The problem, it will be seen, becomes acute in considering multinational companies where a calculative language appears to mask a normative reality. A consequence of the ambiguous influence of power is that the centralized or decentralized characteristics may derive from strengths or weaknesses rather than the requirements of the institution. The characteristics may also derive from the pressures, for results or for survival, under which the organization finds itself. High pressure will produce a drift towards centralization and vice versa, while, in such circumstances, great care may be required to reverse the drift.

A most evident feature of the words 'centralization' and 'autonomy' is that they describe the opposite poles in an unstable relationship. They are employed to record change with the use of statements like: 'we used to be highly centralized' or 'we are aiming towards greater centralization'. A dramatic example of such use was contained in a newspaper paragraph about a change of chief executive. Under the heading 'Imps sack Chief as profits slide' the report stated of the new appointee: 'His mandate is to reverse [his predecessor's] policy of decentralized management. "The time has come . . . to change the balance towards a 'hands-on' style of management from the centre." '[3] The temptation is to see the process of change as a series of freakish reactions to immediate situations like a profit decline, leading to a cyclical reaction in which either centralization or the reverse are blamed for the current problems. The following pages summarize the reason for thinking that there is more than just chance, or the desire for a periodical shake-up of the organization, in the cyclical process.

10.1   THE FORCES FOR CHANGE

Human society can presumably be traced to a condition in which the word 'decentralization' is meaningless—the cave dweller supporting his little tribe in an isolated cave. Similarly, the business company develops from the one-man concern in which delegation is only part of a dream. Autonomy within the organization becomes a live issue as a result of two developments. The first is growth, the addition of members; when the organization begins to break down into identifiable units centralization becomes an issue. The other development derived from growth is the emergence of rival centres of power. In some primitive societies there was the ambiguous relationship between the chief and the holy man, a relationship which dominated the history of the Middle Ages in the form of a struggle between Church and State, the pope and the emperor. A third force already existed, the barons, to be replaced by the landed gentry of the British or the professional classes of the French Revolution and ultimately the representative parties of the modern democracy. The historical message was that opportunity existed to widen the scope of an organization, but that this opportunity would be frustrated if some devolution was not practised. Indeed, primitive societies demonstrated that tribes wandering over large areas and with growing numbers can exist with some form of cohesion but without any apparent central authority. The beginnings of urbanization were accompanied by technological changes, water supply and written records for instance, which made central control possible. In the progress of urbanization other factors produced contrary pressures; for instance, the reduction in role relationships (citizens live different aspects of their lives in different groups), and the centralizing consequences of the alienation that follow.

Through the contradictory pressures and the technical changes the bureaucratic organization gradually emerged.[4] The subdivision of the organization by function or any other method produces units which possess a rationale of their own and which can be provided with a degree of independence if they are, for instance, departments of state, or complete independence if they provide a service to business. The processes of accretion or hiving-off are evidence of the potential for centralization or autonomy. If a unit can be hived off, it can be decentralized. Once the potential is actualized the countervailing forces come into operation. Disaster has been mentioned as a product of decentralization. In government this means a drift to anarchy and lawlessness; in business, bankruptcy. But the reverse does not thereby become a fact. If it is true that 'decentralization was an important reason for the collapse of this company', it does not therefore follow that 'if this company had been centralized, it would have avoided liquidation'. Decentralization enabled a dangerous lack of resources, such as expertise, to become fatal. The purpose of these paragraphs is to chart the give and take of forces, among which the fear of disaster is one.

Table 10.1 shows a selection from the complex pressures already identified and how they can be expected to operate. The pressures are presented in opposites to demonstrate the ways in which the same factor can have opposite consequences. A clearer idea of what is being demanded of the relationship can, thus, be expected to help the understanding and control of the cycle. The table summarizes the following subjects.

Knowledge, which includes expertise and ability, is an issue in almost every type of organization considered. The ultimate need to safeguard the vital truths in religion has been noted, and the extent to which the ability to do this is enshrined in a central body or a local community. In government and in business, the knowledge includes any special expertise only available at the centre as well as the ability to see the total picture. The claim that the whole is greater than the sum of the parts is a centralizing argument that sometimes needs to be treated with scepticism, but it will be seen to have a special relevance in the discussion on the international firm. What is not in doubt is that growing

Table 10.1 The forces for and against centralization

Factors promoting or enabling centralization	Factors promoting or enabling decentralization
The possession of scarce knowledge, expertise or ability, including the ability to see the whole picture. The threat of disaster.	Holding of specialized knowledge in the units.
The need to concentrate on the benefit of the whole when that is greater than the sum of the parts.	Inability of the centre to make decisions fast enough or of sufficient applicability to the units.
The pressure for short-term results (sometimes produced by control systems) (see 4.3).	The ability to leave the units to manage themselves (sometimes produced by the control system).
Complexity of group linkages making decentralization difficult.	Single links make decentralization more likely; *but* produce alienation which reverses the trend.
Acceptability of large-scale organization.	Lack of acceptability of large-scale organization.
Acceptability of authoritarian system.	Acceptability of democratic system.
Organizations with routine work.	Need for flexibility.
Lack of access to the top.	Access to the top.
Growth to middle size.	Growth to large size.
	Legal person.
Care of the organization which leads to entrusting specialists at head office with the duty of a continuous review. Normally their expertise is a centralizing force, but can be used in the reverse direction.	A *laissez-faire* attitude to organization *or* the establishment of a viable unit which has the resources to run its own affairs.
Ambiguity of purpose within organization.	Ambiguity of environment.
Lack of confidence.	Framework of confidence and trust.
Accounting techniques limit autonomy.	Accounting techniques make autonomy possible.

organizations can expect to have to decide frequently about the allocation of expertise between the units, and that the choices made will affect the general decision-making—the next issue.

Decision-making is central to this subject, and its rational allocation in a structured organization often points to decentralization, but there are many countervailing pressures like the fear of disaster. Once the fear turns into a threat, there is an almost irresistible pressure to centralization. On the other hand, complaints about slowness and irrelevance—heard in almost any organization that does have a head office or centre on which subordinate units are dependent—are among the most common arguments for delegation. In a nation such complaints can lead to violence, in cases where there is a national minority, or revolutionary party active, and in business damaging losses can be sustained where subordinate units cannot react to competitors quickly enough. Decentralization reduces the risk of slow decision-making, while centralization reduces other risks up to that of disaster. In organizations where the whole is seen to have the power of achieving more than the sum of the parts the pressures for centralization will be stronger than in those where interrelationships do not exist. Synergy, to use the word of the corporate planners, is a centralizing factor.

Uncertainty avoidance has been noted as a centralizing influence. Powerful pressure to produce greater clarity in the objectives, policies and coordinating arrangements leads to centralization.

This *relationship* of the whole to the parts determines the degree of centralization where a global coordination of resources makes sense, and where the centre can use economies of scale. The countervailing argument is that of motivation in the sub-units. Greater independence and greater responsibility usually produce more initiative and improved performance. In business, tensions arise through the conflict between global coordination and local initiative, but there are other organizations where the usual influences are reversed. One such is the political party where national figures find themselves in the throes of a reselection process in their constituencies. Failure to cultivate the grassroots may render the national position untenable. On the other hand, charities, whose work is designed solely for the local and individual benefit like the Royal National Lifeboat Institution or the National Society for the Prevention of Cruelty to Children, sometimes become strongly centralized. In whatever way the requirements of the centre and the units are reconciled, there is a bargaining process through which the respective positions are eventually determined.

The *control* system was discussed in Chapter 5 where the ability to produce both a centralized and a decentralized system was identified. This subject will be further examined in later chapters; here it is sufficient to emphasize that one intention was to make a restricted delegation possible. The threat of disaster is reduced where the possibility is being monitored, but the effect is often to destroy the intended delegation. The emphasis on short-term results, produced by regular reporting, does not make for local decision-making.

Group linkages have been seen to make decentralization possible. One writer[5] contrasts the numerous and complex links between the various members of a family, including affection, social, support, dependence, education, and the much simpler connections between members of a larger and more complicated organization for employment or leisure. In the latter case there may be only one link, like the earning of a living or the support of a cause. The single link admits of decentralization more easily, whatever the nature of the organization, than the multiple links, a point already noted in connection with urbanization.

The *acceptability of the large-scale organization* is another factor influencing outlooks that help to determine the degree of centralization; this will be a theme of the final chapter.

The *acceptability of authoritarian or democratic systems* also conditions the relevant choice. Not that there is an automatic link between an authoritarian system and centralization; a culture in which such a system is the norm and the democratic approach largely unacceptable is likely also to produce centralized institutions. The reverse is also correct—democratic institutions favour autonomy—but not under all circumstances. In this connection it has been pointed out that authoritarian institutions provide a low repertoire of options in establishing a structure or in responding to the environment.[6] This leads to a constraint on management where flexibility is required, and the *need for flexibility* can be regarded as a pressure towards autonomy.

The *nature of the tasks* the organization has to fulfil has been found to influence the degree of centralization in some studies. If the tasks are mainly of a routine nature, there is little to decentralize and little reason for decentralizing. Contrary pressures, like the need for motivation, are unlikely to be powerful under these circumstances.[7] The hypothesis that the more routine the purposes to be fulfilled, the more centralized the organization, is well supported.

Access to the top is a more personal issue which is important in all organizations, but especially in large global institutions like international companies. Where extra tiers of management are added which reduce access, the result is usually seen to be centralizing.

The influence of *growth* has been found to be more complicated. One study of 257 state, county and city institutions in the United States found that decentralization is higher in the smallest and largest organizations and lower in the middle-sized. This finding contradicts the present author's observations on the effects of growth (see Chapter 19, Figure 19.1), but it aids understanding of the cyclical trends when an organization is growing. Local authority units react differently to growth, as other studies have shown, but the relationship with centralization remains.

The *legal* position is a factor that should not be overemphasized, but cannot be ignored. Where a unit is a legal person, as in a subsidiary of a company, there must be some delegation to ensure that the law is satisfied. Where specific responsibilities, like safety or health, are allocated to named officers in the company, there needs to be sufficient freedom to allow the office-holders to discharge their obligations. In other respects the managerial position may vary considerably from the legal; the corporate structure is determined for commercial purposes while the constitution and the presentation of the accounts have to fit company and taxation laws. The distinction between the legal and the operating systems will be underlined when examining international companies.

Care of the organization is a more elusive category which has been seen to generate centralization. Where the company or political institution, for instance, is led by someone who has a special interest in promoting an effective organization, or where experts in the subject are employed, there is usually a pressure to centralization. The creation of satisfactory arrangements and conditions at head office leads to parallel changes in the units. The opposite is probable where there is a *laissez-faire* approach to organization and each department is left to its own devices. Occasionally, care of the organization may work the other way, where the central authorities are convinced that autonomy is right or where a viable unit with the resources to manage its own affairs is seen to exist.

Ambiguity of purpose within the organization has been identified as a pressure to centralization, while uncertainty in the environment points in the opposite direction. Delegation is favoured when the unit finds itself in a fast changing situation, like a church undergoing persecution or a business faced with particular difficulties of adapting a product to local needs. On the other hand the danger of subordinate units going their own way and breaking up the organization is greatly increased where the purposes are unclear, where, to quote an executive of a thrusting but opportunistic company, 'policies change every night'. Decentralization makes such opportunism hard to tolerate; it can also make the seizing of opportunities in a changing environment and within a strong central control more likely. 'The more heterogeneous, dynamic and uncertain the environment is, the more a decentralized organization structure is favoured.'[8]

Confidence and, with it, an ability to guarantee reactions in the subordinate unit, predispose to decentralization. The highly trained professional, the lawyer or the doctor, does not need constant supervision and probably would not tolerate it. Mistakes are corrected by disciplinary action rather than by supervision. In the civil service and in business, phrases like the 'old boy network' indicate a belief in mutual confidence, produced by a similarity of background or training, which again renders supervision unnecessary. There is no need to keep checking up because the shared instincts can usually be relied on.

Management techniques limit autonomy since they lead to uniformity; at the same time some accounting techniques can provide a framework within which the information flow is adequate to make autonomous arrangements possible. This repeats the claim made under the heading of control; but in business, in general, the emphasis on innovation and the use of advanced management methods is bound to limit autonomy. It provides a central core of knowledge whose dissemination can be restricted.

One technique that has been designed specifically to determine a desirable degree of centralization in companies rests on four questions.[9] The first asks whether the activity is one that can be programmed. An affirmative answer means that senior management can describe, virtually completely, how the activity should be carried out. In this case decentralization is inappropriate. The other three questions are about the motivation, the competence of the unit to carry out its function and whether the added effectiveness of decentralization outweighs the costs. If the answer is yes to all those questions, then decentralization is indicated. One importance of this technique is the admission that decentralization may have a cost, but that the cost may be worthwhile even in commercial terms. The *expressive* view of decentralization would go further and say that the cost has to be accepted.

This general review of the issue, that produce the fluctuations between centralization and decentralization leads to a number of insights, but first a summary of the types of relationship in which autonomy has some meaning.

10.2   A PRELIMINARY TYPOLOGY

For the purposes of this chapter, centralization and autonomy are seen as opposites in, as it were, one dimension. Where one ends, the other begins, even if the beginning and ending are not easy to identify. This limitation to one dimension will be modified in later chapters; for the present it provides a framework for a preliminary classification of the types of situation in which the ideas of centralization and autonomy are meaningful, but have different kinds of meaning. The types themselves overlap, indeed some organizations may have elements of each and it is hoped that this classification may be used to diagnose the vagaries of the exercise of authority and how it changes. Each type is identified by the dominant feature of the relationship and the list includes: personal, traditional, bureaucratic (subdivided into open and close), intermediate, isolated, dual, federal and anarchic. Table 10.2 summarizes the characteristics of each type.[10]

Table 10.2   The types of relationship within which centralization and autonomy have meaning

Type	Characteristic	Main pressure	Basis of autonomy
Personal	Domination by leader	Decentralizing	Delegation
Traditional	Acceptance of traditions	To status quo	Custom
Bureaucratic —close	Structured organization, tightly controlled	Decentralizing	Delegation
Bureaucratic —open	Structured organization, loosely controlled	Centralizing	Custom and delegation
Intermediate	Semi-structured organization	None	Custom and delegation
Professional	Framework of rules rather than organization	Decentralizing	Custom
Isolated	Structured organization tightly controlled	Status quo	Delegation
Dual	Two centres of power within organizations otherwise balancing to one of preceding types	Status quo	Bargaining
Federal	Some *ad hoc* controls	Status quo or centralizing	Agreement
Anarchic	Decentralization complete	Status quo	Acceptance

Personal

The personal organization, led by the charismatic leader or entrepreneur, is the tribe, the village, the newly formed company, the break-away sect or the so-called one-man band. As soon as the band grows large enough to be divided decisions are allocated to the sub-unit. A number of considerations will push the process forward—like the time consumed in settling issues reserved to the leader, the brake these reserved issues impose on expansion, or the difficulty of retaining able subordinates, and it is likely that the personality of the leader will inhibit delegation as will fear of the consequences of relaxing that grip. The personal nature of the authority is emphasized by the fact that succession is a problem and the relationship usually has to be rethought when the leadership is changed. As long as the organization remains personal, the basis of any autonomy is an easily revocable delegation. Personal rule starts and often remains at the centralizing end of the scale.

Traditional

The traditional organization is one in which the division of functions is established by the past, by custom and precedent. There are elements of this organization in societies both ancient and modern, in some communities and in some religious bodies. The subordinate unit regards its place in the decision-making in terms of established rights which it defends, not as delegated authority. There is a considerable pressure against change in such organizations with the consequence that the centralizing pressures do not easily operate.

Bureaucratic (close)

The bureaucratic (close) is the tightly controlled organization with a planned structure that forms the model of bureaucracy in most writings on organization theory. Typically, the power is centralized but the authority is delegated. The aim is to achieve as precise an ordering of functions as possible and to make the reactions of the officials predictable. Governmental and business organizations are frequently of this type which attempts to bring into human affairs the regularity and efficiency of the machine. Indeed Burns has called this type the mechanistic.[11] The establishing of a bureaucratic organization to replace a more personal rule will typically lead to a demand for centralization (unless the personal leader has allowed his or her authority to slip). The delegation may be limited, but it is tenaciously upheld as part of the system; in terms of an earlier discussion, it is also seen as a technique to motivate the participants, an aspect that becomes more significant in the next type. This system is criticized for rigidity but upheld for its efficiency, for providing the goals that society demands even if the methods are open to criticism.[12]

Bureaucratic (open)

The bureaucratic (open) is a more loosely controlled organization that serves the same purposes. It brings a more flexible style of management and an argument from established customs as well as from the rule book. The growth of management education is no doubt among the factors that have led to the spread of this approach in businesses. Once established, the open bureaucratic relationship is decentralized but immediately subject to all the lures to centralization described elsewhere on these pages. The autonomy thrives where efforts are made to retain it, and may be regarded either as a right or a technique. Where the efforts are relaxed, the lures to centralization will take effect.

Intermediate

The intermediate type has been called a repersonalized bureaucracy,[13] and reverses the accepted methods of designing an organization and fitting the people to the offices. In the intermediate type the organization is more flexible and is frequently redesigned to suit its participants. The emergence of matrix organizations in business results from an attempt to combine this repersonalization with a structure that matches the realities of the decision-making. Great stress on training and the acceptance of responsibility is placed in this type.

Professional

The professional is a distinctive relationship, strongly influenced towards autonomy. The professional institutes exist principally to maintain such autonomy, within a disciplined framework which insists on qualifications, competence and ethical standards, even when the professional operates within otherwise centralized organizations. There are companies in which professional units are a source of conflict upholding norms which do not coincide with the corporate aims.

Isolated

The isolated relationship is of a different order altogether and can exist inside an organization where any of the other relationships is normal. The situation arises where a subordinate unit is isolated and not subject to any instructions over a period of time. Some important decisions, including those that can cause life and death, are of necessity delegated but the unit is expected to react in accordance with well-understood instructions. The military unit on operations is a typical example of this along with the airliner, the train and other forms of transport. The delegation is temporary but complete. Increasingly, parts of organizations find themselves in a similar situation, cut off from the main activities, but without the same necessity for temporary delegation. The contractor and the sales unit are examples in business of sections which are isolated but with limited independence.

Dual

The dual relationship exists where there are two centres of power each having authority over the same participants within spheres of influence that are normally understood. This relationship contains scope for conflict, and changes come about through either force or bargaining. Examples of a second source of authority are the holy men in the primitive tribe or the trade unions in the company. In each case the rival source is dependent in the sense that it would cease to exist if the organization disappeared and acts within a limited frame of reference; but the rival authority is tenaciously defended. The identification of independent centres of power may be crucial to the diagnosis of ills in an organization.

Federal

The *federal* relationship is one where the different units have a legally or contractually guarenteed independence on stipulated topics. The best-known example is in government where the central government and the states, *Lände*, provinces or other regional units have control over issues not reserved to the centre. There are fluctuations in the degree of control when one constitutional partner or another wins a battle on a specific question. The equivalent in business is a large firm with unusually independent units or dependent subcontractors. When the fashion for businesses was to absorb suppliers of services into themselves, the trend was to direct ownership. Now hiving-off—privatization in government-owned or financed institutions like the health service—has led to more complex relations, often determined by contract. The complexity of such arrangements arises from the difficulty of attaining a number of conflicting objectives. An arrangement which reduces costs may also lower profits. There is the further difficulty of ensuring adequate information where an *ad hoc* control system is devised and where the contract can never cover all the situations that arise. The complexity makes such arrangements difficult to alter, but the most common problems give rise to pressures towards centralization; companies that operate a federal system often do so only after discovering ways of employing their own control system even where they have no ownership.

At the autonomous end of the scale from centralization to decentralization stands *anarchy*, the reverse of the personal organization, in which no exercise of authority takes place. The small community and organizations with experimental decision-making procedures to allow all participants to contribute are examples. Just as the personal organization is gradually led to delegate through growth, so expansion for the totally decentralized society means either hiving-off into new and independent units, a common procedure for both established Tolstoyan-style communities and modern cooperatives, or some compromise of principles. There still remain many interesting organizations at or near the end of the scale.

The ability of the various forms of relationship to coexist in the same institution derives partly from the fact that some are complementary to others. For instance, the isolated is virtually never the only form of relationship within a company. There are also occasions when an organization is in transition, for instance from a personal rule to a bureaucratic structure. The fact of coexistence itself produces stresses and is one of the factors which results in apparently aimless changes. Identification is not made easier by the fact that the various types shade into one another, and the same situations can easily be interpreted differently. Officials in a close bureaucracy, for instance, claim that the tight controls are maintained because of the difficulty of producing viable units which can cope with autonomy. With the more open systems, on the other hand, acceptance of responsibility may be seen to give rise to comments like 'the will to make it work'. Such phrases are heard as organizations become more complex.

The process of development does not start with the personal and end with the federated; organizations may change backwards and forwards over time as well as containing mixed relationships; but it would appear that historically most institutions would fit the personal, traditional or close bureaucratic types, and that nowadays there are moves towards the flexible arrangements of the open bureaucratic, intermediate and federal as well as a special form of the isolated in which there is great independence within narrow constraints. There are some who would argue, however, that the more flexible organizations have always existed and that to deny this is only to look at the formal, official, aspect, ignoring what really happens in spite of constitutions, manuals, orders and regulations. This objection is met by repeating that there are mixed arrangements and that the unofficial working of an organization can be different from, even contradictory to, the official. This must be so, otherwise the many organizations (including some companies and churches), in which the rules gather dust in unopened files, would be inexplicable. If the official organization is close bureaucratic, but in practice it resembles the intermediate, this confirms the need for observation as part of the diagnosis. The nine types remain both comprehensive and explanatory, a basis for a fresh look at the problems of measurement.

10.3 AUTHORITY AND MEASUREMENT

A number of considerations required for measuring centralization were listed in the last chapter (see Table 9.1) in a how-to-do-it context. Some of these considerations are restated here to integrate them with a theoretical statement of the subject and to lead into the discussion in part II.

The unit whose relationship is to be measured
Confusion has been caused by assuming that an organization is decentralized; it is a number of specific relationships within the organization that are subject to greater or less authority and the position can be reversed with sub-units. An organization is decentralized only to the extent that the sum of the relationships of its units (and sub-units) are more decentralized than that in the standard of comparison. References to decentralized organizations in this work normally refer to a typical relationship within the organization.

The characteristic to be measured
The difficulties of this have been discussed at length; the conclusion so far is that the degree of authority is most accurately represented by trying to fix a locus of decision-making. Some cogent objections to this procedure are met by allowing fractions in the measurement. The underlying factors rest on judgement and common sense, but this does not invalidate the use of sophisticated scaling and regression techniques to identify, integrate and test the variables. This view has been reinforced by the discussion on the relationship between power, authority and centralization.

The variables to be used and how they are defined
Straight answers to questions about who is entitled to take a particular decision are too simplistic. A composite measure needs to be assembled from questions that seek to find out where the decision had been taken and what were the constraints. The informal as well as the official procedures need to be taken into account.

The standard of comparison
A measure of centralization that claims to be absolute is meaningless; the questions to be answered usually concern the effects of more or less centralization. There are three possible standards of comparison, each of which has its particular difficulties in practice. Two provide comparisons with the same organization, firstly with other relationships within it and secondly with its past. The third provides comparisons with other organizations where there are comparable relationships.

Identify the optimum measure, if it exists
The earlier sections of this chapter have emphasized a number of points, especially the kind of situations where either centralization or autonomy are to be preferred and the relationships for which autonomy is a meaningful idea. From this a relevant or desirable degree of centralization may be deduced against which any measurement is compared.

These five points together provide a scheme within which some form of measurement can be devised to provide answers to questions on the subject. The result may be compared to a thermometer registering fluctuations between boiling and freezing. Between the extremes of centralized decisions which become less and less related to reality, and autonomous decisions that ultimately destroy the organization, there is scope for endless fluctuation. These pages contain a sustained attempt to demonstrate that the fluctuations are not also aimless, that they can be tracked and predicted within identifiable limits. Figure 10.1 illustrates those limits within which the pressures have been seen to

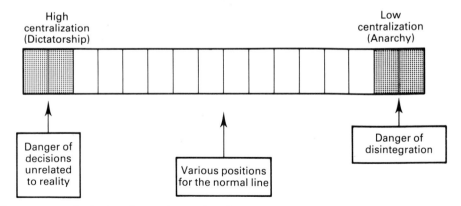

Figure 10.1   The limits of centralization and autonomy

operate. For any particular organization the contrast between the actual and the desirable positions along the line can be plotted along with changes over time—the situation is seldom static. The desirable position will be determined in the light of the issues summarized in this chapter.

A hypothesis that stems from detailed observations is that there is some *normal line*, some point along the scale to which a particular organization will attempt to return. This is a similar idea to that of the *compliance structure*,[14] where each type of organization is seen to have a distinctive relationship between the kind of power and the method of obtaining compliance, and there is a pressure to revert to that relationship. The normal line will be fixed by the way the factors outlined in Figure 10.2 operate in a particular instance. No doubt a protestant church will have a normal line near to the decentralized end, as will a professional organization. In a manufacturing company the normal line will be towards the centralized end. If the normal line has been correctly identified, then an explanation for the fluctuations between centralization and autonomy has been found—as one force becomes sufficiently powerful to push the organization's balance towards one extreme or the other, powerful pressures move in to restore the *normal* position. This is a refinement on a hypothesis already proposed and Figure 10.2 presents some of the forces that operate along the spectrum and the movement of the normal line as a consequence of changes in organization style. This shows only major changes simplified for illustration in diagrammatic form.

Part (i) of the diagram shows first a cycle of changes which move the normal line itself—a kind of macro-process within which other more limited cycles are constantly operating—and secondly where the normal line is fixed as a result of the changes. Part (ii) shows another such cycle, this time the wider influence is organization need rather than organization type. The smaller cycles around each fresh positioning of the normal line are influenced by all the factors listed in Table 10.1 and already discussed. A different kind of spectrum will be designed for the various types of relationship and again the reasons for upheavals can be identified. Figure 10.2 also illustrates that the normal line is not regarded as some middle way in the centre of the spectrum, a kind of classical happy mean. It is to be regarded as the appropriate balance of forces for a particular organization—one the organization will seek, and whose identification can break the cycle of upheavals.

10.4   FINALE TO PART I

This chapter has assembled some of the issues to emerge from the rest of part I that will be re-examined in part II in the light of their relevance to the international company. In particular, the pressures and counter-pressures for and against autonomy have been listed and the concept of the normal line has been identified. Various kinds of autonomy have also been explained to show that a straightforward distinction between centralization and decentralization cannot be applied to all circumstances. Other classifications are possible, including one that concentrates on the limitations to autonomy. These have

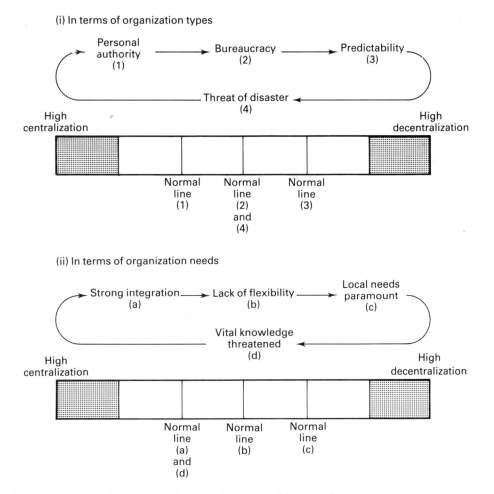

Figure 10.2 The forces towards centralization and decentralization

been seen to include special or sacred knowledge, the threat of disaster, the time scale, some general policies or principles, as well as a number of predetermined (and perhaps agreed) constraints.

The word 'flexibility' has been used frequently and signals one of the many paradoxes inherent in the subject. Where quick action is required at the centre, the need for flexibility suggests centralization, but the reverse is true when the units have to be able to respond fast to changing or competitive conditions. In company organizations, the intention to build-in flexibility is often frustrated because an unwritten constitution designed not to hamper change allows the emergence of procedures which can be hard to alter, whereas a set of written regulations or a manual of operating procedures normally includes provision for amendment.

A paradox that has already been considered, but that is especially relevant to the international firm, is that decentralization is sometimes considered to be part of the structure and sometimes a technique. This theme will be developed in connection with the various aspects of management to which centralization is relevant, like the handling of communications. No doubt there are often mixed motives, and the results will reflect other factors as well, but the general idea of 'care of the organization' is relevant whatever the attitude. This care emanates from a central function, but includes attempts to mitigate the effects of centralization.

A theory of the fluctuations between centralization and autonomy, then, starts from a statement of relationship whose complexity and ambiguity leads to misapprehensions which can be wasteful of an organization's resources. The ambiguity arises from the contradictory pressures which have been identified in general and which prevent the organization being deflected too far from its goals, but at the same time produce a bewildering series of changes; these changes are explained by identifying the pressures which pull in opposite directions and whose force can then be understood and anticipated or controlled.

Part II
The International Firm

The relevance of centralization and autonomy to a particular kind of organization, the business enterprise that operates affiliates across national frontiers, is examined in this part. The multinational firm (the phrase is used of any company with directly managed investments in more than one country) has particular problems of relationships across political, legal, fiscal, geographical, cultural and many other kinds of barrier. The problems are examined with a view to determining the extent to which the various attempts at their resolution influence broader statements on the subject of centralization and autonomy.

11 Studies of the International Firm

The focus of attention now turns to the international firm. The phrase includes all enterprises which operate outside their own country, by whatever means, while those which employ direct investment are called multinational firms. Most of the present discussion is about this type of company, but the question of organization boundaries is itself an important theme, and to limit the discussion to foreign investment would be to ignore that theme.[1] The international firm is here regarded as a kind of laboratory in which the issues examined in Part I are reviewed in a number of working organizations, and the implications of this review are considered. The starting point is a survey of some concerns of current literature on the subject and an introduction to the sustained series whose results are presented in the following chapters. The principal subject is the decision-making system, and how it works across frontiers and across products. The combination of long lines of communication with the frequent need for rapid action epitomizes the complexity of the organization.

11.1 THE SUBJECT

The study of decentralization across frontiers is of a one-to-one relationship—that between a controlling, and usually owning, unit in the home country and a closely related unit abroad. This must appear to be a simpler undertaking than the examination of the many links in the hierarchy considered in an earlier chapter. The one-to-one relationship, however, turns out to be less simple than anticipated; it contains a number of lines of authority with varying emphases and interpretations. The standpoint of executives influences their view of the system, while individual perceptions of centralization are shown to be unreliable in a number of ways, of which one is that managers at head office tend to think that any delegation from the top of the company is a process of decentralization. In the eyes of the foreign subsidiary, however, decentralization to a product division in the home country looks like centralization, and any lengthening of the lines of communication between those who run the subsidiary and those at the top of the company is likely so to appear, even where the opposite is genuinely intended (see Chapter 15). It is also apparent that a process of decentralization could be effectively frustrated by the actions of subordinate managers in individual functions. These latter sometimes go to great lengths to ensure that the techniques they have evolved for their own functions are used worldwide. Hence, a redefinition of the concept is needed in order to conduct a viable study of centralization internationally. The legal relationships between the parent and the subsidiary are usually clear, both as defined by the laws of the respective countries, and by the regulations of the companies themselves. The problem is to penetrate the complicated network of coalitions and sub-coalitions which make up the organization and whose interrelationships determine how it actually works.[2]

In spite of these complications it remains that the international aspect is easier to handle in a research context than others, for the researcher is not investigating the delegation process through a series of levels but the straight sharing of responsibility across frontiers between one company and another, when the latter is owned by the former—the one-to-one situation already described. This should simplify the issues, but other factors intervene to produce difficulties. These factors include sub-coalitions which stretch across national frontiers, such as functional interest groups like finance or new product development. Other factors range from the relatively simple to some highly elusive theoretical and conceptual issues. Among the simpler is the advice that companies are given by their financial experts not to send direct instructions to their foreign subsidiaries. Such instructions can have legal, and in particular tax, implications. Hence, head office is able to argue that the company must be regarded as decentralized because no instructions are sent abroad. This situation does not correspond with reality either in the eyes of head office or of the foreign subsidiaries; a code is developed, which is well known inside the firm, through which instructions are sent. The researcher has to become familiar with the code used in any company which he or she is reviewing. Another subject where the accepted wisdom contradicts itself concerns the speed of decision-taking. On the one hand it is believed that a decentralized system is too slow when urgent decisions have to be taken at the centre; on the other, it is alleged that centralization produces blockages in head office which slow down the decision-making when the subsidiary has to seek permission to respond urgently to an opportunity or a problem.

What is clear and agreed on all sides is that the relationship between the head office management of the international company and the management of the foreign affiliate is both puzzling and important, and that this will remain the case in spite of growing internationalism and the impatience of business people with national constraints. It is this relationship that the studies detailed here set out to explore. However loosely the phenomenon may have been discussed, no one can deny its significance both in theory and in practice or its many implications for understanding the behaviour of complex organizations and the political and commercial consequences of this behaviour.

11.2   OVERVIEW

International studies of the subject are not usually concerned with the relationship of the company to the subsidiary alone. With some exceptions, they are to be found in writings whose main themes are organization or strategy or some other aspect of international management, and where the need is to indicate only an approximate degree of centralization and the implications are not investigated in any depth. Nevertheless, a number of generalizations are made which deserve comment.

The following paragraphs identify the main themes and discuss the assertions. The writers to whom reference is made are using different words and various definitions, but they all have some interest in centralization and the autonomy of the subsidiary.

Measurement

The question of measurement is not considered at all by some authorities. There is an assumption, not always stated, that the degree of centralization can be identified by some process of observation. Among those who do accept an obligation to quantify there are a number of approaches. One is the *search for an objective measurement*. This means the use of some readily calculated factor which is held to be a proxy for centralization or at least related to it in some inescapable fashion. In an early work, Dunning[3] attempted to relate the profitability of United States owned companies in Britain to the degree of head office influence on the 'decision-taking and control'. The profitability of subsidiaries in the sample was linked to five indices:
(a)   the proportion of the firm's equity capital owned by the parent company;
(b)   the proportion of the non United States executives that received training in the home country;
(c)   the nationality of the directors;
(d)   the extent to which the management techniques are based on current American practices;
(e)   the extent to which the parent company retains control of the decision-making.
Since the author is examining profitability, he naturally does not enlarge on the model of authority implicit in the indices. Numbers (a) to (c) may be called pure objective indices in that the figures can be obtained without the use of a participant's perception, although this does not rule out ambiguities. Profitability is notoriously difficult to define convincingly in a sub-unit, while even nationality carries question marks. What is the score, for example, if a director has dual nationality or if he has lived in a country most of his life without acquiring citizenship? Such situations are not uncommon among international executives.

The query with these three indicators is that they show that one particular decision has been taken centrally without thereby telling us anything about other decisions. A low proportion of equity, for instance, can be accompanied by high centralization. There is evidence of firms that have developed a facility for central decision-making even where they own only a small proportion of the equity in their foreign affiliates, or even none at all. There is also evidence that various staffing arrangements can accompany both centralization and decentralization. Some senior executives are moved from one foreign subsidiary to another throughout their careers because of their special competence, and the presence of expatriates at the top can, under such circumstances, ensure greater autonomy for the subsidiary.[4] The trusted manager from head office who knows his or her way around the company is proof against interference, while local nationals appointed because of a legal obligation may not be considered capable of managing autonomously. In a regional centre, it has been said, the presence of expatriates from the home country means decentralization to the local subsidiary. The reverse is signalled by the appointment of staff from the region.

The other two indices, (d) on the use of head office techniques and (e) on parent company control of decision-making, are a mixture of objectivity and observation. The transfer of management techniques may arise in a number of ways, including the decision of the subsidiary to buy them either by internal appointment or through outside consultants, and the extent to which authority is reserved to the parent company is a matter of perception. This index is a much broader one and illustrates the trade-off between the objective indicator with its limited reference and the subjective which may reflect more accurately the state of the company. The fifth, the parent company control of decision-making, is the principal index used on these pages, but the scope for objective determination will be seen to be limited. The fact that this last is preferred here and that all five were put forward tentatively in the first place should not be taken as dismissing lightly the search for objective indicators; and the word 'indicator' is more appropriate than 'index' in a situation where a convincing statement about the degree of centralization in a particular company can be assembled by means of a number of pieces of evidence rather than one consistent measure. Relevant pieces of evidence are scattered through the following chapters and include exact adherence to head office patterns of organization and management by the subsidiary as well as the adoption of internationally integrated policies. One objective measure that could be used is the frequency of submitting budgets. One reason why this is not frequently employed is that most of the larger American companies, the usual subjects of research, insist on a monthly presentation. The result is that, for them, this indicator does not distinguish between centralization and autonomy. In one study that does show the frequency of budget submissions, the results demonstrate that the Australian subsidiaries of British companies are decentralized. These vary by industry sector but half (26 out of 52) submitted annually, while only 4 (7.7 per cent) submitted monthly.[5] The same study refers to another indicator which is considered later in this book—the person to whom reports are sent. The proposition is that the more decentralized the subsidiary, the higher the level of head office executives to whom reports are addressed.

This study also selects a number of 'key areas' and investigates the head office and the subsidiary view of 'decision' responsibility for these areas. The results are set out in Table 11.1. In this table, the variables may appear eccentric and some vague ('marketing'), although the selection is partly justified by the relatively small companies being considered. On the basis of these variables, two conclusions stand out. One is that a sample of companies that are decentralized by any standard has been identified, and the other is that there are considerable differences between head office views on where decisions are taken and those of the subsidiary. Both points will be picked up later and, with regard to the former, the fact that this was a sample of new investors tends to confirm the view that the degree of centralization increases as the subsidiary grows older.

Staffing and ownership are also used by Robinson[6] as indicators of centralization. Another objective indicator, he suggests, is 'the level of external political pressure to relinquish control'. The evidence shown below, in Chapter 13, demonstrates that such pressure can have the reverse of the intended effect. At the least it proves highly resistible, and may induce stricter regulations within the company. Other objective measures are covered by Robinson's definition of centralization. They include the number of organizational levels above the foreign subsidiary as well as the use of profit centres, job descriptions and standardized information systems. The first will be considered again, but it does seem that a greater number of levels is perceived by the subsidiary as meaning less independence. The objective measure, in other words, is also supported subjectively. But if it is to be regarded as totally accurate no doubt a review of the allocation of expertise and responsibilities at each stage would be required, and this adulterates the objectivity. The other problem of this measure is that it cannot distinguish sufficiently between firms when the international organization is being considered. There are not likely to be more than four levels, and the majority of companies only have two. The other issues listed are not straightforwardly objective; the rules regarding profit centres, job descriptions and information systems have to be interpreted if they are to indicate centralization. In terms of the review in the last chapter, standardization is being measured rather than autonomy. The other measures proposed by Robinson are in terms of perception, and bring us to the second theme—*the measurement of centralization by questionnaires designed to elicit the locus of decision-making*.

Those who take the view that a reliable measure must be subjective, through the perceptions of the managers concerned, sometimes make considerable efforts to reduce the uncertainties that can arise. The efforts include interviewing managers at different levels and cross-checking their responses, examining the correspondence, and developing elaborate questionnaires providing a range of choices to be selected. Franko,[7] for instance, uses an index of standardization to demonstrate the influence of head office policies and practices on the foreign subsidiary. That standardization does not necessarily correlate with centralization has already been argued at some length, but there may be a confusion of words here. The questions on which the index is based are not framed so as to clarify the issues, and the managers investigated may well have answered in either sense. They were asked to mark on a seven-point scale

Table 11.1 Decision responsibility for 10 key areas in one empirical study

As seen by:	Head office				The subsidiary			
Decision rests with:	Head office	Subsidiary	Joint	Not available	Head office	Subsidiary	Joint	Not available
Prices	7.6	73.1	17.3	1.9	2.1	85.4	12.5	0
Wages	0	84.6	13.5	1.9	2.1	81.3	14.6	2.1
Advertising budgets	5.8	61.6	23.0	9.6	2.1	87.5	6.3	4.2
Management recruiting	3.9	63.5	30.8	1.9	0	72.9	20.8	6.3
Marketing	0	75	25	0	0	93.8	6.3	0
Purchasing	3.9	67.3	17.3	11.5	0	89.6	8.3	2.1
Labour training	0	78.9	9.6	11.5	2.1	89.6	6.3	2.1
Product range	19.2	34.6	46.2	0	12.5	52.1	35.4	0
Quality levels	19.2	46.2	27.0	7.7	20.8	47.9	27.1	4.2
Remittances	65.3	9.6	25.0	0	35.4	22.9	37.5	4.2

Compiled by the author from data provided in Mathew (1979) (pages 185 and 205); the sample is 52 British companies operating in Australia and all figures are percentages of that. Discrepancies are due to rounding.

ranging from 'policy totally different' to 'policy identical' a short list of marketing and financial decisions. More substantial questioning in a study which included many other subjects could hardly be expected, but it must be doubted whether the results shed much light on the question of centralization. In a later work, Franko expresses the view that relationships with the foreign subsidiaries of numerous European companies are informal but centralized. This coincides with the present author's observations, which arise from interpreting numerous statements by executives rather than by direct answers to questions. Servan-Schreiber[8] takes the view that the success of United States companies in Europe is partly due to their greater decentralization. Against this there is a general assumption—Franko calls it a 'truism'—that, on the contrary, United States firms are more centralized than others. There may be a further confusion between centralization and formalization. Some of those who assert that United States companies are more centralized may take formal reporting procedures as a sign of this. That such procedures can lead to less autonomy for the subsidiary will be suggested later, but the procedures themselves do not prove this.

More elaborate questionnaires have been undertaken by other writers, including Schöllhamer, Garnier, and Ondrak.[9] In Schöllhamer's work the measurement of a degree of centralization is accompanied by a measure of intensity of conflict between head office and the foreign subsidiary, and thus ties up with a theme of the present study. A selection of 98 decisions are chosen and questions about them asked of head office and the foreign subsidiary in a number of companies originating in the United States, Britain, Germany, Switzerland and Japan. Each decision was subject to a five-point response ranging, in the case of centralization, from decisions made by the parent company alone through three grades of participation to decisions made by the subsidiary alone. On the causes of conflict, the same decisions are rated from very seldom or never through to very frequent. The five-point questioning provides a route to fractional answers while retaining the advantages of the locus of decision-making approach. The evidence so far available is inconclusive, although some decisions stand out as more likely to be taken at head office and some with the subsidiary through all the nationalities of origin.

Garnier takes United States companies and their subsidiaries in France and Mexico. The research began with three-point questions and then changed to seven so this work also allowed fractions while being rooted explicitly in the locus of decision-making approach. The initial list of decisions was picked out of the literature and then reduced to 38 after discussions with seven managers. In this study the word 'autonomy' is used and is described as a sub-scale of 'overall centralization', the measure that is reached by adding the scores achieved by the answers to questions about where the 38 decisions are taken. The autonomy score, it is pointed out, is very sensitive to the kind of decisions that are included. A bias towards personnel decisions, for instance, may bias the whole research towards decentralization. This is, of course, why a rating of the decisions by significance is required. Unlike some studies, this one did attempt to reach a sample based on a total population, but it was conducted by post and the proportion of replies was small (less than 10 per cent). Thus, a double bias is introduced—the small number of replies is compounded by the unreliability of answers to a postal questionnaire. However, the results do provide evidence for differences of national background (the replies resembled one another within each country more than between the two) and at the same time against a determinist view. Given the same situations, managers were found to react differently. This combination of an element of predictability with an element of uncertainty is a common thread through a number of studies.

The work of Ondrak is more modest in scope than that of Schöllhamer or Garnier—nineteen small Canadian firms in one industry are examined with only twelve decisions—but more ambitious in that a time scale is introduced by asking the questions twice at an interval of four years. In this case a four-point questionnaire was used, ranging from 'largely a matter of subsidiary autonomy' to 'largely a matter of HQ responsibility'; and this gave rise to a classification of subsidiaries into:

(a)   autonomous subsidiary;
(b)   holding company subsidiary;
(c)   profit centre subsidiary;
(d)   integrated subsidiary.

Of the fourteen companies analysed in detail, eight had changed classification during the four years, thus showing a relatively high rate of change and freedom of choice, but also showing the need to investigate closely the reasons for the alterations.

Communication

The implications of both centralization and autonomy for the communication system have already been demonstrated. The lack of knowledge of head office that can develop after a subsidiary is decentralized is a known cause of disaster; this can arise either because the facts were not known, or were misunderstood, at the centre or because there was deliberate deceit on the part of the foreign affiliate. An example of ignorance and misunderstanding, and perhaps some deceit as well, was the series of problems caused for an English car component manufacturer (Wilmot Breedon Ltd) by its French subsidiary in the early 1960s.[10] In this case the parent company was small and the French company was its first substantial investment abroad. As the subsidiary was an existing company, considerable autonomy was allowed. A serious problem followed without the parent company being aware of what was happening. Indeed, the seriousness was such that the British owner failed to pay a dividend to its shareholders for some years. The parent company and the subsidiary survived—probably as a result of the chance circumstance that a Swiss bank had contributed to the financing of the subsidiary and was willing to continue doing so. In a number of cases more recently the liquidation of the parent company has demonstrated the dangers of decentralization.[11]

As against the occasional dramatic consequences of autonomy, the problems of centralization are constantly being demonstrated. In view of the earlier discussion, it would be expected that centralization would cause problems of communication, but that these would be exacerbated where downward messages greatly exceeded upward. The international studies examined do not consider this point, but do identify a number of misunderstandings. For instance Slipsager[12] conducted research into a Danish international company. In this company there was an unexpectedly favourable view of the state of communications, both in head office and in the foreign subsidiary. Even so 50 per cent of the corporate and 56 per cent of the affiliate executives questioned considered that the 'boundary of the decision power' between the two was ambiguous. More predictably 40 per cent of the host country executives considered that the subsidiaries had too little influence on policy decisions, compared with only 14 per cent of those in the home country. There was a similar response to a direct question on centralization (44 per cent–16 per cent considered the 'attitude of the parent company too centralized'). This study was into one company and the report produces no comparative data, but the results show typical perceptions arising out of a centralized situation and its effects on communications. Other writers make the suggestion that will be picked up later that management development schemes may produce informal communications.

Ownership

Studies of the advantages and disadvantages of joint ventures usually start with the assumption that undivided authority is the aim that leads to 100 per cent ownership; this view explains the instability of many ventures, and is supported by evidence showing that certain decisions do change when local partners or shareholders are bought out.[13] The extent to which companies achieve a centralized authority without complete or even majority ownership is seldom discussed. More discussed are the conditions under which different forms of ownership may be acceptable to corporate executives and government officials in the countries where they operate. Thus, Salera[14] refers to the 'risk-fit' situations. In some cases, he asserts, high risk means that managers are unwilling to share decisions. In others the effect of the risk is to make companies welcome partners. The 'risk-fit' analysis is proposed but not pursued; the interesting implication of the proposal is that it may explain why companies are prepared to go to some lengths to produce this difficult combination of central control and local ownership. The required 'fit' may indeed involve local funds but central decision-making.

Another approach to the question of joint ventures considers the objectives of the partners and the extent to which they are fulfilled.[15] As long as the identity of purpose remains, the partnership survives. The lure of undivided authority, it is suggested, will break the arrangement unless the company has a strong interest in the particular operation. However, some units are relatively easy to hive off, and the decision-making will be determined by such considerations. Since the publication of that view, joint ventures have become more frequent, but recent surveys continue to record their unpopularity. One of these emphasizes two sets of reasons for failure. The first is where the nature of the business dictates that important decisions cannot be delegated, and the joint venture partner is left with a part in the decision-making which is not commensurate with the equity holding. The other set has to do with the relationship between the joint venture and other parts of each parent company in the formulation of policies on issues like dividends, debt-equity ratios, marketing methods and quality control. The problems are further subdivided into strategic, management style, financial, accounting and control, marketing, production, personnel, research and development and relationships with government. The answers are seen to be the taking of a number of steps to reduce the risks rather than to try to remove the problems.

Strategy and planning

The part that the subsidiary plays in the development of corporate strategy features in much of the literature. The centralizing influence of the realization that global strategies are possible, profitable and perhaps necessary is mentioned by Robock and Simmonds, and Robinson.[16] The latter work quotes an earlier study on United States companies which related the degree of centralization firmly to strategy, mainly to factors inherent in the product. Thus, pharmaceutical companies are said to be centralized because they required product consistency. Other factors included function, size and distance. This writer traced a trend towards more centralization which was related to technology, growth and performance. Other authors also suggest such a process of development.

Stopford and Wells[17] take it for granted that decentralization is normal for a newly established foreign subsidiary of a United States firm. They also state that the subsidiary manager strives hard to maintain autonomy but that there is a gradual erosion. This erosion, in their view, begins with the formation of the international division, although it takes place slowly. The evidence for these assertions is not spelt out, but the lure towards centralization is strongly supported—although connected with a particular organization structure, a subject to be considered in Chapter 15 where the connection is seen to be more complicated. The insertion of the new level of management, whether in the form of an international division or any other unit between the subsidiary and the ultimate authority, will appear as centralizing by the subsidiary.

Salera[18] relates decentralization to product, suggesting that consumer product firms are more likely to be decentralized. He also asserts that the more experienced international operators allow more autonomy for their subsidiaries. This view is contrary to that of the authors mentioned above and most others who see experience, and particularly the emergence of a global strategy, as a key element in the lure to centralization.

Another aspect of the subject has been considered by Prahalad[19] and his co-authors in a series of papers that relate centralization to strategic decision-making and control in the matrix organization. He distinguishes companies which are salient (in other words they attract the attention of local governments on account of the nature of their products, their market power or their exports) from those that are not. He further contrasts those that are independent with those that are interdependent. The studies were carried out over long periods with a small number of large companies. One of the results is to indicate how the movement of the locus of authority in the matrix can change the strategies of the company along with its bargaining position, both internally between head office and subsidiary and externally with governments. In particular, the influence that the host country government can have on subsidiary policies is demonstrated. A company may move into a business unrelated to its own in order to safeguard its main business. The example of Union Carbide moving into shrimp fishing for export because the Indian government regarded that as a priority sector is mentioned. On the other hand, subsidiaries can gain independence from head office by, for instance, quoting privileged information from the government which head office has no way of verifying.

Corporate attitudes

There have been attempts to identify corporate types along lines similar to those used in personality studies—the drafting of a profile of characteristics to identify a particular psychological type. These attempts involve the theoretical difficulties which have already been discussed, assumptions have to be made about the means of discovering the attitudes of companies, and whether it is possible to speak about the personality of an organization at all. The basis for such an international company typology usually derives from a firm's alleged attitude to international operations and especially to the role of the subsidiaries. The word 'multinational' itself is sometimes used in this attitudinal sense, although not in this book. Some writers discuss 'degrees of multinationality' or employ phrases like 'truly multinational'. Such phrases are frequently used by managers as well and assume a profile containing a mixture of objective and subjective indicators. Proportion of investment abroad, number of foreign subsidiaries and numbers of expatriate executives are the most common among the objective indicators. The subjective include a range of attitudes to the foreign operations, including the degree of priority given to them. A mixture of both the subjective and the objective may be found in statements about the bias in the corporate planning system as well. There may be evidence of the kind which shows that the plans are compiled at the centre with little consideration for the special interests of the foreign operations. and there may be features of the organization of the planning departments which make much subsidiary participation unlikely. 'Greater multinationality' will then be seen as a move to a greater bias in the system towards the subsidiaries and their involvement in the planning. There may also be evidence from managers' perceptions about how the planning system works which supports or contradicts the objective evidence. The relationship between the degree of centralization and the degree of multinationality according to these theories is complicated. There is a view, sometimes included in the profiles, that the more 'truly multinational' company is a federation of semi-autonomous units. But, on the other hand, the company's greater commitment to operations abroad may well bring greater centralization—the more that is at stake, invested outside the home country, the more the lure to centralization is increased. Hence, the subjective and the objective indicators may contradict one another.

A well-known application of personality types to international companies is that of Perlmutter[20] who coined the words 'ethnocentric', 'polycentric' and 'geocentric'. Each type has its own set of profiles organized around seven main categories including: complexity, central communications, nationality and staff. All the categories are assessed by the perceptions of the managers and one is entitled 'Authority: decision-making'. The ethnocentric type is the one with a strong bias towards head office; it is home-country centred and centralized. The polycentric has an orientation towards the host country, and is decentralized. The geocentric type is less straightforward. This is described as 'a world-centred concept' but the authority profile is summarized as: 'aim for a collaborative approach between headquarters and subsidiaries'. This phrase is an example of two of the difficulties of this line of reasoning. Whose aim are we talking about? What evidence is there that any moves are being made in the direction indicated by this aim? The difference between the expectation, let alone the 'aim', and the reality makes it hazardous to classify companies in this way, but the problem of determining what constitutes a company aim is even greater. Is it the aim of the chief executive, the joint aim of members of the board, the objective of the planning department, the principal shareholder, the public relations officer or who? Evidently, the two difficulties compound one another.

However, an attempt is being made to develop a typology which relates company attitudes to authority. There should be a relationship, even if pioneering attempts to uncover it produce more problems than they solve. Some writers, and many managers, state the issue in moral terms. Perlmutter himself wrote an article entitled, 'How multinational should your managers be?' The introduction of the word 'should' suggests a moral approach, although in that particular article the reference was rather to the contrast betwen a firm's acceptance of geocentric aims while continuing to use inconsistent staffing policies. The moral statement is clearer when companies are expected to conform to certain norms of non-interference in subsidiary affairs, or the reverse. This is most commonly related to separate functions. The appropriate degree of interference or non-interference is considered different for finance than for production or marketing, while personnel is different again.

Support and conflict

The other side of the centralization-decentralization question concerns support and alienation. To questions about autonomy in the subsidiary, some head office executives will reply that the real problem is forcing the local managers to accept responsibility. Equally, the latter may say that the centre is too detached and does not provide adequate support. These may both be regarded as examples of pressures towards some form of inverted centralization, arising from dependence attitudes in the foreign affiliate. One author who has collected evidence on support and alienation in the company-subsidiary relationship is Hofstede.[21] In one company he surveyed, 'not enough support' and 'too much interference' rate roughly equal answers from subsidiary managers; they also rate similar responses from sales offices abroad. This evidence may not be representative and was, in any case, collected as part of a study of executive satisfaction and dissatisfaction. Nevertheless, its existence is a warning against assuming too readily that the pressure of the foreign executive is always towards decentralization.

A related issue which forms an important theme in this book is that of conflict. The degree of centralization, like the type of organization, can be seen to emerge from the various conflicts in which the executive groups are involved. These interlock and operate both inside the company and between management and governments and other external organizations. Neghandi[22] has listed seven issues betweed companies and host countries which may influence the autonomy of the local subsidiary. These included ownership, control and economic planning, which together cause considerable tension. The results of Neghandi's survey show differences according to the nationality of the parent company. The influence of competition is also emphasized. A higher level of competitiveness accompanied a lower level of conflict with government. The relationship of this to centralization will be examined in more detail later. Indeed, a substantial number of writers have considered the subject of autonomy only in connection with the relations between companies and governments, a subject which is considered in the next chapter. Meanwhile, the series of researches the result of which form the main subject matter of Chapters 12–17 will be introduced in the pages which follow.

11.3   THE MANCHESTER STUDIES

A series of studies, based on the University of Manchester Institute of Science and Technology[23] and beginning in 1964, set out to unravel some of the perplexing issues underlying the company to subsidiary relationship. These studies did not start from an interest in centralization, but from a project designed to investigate the policy-forming procedures of the multinational firm. Early in this project, discrepancies were noticed between the way the system was alleged to work and the way it appeared to be doing so. This led to a realization of the importance of understanding where a decision was made, what conflicts arose within the decision-making process itself, and how the outcome was redirected. At the same time it was noticed that statements were being made about the advantages of a devolution which did not exist. 'Since we decentralized the performance of our subsidiaries has improved' was a typical statement. In the event, there was often no sign of the decentralization, so the reason for the improvement was presumably to be found elsewhere. Two paradoxes were identified in the course of the research. One stated that an ideology of decentralization masked a centralizing reality, and the other that the centralizing reality was yet practised without effective sanctions. The final insight was that powerful as the lures towards centralization were, there were also pressures the other way. As a result, companies did not exhibit a steady progress towards one condition or the other, but were moved backwards and forwards by the opposing forces. The studies of the subject started from these observations, and were aimed to test out the truth or falsity of the many statements suggesting that success or failure in a multinational company depended on the autonomy granted to the foreign subsidiary. The attempt to answer these questions produced the research projects discussed below. Because they started from assertions about where a decision was actually taken, the projects also started from the locus of decision-making approach.

Methodology—general

The problem of conceptualizing centralization and decentralization is modified when the research is directly geared towards understanding the relationship between parent companies and foreign subsidiaries, the relationship upon which researchers have to focus their interest.

Although matrix and other similar types of organization may produce complications in some multinational companies, the researcher need not delve into the workplace structure of authority within the subsidiary or the particular degrees of staff decision-making at head office. The focus is on the specific decision-making responsibility, power, authority or influence of one group over another separate and distinct from it, each with defined geographical responsibilities. Further, since the analysis of centralization is conducted in order to elucidate the parent-subsidiary relationship, the majority of writers dealing with the subject have not felt it necessary to go into the great detail needed to examine the workings of a hierarchy. For instance, the concept of the *normal line* is used to illustrate that control varies between companies and in the same company over time but that the pushes and pulls (the lures) restrict the variations.[24]

Most of the literature dealing with centralization in multinational companies has relied upon a general definition of the concept in terms of decision-making at the top, implying that this is the equivalent of the centralization of authority, and left it at that. The rigidity of definition required for measurement has not been attempted. Since most writers on multinationals belong to the school of management scientists there is a tendency to identify the issue with the particular structure adopted by the companies studies, and to see it as a management technique. The fact that the issue of centralization lies between two distinct and easily divisible parts of a large organization has consequences for the mode of research chosen. While the problem of the precise location of a decision is still difficult, given the continuous flow of influence and suggestion from headquarters to subsidiary, it is, nonetheless, possible to determine whether the bulk of the significant decisions are made either at home or abroad; this is not the case in a single organization where decisions have to be traced to somewhere in a particular department. It is the task of the compiler of research questionnaires to define the degree of influence created within and from headquarters clearly and estimate this in order to show those areas where the subsidiary has autonomy.

There will be some areas where the subsidiary is virtually autonomous, and likewise some where the headquarters will order actions without any attempt at consultation. These areas are represented diagrammatically by (A) and (D) in Figure 11.1. Likewise, there will be subjects on which the debate between the subsidiary and headquarters is more like that between partners. There will be other subjects in which the interests of the group as a whole are concerned, and on these the subsidiary managers can be assumed to have less influence. This statement needs testing in individual cases, but diversification policies and major new investments which have emerged as a result of global scanning from the centre are examples. The first problem in attempting to discover this area of autonomy—(A) in Figure 11.1—is to collect a range of typical decisions common to all the multinationals under investigation. This is more difficult than it sounds, since the check-list must be validated to prevent the possibility of error caused by trying to determine the locus of a type of decision not made either within the subsidiary or at head office. For example, questions regarding the decision to change production processes are not relevant to an insurance company; the check-list of decisions must be chosen to fit the sample, or vice versa.

Secondly, with regard to the check-list, the researcher has to be aware of problems connected with the repetition of specific decisions. A correlation, though only approximate, is assumed betweed the importance of a decision to a company and the frequency with which it has to be taken. There is a

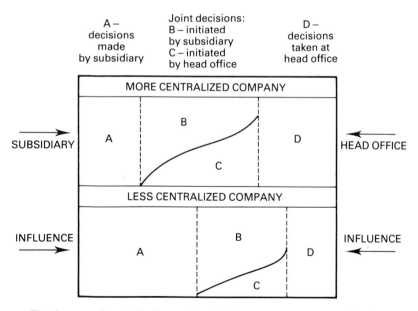

The degrees of centralization and local autonomy are represented by the widths of A and D and the areas of B and C.

Figure 11.1   Areas of influence in decision-making

rudimentary similarity between this time span of frequency of decisions and the span of control of middle and junior management. For a full comparison between organizations, the check-list of decisions must try to avoid those questions the locus of which varies not according to the degree of centralization, but according to the company's products. In a labour-intensive industry, for instance, the decision to set up a new plant will be less important than if such a decision required an enormous injection of new finance. The decisions should be of comparable importance across the sample; otherwise there is a danger that the difference between types of manufacture is being measured rather than centralization. Nevertheless, industry-specific indicators have their place, so long as the facts are recognized. Such indicators show centralization within the industry or demonstrate that one particular sector is more centralized than another.

This discussion raises again problems that bedevil centralization analysis like: are we measuring the locus of a set series of decisions—regardless of their importance in the individual setting? or are we trying to measure the centralization of authority?

If the latter, then clearly the importance of a particular decision to the company as a whole will vary its location in the decision-making hierarchy. There is not one variable here but two: the degree of centralization of decision-making authority in the company and the importance of the particular decision to the individual company. For this reason it is absurd to put a set figure on the amount of capital expenditure which a subsidiary manager is allowed to authorize, as a symptom of decentralization, since a figure that constitutes decentralization in the case of General Motors could constitute centralization in Guest, Keen and Nettlefold. As a consequence any list of important subsidiary decisions has to be found in terms that take account of the variation in importance to individual companies, and the research must cope with the difficulties that result.

Further, the division between the *reasons* for centralization or decentralization and the *effects* must be isolated from the search for the *symptoms* or indicators, in order to make any statements relating to performance under centralization or in order to search for the normal line to which the system moves in a particular company. For example, the degree of technology or the controls used could be either a reason for centralization or an effect of it; in consequence it is not possible to take the questions of size and technology as a part of the programme to discover if a company is centralized if one wishes to use such evidence as an explanation.

In examing the methods actually used to assemble the evidence it must be said that some of the questioning is bedevilled by the viewpoints of the respondents. One of the discoveries that stimulated this research in the mid-1960s was the incompatibility of answers to the same questions when asked at head office and asked in the foreign subsidiary. Head office would say: 'We have adopted a considerable degree of decentralization in recent years.' In the subsidiary a question on the same subject would be answered: 'We are subject to constantly increasing interference.' These responses demonstrated the unreliability of studies in which questions are only asked at head office and demanded an explanation of how the contradiction can be expressed in such an extreme way. Naturally, any attempt at maintaining relationships on the part of head office, however well-intentioned, can be regarded as a pressure towards centralization by the subsidiary. Similarly, an exhortation to set up their own planning system, a decentralizing message from head office to the subsidiary, can be ignored where experience has taught the wisdom of simply fitting into the central plans of the corporate staff. Nevertheless, there remains a difference in viewpoints between that of head office and that of the subsidiary which demands and will receive further explanation. But first the method of approach is examined in more detail.

The centralization issue and the multinational firm

The principle that more accurate results are obtained by approaching the same question by a number of different methods has long been established in the social sciences.[25] In the studies under review three principal methods of investigation have been used. One is the interviewing in depth in various units of a number of companies to establish standards of comparison as to the degree of centralization and decentralization perceived by executives to exist inside those companies; another is by a case study of one firm which involved an analysis of all communications within that company; and the third is by extensive interviewing within a small number of large companies to elicit where decisions on a standard list are normally taken in the firms questioned. Relevant data were also collected in a number of other studies—some sectoral (such as retailing), some strategic (such as personnel policies of international companies). The list of decisions is printed at the end of this chapter.

Under the first method, about 40 manufacturing companies were interviewed in depth, another 42 in less depth and a similar number of retailing firms with stores in various countries were also interviewed. By 'in depth' is meant meetings with at least three executives in head office and in no less than two foreign subsidiaries. The manufacturing companies were guaranteed anonymity in order to persuade them to allow executives to talk freely on delicate issues. Their conversations were checked against a study of documents: correspondence, company manuals and internal circulars as well as publications such as annual reports. The delicacy of the issue can be illustrated in many ways. For instance, some of the questions were the subject of acute controversy inside the firm. Some, like transfer pricing, where also controversial outside the firm. No company would provide full details of pricing policies; in some this was the *only* decision where such details were refused; even so, most were willing enough to discuss who decided about pricing policies. This issue caused considerable discussion internally because every transfer of goods across frontiers could improve the figures of one unit of the organization and worsen those of another.

This internal dispute, which lies at the heart of the centralization debate, is one which many writers on transfer pricing ignore. Any manipulation of the prices affects appraisal and control methods, and generates considerable argument; companies are not the monolithic organizations they are often assumed to be.

The temperature of the debate on this point is, of course, raised by the interested authorities of the countries in which the units are situated. One country's tax gain is another's loss, and the tax administration will be concerned about the internal argument on pricing. On the other hand if the goods are dutiable, the pressures of the customs and excise in a particular country may be contrary to those of the tax authorities. Thus, components pass from subsidiary A in country X to subsidiary B for local assembly in country Y. The management of subsidiary A holds out for a high price in order to improve the results of that subsidiary, for the same reason that the managers of subsidiary B argue for a lower price. However the argument is settled, a number of considerations will be involved—the state of the business in both countries, the price for which the finished products can be sold in country B, market share considerations and so on. Only where there is a known market price for the component in both countries can the decision be avoided, and this will rarely be the case in the high technology industries which are especially dominated by multinationals. The tax authorities in each country have similar interests to those of the subsidiary management since company taxes are usually levied on profits, but the customs administration in country Y is likely to take the opposite view as duties are usually levied on import prices. The tax officer examines the price to see if it is too high, as this would reduce the profit and thus the tax, while the customs representative suspects that the price has been artificially reduced to lower the duty. Caught in such a maze of conflicting pressures from within and without it is hardly surprising that strict confidentiality is called for.

Examples of delicate information considered vital for this study included information about arrangements between separate companies with regard to trading areas, market share and licensing agreements. Such arrangements are now coming under the review of many governments as well as the European Economic Community; nevertheless, it is still true that an understanding that is acceptable in Europe may be illegal in the United States. If, therefore, a European company which has such agreements also has a subsidiary in the United States, that subsidiary must be kept in ignorance of such agreements, otherwise its executives might be liable to prosecution.

The questions asked were about the communications routes, the decision-making and the controls exercised between the parent company and the foreign subsidiaries. These were asked according to standard check-lists,[26] but each company was treated as an individual case study. This does not claim to be a cross-sectional analysis for reasons which will become apparent later. The comparative element at this stage was provided by the judgement of the researcher. This judgement was informed by two considerations. One was an organization pattern in the researcher's mind, a sort of neutral company that was neither centralized nor decentralized. The other was the accumulated experience of interviews which showed where exaggeration and underestimation were likely to occur.

Recognizing the relative nature of the subject, another danger lies in the problem of how far to include a historical overview in estimating the degree of centralization. Without a historical overview it is difficult to avoid seeing centralization in an absolute and static sense, but the purpose was to describe trends. These trends, furthermore, are contingent on a number of factors which are a part of the estimate of centralization. The political, social and economic conditions of two countries in which a multinational company operates obviously affect the degree of centralization adopted by that company in those countries. Without some perception in time and knowledge of how those subsidiaries developed it is difficult, however, to identify precisely what effect the conditions have, but preoccupation with the time dimension produces different problems. Some research regards the historical background as so important that it is considered necessary to probe back into the past to search out the trends. Some companies encourage this. Executives will say that there used to be a high degree of centralization that has now decreased. The trouble about accepting such encouragement is that the evidence becomes more unreliable and difficult to compare just at a time when efforts are needed to minimize the discrepancies. Memories operate curiously, and people questioned may be repeating traditions that they heard when joining the company or giving their view of a situation that existed at a time when their own perspective was different. They were then in a subordinate position, and a company is likely to appear less centralized when viewed from the top. If, on the other hand, they are describing a change process that they have lived through, their views may be biased. In this research, the main enquiries have been into crucial decisions taken and arrangements made in the present or in the recent past. In the following pages this is called the *first method of research*.

Questioning about the degree of centralization continued and proved of considerable interest, but some of the trends identified needed to be checked in other ways. Hence, two other studies were established. One was designed to examine what was going on inside a company in much greater depth and the other was intended to establish more rigorous means for comparing companies.

The second method was a study of one company in which a researcher worked through all correspondence and telex messages that passed between the company and its foreign subsidiaries over a four-year period.[27] This correspondence was then classified under a number of headings: mandatory orders, suggestions, advice, queries, apologies, information, requests, complaints and congratulations.

The final classification was discussed with the executives concerned, and definitions agreed with them before the correspondence was analysed. Afterwards the head office managers who had originated the letters, as well as some subsidiary managers, were interviewed and their perceptions checked against the analysis. The company chosen had an international division and kept on a central filing system the correspondence, telexes and even notes on telephone calls; only a limited number of executives communicated abroad. Most companies would not lend themselves so conveniently to this method, nor would it ever be possible to claim that they were representative. There is, further, a possible theoretical difficulty in that the use of this method stretches still further the definition of centralization. The assumption on which this method rests is that the percentage of mandatory orders to other messages in the communication system is an indication of centralization—a high percentage indicates that head office is communicating decisions rather than the raw materials of decision-making. So long as this is taken as an indication only, agreed by the researcher and by the executives who cooperate, there should be no serious problems. In the following pages this is called the *communications survey*. With the reservations mentioned, this method has provided a fruitful approach which has produced some important correctives to generalizations supported by other methods.

The third method used was designed to provide both a different approach for scrutinizing hypotheses that were already emerging and to explore the possibilities of a wider-scale comparative survey. A limited number of British-based multinationals were approached. Executives were interviewed in several European countries, and in three languages, using a standardized list of decisions. Questions were asked about the taking of these decisions—by whom they had been taken recently—and related issues.

The study aimed to produce a diagnostic tool—a way of analysing the situation within a multinational company, its structure and performance. Another aim was to discover why the structure was as it was—the influence of factors like environment and personality. This particular research was confined to British-based multinationals and their majority-owned subsidiaries on the continent of Europe. Companies mainly in finance, petroleum and retailing were omitted; but otherwise a variety of industry sectors was included.

In a study of this kind there is a choice of relevant subjects. One could be concerned with the process by which a specific decision, such as the dismissal of a senior manager, was taken in a number of different firms, or the means by which decisions were taken in a particular functional area, such as marketing, could be investigated, or again the research could concentrate on the way major decisions were taken as a whole, across all the various activities of companies. All of these subjects were investigated, but with an emphasis on the third. One reason for this was the fact that it could not logically be argued that any one decision or any one particular function adequately represented the whole of a company. The way in which, for example, marketing decisions were taken might be different from the methods used in production. The study aimed to discover the differences and look for their reasons. The design of the research recognised that the decision-making process was not a simple one, that any single decision involved many different people and levels in a company. However, when a decision was arrived at, there was usually one senior executive who had ultimate responsibility for that decision. The people studied were therefore the top half-dozen managers of national subsidiaries covering each of the key functions, such as marketing, manufacturing, finance, personnel and so on, as well as the executives to whom they report in the head office in Britain. A distinction was made between the senior line management at head office and their staff advisers.

The research did not seek to obtain from these respondents answers about decisions they made, as decision-making is not necessarily a one-man process, but rather their opinion as representatives of their group about where decisions were made. To assume that one manager adequately represents a group may be dangerous, but was a simplifying assumption in order to carry out the research. One advantage arising from the choice of respondents was that the interview load upon any one person in the subsidiary, or in head office, was reduced. The researcher obtained a composite picture from several senior managers, while any one manager only spent an hour or two talking to him in confidence and might thus feel free to talk about his or her own function and to give opinions about others in the company. In the case of each subsidiary and each head office the maximum time necessary to obtain the data was two days per unit.

Before visiting any of the companies, two further questions had to be answered—how to establish where the decisions were normally taken and what would be considered the major decisions. To establish an answer to the first question, Figure 11.2 was used. This shows five types of authority exercise (I—Independent, CI—coordinated, APD—only approval required, CC—head office decision with consultation and WCC—head office decision without consultation). It is a possible criticism of such an approach that any particular decision may sometimes be an 'APD' and sometimes a 'WCC'. This was partly overcome by asking the managers: 'What usually happens at the moment—say within your experience of the last half year?' A question asked in previous research—'Have there been cases of the reformulation of policy by the subsidiary?'—was also used here, in order to concentrate attention on the actual

	Decision*	Local management	Head office management †
Local	I	Decision	–
	CI	Decision	Consultation
	APD	Decision	Approval
HO†	CC	Consultation	Decision
	WCC	–	Decision

† However head office is represented – by division, function, region or central body

* I : Completely independent.
CI : Coordinated authority – take decision after consultation with higher management, but not binding on local management.
APD : Decision submitted to previous approval.
CC : Decision of HO after consultation with local management.
WCC : HO decision without local consultation.

Adapted from Eugster, C. and Uytterelst, L. (1973) 'Les Sociétés multinationales', *Revue Economique et Sociale*, March.

Figure 11.2   Levels of authority

initiatives taken by the subsidiary. The replies to this question were used with caution in view of the tricks that memory can play. For the second question—what are significant issues?—this study used a list based on many discussions with managers at all levels of multinational firms. The list avoids mundane issues but does embrace activities in all three of the decision-analysis processes—strategic planning, management control, operational control—mentioned by Anthony.[28]

It was assumed that the views of the managers in the subsidiaries and those in the head office were of equal significance, on the question of what were discussable issues between the parties and what were not, what were significant and what not, and where decisions were taken. Thus, it was hoped to avoid presuppositions which might distort the results, a problem well demonstrated by Bacharach and Baratz.[29]

Since only half the companies approached agreed to cooperate fully at this stage, a question arose about the extent to which this had biased the results. Did those companies which did not cooperate differ from those which did in being, for example, more restrictive in their internal relationships as well as in their relationships with university researchers? Is it possible that those groups which did allow research to be carried out, answered the request of the researcher to enter two of their subsidiaries by consciously or unconsciously giving only the names of the two most respectable or well-behaved subsidiaries? Since the results of this research are integrated with the other methods used, it is hoped that doubts raised by these questions are satisfactorily resolved.

The method of approach in this study was:

(1) Make contact with one person in the head office of the group, who can give names and addresses of managing directors of subsidiaries.
(2) Visit this contact and explain the project briefly.
(3) Obtain permission from the contact to visit the subsidiaries.
(4) Approach managing directors of subsidiaries, directly and not through head office.
(5) Carry out fieldwork in subsidiaries.
(6) Report on findings to managing directors of subsidiaries.
(7) Carry out fieldwork among head office managers.
(8) Report on head office fieldwork to main head office contact.

It is not practical to enter subsidiaries without having the permission of a senior manager at the group head office, but this method of talking to the subsidiaries first was designed to check any bias that may have crept into the other researches in which head office executives were interviewed at the start. It is not considered likely that such a method will lead to research biased in the direction of the subsidiary managers, since a full list of decisions is placed in front of those in head office. Obtaining details from the subsidiary first may help to reveal those informal contacts, either set up by managers in the subsidiaries or in head office, which are not part of the official links between the two sides. This may mean that questions can be asked of a different set of people at the head office to those appearing on official organization charts. Such an approach raises a further problem. Subsidiary managers may be more willing to give the names of those whom they regard as friendly contacts in the head office than those with whom they have an equal amount of contact, but in ways which are less comfortable or represent for them the disciplinary function. Such differences should emerge as a result of fieldwork at head office level and are in themselves signs of the relationship between the two parties.

It might be preferable for researchers to obtain from their parent company contact an open letter with which they would then visit those subsidiaries they select in the group. This was not found to be practicable. Where the head office contact is specifying those subsidiaries to be visited, there is clearly the possibility of collusion between the two sides. The skill of the researcher must play an important part in overcoming this problem; also helpful is the fact that little detailed information was given to the head office contact before entry to the first subsidiary.

A particularly important principle of the research was confidentiality, which was safeguarded in two ways. Firstly, all those in the groups surveyed had to be assured that no information would be published either in the university or in book form which could identify them in any way. Secondly, and no less important, managers in head office had to be assured that anything they told the researcher would not be communicated to anyone in the subsidiary and vice versa. As a research method, it would perhaps be fruitful to pose a conflict at the level of the head office: 'You, Mr X, are telling me that this is what happens in the subsidiary. But Mr Y in the subsidiary told me that another thing happened. How do you account for this difference of opinion?' To do this after promising confidentiality would clearly be unethical; such an approach was rejected in favour of the theoretical question and the impersonal doubt: 'I understand that this situation has occurred in other companies, can you conceive of it happening here?' Verifying the contents of interviews through sending a report to the managing director of each subsidiary, of the interview in the *subsidiary*, and a report to the contact at head office of the head office interviews was considered the most reliable way of ensuring accuracy on each side. Any misunderstandings, or gaps in the information collected by the researcher, can be corrected by the respective parties before processing the information.[30] On later pages this is called the study of *British Companies in Europe*.

While the three research projects were being conducted, a number of shorter-term related studies were being undertaken for specific sponsors. One is *the retailing project*. This studied the particular problems of foreign investment in retailing, and the types of control and expertise that emerge. Here is a case of an industry which has only recently begun to invest abroad on anything but a very small scale, and has done this specifically to make money out of hard-learned expertise. Under these circumstances decentralization on fundamentals would make little sense, while centralization on many issues would be absurd given the local character of shopping habits. The issue of vital knowledge discussed in earlier chapters is relevant here. Another related research looked at one specific decision, that of disinvestment.[31] This is naturally assumed to be a centralized decision, indeed one which may well disprove claims on the part of the company to leave subsidiaries to take their own decisions. Such a commonsense conclusion does not, however, turn out to be the whole story. A comparatively decentralized company may have procedures for negotiation between subsidiaries designed to enable agreement on rationalization across frontiers—one form of disinvestment and a delicate subject which, some would argue, cannot be effectively achieved in a firm which is too centralized. An obstinate subsidiary can easily block compulsory rationalization, although the parent company's withdrawal of support may lead to its insolvency.[32] Thus, the disinvestment project provided invaluable evidence and was conducted on similar interviewing and cross-checking principles to the others.

A number of other approaches were possible. A quick route to a comparative study would have been a postal questionnaire. Given the depth of the previous research, some of the problems of questionnaire design could have been overcome, but there would still have been considerable differences of interpretation. In fact the Manchester researchers gave guarantees to all firms that agreed to cooperate in the research that no postal questionnaires would be used. The nuisance and resentment caused to executives by this method is in no way compensated by the results obtainable even under the most favourable conditions. A spurious appearance of accuracy may be obtained in return for hostility and the closure of doors to more fruitful investigations.

None of the methods by itself produced an overall and convincing measure of centralization so that any particular company could be readily placed along a scale. One company had already used questions based on a list of predetermined decisions for its internal purposes. The management of that company was satisfied that the results were sufficiently valuable to justify repeating such an exercise, but naturally were only able to make internal comparisons. This supported the view that this method, supplemented and cross-checked by the other two, gives the best hope for producing definite results in the future. These results are achieved by blurring to some extent the difficult distinction between the locus of decision-making and influences on the decision. The position is now foreseeable when a measure can be offered that will apply to numerous sets of circumstances. In order to use this comparatively, and thus further the aims of the whole project, it would be necessary to arrange some form of continuous monitoring in selected companies. The provision of continuity which identifies more realistically the process of change is critical to future research. While there is some truth in the widespread belief that the parent-subsidiary relationship differs according to the function, the type of subsidiary and the like, there is also evidence brought together on these pages that management is all of a piece, and a company that rates high for centralization in one function or one subsidiary is likely to rate high for most, although the degree may vary within each function.

This identification of the trends and variables was assisted by projects, often short-term, conducted on a consultancy basis for companies in which various aspects of corporate planning as well as relationships between head office and the foreign subsidiary were examined. Many advantages have been gained from these projects, sometimes undertaken as a *quid pro quo* for research facilities and sometimes in return for funds to support further research. A beneficial circle developed in which the initial research produced credibility which led to openings for consultancy; the results of the consultancy then stimulated further research and provided evidence for it. Some of the most valuable insights gained over the years have first become apparent through a consultancy operation. Examples of this are noted later under headings like *inverted centralization*, first noticed in 1968 in the course of a project, and the *different time horizons of the different management projections*. Naturally, there is a danger of bias in adopting project-based insights, and these must be rechecked from as detached a viewpoint as possible and incorporated into research where opportunity offers. Equally, there are truths which can only be discovered by actual involvement with firms; they are not visible to the outside observer, however skilled or sensitive.

Evidence for this chapter has been collected from the many sources outlined, which has meant some difficulty in cross-referencing. As already explained, the main projects are referred to in the following way:

The first method of research. Which refers to the intensive interviewing of executives in 40 companies, and less intensive investigations in a further 42.

The communications survey. This refers to the detailed study of centralization in one company.

The study of British companies in Europe. This refers to the survey of the locus of decision-making in six British international companies.

The retailing study. This refers to the examination of foreign investment in all British retailers with investment abroad and foreign retailers with investment in Britain.

The personnel policies study. This refers to a survey of the foreign control of personnel companies by non-British companies operating in the United Kingdom.

These studies were all conducted by members of the International Business Unit in Manchester using similar methods and criteria and contributing to common results. Other projects of the Unit which contributed in some way to the present report are mentioned in context. Where the word 'evidence' is used, this refers to facts collected in these studies or others whose results have been used to check the present data. In the following chapters the results of these studies are used to generalize, where justified by the evidence, about the relationships between the decision-making process of the multinational firm and its political environments, its own management and planning systems and a series of other factors.

11.4 CORPORATE DECISIONS

The following check-list of decisions was used to verify the locus of decision-making in the eyes of both head office and of the subsidiary. The list was submitted to a panel of 20 experts who were asked to score for significance (that is importance; they were asked to score low those items that were insufficiently important to rate with the others) and ambiguity (that is doubt about their meaning; they were asked to score low those items that would be likely to produce contradictory answers). As a result those marked with an * were deleted.

Does this subsidiary decide:
1. on its own sources of funds?
2. on the allocation of its own profits?
3. its own depreciation calculation?
*4. its own credit arrangements?
5. its own accounting system?
*6. on the appointment of its own auditors?
7. its own costing system?
*8. on the choice of its own bank?
9. on new capital investment under . . . for: land?
10. on new capital investment under . . . for: buildings?
11. on new capital investment under . . . for: equipment?
12. to initiate its own capital budget proposals?
*13. to market one of its products in a fresh region in its own country?
14. to enter a new export market?
15. to fix its own prices/discount structures?
*16. on its own promotion techniques?
*17. on its own advertising?
18. on the image of the company it is going to present?
19. on its own sales objectives?
20. on its own distribution channels?
*21. to adapt the company's products to local conditions?
22. standards of quality in its domestic market?
23. on its own trademarks?
*24. plans up to 2 years ahead?
*25. plans from 2 to 5 years ahead?
26. plans more than 5 years ahead?
27. on its own expansion targets?
28. to take over another company in its own country?
29. on the appointment of its own chief executive?
30. on the dismissal of its own chief executive?
31. on a temporary replacement for its chief executive?
32. on the appointment of its own finance director?
33. on the dismissal of its finance director?
*34. on the temporary replacement of its finance director?
35. on the composition of its board or executive committee?
36. on the appointment of other senior executives?
37. on the dismissal of other senior executives?
*38. on the temporary replacement of other senior executives?
39. on the hiring of its own expatriate staff?
40. on the dismissal of its own expatriate staff?
41. on its own management development programme?
42. on its own personnel promotion policies?
*43. on the creation of a new department?
*44. on altering the responsibilities of a department?
*45. on the abolishing of a department?
*46. on the allocation of senior management posts?

47.   on its own recruitment policies?
*48. on its own selection policies?
*49. on its own employee training programmes?
50.   on its own policies with regard to joint consultation?
*51. on its own policies with regard to trade unions?
*52. on the use of attitudinal studies among employees?
53.   on its own production methods?
*54. on its own industrial engineering techniques?
55.   on the negotiation of its licensing agreements?
*56. on the changing of product specifications?
57.   on additions to its product line?
*58. on deletions from its product lines?
*59. on its own quality control procedures?
60.   about the purchasing of new machinery?
*61. on the sale of machinery?
62.   on the establishment of its own research department?
63.   on its own applications for patents?
64.   on its own research projects?
65.   on the abandonment of research projects?
66.   on the use of external research and development agencies?
67.   on its own insurance arrangements?
68.   on its own purchasing policies for materials/components produced within the group?
69.   on its own purchasing policies for materials/components not produced within the group?
*70. its own stock levels?
*71. on its profitability objective?

Are there any other decisions which you think should be included on this list?

Note: This list was drafted in the early 1970s, so the figures in items 9, 10 and 11 have been omitted as they would be meaningless today, and in any case this question cannot be used in comparing companies of radically different size as explained earlier in the chapter.

12 Organization Conflict and Performance Appraisal

Every company with direct investment abroad finds itself involved in conflict on four fronts. The evidence for this has been distilled from many hundreds of interviews in the research projects just described. The conflict may be latent much of the time and (when actual) may take a variety of forms—some harmful and some beneficial. The four fronts include two within the company, within head office and between head office and the foreign subsidiary; the other two are between the company and outside organizations, the first in the home country and the second in the host. The main characteristics of each conflict front are described below.

12.1 CONFLICT

(1) The conflict within head office
The disagreements within the parent company are mainly concerned with the decision to go abroad and the implications of that decision; these include the priority to be given to sales and production abroad, their development and management, including coordination with the domestic operation, the resources to be allocated and the disinvestment decision where appropriate. This conflict becomes institutionalized, built into the management system, through the so-called projections of management.[1] This phrase refers to the three major groups of responsibilities around which management titles are named to match up to the three principal areas of decision-making: the functional (finance, marketing production and so on), the product group (the main businesses of the company) and the geographical (international, regional and national). Where a company has, for instance, a corps of managers appointed to develop the overseas business, there will be a lobby in head office dedicated to promoting the business. That was one of the reasons for their appointment, and companies with specialist international or regional departments have been found to grow fast in foreign investment but less rapidly in profits from abroad. A point to note in considering this form of conflict is that issues with three dimensions are much more complex than those with two which, in their turn, are more complex than

those with one. Disagreements between marketing and production provide an example of the single dimension, which becomes double when the company appoints senior managers with product group responsibilities. The addition of the geographical management provides scope for disagreements on strategy and resource allocations by function, by product and by geography with all the network of interlinked decisions that can arise.

(2)   The conflict between head office and the subsidiary

Once a national subsidiary is established, it becomes a pressure group for the development of the business in its country. The management style, including the degree of decentralization, is also at issue along with other implications of the subsidiary's place in the corporate system. The general struggle for corporate resources means that this conflict is also seen as inter-subsidiary.

(3) and (4)   Company and government

The two other conflict fronts are between companies and governments in the home (3) and host (4) countries; these are considered in more detail in the next chapter. There considerable interlocking is demonstrated as well as mutual influences which are always latent and can become actual in many different ways. With governments should be included other institutions and pressure groups.

Conflicts and decisions

The complexity of the interlocking conflicts is simplified in Figure 12.1 which shows how some of the elements of the four conflict fronts affect one decision, in this case the siting of a new plant. The decision is first debated within the parent company where the arguments are rehearsed for placing it at home or abroad and where the investment appraisal procedures will be implemented and the necessary consents eventually given. The project is also likely to be the subject of lobbying from one or more subsidiaries (conflict area (2)) who will also have carried out investment appraisals as well as being able to point to market growth, cost reduction and other advantages of their countries. Governments and other interest groups in the countries concerned will be looking at the revenue, employment and other implications and may also nominate representatives to lobby the company for or against the project. Although limited to this one decision, the figure suggests numerous general propositions. For example, the resolution of questions implied in conflict area (1) will affect the autonomy of the subsidiary just as much as those that come more obviously in area (2). The exact relationship of the external with the internal conflicts is also the subject of discussion, and it will not be overlooked that the word 'conflict' is being used in a broad sense. A government may intervene in the corporate decision-making process through incentives as well as constraints.

In the figure, as in the text, the conflict zones are numbered from (1) to (4), but

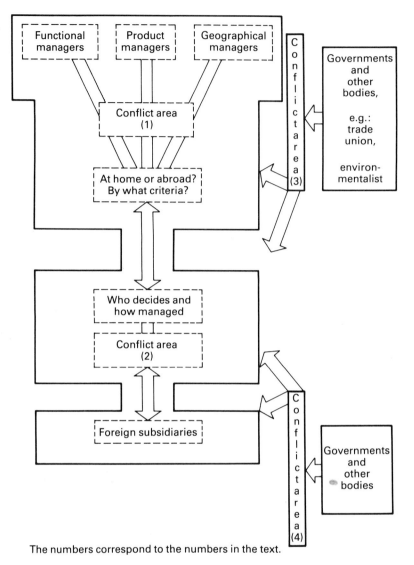

The numbers correspond to the numbers in the text.

Figure 12.1   How conflicts may arise in answering the question: where is this company
going to place its next plant?

the numbering must not be taken to suggest that there is a necessary sequence of
events. All the possible conflicts can become actual at the same time, with the
company finding itself under intense and conflicting pressures; or the project can
begin with a proposal from a host country government which then begins to
lobby the company. Similarly, although the measurement of centralization may
attempt to isolate the internal decision processes from the external influences,
there is little hope of producing this isolation in practice and the significance of
any hypothesis which relies on it will be limited. This is a difficulty of
propositions in the form of 'greater decentralization increases motivation in the

subsidiary'. Even if the company kept such a low profile that its operations were totally uninfluenced by government or public opinion in any of the countries in which it operated, the process of recruitment brings in outside influences, including beliefs and expectations that stem from the different cultures in which the company recruits. Indeed, an attempt to reduce the potential cultural conflict can be observed in a number of different arrangements—bringing managers to head office for lengthy periods, arranging international training programmes, a regular routine of visits and intra-company conferences, and other similar devices. Some of the disillusionment that companies find with these devices arises from exaggerated expectations. The promotion of a better understanding of one another's points of view may make more plain the hard core of conflict which was less difficult to handle when blurred.

This danger of exacerbating conflict through improving communications is even more evident in coping with outside influences, and the hostile climate of opinion in which companies are operating is a factor that produces greater centralization. The process is clear. The maxim that private soldiers cannot be allowed to start wars is translated into corporate terms in the view that relations between companies and governments cannot be entrusted to a local subsidiary. A corporate overview of political relationships is needed to ensure that controversial issues are skilfully negotiated. This is a reversal of older methods whereby orders were issued from head office and the local subsidiary was left to sort out the problems. A pattern is now emerging of central management of relations with the environment, and in some large companies this is accompanied by the establishment of a central department—often called external affairs—to mastermind relationships with all facets of the non-commercial environment.[2] Although, in some cases, large local subsidiaries do have similar departments, this development is almost always a symptom of centralization. Central policies for handling delicate questions are being set and often the actual negotiations are being conducted by head office executives. Indeed, this is expected by world opinion as companies operating in South Africa have discovered—it is head office as well as the local subsidiary that comes under attack when controversial labour or marketing policies are followed. Increasing hostility on the part of governments and of public opinion leads to centralizing measures on the part of the companies most affected, and this occurs in spite of concessions to local regulations and of any increased bargaining power the subsidiary may acquire through government action.

The concept is one of policy-forming areas that overlap and is illustrated diagrammatically in Figure 12.2. This figure, too, encapsulates a complex process. The areas of policy-making where conflicts can occur are enclosed when the lines overlap. It will be noticed that there is a small area (MRQJ) where all the conflicts overlap. This reflects a small number of inter-governmental conflicts on subjects of competition or trading policies, where, for instance, a company will break the laws of one country or the other whatever it does. For the rest ECD represents the area of potential conflict between head office and subsidiary, AVJU with the host country government, and MNSHT with the host country government.

A reaction, then, of the companies to the changing environment is increased centralization. This is ironical because one of the complaints is of over-centralization. Governments object to decisions taken outside the country which have a significant influence on the national economy. Trade unions are irritated by their inability to reach the decision-maker. Employers' organizations find that foreign firms do not support them. The list could be added to, but the point is clear: some complaints, including those of over-centralization, have led to increased centralization. At the same time, in its conflict with head office, the subsidiary has a powerful identity of interest locally. In this sense the conflict with government may reflect and influence the conflict between head office and the subsidiary. The growth and expansion of the subsidiary is likely to be welcome to the country in which it is located. Investment and employment are involved. As against this the use of local funds, the control of exports and the payment of excessive royalties are sources of complaint. Further, international organizations are increasingly involved. Regional associations like the Latin American Free Trade Area or the European Economic Community, international organizations like the United Nations or the Organization for Economic Cooperation and Development, are taking a share in the restrictive role of

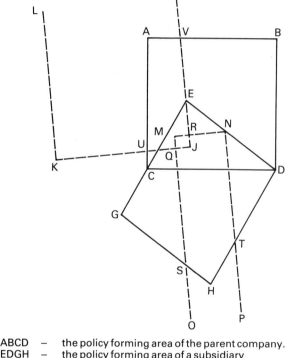

ABCD	–	the policy forming area of the parent company.
EDGH	–	the policy forming area of a subsidiary.
IJKL	–	part of the policy forming area of the home country government and other interest groups.
MNOP	–	part of the policy forming area of the host country government and other interest groups.

The diagram is illustrative only, not to scale.

Figure 12.2   The potential conflicts in the policy-making of the multinational company

government; this means that action by individual governments is less likely to drive away wanted investment where restrictions are imposed. The phrase 'taking a share' has been used advisedly because governments are still free to go their own ways; the codes of conduct agreed by international organizations are used by governments to influence corporate policies but are not obligatory on the member states. The trend to inter-governmental decisions does, however, make a global response on the part of companies more likely.

The foregoing discussion, summarized in Figure 12.2, which shows that the strategies and decision-making are influenced by the interlocking conflicts, has attempted to explain how the controversies reinforce the pressures to centralization rather than maintain the tension between greater and less autonomy. Nevertheless, there are powerful pressures the other way, not least the belief at head office that decentralization improves performance. This brings another element into the discussion; performance can be understood in many senses. Indeed, it is easy to assemble facts which produce a spiral argument. For an improvement in the *performance* of the subsidiary, defined as a short-term improvement in its operating figures, may be disadvantageous to other parts of the group and may lead to greater centralization. Figure 12.3 shows some of the contradictory pressures which recur in conversations with executives in appropriate posts.

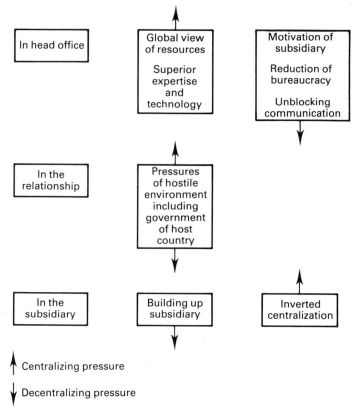

Figure 12.3   Some contradictory pressures

A particularly interesting occurrence is here called *inverted centralization*. This occurs when the parent company intends a decentralized arrangement, but where action in the subsidiary forces a more centralized arrangement than that intended. Inaction might be a more suitable word for the simplest form of this phenomenon, when the subsidiary simply fails or refuses to accept the responsibilities delegated. There are several more subtle forms. Conscious decentralization implies certain organization arrangements. For instance, the decentralized subsidiary will have the range of functions required for the total management of its business; if there is no purchasing department, that function cannot be said to be decentralized. Another feature of the autonomous subsidiary is that communications with head office are relatively fixed and formal, and it is not possible for an unauthorized executive or unit to seek instructions from the foreign head office. The subsidiary cannot be autonomous if its senior management can be bypassed. Where this does happen in fact, although against the intention, there occurs inverted centralization. The decision-making is being forced back to head office by subordinate managers in the subsidiary who are effectively ignoring their own superiors. The conditions under which this happens are usually the existence of a common bond of knowledge or expertise. The professional affinity may be more important than the national, and this is in fact an important aspect of the transfer of knowledge as well as of centralization.

The discovery of inverted centralization has methodological implications; it first came to light in the course of a consultancy exercise. It was noticed that a technical support function in an operating unit of a subsidiary was consulting, contrary to the rules, with the foreign head office over the heads of the national executives in the subsidiary headquarters, whose efforts to become involved were largely frustrated. Clearly such an arrangement required at least the connivance of the head of the unit concerned, and in this case he was on secondment from head office and was sympathetic to centralization. Figure 12.4 illustrates the position, the dotted line showing the unofficial but close link that was established in spite of company policies. The usual assumption is that decentralization is the aim of the subsidiary, but this aim may only apply to part of the subsidiary, and all the supposed benefits of autonomy can become disadvantages under certain circumstances. In this case, the autonomy was not boosting the morale or efficiency of all the subsidiary managers; on the contrary, it was causing frustration and annoyance to some. The local experts were more interested in links of knowledge and skill rather than those of nationality and found them in the parent company rather than in the local headquarters.

Once discovered, examples of inverted centralization can be detected in many companies, but the methodological significance is that it is doubtful whether this would ever have come to light through the normal procedures of research. Certainly, it would never have become apparent in answers to questionnaires, and probably not in less structured enquiries either. It needed a closer relationship with a company to bring to light an aspect of the subject which, although well-known to those concerned, was seldom articulated.

Inverted centralization, then, is one of the less evident pressures deriving from the conflicts in which the international company finds itself. Figure 12.4

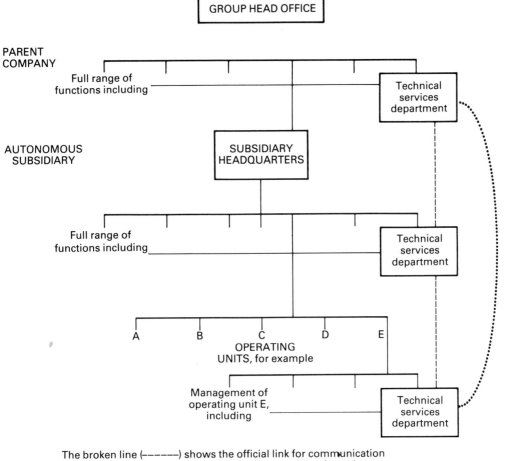

The broken line (------) shows the official link for communication and consultation on technical policies, the dotted line (.........) the unofficial.

Figure 12.4   An example of inverted centralization

picks up a number of others like government relations and organization. These are both discussed in subsequent chapters. Yet another issue is the role of head office as the depository of the business idea and the commercial expertise which gives the company its own niche in international trade, a role which places an upper limit on autonomy by including discipline and nurture, and the safeguarding of the vital knowledge. These two are inseparable from direct investment where the management relationship has, by definition, to be closer than the legal one of the shareholders and their property which is administered for them by others. This latter relationship is portfolio investment; the direct investor is interested in management as well as ownership and the conflicts derive from this.

The means of restricting conflict

That some conflict and dispute is inevitable is beyond doubt. The allocation of scarce resources has to involve disagreements and probably rival interests. There is no possibility that a company concentrating on providing a secure income for its shareholders can satisfy the aspirations of every sub-unit let alone the governments with which it has to deal. The inevitability does not, however, mean that there is any certainty about how the disagreements are resolved. There are indeed a number of considerations which include latent as well as actual conflicts, but also include a variety of ways of waging the dispute and attempting to restrict the consequences. The formation of an external affairs department to mastermind the corporate response to external influences has already been mentioned as one of the many responses that turn out to have a centralizing influence whatever the intention. The opposite response, to decentralize to the extent of leaving a subsidiary to manage its own affairs completely in effect to produce an investment relationship only, is also possible. The problem of this response is that the company is still held to be responsible for the activities of its affiliates, and can lose both the benefits of the international investment and its reputation at the same time—another reason behind the lure to centralization.

The internal conflicts are reduced by employing consultative and other procedures. If these increase the amount of central machinery, this may itself be a centralizing pressure and it is not unlikely that to recognize the force of the disagreements and allow the arguments to take their course is more effective. Whether this is so or not will partly depend on the view that those concerned take of the subsidiary performance; the method of appraisal can either enhance or modify the conflict.

12.2   PERFORMANCE APPRAISAL

To review performance haphazardly and in an unconvincing manner is likely to exacerbate the internal conflict—the external as well if the appraisal leads to disinvestment. Yet the methods used for monitoring performance across frontiers produce notorious difficulties. These difficulties are in part legal, coping with the consequences of national legislation on matters like the consolidation of accounts and the transfer of funds, and are compounded by regulations issued by accounting and other professional bodies. Factors like fluctuating exchange rates also play a part; but without all these problems there would still be the overriding consideration of corporate policies that make appraisal difficult when performance is judged solely by financial returns. In fact questions about appraisal do produce a variety of answers that run from the purely financial and quantifiable 'return on investment' to the more subtle and qualitative 'inspection of planning procedures'. The latter may appear over-subjective, but may turn out to be more realistic than the former and just as objective in practice. It is frequently assumed that the multinational firm produces its best results when the interests of the parts are subordinate to the whole, a centralizing argument; but it is characteristic of centralization that its increase makes a reliable appraisal of subsidiary all the more difficult.[3] When the choosing and implementing of policies are increasingly carried out at the centre, while instructions are given to subsidiaries which effectively ensure that they show poor results, there is an incentive to further centralization on the grounds that the subsidiaries cannot cope. One well-known instance of a subsidiary showing poor results apparently on instructions is that of the British subsidiary of Hoffman Laroche.[4] A high transfer price not only kept up prices in the United Kingdom, but also limited profits there, thus keeping down the taxes the company paid in a high tax country. Pricing policies were understood to be determined at head office; they usually are when a subsidiary is instructed to operate at a loss as a means of transferring funds to another unit of the firm where it is desired to place new investment. To make the required loss may involve as much managerial skill in the subsidiary as making a profit. So many interests, internal and external, are likely to be watching the company and the loss has to be achieved without shattering morale or destroying incentives.

Difficulties such as those described mean that the most convincing way of appraising subsidiary success is to include non-quantitative issues like the setting of plans and targets. Aggregated information across a sample of subsidiaries is distorted towards short-term or biased results. The less autonomous the subsidiary, the more the need for qualitative appraisal, while the more detailed the system used for reporting subsidiary results, the greater the suspicion of centralization. Transnational accounting is, however, a highly technical business and often disguises more than it shows even to the company concerned, let alone outsiders. This is another barrier to assessment which leads to centralization through a limited consideration of financial performance.[5] Nevertheless, decentralization is often considered as a consequence of high performance and, if this is so, a broader review is required. In practice, a mistaken belief that decentralization exists is often related to a restricted measure of centralization.

Take, for instance, the assumption that *decentralization improves performance.* In one example investigations clearly demonstrated that the company was not growing more decentralized as was assumed. After examining the research evidence, which demonstrated that they were issuing many more orders than they realized, the head office executives themselves agreed that such was the case.[6] Whatever may have been the reason for their success, it certainly was not the high level of autonomy. Another company reported the reverse worry, an assumption that over-centralization was causing sub-standard performance. It may have been, but the company as a whole was outperforming its rivals in a highly competitive market; hence the handicap, if any, cannot have been too severe.

The relationship between centralization or autonomy and the effectiveness of the organization is influenced by at least two other issues.

Care
The recognition of the potential conflicts and the attention paid to their

implications in organizing the company could be expected to mean that the relationship with the foreign subsidiary was centralized when that was required and decentralized when autonomy was more suitable, but in practice special emphasis on organization usually leads in the centralizing direction because expertise in administering semi-autonomous units is developed at head office, and the specialist department set up for the purpose is itself a centralizing force, dedicated to ensuring that its wisdom permeates throughout the enterprise. The consequence for performance will have some connection with the structure produced.

Contact

The amount of contact between head office and the subsidiary in the form of visits and conferences, can influence performance whatever the degree of centralization or autonomy. Sensitively handled, the advice, assistance and discussion of difficulties should remedy any shortcomings caused by autonomy, while insensitivity can produce a more centralized position than intended. The possible effects are sketched out in Figure 12.5, where the roman numerals are used to indicate an expected order of performance, from I high to IV low, if autonomy has the greater influence; the arabic numerals show the order if contact is more important. Naturally, there are other influences to be taken into account, and conclusive evidence is not available. There remains, however, the suggestion that contact is as important as autonomy in its influence on performance and that the two need to be practised together. Autonomy (lack of interference) with isolation does not produce the same result as autonomy with contact—advice, assistance and the ability to discuss problems.

Autonomy / Contact	High	Low
High	I 1	III 2
Low	II 3	IV 4

Figure 12.5 Possible influence of autonomy and contact on performance

The decision-making will also be influenced by yet another conflict, that between the differing objectives of the individuals and groups that exist both in head office and the subsidiary. Thus, the corporate aims, the subsidiary's objectives and the personal objectives of individual managers do not always coincide. Entry into new products or localities, for instance, is likely to mean a cutback in resources for those that already exist. There may be conflict because of the different expectations of various groups of managers (according to experience, qualifications, age group or nationality for instance); there will certainly be the conflict of projections with which this chapter started, and which was followed by a review of the conflicting interests through which the decision-making has to be steered and which influence the degree of centralization. The means of ensuring that the conflict is constructive rather than destructive were then considered as was the effect on performance. The following chapters will expand the subject in the context of the various influences already detected beginning with relations with governments and other interest groups in the companies' environment.

13 Company – Country Relations

The multinational firm has become an object of controversy partly because of its size and partly because its policies are not confined within national frontiers. The large organization, always an object of criticism for its effect on the human spirit, has come under fire in recent years.[1] Doubts have been cast on its efficiency as well as its humanity. When a particularly large organization appears to threaten policies determined by a democratically elected government, the censure can be expected to grow more intense. Indeed it was the fashion, some years ago, for multinationals and their supporters to emphasize the advantages of a corporate internationalism which was making national frontiers irrelevant and obsolete. A Hungarian writer in the early 1970s listed numerous quotations from Western writings stating that the multinational corporation had rendered the nation state an anachronism.[2] The arguments quoted are little used today and the nation state can be said to have staged a come-back, at least temporarily.

The problem governments now face is to find a means of restraining the multinational company without driving it elsewhere. Foreign business brings to a country much-needed investment, high quality employment, advanced technology and other benefits, including improved standards of management and methods of commerce. That a high price is charged for these benefits does not lessen the dilemma of government; on the contrary part of the price is made up of international competition for corporate favours, the incentives and concessions aimed at luring companies. A result of the dilemma has been the growing demand for a framework of international regulation to compel companies not to exercise their powers to the national disadvantage, and not to play one government off against another. The rules or codes are usually voluntary, except in regional treaty organizations (like the European or the Andean common markets) where they may be incorporated in the laws of member states, and are directed towards countries as well as companies; there are clauses, for instance, aimed at restraining countries from competing for foreign investment in the way they offer incentives.

Meanwhile companies face their own dilemmas. If they fail to create a mass market and charge accordingly, they are accused of overcharging; if they do produce a mass market, they are accused of dubious sales methods. If they do not promote local nationals from various parts of the company, they are accused of nationalism or racialism, and if they do they are accused of fostering a brain-drain. Another dilemma is that the various interest groups in a country—finance, labour and consumers among them—have different aims and different criteria of success, but manage to agree among themselves in advocating restrictions on the foreign firm.

One demand is that the subsidiary be allowed autonomy, that it is intolerable that a foreign company can issue instructions to a locally registered organization which can harm the local economy. The transfer of funds between units of a company is cited as an example. Funds are frequently transferred into a strong economy where the company wants to develop its business and out of a weak one, which is thus further weakened. In April 1983, for instance, it was announced that Ford of Britain had lent £981 million to the parent company during the preceding two years. This represented a large amount of capital at a time of high unemployment in the subsidiary's country, and could be considered a form of involuntary aid from a poorer country to a richer one. Of course there is no evidence that it was 'involuntary' on the subsidiary's part or that any instructions were issued; the deal may well have been regarded as a profitable use of spare cash at a time of high interest rates in the United States. It could further be argued on behalf of the companies that this is an unrepresentative case. The reverse transfer was a return for earlier support when funds had been passing into Ford of Britain; the company was, in any case, fortunate in being able to draw on the resources of a subsidiary in a time of need. Companies more often find themselves caught with unused funds in parts of the world from which exchange control regulations make it impossible to move the money, and in a currency with little value even if it could be moved. Many an exercise which is criticised by host country interests as over-greedy is difficult to justify to shareholders because it is unprofitable due to blocked remittances.

Whatever the implications of a particular instance, the demand of governments is that the national subsidiary should have more independence to decide what is best for its own development, but a consequence of the atmosphere created by the controversies is that companies are unwilling to leave a subsidiary free to deal with delicate political issues. Only head office, it is thought, has the resources to produce executives with the ability and knowledge to negotiate with governments. The fear is that an autonomous subsidiary, whether through ineptitude or prejudice, will cause unnecessary trouble. The company acts on the military principle that local commanders cannot be allowed to start wars. Where a local problem does arise, the company as a whole is blamed and one more is added to the list of accusations against the multinational firm.

13.1   DECISIONS THAT CAUSE SCANDAL

The word 'dilemma' has been worked hard already, but its use indicates why the troubled relations between companies and governments particularly influence the degree of centralization. A normal response to any serious dilemma is to decide that this is a head office issue and that special skills and expertise are required. When the dilemma concerns non-commercial questions which yet have vital commercial consequences, the centralizing response becomes even more probable. Some subsidiaries are big businesses in their own right, able to afford a range of services and specialist advisers, but most are not. The services that are able to wrestle with political, legal and social problems cannot be provided in a typical small subsidiary, especially where companies find themselves involved in an almost irreconcilable conflict. The clash may be completely outside the control of the company, like the American-owned bank operating in Paris in the early days of the Second World War caught between contradictory regulations. The pressure in this case was between a French emergency law instructing all banks operating in the country to place a proportion of their deposits in government securities and the American Neutrality Act which forbade United States companies from investing with belligerent governments. The resultant legal action was left unresolved when France fell in 1940, but 25 years later a case involving the same two countries had a different outcome. This instance came at a time when the French government was actively encouraging trade with China, but the American government was still placing an embargo on trading links. The company was the Detroit-based Fruehauf Trailers, whose French subsidiary won a subcontract to the state-owned concern Berliet, who were selling lorries to China. The parent company brusquely telexed the subsidiary instructing the non-fulfilment of the order. The French reaction was one of outrage,[3] and the chief executive of the local subsidiary resolved to take his company before the commercial courts which instructed the fulfilment of the contract. The same company had a serious difference with its British subsidiary some years later which had a different outcome. In this case the issue was internal to the company, a row over the purchase by the parent company of shares previously available on the local stock exchange. The eventual outcome was the dismissal of the British board after the Monopolies Commission had reported that there were no grounds for intervention.[4] A more recent example was over the supply of materials for the Soviet pipeline bringing natural gas to Western Europe. In this case United States companies were ordered to stop supplies as part of sanctions imposed after the invasion of Afghanistan and the imposition of martial law in Poland. The Dresser Corporation was one which found itself under attack on both sides of the Atlantic. Officials of the parent company were refused immunity from prosecution in the American courts if their French subsidiary delivered the compressors they had been contracted to supply. At the same time Dresser (France) was ordered by the French government (under an Act of 1959) to despatch the compressors. In Britain a licensee of General Electric, John Brown Ltd, was in a similar position over turbines. The British government (under an Act of 1980) forbade the company from obeying the United States embargo order. These instances showed not only disputes within a company over where decisions are taken, but between governments as well. The fact that the host country government won in both cases shows that sovereignty can ultimately be upheld, where the government is strong enough and the country rich enough.

Other cases that demonstrate similar issues involved international organizations as well like the dispute over formula milk.

The formula milk controversy

The incidents already mentioned are among those which have aroused demands for greater autonomy, but recently there have been examples of cases in which the opposition has effectively demanded greater centralization by blaming head office for the sins of the subsidiary. One such is the long-running controversy over the high-pressure selling of formula milk for babies in developing countries. The manufacturers involved, Nestlé, Bristol-Myers, Abbott Laboratories, American Home Products, Borden, Cow & Gate and Glaxo among them, were accused of damaging the health of infants in the poorer countries by the measures used to sell formula milk. The problem for the companies was that they would have been even more severely criticized if they had refused to allow sale of the product. Formula milk is vital to a baby's survival where breastfeeding is impossible, not an uncommon situation in rich countries and even more likely to occur in countries where the mothers are inadequately fed; it is also safer than unprocessed milk from cows or goats. The companies' position was made more difficult by the fact that a considerable sales effort was needed in an impoverished and tradition-bound society to create a mass market. Without this the price would have been too high, and the manufacturers would then have been accused of over-charging.

As it happened this accusation was made in any case, but the main charge was that the selling methods gave the customers the impression that good mothers must make every effort to provide their babies with this product, but did not give them sufficient instruction in its use. On the tins were details about the strength of the mixture required, for instance, but these were hard to follow and impossible if the mother was illiterate. It was also improbable that the water would be sterilized, especially if a long walk to a scarce well was necessary, and the formula product did not provide the babies with the immunity carried by the mother's milk. The salesmanship included broadcasting, free samples at the clinics and the dressing of sales ladies in nurses' uniforms.

The controversy began in the early 1970s when publicity was given to research results which produced evidence that harm was being done to infants by the formula milk. There were also counter-arguments, such as the statement that the product had also made a large contribution to improved health, that abuse could easily be cured and that the fuss was greatly exaggerated in any case; a mother's instincts usually told her when a product was harming her baby before it was too late. The World Health Organization began to consider the issue in 1972, but in 1974 the publication of a leaflet in Switzerland entitled *Nestlé Kills Babies* and the subsequent libel action brought the matter to the attention of public opinion in many parts of the world. Boycotts against the manufacturers were undertaken in North America and a variety of organizations entered the argument. Finally, in January 1981, the World Health Organization adopted a code of conduct for the promotion of formula milk. This code was accepted by all the delegates present except the United States and was subsequently adopted by the General Assembly of the WHO. During the controversy Nestlé, the company which bore the brunt of the attack, held a number of internal investigations. Instructions to subsidiaries in countries at risk followed these investigations until finally, in February 1982, the company sent a directive threatening 'appropriate corrective action' against any affiliate which did not comply with the World Health Organization's code.[5] This example brings together a number of emotive issues—breastfeeding, infant mortality and big business—and well illustrates the consequences of external pressures on centralization. Food companies have less reason than most for central control; on the contrary the local subsidiary has to fit into its national culture and to be able to take decisions in the light of changing tastes and fast-moving competitors. The centre might give advice on marketing techniques, but to determine sales promotion centrally would make little sense. Nestlé was already more centralized than many food companies in possessing international brand names, but the need to defend itself against so much hostile opinion and threats to the business certainly produced more centralization, culminating in the instruction quoted.

Dismissal without compensation

A debate in a much lower key, but with an even more subtle implication for the subject of autonomy, occurred in 1977 as a result of the bankruptcy of Badger (Belgium) SA.[6] This firm dismissed its 250 employees, mostly professional engineers, without notice or compensation, and the liquidation was confirmed by a court of law. The employees' representatives argued their case with strong support from the Belgian government, but the company refused payment on the grounds that there were no funds with which to pay. Badger (Belgium) was a subsidiary of the Badger Corporation of Massachusetts which, in its turn, was a subsidiary of the Raytheon Corporation. Both parent companies were profitable at the time and Badger was actively recruiting staff in at least one other European subsidiary. In this case it was the company that argued that the subsidiary was an independent entity and that the parent's responsibility was limited to that of a shareholder. The principle of limited liability meant that the shareholder could not be held accountable except for the funds invested. Indeed, the accusation that critics of the company were calling in question the principle of limited liability was made repeatedly in the debate.

The opponents argued, on the other hand, that the principle was being abused anyway when a rich company allowed a subsidiary to go bankrupt. It was alleged that an important reason for the bankruptcy was the manipulation of international contracts between affiliates by the parent company, and that the ability of the subsidiary to control its own destiny had been impaired; so a lack of autonomy was being alleged and the company was simultaneously being asked to accept responsibility for its affiliate and to pay its debts. It so happened that six months earlier the member countries of the Organization for Economic Cooperation and Development had finally signed a code of conduct agreeing, if tentatively, that profitable firms should not disclaim responsibility for subsidiary debts. Representatives of employers and trade unions had both agreed to the final draft of the code, itself a compromise. The important clause was mildly worded in the adopted version. It did not demand that units should not be closed, but that appropriate warning should be given of any changes 'to representatives of their employees, and where appropriate to the relevant governmental authorities so as to mitigate to the maximum effect practicable adverse effects'. The code itself was voluntary and specifically stated that individual companies could not be arraigned under its terms, but after the debate the company eventually agreed to pay compensation to the employees, a result which previous approaches by the Belgian government had failed to secure. A number of cases since have demonstrated that a voluntary code can in fact produce results in the form of cash for an aggrieved party.

An incident that demonstrated yet another facet of the political pressure for centralization occurred when a British company appointed a local national to take charge of a South American subsidiary. Satisfactory results from the subsidiary led to the company decentralizing thoroughly and only reserving a minimum number of key decisions to head office until it was discovered that the chief executive of the Latin American company was using his position to support plots against the government. The main board had reaffirmed a policy of strict non-intervention in local affairs and was horrified to learn that the policy was being contravened, especially in a newly industrialized country of Latin America. The dismissal of the executive was followed by one of the ironical turns of fortune which so often accompanies such incidents. The dismissed executive sued in the local courts for wrongful dismissal—the country at the time possessed a law specifically protecting local managers from ejection by foreign companies—and was reinstated. In the end the company acquired a reputation for intervention which would have been avoided had it remained more centralized in the first place.

These examples illustrate a number of ways in which a company can find itself involved in a scandal through insisting that the subsidiary is an autonomous part of the corporate system. For the subsidiary itself there is a two-way struggle according to whether it is regarded as integrated into the company or to the national economy. Of course, it has a measure of integration with both, and the struggles to which these examples witness are a consequence of this two-way integration, or lack of it.

13.2 THE TWO-WAY AUTONOMY

The logic of commercial policies is increasingly influenced by government action, a fact which has introduced this action into the discussion. Inevitably, the significance of a word like 'autonomy' is widened when it is applied to a unit with rival claims on its allegiance, while disentangling the relationships is complicated in what is clearly not a zero-sum game. Solutions are possible that benefit all the parties, but only under certain sets of circumstances. A closer look suggests that when the country and the company are prospering, there may be a mutual interest which promotes the prosperity of both, but there is little chance of mutual benefit when a company moves money out of a country, especially if that country is already suffering from balance of payments problems. At the same time consideration for their own corporate citizens and for the benefits that foreign investment brings inhibits restriction.

The friction is increased by mutual incomprehension between company executives and government officials. Each regards the other as wielding excessive power. Executives of the subsidiary see the two-way conflict clearly enough. They have to obey the rules of the company and act in its best interests unless there is a specific government instruction to behave differently. If there is, they will obey it, however unwillingly. The government is sovereign and they cannot understand statements to the contrary; their attitude is normally reinforced by the certainty that their career with the company will be endangered if they acquire a reputation for arousing hostility in the country.

The officials, on the other hand, and the politicians are constantly aware that the company can withdraw its investment when it wishes and move elsewhere. The exercise is more difficult than is sometimes imagined, but that is beside the point since the threat determines the reactions. The company is seen as holding all the cards against the poorly placed government whose authority is sapped by the footloose firm. Other interest groups take the same view and one reason for the bad publicity that the multinational has received in recent years is surely because a variety of groups see themselves to be threatened. Financial interests, for instance, regard foreign multinationals as a danger to the domestic money market. The fact that companies prefer 100 per cent ownership where this is possible means that shares cannot be bought in attractive local concerns, the well-managed high technology firms which are worth taking over. This is disappointing to financial institutions and other shareholders who do not find the ability to bid for high-priced shares in the parent company a desirable alternative. This inability to buy shares, while the foreign company also rates high priority for local loan finance, has built up opposition among those who are certainly not opposed to big business but are concerned with the interests of local entrepreneurs and those of the local money market. Opposition on the part of labour interests is more expected but not necessarily more determined. Trade union reaction to employers who switch production across frontiers is vocal rather than effective. The workers of one country gain what those of another lose, and there is little proneness to unity where interests are so divided, except where the transfer of investment involves either a reduction of the overall labour force or a move to a low-wage country. What does exist, and this makes the unlikely alliance between capital and labour a pressure on the company, is a motive to promote international restraints. In view of the balance of power, the unions have seen political action to be more advantageous than industrial.

Other organized groups, like consumers and churches, also find that companies affront their interests or principles, while educationalists (especially those concerned with science and technology) notice the implications for education of the way firms concentrate their research in the home country. In Canada, for instance, there are mutterings about the consequences of having to live with a 'branch economy'. At least an industrial country like Canada has a foot in both camps, as the home country of many multinationals. For most of the developing countries this is not the case, although the number of small-scale foreign investments is growing. By the same token, the less-developed countries which do have markets, labour and infrastructure sufficient to attract investors are not inhibited by the threat of reprisals. Hence, they have been able to impose regulations that insist on the sale of local equity and on safeguards for the local employees.

The situation facing governments is one of a balance between benefit and damage to national interests, and the search for a form of regulation which will not involve a loss of benefits has further increased the demand for international action. This demand has been met in two ways; both are designed to integrate the subsidiary more closely in the national system, and thus to ensure for it more autonomy in the corporate system as well. One way is by regulation on the part of regional bodies, notably the European Community and the Andean Common Market on specific issues like competition, restraint of trade and local financing (see the list in the notes on issues between companies and governments at the end of this chapter).

The general codes of conduct

The other international method of achieving national regulation is by codes of conduct which are voluntary by nature and depend on the united opinion and pressure of the signatories. These again are of two kinds: the general and the specialized. The first general code of conduct was promulgated by the Organization for Economic Cooperation and Development (OECD) in 1976.[7] This was relatively brief, confined itself to general principles and contained prescriptions for governments—they were not to compete with one another in offering incentives and they were to treat foreign firms on the same basis as domestic firms—as well as companies. The special significance of the OECD code was that it partially reversed one of the principles on which the Organization was founded, the increasing liberalization of capital movements. The liberalization was decreased to the extent that countries were to be encouraged to demand and companies to accept a number of conditions for such movements. These included the upholding of the laws, the economic policies and the interests of each country of operation, the observation of local standards and practices on labour relations and other social policies, and the mitigating of any harmful consequences that global strategies might have for local subsidiaries. A practical consequence of the acceptance of this code was seen in the Badger case already discussed.

A more ambitious and detailed framework of regulation is proposed by the United Nations. This is still under discussion, but the main outline and most of the clauses have been agreed.[8] These fall into six main parts. The first three declare that the code is aimed at policing the multinationals and ensuring that their activities contribute to international development, that the scope of the code is any enterprise from whatever nationality or type of ownership that has substantial authority over an affiliate abroad, and that companies must respect the sovereignty, laws, policies, cultures and traditions of the countries in which they operate, while opposing apartheid. These clauses are clearly designed to transfer as much authority as possible from the corporate head office to local institutions, while the fourth section lists the policies which concern governments most. Political interference and corrupt practices are condemned, while the subsidiary is to be 'structured' in such a way as to allow it to make a full contribution to a country's social and economic plans. Personnel policies and training programmes are to be arranged for the benefit of local nationals.

The trading policies of the subsidiary are to include freedom to export to any markets in which the products can be sold, while financial policies must conform to the laws of the host country and not harm its economy. In particular the repatriation of capital, the transfer of profits and other cash transactions are to be timed to minimize the damage to the balance of payments. The subsidiary is also expected to avoid practices unhelpful to the national capital markets, to consult with the government when engaged in share issues or long-term loans, and to cooperate in efforts to establish local equity participation. Transfer prices should be based on the arm's-length principle that trading with other units of the company should be at prices, and on terms, that would apply if they were separate firms. Restrictive practices are condemned, while technology is to be transferred at a reasonable price.

The protection of consumers and of the physical environment is also called for. Detailed clauses demand that information is disclosed for the enterprise as a whole, for each subsidiary as a separate company, and (with some reservations) by region for all products and by product for the world. The information is to be presented under the following headings (for the whole company and for each unit): balance sheet, income statement, allocation of profits, sources and uses of funds, new long-term investments, research and development expenditure, the structure of the company, the shareholding, the operations, employment provided, the accounting practices employed and the principles used for transfer pricing. Representatives of labour are to be kept fully informed of plans and developments likely to affect the employees, subject to safeguards where confidentiality is important.

The final sections of the code emphasize the relationships between companies and countries. In return for a responsible attitude to their role in the country, companies can expect the same treatment as domestic firms with freedom from arbitrary expropriation and adequate compensation in the event of nationalization. Governments can prohibit the entry of foreign firms into certain sectors of the economy. Procedures are to be agreed for solving problems of jurisdiction which may cause difficulties for companies, and there is provision for the development of bilateral and multilateral agreements between states to implement the clauses of the code. Governments agree not to use companies in the furtherance of their policies in other countries but, on the contrary, to use their influence to prevent firms from interfering in the internal affairs of host nations. The final clauses deal with implementation and reconsideration.

A thorough-going implementation of this comprehensive code will undoubtedly mean greater independence for the individual subsidiary on specific issues. Changes in ownership policies, for instance, will open up other forms of devolution. But these changes are coming in any case (see Chapter 15) and some of the other proposals will not always lead to the hoped-for results. The disclosure of information, as an example, will provide more detailed information to the government, the trade unions and other interested parties. It will also provide more information to shareholders, and ensure within the company a more immediate response to issues that could previously be fudged. On the other hand, highly centralized decisions like disposal or closure become more likely. The clean break is easier in a hostile environment. In any event, companies will devise fresh modes of operating within the new constraints. It is the clauses about training local nationals and permitting more local centres of research that are likely to have more long-term influence rather than the establishment of a series of constraints that are hard to enforce. The positive clauses are mainly ones whose implementation depends only partly on the companies. National educational, technological, industrial and other policies will have as much influence.

The specialized codes of conduct

The code that resulted from the controversy over the sale of formula milk in poor countries has already been mentioned.[9] This called on manufacturers to restrain their sales promotion. Companies as a whole were blamed for the damage caused by subsidiaries in developing countries, hence head offices were asked to exercise more authority over their foreign affiliates. A year earlier, an agreement had been signed on an entirely different issue—restrictive trade practices.[10] This aims to reinforce and supplement national competition policies, above all in making sure that the benefits of measures aimed at trade liberalization are achieved. The code includes the provision of technical assistance when required and considers a number of issues on which the national influence on the local company may need strengthening against that of the head office. The same organization (UNCTAD) is developing a code concerning the transfer of technology which attempts to facilitate access to technical knowledge and patents. The code covers all transfers, with an emphasis on the interests of developing countries, but is mainly aimed at the multinational firm, especially at increasing the autonomy of the foreign subsidiary. Indeed this code originated in a more general proposal for regulation.

The International Labour Office is yet another organization which has produced a code[11] on labour and other social policies. This is divided into six sections, of which the first declares that the code covers all types of company (whether in private, mixed or public ownership) and is aimed at supporting the positive contributions to national well-being and reducing the harmful ones. Companies are expected, in the following sections, to respect the sovereignty of the states in which they operate and especially to support freedom of association, collective bargaining and non-discrimination in labour and social policies; they are urged to go beyond the local norms in these policies and to provide relevant training at all levels together with high standards of safety and health. There are provisions for enforcing agreed best practices in industrial relations, and governments are required not to offer incentives in the form of anti-labour measures. The code ends with procedures for regular consultation and the settling of disputes.

The United Nations also has expert groups working on accounting and reporting practices and on the subject of illicit payments,[12] while the long-running saga of the United Nations Convention on the Law of the Sea looks like heading the list of topical issues into the late 1980s. Most of the codes and agreements, it will be noted, are of recent date and represent a gradually increased pressure on corporate decision-makers. The intangible effects are, of course, incalculable, although it has already been indicated that they are double-edged. Companies react to pressure for greater devolution by greater centralization—out of fear of allowing autonomy to units in delicate situations. The tangible results are detailed and have consequences for individual companies rather than producing a general trend. An engineering consultancy firm did compensate its employees in Belgium and some formula milk producers did give instructions to their subsidiaries in Africa. At the same time some cherished principles are being dinted. It is doubtful whether the principle of limited liability will continue to be applied in its pure form to companies who are taking to themselves a more interventionist approach than is expected of shareholders, any more than subsidiary privileges will be granted to units that are being treated as branches. Some international efforts to redefine the principle in both cases for direct investment are probable.

In this discussion it has become clear that the statement that governments exercise pressure for decentralization has to be modified. That is true of individual governments seeking greater influence on the policies of subsidiaries; as members of international treaty organizations the same governments are working for centralization on some issues—the forcing of head office to accept responsibility for any shortcomings in subsidiary activities. This dual pressure is tending to call in question statements affirming that policies are centralized and operations autonomous. That the distinction is hard to maintain is asserted elsewhere, but for inter-governmental pressures on companies the implications may well be reversed. Meanwhile the balance of the countervailing powers will be examined in the rest of this chapter.

13.3   PRESSURES FOR DECENTRALIZATION

The conflicting pressures on the subsidiary towards integration with the rest of the company as well as within its own country have been demonstrated both by examples and by moves towards international regulation. The discussion so far has been designed to emphasize the contradictions in the political environment; it remains that the demands heard most clearly outside the international bodies are for greater devolution to the host country. The international expertise is taken for granted, it is the local benefits that are sought.

In some countries, especially the newly industrializing, there is a straightforward demand that the companies should show themselves more adaptable to local conditions. These countries hold out the promise of rapid expansion with an improving infrastructure and increasingly well-trained labour forces who only expect modest wages. Within substantial national differences most are using their attractiveness to the foreign investor to impose conditions. The countries include India, Nigeria, Egypt and other Middle East states, the richer countries of Latin America, and the five members of the Association of South East Asian Nations (Singapore, Malaysia, Indonesia, South Korea and Thailand). Of these the last-named group have the most lenient regulations from the company's point of view, but their increasing wealth and growing self-consciousness as a group means that more regulation is likely. This can be expected to extend to other developing countries, although most are in a weaker position to enforce restrictive measures. Nevertheless, the bargaining power of all the developing nations is increasing, and with it the ability to insist on less foreign authority over subsidiaries operating within their boundaries. This trend is coming about as a result of a number of changes, not the least of which is Japanese investment, which is usually more amenable to local aspirations, including the wish for participation. There is also the discovery by foreign companies that non-equity arrangements can be profitable and relatively free of risk, while national administrators are gaining experience of workable policies and are, be it said, being driven by increasing balance of payments difficulties to make demands on companies. These demands include the need to purchase locally, the need to control cash movements, and the need to control all expenditure of hard currency. All these measures together are ensuring that business in the developing countries is acquiring ground-rules that resemble those in industrialized countries less and less.[13]

Undoubtedly, the more concerted international effort is another factor in enabling the developing countries to adopt restrictive measures, but some go well beyond the requirements of the codes. For instance, regulations in India have forced some local subsidiaries into adopting strategies unrelated to those of the parent company. The regulations in question compel the company to reinvest a proportion of its earnings within the country, and then to reinvest in industry sectors on the government priority list. High technology companies can usually find related products to develop, but others find themselves led into a number of product lines which the subsidiary would not have entered if the regulations had not existed. Indeed the search for appropriate (and conglomerate) diversification has been a feature of recent developments in a number of countries, as has been the emergence of local assembly plants to match another set of regulations and tariff arrangements—those controlling imports. Companies like General Motors and IBM have withdrawn from some of their operations rather than grant the required autonomy to their local subsidiaries. Such withdrawals, which occurred mainly between 1965 and 1975, bear witness to the strength of the centralizing policies, but they are becoming more improbable as the regulations are spreading and as companies learn to live with them. Nevertheless, the pressures for decentralization remain strong and are often the subject of deeply held convictions and powerful speeches. In the last twenty years, the debate has echoed with allegations like 'the third greatest industrial power in the world, after the United States and Russia, will not be Europe, but American investment in Europe' or 'national governments, including our own, will be reduced to the status of parish councils in dealing with the large corporations that will span the world'.[14]

13.4   PRESSURES FOR CENTRALIZATION

The countervailing pressures have already been outlined. Commercial considerations, as companies see them, usually indicate the need for centralization. That is a theme of these chapters and is reinforced by non-commercial considerations, like the fear of being plunged into controversy by inept actions on the part of local subsidiaries, or the fear that their managers do not have the knowledge or experience to negotiate with governments. Growing competition and increasing criticism both induce companies towards globally integrated policies and management. Their ability to implement the global policies depends upon their bargaining position for the time being, and shifts in the balance of power (along with the ability to cause the shifts to happen) underlie most of this chapter. In 13.2 efforts to tilt the balance towards governments through international action were described. These efforts are countered when the company has attractions which prove irresistible to host nations. A prime bargaining counter is knowledge and expertise, especially technical knowhow, and international agreements on this subject have proved difficult to finalize or enforce. One authority writes about the 'counteractive response' whereby companies can override restrictions, citing the ability of an electronic manufacturer to negotiate a wholly-owned venture in Japan before that country's regulations were modified to permit such ventures; also cited is the refusal of American aerospace manufacturers to enter into arrangements which allowed their partners more than subcontractor status.[15] The ability not only to provide technology, but to offer it in a commercial package which includes marketing, after-sales, financing and updating knowledge, is a particularly strong bargaining counter. For this reason efforts have been made through the ILO code to make provision for the unpackaging, the use by developing countries of a number of different agencies in bringing a particular innovation to their markets. Numerous small consultancy operations have come into existence in the energy industries, for instance, and equipment can be hired on charter. Another counter to the bargaining effect of high technology is for a country to accept a less advanced product. In spite of the emphasis on intermediate or appropriate technologies, this has proved difficult in practice.

Sources of bargaining power for the multinationals are their economies of scale, where these apply, and in particular their ability to establish specialized plants for components or limited product lines in different countries linked by a sophisticated logistic system. Such a system depends upon a high degree of centralization, but the attractiveness to a country of a specialized plant makes it relatively easy to negotiate. Yet another source is that of product differentiation based on technology, rather than that based on marketing considerations.

The competitive situation has already been mentioned with the suggestion that intense competition works differently according to the size of the company. The large firm usually reacts by greater centralization; the smaller firm may react in the same way, but may instead respond by seeking an alliance with government. As part of any deal for assistance or cooperation, the authorities will almost certainly demand that they are able to deal with an autonomous subsidiary. In fact government officials are usually looking for reliability and may be suspicious of approaches from any but the largest firms. A smaller firm will usually need to possess a reputation which it would be unwilling to lose, or an outstanding invention, before it has much bargaining power; although the preference for larger firms may be modified by another—that for companies from neutral countries like Norway.

External affairs

One reaction of the larger company, especially where government contracts are at stake is the external affairs department.[16] The growth of an institution within the company (the exact title varies) to cope with the non-commercial aspects of the environment sets the seal, as it were, on the centralizing effects of the controversies that surround the multinational. The department takes under its wing all aspects of the corporate relationship with those parts of the environment which are not primarily the concern of the technical or marketing functions, and where non-commercial skills are required. Included are relationships with governments, educational, charitable and other organizations, as well as the public relations function. The department also conducts research into public opinion and other aspects of the environment, feeding information into the company and making proposals for speeches by directors and others who have to express corporate opinions to the public. The department is normally a centralizing force; it is expensive to run and suitable staff are hard to recruit, since the work is conducted outside the normal commercial disciplines but within a commercial hierarchy. Some subsidiaries do have their own external affairs departments. If they do, this normally suggests a degree of decentralization unless (like some foreign research departments) they are closely locked into the head office department. In this case they are being used to ensure that central policies are being closely followed abroad.

13.5 CONCLUSIONS

This chapter is constructed around two themes. The first is that the subsidiary's autonomy is under attack from two sides: its corporate head office and its national government. The same is, of course, true of head office to a certain extent. There are pressures on companies to play or to refrain from playing a particular role in world affairs according to the policies of its domestic government.

The British government, for instance, has been attempting to promote more investment in developing countries while reducing aid, thus, it has been suggested, transferring the cost from the taxpayer to the shareholder. The resolution of the conflict depends on the bargaining strengths of the two sides, but the success of one is not necessarily the failure of the other. There are matters of common interest as well as of conflict. A relevant issue that has not been mentioned is the possibility of the subsidiary playing its head office and its government off against one another and thus achieving a degree of managerial autonomy from both. A satisfactory record of growth and profitability may mean that it is dangerous for head office to interfere, that any change has to be for the worse, and if the parent company has restricted horizons, there will be little incentive to bring pressure to bear on the subsidiary. There will be greater emphasis on conformity in a company with a global planning system. Lack of interest on the part of the government is more likely to arise from issues outside the subsidiary's control, like its relative unimportance to the economy. In the studies reported in Chapter 11, few subsidiaries argued convincingly that they were able to modify head office threats by quoting regulations or policies. Nevertheless, the corporate system is strained by having to cope with the different requirements of different countries, and numerous exceptions to global policies are required to enable the subsidiaries to live within the law. A special case was cited by a European company which had entered into collaborative agreements with domestic competitors. These arrangements were legal at home, but it was feared that they might fall foul of anti-trust legislation in the United States, so the arrangement was kept secret from the North American subsidiary.

In the main, then, there is a process of manoeuvring and manipulating between companies and governments in which the company's main bargaining counter is its superior knowledge, which enables it to bring wealth and employment to the country. Governments are increasingly relying on international codes to support their demands for greater control of national subsidiaries. The countries which are in a strong bargaining position are the newly industrializing countries, especially those on the Pacific rim. These possess markets that are attractive to the multinational and are not as inhibited as the industrialized countries by being also the home countries of foreign investors. This favourable situation can be expected to change slowly.

The other theme of this chapter has been the recurring paradox that controversies provoked because companies are considered over-centralized have led to greater centralization. The ultimate stage in this process was the emergence of a department to handle external affairs, a department which is usually centralized and a centralizing influence.

Issues between companies and governments

This chapter concludes with notes on the issues on which controversies occur, where either the practices or the expectations of the companies conflict with the policies and aspirations of nations. This list does not claim to be exhaustive; included are those issues which most clearly indicate the contradictory pressures on centralization and autonomy.

Competition
The company is alleged to exercise too much power in the market place, but

companies counter-claim that globally they promote competition. A degree of centralization is needed to justify this claim.

Employment

Multinationals are sought after because they provide employment and jobs of high quality in progressive industries; the opposition arises when plants and other facilities are transferred across frontiers, especially for non-market reasons that appear to be anti-government or anti-labour. In this case the accusation is of over-centralization, not allowing the local operation to develop within its own market.

Environment (physical)

This is one of the non-commercial issues on which multinationals are accused of taking central decisions. Plants are moved to countries which have lax pollution laws. Companies reply that, on the contrary, they have the resources to go beyond the demands of the law, and that the expense of anti-pollution equipment demands central development and purchasing.

Finance

Among the most controversial subjects is the movement of funds and the payment of remittances. A problem for a country is that the movement of substantial funds—the repayment of a loan or the payment of a large dividend—can come when the country is itself in economic difficulties. If, at such a time, the company decides to move the money to another country to invest in greater prosperity there, the transfer hits an economy that is already troubled. A domestic firm could be expected to reinvest a high proportion of its earnings instead of paying out dividends which would weaken the company and the country. A problem for a company is that of blocked remittances. Some companies are in need of funds which they possess but cannot move to the operation that needs them.

Information

Discussed with less passion than subjects like pricing and employment, but as frequently on the agenda when multinationals are being criticized, is the demand for information. The demand comes partly from the frustration of administrators and trade unionists who are unable to find out the relevant facts about the local operation—what it can afford, for instance. The international and regional codes include a demand for more information, which is often difficult to supply, information being expensive in its own right, but an attempt to meet the demand revives the conflict between central and local authority in a different and enigmatic form. Take the example of a United States based multinational with a subsidiary in France. At home the company is accustomed to being open with its operating figures. The local mores and the stock exchange regulations both demand openness. In France, on the other hand, the subsidiary is in a climate of opinion which respects privacy in business affairs, where regulations about publishing information are undemanding, but where there is considerable hostility to foreign investors. In this situation the local company is likely to play safe and to take advantage of the permitted secrecy lest openness leads the critics to find occasions for further hostility. The object of demands for greater information in such a case would be the centre, demanding that head office persuades the local affiliate to reveal its facts and figures.

Labour

The personnel function is often described as the most decentralized, but trade unions allege that companies use their global facilities to strengthen their position against organized labour. The movement of jobs across frontiers and the development of more than one source of supply are just two of the measures taken. This subject is discussed more fully in Chapter 15.

Ownership

A persistent demand of the critics is for local shareholding in subsidiaries. This subject is discussed in detail later where it is seen that local shareholding does indeed result in a relaxation of central authority on some issues, but that it is often accompanied by less autonomy than either the companies or the critics expect. Against this is the move to two-tier boards in European countries, notably Germany and the Netherlands, on which the shareholders (in the case of the multinationals, the parent company) do not have a majority.

Pricing

The policies a company pursues over the pricing of sales between different units is a subject which has collected to itself a number of legends both inside and outside the company. The government argument in this case is unequivocally towards decentralization. Dealings between units of a company are supposed to be as between independent entities and corporate taxes are levied on the assumption that this is so, pricing at arm's length as it is called. The tax administrations of many countries have the right to make an extra levy where it can be shown that the company is saving tax by not pricing in this way.

Regional development

An important aim of government policies in countries with any degree of industrialization is to steer industry into areas of unemployment or where other regional considerations make further industrialization desirable. Evidence has been assembled to show that foreign companies are more responsive to the inducements offered than domestic companies, hence this can be presumed to be a subject on which governments welcome centralization. Instructions from abroad appear more likely to help regional policies than the instincts of the native business people.

Taxes

The effects of transfer pricing have already been mentioned; in general companies benefit from central tax expertise in spite of local variations. The ability of the company to move its main facilities to avoid what it considers to be countries of heavy taxation is a problem for national authorities.

Technology

This appears to be one issue on which companies and countries have a common interest. Countries obtain the benefits of the knowledge and the companies are able to derive additional income from the results of expensive research. The situation is not always so satisfactory in practice. Countries take the view that the wrong kind of technology is being transferred and that excessive prices are being charged, while companies find it harder than expected to make the transfer profitably. Hostile attitudes to innovation and the difficulty of ensuring that new methods are used effectively are among the causes of this. The benefits derived from the diffusion of new technology usually cause governments to be tolerant of centralized decision-making by international companies on this issue; but sometimes there is pressure for local filtering and adaptation.

Trade

A main objection to corporate centralization, it has been pointed out, is when instructions are given to a subsidiary not to export or to service only limited markets. Although some operations may have been established with the object of import-substitution, the prevention of exports is naturally considered a scandal by government. In a selection of 34 companies that the present author examined, only one said that there was no control over the export policies of their subsidiaries, and most took it for granted that there had to be. Numerous problems were mentioned including customers confused by different terms offered by sales representatives working for the same company or by units promoting the same product to different segments of the market. Other studies have produced different figures, but the restrictions on the subsidiaries are always evident.[17] To add to this trend is a threat posed to government policies by the increasing proportion of trade that is between parts of a company and can be changed readily to the disadvantage of the country. The proportion of American exports despatched to another unit in the same company is over 30 per cent, while a similar proportion of the exports of British multinationals was going to their affiliates some years ago.[18] Masterminding the logistics of this considerable intra-company trade can be expected to restrict autonomy.

An attempt to mitigate the various effects of centralized trading and research policies that is mainly relevent to industrialized countries, is the World Product Mandate, the arrangement whereby responsibility for the total management of a product group is moved out of the home country.[19] Although there are only limited examples of this—Philips in Italy and Black & Decker in Canada among them—there would seem to be advantages both for companies and countries. The latter obtain a complete business, with all its skills and outlets, including research, while the company is able to take advantage of the location, workforce or funding opportunities offered by a particular country. The authority problem arises when the allocation of resources is under consideration. Whether this product will be able to count on an unbiased allocation of funds when it is out of the country, and whether its location will bring in extraneous considerations to this allocation are questions that are directly relevant. If the product division does not thrive on its own, then the world product mandate will produce problems for the company. If it does, the mutual benefit can be expected.

One other issue does not fit under those headings and that is change of government. In a democratic system, an election can produce a reversal of a policy that has led to foreign investment in a country. Consents to oil or mineral exploration, for instance, may be modified or ended if national policies change, and policies or nationalization or indigenization may harm long-term plans on the basis of which the market had appeared worth entering. In less stable countries, changes in leadership may make contractual relationships unreliable.

The issue-by-issue examination of some of the elements in the controversy between companies and governments exposes even more clearly the ambiguity of the demand for decentralization. Governments are seeking efficient and reliable management which shows consideration for the national interest. This will often come from head office rather than from the subsidiary. An issue that has not been mentioned, but where the central–local conflict is seen at its most acute is examined in the next chapter. Corporate planning is a function around which a number of conflicts gather—conflicts about methods and timing as well as interests.

14 Planning, Control and Pricing

Three subjects are brought together in this chapter, subjects which have many mutual influences as well as implications for centralization. Corporate planning, here taken to mean the reasoning behind initiatives that concern the company as a whole or the major interests of its sub-units, and control—the monitoring of performance—are closely related and can both be used as tools to aid either centralization or autonomy; the pricing policies, adopted for payment of goods and services within the company, reflect the planning, can sabotage the effects of the control system and are often regarded as critical to the parent–subsidiary relationship.

14.1 CORPORATE PLANNING

Corporate planning, it has been said, is the issue over which the question of centralization and decentralization becomes most acute. One view is that the allocation of resources is determined centrally through a process in which the foreign operations play little part, and the consequent decisions make a mockery of autonomy. This, the opinion held by many subsidiary managers, will be regarded as a caricature by the corporate planners. They will be conscious, on the contrary, of the time-consuming and expensive effort that has gone into plans which are then sabotaged by the determination of the subsidiaries to go their own way. Planners, like other professionals, will affirm that their work is neutral, that they are recommending optimal measures as a result of objective studies, and that most of their proposals are based on information supplied by the subsidiaries. All of these statements bear further examination.

The place of corporate planning in an international company can be explained under five headings. These are listed in Table 14.1 and do not differ from domestic companies except that the tasks set out under each heading are differently defined.

Approaches
The first item on the list, the approaches, relates most closely to centralization and provides an underlying philosophy which influences the other items.

Table 14.1 A summary of international corporate planning

(1) Approaches:	Indicative: aggregating Professional: non-professional Active: responsive
(2) Activities:	Decision preparation Translation Implementation
(3) Services:	Making objective Balancing Linking
(4) Techniques	
(5) Organization and staffing	

Corporate planning is something that every company does; it is not just an optional extra to improve performance. In the simplest of one-person businesses, proprietors have an idea in their heads of what the business is all about and where they intend it to go—that is, a corporate plan, albeit unwritten and possibly ill-informed. From this rudimentary start the process gradually becomes more elaborate, although not necessarily more sophisticated, until the point is reached where companies hire professional planners, sometimes highly specialized. The essence of corporate planning remains the same, an idea and an intention, but the practice changes from the spare-time activity of line managers to a function staffed by professionals. One distinction to be considered is that between the part-time and the full-time planners; another derives from it, whether the role of the planner is that of adviser or that of manager, requiring the ability to direct the implementation of the plans. The distinction has traditionally been blurred, but the development of large-scale international organizations has led to a rethinking of the planning role into one which is regarded as advisory in two senses—in the sense that the planners are not decision-makers, but also in the sense that they are not planners either. Their role is the provision of advice on techniques and the use of information sources (including data-bases) to enable the line managers to carry out their own planning more confidently. Whether this approach to planning is centralizing or not will depend on a number of factors, including the organization.

Another distinction is between indicative, that is, planning from the top, and aggregating, where the corporate plans are a bringing together of the plans of the subsidiaries. The distinction is often referred to as top-down or bottom-up planning; these phrases oversimplify but express the opposite poles in a range of options. The top-down planning is not, of course, conducted in isolation; head office will be basing proposals on information fed in through the control system, but the amount of consultation is limited, and each subsidiary is informed of its share in targets and lead-times which it has had little part in drafting. Aggregate, bottom-up, planning for its part is not uninfluenced by head office but is essentially the product of the plans of the subsidiaries. It is put together market by market with some global coordination, but not as a result of imposition from above. In some cases head office acts as little more than an arbitrator between requests for resources from the subsidiaries.

More fundamental than these distinctions, and in a sense comprehending them, is that between active and responsive planning. In a majority of companies the planning is mainly responsive—sifting proposals made from internal and external sources and providing advice on their viability and suitability. This is relatively neutral when it comes to considering centralization compared to the active planning where the company initiates more frequently.

Activities
Corporate planning is part of a continuous process which runs from the first germ of an idea until its final implementation or abandonment. The stages are:
(a)   the original idea;
(b)   the decision preparation (1);
(c)   the decision to proceed;
(d)   the translation (2);
(e)   the further decisions including the allocation of resources;
(f)   the implementation planning (3);
(g)   the operation.

Naturally, the planner may also be involved in the original idea and in any of the other stages—in a small firm he will be into all of them—but the principal contribution is at the numbered stages (the decision preparation, the translation and the implementation planning) where the specialized skills are required. Moving from one stage to another means moving from the general to the particular, from the broad-based qualitative to the detailed quantitative and this demonstrates the breadth of expertise the professional planner requires. The decision preparation, also called strategic or long-term planning, takes a look at the overall implications of the original idea. This will first of all be scrutinized in the light of existing strategies and operations, and how they would be affected if the idea was put into practice. If, say, the proposal is for moving into a new group of products, or a new part of the world, the review will include a summary of its appropriateness to the company in terms of strengths and weaknesses; these will be matched with the opportunities and constraints in the business environment of the new product or region. A consideration of the long-term market will also be required as well as information about how that market is currently being serviced. A simple check-list can be used to indicate which are the more promising projects, or a more elaborate scheme derived from portfolio investment or other relevant techniques. If the project is designed for the company as a whole, considerations like the need for confidentiality may preclude even consultation with the subsidiaries. The likelihood of the subsidiary being able to initiate substantial projects itself will depend upon the approach. If the company operates an indicative system, keeping the subsidiaries fully occupied with their share of central plans, then there is likely to be little scope for strategic planning at their level except in feeding information to the centre or in adapting projects or products for local use. There is a multiplier effect against autonomy, because there is little use hiring people with the appropriate skills where no long-term planning is being carried out; but their absence will ensure that subsidiary initiatives are limited. This is a subject on which practices differ considerably, and is reflected in the options for organization; as a rule the existence of long-term strategic planning in the subsidiary is a satisfactory indicator of autonomy.

The translation planning is a process of specifying the implications of the decision once taken. The amount of extra investment required in each function—production, research, marketing, personnel and the rest—as well as in the subsidiaries and other units. The generalized expectations produced in the earlier stage will now be supported by cash flow projections and the marketing effort needed to support the projections. The process is one of breaking down the outline strategic plan into a set of tactics for each department and then bringing them together again into a coordinated whole. The marketing implications start with guidelines for market research, and an outline of the scale of the promotion effort that will be needed to meet the targets for the project. The market segment, the image, the pricing and other marketing policies are also suggested.

Once the market information begins to filter through, manufacturing planning can begin with the costing of the various factors of production including the workforce, supplies and equipment; action by the research and development department will also be required if a new product is being investigated, and the necessary development work will extend the time horizons and the costs. Location studies will build on those already carried out to determine suitable sites for both production and selling facilities. At the same time purchasing plans are being made, including the arguments for and against purchasing within the company (if relevant) and the finding of other sources of supply in case of breakdown. Recruiting and training programmes will also have to be organized. Through the whole process the financial policies will gradually be worked out. From the initial guidelines about the scale of the project to the calculations about the sources of funds, the proportions of the various kinds of funding (retained earnings, short-term borrowings, long-term loans and equity) and the timing of the capital requirements, the cash flow projections and so on.

The considerations set out briefly in the last two paragraphs illustrate why corporate planning has come to be considered a centralizing function. Also assumed is the search for new products; where cutbacks are the order of the day, the planning is likely to be even more biased to head office. The possibilities of reducing risk and wastage in both new projects and cutbacks are increasing with more refined techniques for judging investment and disinvestment proposals, and the growth of data banks able to provide market information rapidly and in quantity. Logistical considerations capable of providing a competitive edge, including the careful timings required, all add up to the impression that only small-scale planning is viable in the subsidiary. But these arguments are met by scepticism about the actual savings to be gained, and a belief that planning restricted to the centre can produce errors to match the scale of the planning. A book entitled *Great Planning Disasters* contains a number of instances of large-scale planning and how remote it can become from its consequences.[1] Some would argue that an element of decentralization in planning keeps the exercise closer to reality and is a safeguard against major blunders. This argument is supported by the fact that only a minority even of large companies (below 40 per cent in one study of large American firms) actually conduct a global search when conducting market appraisals, although the practice of central planning is growing. In other words, centralized planning can exist without the use of the very methods which provide justification for the centralizing. These considerations raise the spectre of a trap in which the central expertise is not being used in a way that will take advantage of its specific strengths, while the subsidiary is robbed of the ability to take initiatives. When recognized, the problem is solved either by strengthening head office or the subsidiary, and in the latter case the staff of central corporate planning may well be reduced considerably (another sign of decentralization). Decisions to change the bias in the planning system can be taken as a result of personal choice or of the attempt to remedy perceived problems; there is, however, a logic by industry sector and by other factors such as the distribution of existing facilities. In industries like food processing, which demand a large number of small plants, it may be more suitable for the translation planning to be carried out in the subsidiaries rather than the centre, while some coordination deals with questions about intra-company transfers. Heavy equipment may need a more centralized approach; changing techniques can result in today's large-scale manufacture becoming small-scale tomorrow, as has happened in parts of the electrical and electronics industry. Statements like 'we have traditionally been a centralized industry' may mask an inability to change with the technology.

Implementation planning is the other corporate planning activity (number (3) on Figure 14.1) and the one in which the most specialized techniques are used. At the earlier stages there is the chance of taking a global view to support centralization, but there are few other problems about remitting the activity to the subsidiary. If this is done, the larger company may wish to employ experts on forecasting, investment and country appraisal techniques to provide an advisory service to the subsidiaries. At the implementation stage, when the sub-units are most likely to play a part, such an advisory service is required still more. The difficulty of producing effective advisory services tends to make even this stage centralized, especially since precision is also needed. The actual transference of the plans into budgets will naturally be left to subsidiary management, but there is another aspect of implementation planning which frequently calls for central involvement—the adjustments to be made when plans go astray. If a company employs a full-time planning staff, this is likely to mean emphasis on contingency planning, reviewing the options available to match unexpected changes in the market or in the competition. The development of criteria on which to base reactions to the changes may be an activity outside the scope of the subsidiary which will at least need advice on this subject, but the degree of centralization will, in the end, depend on the approach rather than on the implications of this stage of the planning.

Services
The progress of a company is a mixture of intention and opportunism. Planning, as popularly conceived, provides guidance so that progress is by intention—the

(1) Decision preparation   (2) Translation   (3) Implementation

Corporate planning centralized

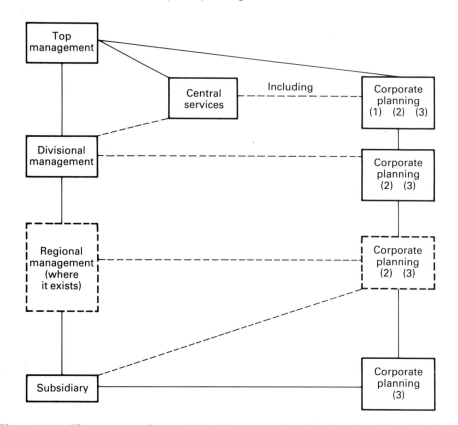

Figure 14.1 Three ways of organizing the corporate planning department in large international firms

way to thought-out objectives, albeit with some allowance for contingencies along the route. In fact the services of the corporate planner are more frequently used to provide guidelines indicating, for example, appropriate responses to an approach from a company for sale. For this purpose a corporate strategy, the generalized long-term set of plans, is rewritten into criteria so that any proposal, whether demanding positive action or responsive—can be tested for its compatability with what exists. The criteria are designed to reduce the risk of disaster and increase the hope of synergy. Another service is to provide an objective review of opportunities and progress. This objective view should be incorporated into the criteria, but is useful in other ways as well. It is also difficult, and will merit further discussion under the heading of organization and staffing.

The services known as balancing and linking are also provided by corporate

II
Corporate planning decentralized in a centralized firm

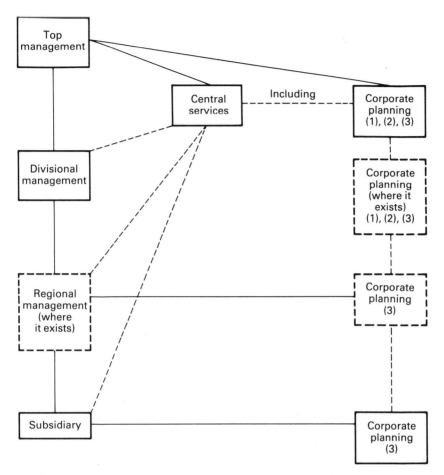

planning. Linking is the bringing together of the various activities which are required in a successful business venture, including market research, manufacture, finance, promotion and distribution. This service is less needed in a small firm but has to be carefully engineered in a large one. The professional corporate planner provides a system of coordination with methods for identifying deadlines and other guides to achieving an integrated project. Balancing is a more subtle exercise in ensuring that there is an equilibrium in all departments between the needs of the customers and the resources of the various units together with those of their suppliers. Objectivity is relevant in this connection, since there will be commitments at various points in the international chain which are emotionally held ('we have always used those suppliers', 'that country provides a more reliable market'). These commitments are used by subsidiaries as bargaining counters against the centre.

III
Corporate planning decentralized in a decentralized firm

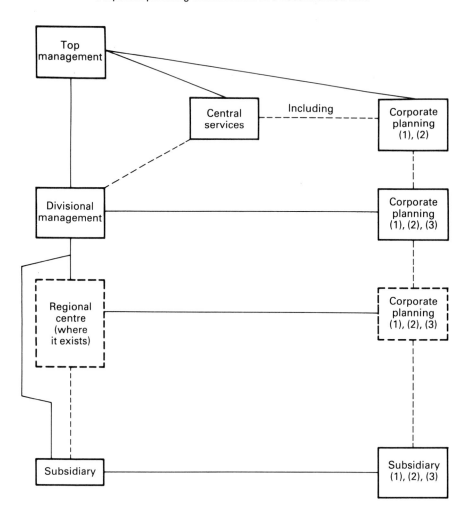

(Adapted from Brooke and van Beusekom (1978) p. 226)

Techniques

Planning is a mixture of a systematic understanding of the company and its environment with an ability to provide criteria for investigating proposals and scheduling the results. A broad general grasp has to be accompanied by the use of analytical techniques which are growing in complexity. At the earlier stages technological, demographic, social and other forms of forecasting will be valuable along with the ability to produce scenarios and analyse contingencies; at the later stages a considerable battery of techniques, including simulation exercises on the corporate strategies and on those of competitors, are used to ensure a smooth and successful implementation. There is a conflict between the centralizing effect of the techniques, some of which will have to be brought in from outside, and the need to win the cooperation of those who must operate the resulting proposals. This appears to be the subject on which the Japanese style provides distinctive and useful insights with the closer involvement of all concerned in the planning itself as well as providing the required data. The more initiatory role of middle management, bringing together a variety of skills, aids this process.[2] However the Japanese experience is judged, the problem of gaining cooperation cannot be avoided and is harder to solve in the centralized system. A technique is valueless if its results do not carry conviction.

Organization and staffing
The discussion on the activities, approaches and techniques implies questions about their effect on centralization and autonomy which are partly answered by observing how the whole system is fitted into an organization structure. This may be rudimentary, a few busy line managers detailed to spend part of their time producing plans. This arrangement marks the first step towards a formal system which eventually grows into a fully fledged professional department. Assuming that the company has a full-time planning staff, there are a number of organizational options which will indicate the degree of centralization intended as will the staffing arrangements. Figure 14.1 shows three possible structures for corporate planning in a large international company with I being the most centralized in intention and III the least. Naturally, there are many variants on these three and the intention does not always correspond with practice, but in types I and II all the decision preparation is intended to take place at the centre.

In the first option (I), the subsidiary department is virtually regarded as a part of head office located in the subsidiary; indeed the divisional and regional stages may be bypassed. At the same time there is a dual allegiance at the local level where the planning staff report both to region or division or even direct to head office, and to their subsidiary management. At the lower levels only implementation planning is carried out; all the decision preparation is at the top. This form of organization is centralized by intention, and the powers of the subsidiary are closely circumscribed.

In option II the authority of the subsidiary is also restricted, but the local planning department is unequivocally subordinate to subsidiary management. The position is totally different in option III where the organization is framed to promote autonomy in the subsidiary. Decision preparation, translation and implementation are all carried out at local level. In companies with this organization the central department is usually small and does not necessarily have the word 'planning' in its title. The department, whatever its name, provides support to top management and a service throughout the company. This option is less common than II and is usually to be found in consumer goods companies or divisions.

Both the latter types occasionally produce instances of inverted centralization; the growth in specialized planning staff makes such a development more likely.

This arises when experts at national level attempt to circumvent the design and concentrate their allegiance on the central planning department. When moves to inverted centralization are noticed, the observation is itself used as an argument against over-emphasis on expertise in staffing. There is a widespread view, on other grounds, against over-specialization or at least for movement between planning and other departments. Planning uses some esoteric skills (in scheduling or forecasting, for instance) but can easily grow out of touch with the mainstream of the business. In particular, the planners may lack the understanding or the political aptitude needed to ensure that their proposals and criteria are used. The conclusion that senior planning staff should be recruited from other departments inside the company rather than outside experts is reinforced by the observation that planning provides an excellent training ground for general management. Individuals on their way from a functional department to a senior line position can obtain an overview of the enterprise's activities as well as the experience of management in a department where their abilities will be tested. Hence, the pressure for a mixture of specialist personnel, who may be making a career in planning, and a leavening of more transitory members of staff, is becoming normal in planning departments that are large enough to accommodate a suitable mixture. The importance of this development for us is that the specialists are more likely to be a centralizing influence. So the initial comment that planning is regarded as an influence against autonomy stemmed, at least in part, from the years (say, 1960–1972) when corporate planning departments were being installed, years in which both the organization and the staffing arrangements led to a centralizing approach. More recently this has been modified and the role of planning made to conform more closely with the general approach of the firm. This means a small but noticeable increase in type III systems supported by central departments reduced in size.

The action and reaction within the planning department is illustrated in Figure 14.2 which summarizes the discussion. The diagram, for simplicity, shows a number of pressures within one cycle. In fact, there are two cycles: the forces towards centralization and autonomy within the planning department itself, and the influence of the department on the general level of centralization in the company. The first cycle should be expected to reinforce the second, but the two do not always move in unison. Some of the charges against a corporate planning system as such arise from experience in companies where the two cycles are out of phase; this can happen, for instance, when a strongly centralized planning system is retained in a company which has made conscious efforts to encourage autonomy in the subsidiary in all other decision-making areas. A degree of inverted centralization can make this worse. The opposite, decentralized planning in a centralized system, is likely to prove unworkable. Some correspondence between the planning and the rest of the corporate structure is required. One way in which this correspondence is made easier to achieve is in diversification planning, where the translation and the implementation can be shared between head office and the subsidiary in a banker–client relationship. The former proposes the product areas and the funding methods while the subsidiary reviews the local opportunities.

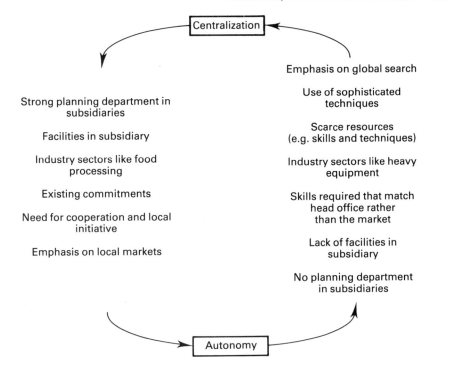

Figure 14.2 The pressures towards centralization and autonomy in the planning system

14.2 CONTROL

Control and planning are two parts in one series of activities. In fact their deadlines determine the calendar for managers at head office as much as those in the subsidiaries; so the timetable is hardly to be considered a centralizing influence, dominating though it can be with the control system recurring each month and the planning meetings spaced through half the year. The control system monitors the results of the implementation at the same time as it provides data for further planning. In the earlier discussion on the subject, the importance of identifying the unit of control was stressed. This identification is straightforward in the case of the multinational company. There is a head office in one country which, for the purposes of the subsidiary, includes all the units in that country that carry out monitoring. There is an affiliate in another country which is required to make regular reports to the head office either as a result of ownership or of a contract. Essentially, there is a one-for-one relationship in the cross-frontier reporting although different levels may be involved on both sides.

The means of control begin with the regular transmission of operating figures. These may be at any frequency from one week to two years. Most research, including all the projects on which this section is based, found monthly transmissions to be normal, but there are many exceptions. An investigation into British firms operating in Australia found a majority of the local subsidiaries were only required to report annually.[3] This may have been a result of their small size and limited overseas operations. The companies that feature in most samples are experienced overseas operators who have usually gone over to monthly reporting, a fact that does not necessarily make them representative. Certainly the longer period leaves more local discretion, and is not usually related to close supervision. Where closer supervision is required, there will be reporting in all functions as well as a narrative account of progress. The financial reports will include capital and revenue accounts as well as variants from budget and whatever ratios and cash flow statements the particular company's system calls for. Other elements in the system are visits both ways between head office and the subsidiary in which the details are inspected. The inspection may go beyond the operating figures to include a review of planning procedures and the making of more impressionistic judgements on the management skills. A manager of a joint venture between two powerful international firms noted the different responses received from each of the partners. One would simply telex approval if the overall revenue statement was in line with the budget or an improvement on it. The other would query additional income as well as a shortfall, enquiring about the planning implication of any variance. So easily can the control system become a tool of centralization. Another means of control that has the merit of simplicity without necessarily limiting the discretion of the subsidiary unduly, is to insist that each affiliate uses the parent company's internal auditors. Naturally, that particular decision, the appointment of the internal auditors, is taken centrally but the extra confidence that such a measure gives the parent company compensates in other ways. This method also means that the subsidiary's problems of translating accounts into head office requirements are better understood, and the appraisal regarded as fairer.

The working of the control system has already been examined (see pages 73 to 80) and ten assertions listed; these affirmed that an adequate system: (1) makes possible delegation, (2) provides evidence about the performance of the subsidiary and (3) of the individual executive, who (4) gains in job satisfaction where the system seems fair, (5) provides information for planning and (6) education for managers, (7) stimulates the use of new ideas and techniques, (8) directs top management attention to areas of need, (9) is no substitute for clear direction and (10) can be dangerous if given an incorrect orientation. All these assertions are relevant to the parent–subsidiary relationship in the international firm; some of them operate differently in a domestic concern. A notable difference is concerned with (1) delegation. For the domestic company the evidence for a relationship between the control system and decentralization is mixed. The statement that an adequate control system enables greater decentralization is generally supported, albeit with some reservations. For the international company the reservations are much greater. It is likely, for instance, that the financial reports have to be produced according to alien accounting methods. Most companies insist that head office accounting conventions are used by all the subsidiaries—the figure was over 85 per cent in one sample investigated.[4] The purpose of this insistence is to facilitate consolidation at head office, but the effect is to restrain at least the financial department of the foreign subsidiary. In most companies head office has the better facilities for translating foreign accounts, but to undertake the translation there would increase central overheads which the subsidiaries dislike having to pay. The method used is more expensive for the company, but cheaper for head office. Further, the control system is part of a general pressure for uniformity which diminishes the discretion of the foreign affiliate. The pressure for ever greater speed also contributes to this effect, but there are good reasons for both pressures. The information is already out-of-date when it reaches head office in any case and an elaborate reporting system at frequent intervals provides more up-to-date guidance of the progress of the subsidiary and data for the use of the planners. Some disasters would have been avoided if more recent information had been received in a form that was easier to interpret. Wilmot Breedon[5] was an example of a company part of whose troubles stemmed from a misunderstanding of the reports which came from a subsidiary in the accounting conventions of the host country.

There is also the difference in specialist staff available to head office as opposed to the foreign affiliate. This is not always the case; there have been moves to reduce the central staffs, but usually the difference is great and a standardized reporting system can be a burden to a small subsidiary. A local marketing manager once told the present author that the competition he faced was negligible; his company had over 80 per cent of the market, and his competitors were about 200 small firms whom he could not attack because of the danger of an anti-monopoly action; but the monthly report on the competition he had to present to head office was 'terrifying', involving, as it did, the completion of long and elaborate forms which added up to many hundreds of pages a year. This is an example of a common occurrence. The pressure to centralization is that the subsidiary has to employ skills that match the demands of head office, not necessarily those of the market.

Fair appraisal through the control system (numbers (2), (3) and (4) on the above list) is more difficult internationally than for a domestic unit, where it already causes problems. The list of difficulties includes the side-effects of international policies, including pricing measures and loans, the difficulty of translating international currencies, as well as regulations about the transfer of funds and other government measures to redress the balance of payments. If the companies do not adopt arm's length pricing and instruct subsidiaries to sell to head office or other subsidiaries at disadvantageous terms, then fair appraisal involves complex calculations if it can be made fair at all. All pricing contains an element of playing the market, bargaining or guessing what the customer will pay, and if this is removed the manager is unable to produce satisfactory figures on return on investment or any other measure required.

Another difficulty of appraisal through the control system is that of time scale. The manager who goes exclusively for quick results, fails to provide for proper renewal of the equipment and moves on before the results of his short-term measures catch up with him is a familiar figure in domestic business. He acquires a reputation for success at the expense of his successor, who has to clear up the mess. On the international scene such a character may be much harder to detect; in lower labour cost countries, for instance, the formula for determining fresh capital needs will be different from that used at home. The manager who is looking to the future, on the other hand, may be slower to achieve profit targets than head office expects. Returns that come too quickly may sabotage the future.

In foreign operations, too, there is a distinction between appraisal of a unit and appraisal of its management. In domestic management the same figure may apply to both, but not in a business environment, where the competition is of a different kind as are expectations about prices, costs and returns. Hence, the operation may be showing too low an income by the standards of the company which is making international comparisons, while the managers may be showing returns well above the average for the industry sector in their country. The subsidiary is then judged a failure, perhaps ripe for disinvestment, while the managers have proved successful. In the end judgement is made on a variety of indicators and, apart from isolated individuals with strong prejudices, financial executives often find it hard to say on what principles the judgements are being made. If the appraisers cannot articulate the reasons for their appraisal, it is difficult to see how the subordinates can consider that the judgements are fair or definitive.[6]

Among other assertions about the control system, the educational aspect works well, it appears. The form-filling required concentrates the minds of the foreign managers on those parts of their jobs which headquarters considers to be most important. This can hardly be considered a decentralizing influence, but one consequence is that the system proves difficult to change. The process, observed in many companies, is one of generally increasing the number of items of reporting. At first only a minimum of reports are required: income and expenditure in general terms, surpluses, cash flow, the tax position, market share and some production statistics. The number of reports increases either through experience, which demonstrates shortfalls in the subsidiaries or because head office managers are collecting global statistics on a greater number of issues. Fresh items are added, but seldom are existing items deleted; hence, the forms grow longer and longer. The length will be further compounded when monthly, quarterly and annual reports are all required on different forms. The results add up to hundreds of pages a year, sometimes of esoteric information which the subsidiary does not need for its own purposes. The growing protests eventually produce an exercise in which the control forms are scrutinized and the number of items drastically reduced. Then it is discovered, usually after a considerable lapse of time, that some subsidiaries have ceased managing carefully the items that have been axed. More attention has been concentrated on those that survive. If head office regards the others as sufficiently unimportant to be deleted, then *some* subsidiary managers assume that they no longer need to worry about them. One company, for example, found that the debtors were increasing with a devastating affect on the cash flow after the subsidiaries were no longer required to report on the subject. Naturally, the increase in money owed came to light only gradually and many months after the forms were changed.

Limiting the demands to those which the subsidiary itself requires for the effective management of its business would appear to be a means of reducing the burden of the formal control system, and removing some of the centralizing effects. The literal following of this suggestion might not adequately fill all the demands on the control system, like the educational and the planning, but it is followed in many companies. Where it is not followed the control system not only makes for centralization, whatever the intention, but in an exaggerated form. So much subsidiary attention is turned away from its market and towards its proprietor. The main pressures each way are summarized in Figure 14.3.

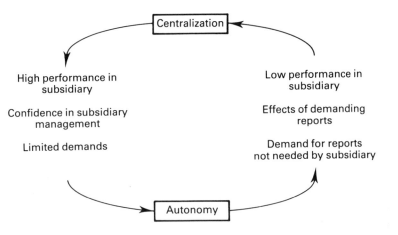

Figure 14.3   The pressures towards centralization and autonomy in the control system

14.3   THE MOVEMENT OF FUNDS AND TRANSFER PRICING

The Achilles' heel of international corporate planning and control systems is the need to move funds across frontiers. This 'need' arises both from the nature of international operations and the special opportunities for the profitable sourcing and use of funds. The unpredictable nature of interest rates, exchange rates and the other influences on the viability of a project is a source of setbacks in planning, while transfer pricing can make a mockery of the most carefully prepared control system. It used, for example, to be stressed that the duty of the finance department was to seek long-term borrowings in countries where interest rates were low. 'Even saving a 0.5 per cent on the interest rate on a large new development can make the difference between a profit and loss, especially where the competition is keen . . .' Such was a typical, if exaggerated, sentence heard in many a speech. Nowadays the list of disasters to companies which followed that advice literally is growing. A saving considerably greater than 0.5 per cent can produce an enormous loss if the currency exchange worsens by over 30 per cent (as happened in one two-year period between the pound sterling and the Swiss franc) by the time the loan has to be repaid. Indeed the continuing uncertainty about currencies has led to the advice to borrow when possible in the country in which the funding is required. There has also been a certain, but slow, increase in international currencies mainly (but not exclusively) used by banks and governments. However, most international companies have to move funds that are substantial in proportion to the size of the companies, and have only limited control over the timing of any movement. The risks can, it is true, be mitigated by various devices, like buying money forward and by insuring against loss of investment or export credits, but these are not simple exercises, and the degree of expertise required is costly whether employed internally or bought from external advisers. Hence, the sourcing and use of funds is likely to be controlled centrally by managers who have some familiarity with international and local money markets.

A piece of conventional advice that is often ignored is to develop a range of methods for transferring funds. Any particular route can be blocked, taxed, discriminated against in other ways and find itself a source of attacks upon the company. This especially applies to dividends. There have even been cases where strong-minded subsidiary executives have blocked the payment of dividends, and these dividends (or the profits on which they are based) are usually taxed more highly than other forms of transfer. Usually, but not always, for increasingly countries—especially those in the strongest bargaining position like the more advanced developing countries—are detecting what are considered to be excessive movements of funds by other means and so block the transfers or impose additional restraints like withholding taxes. The methods of fund transfer in addition to the transfer of profits by dividends include: intra-company loans and interest payments, royalties and other payments for knowledge, fees for management services including head office charges, prices and credit terms for intra-company sales. *All* of these items, apart from dividends, come under the general heading of transfer pricing; that is, discretionary prices charged by one unit to another for goods and services.[7]

The term 'transfer pricing' has come to symbolize a whole area of criticism of the multinational, and many of the uses connected with it are strongly criticized within companies as well. The central administration of price controls inside the firm cuts across the normal bargaining process, defeats attempts at fair appraisal and distorts decision-making on fresh investment or disinvestment. Naturally, every transfer must have a price; it is the distortion of that price that causes objections, a distortion which is also an interference with the workings of a free market.

Intra-company prices are paid for both goods and services. The transfer of goods includes finished goods sold by a manufacturing unit to a marketing subsidiary, and the sale of components or raw materials between manufacturing units. Almost all the hard evidence, the actual examples or well-founded allegations of overcharging, concerns sales of goods between manufacturing units and marketing subsidiaries. These examples include court cases in the United States and Japan, official investigations in several other countries and reports such as one into the pricing of pharmaceuticals in Colombia.[8] On principle these cases do not differ greatly from overcharging to agents or other third parties. The case is one for anti-monopolies legislation or the encouragement of competition; as it happens most of the examples come from an industry sector (pharmaceuticals) where entry costs make competition especially difficult. Indeed the practices complained of are often encouraged by governments who provide protection for pharmaceutical products and state purchasing agencies who are prepared to pay a high price for scarce and effective products. The internal problem of appraisal and control is readily overcome with this kind of transfer, as it is easy to make allowances for any unit whose profitability is reduced.

The transfer between production units of intermediate goods and raw materials presents problems of a different order. In this case there has to be a decision—transfer pricing is not to be regarded as an optional extra—and the decision can take a number of forms. Which form it does take in any particular company is seldom known outside because this is a subject of complete secrecy. Many were willing to reveal all other aspects of their international trading policies except their pricing methods; however, the limited evidence compiled in the studies reported here confirms the view expressed by other investigators that large companies mainly use some variety of cost-plus policy.[9] It is medium-sized firms that are more inclined to use transfer pricing policies to move funds or reduce taxes. The theoretical possibilities are endless, but so are the difficulties and expenses. The option overtly favoured by governments, incorporated in the codes of conduct and declared as company policy by the limited number of companies willing to declared a policy, is that of arm's length dealings. This is supposed to mean transfer at market prices, but it is difficult to decide a market price for an intermediate product. In some cases it will be unique: in all cases it will be subject to discretion. The price charged to a large buyer in a competitive market might be totally different from that to a small customer in a market that was price elastic, and neither transaction might be relevant to fixing an internal price. One option is to take the view that there is only one profit to be made—the sale to the outside customer. This produces the cost-plus pricing for the larger companies. But this still may not appear satisfactory to governments along the route who see all the profit being shown in another country. It has to be remembered, too, that the organs of government do not speak with a single voice. A high price in a vendor country may produce low profits, and thus low taxes in the buyer country; but that country's customs officials will levy a higher duty if they are working on percentage import tariffs. A reduction in price would, in this case, be acceptable to one arm of government but not another, and these are not necessarily the only government departments concerned with the pricing. Industrial strategy, national planning, competition and price control authorities can all have an interest, and these interests can pull in different directions, which proves expensive for the company. A suspicion of tax evasion can lead to a company having to host a team of revenue investigators for many months, while tax authorities in several countries can charge tax on an assumed income if they suspect that profits are artificially reduced. Such a power, although not often used, means a prolonged appeal on the part of the company, which is left to establish its innocence.[10]

Within the company, artificial influences on the transfer prices are strongly resisted on the grounds that an executive's reputation can be damaged at random. The opposition is countered by staff in the finance department who are well-versed in the theoretical advantages to be gained, especially for tax saving, which is always an appealing claim. That such arguments seem to cut less ice in large companies, where the level of experience and expertise is likely to be higher, suggests that the costs outweigh the benefits; this will be especially the case where a long-term view is being taken, a luxury not always available to the small firm.

One of the benefits of decentralizing the pricing issue is that the subsidiary builds up a bargaining facility for use within the company, which produces the ability to bargain with government as well. The transfer pricing policy is not abolished by a declaration of adherence to arm's-length principles, but it is moved into a different sphere of activity where the difficulties can be handled by the normal processes of management. The global view, in this case, has less obvious advantages than in the allocation of resources; this latter includes decisions about the movement of funds which would normally have been taken even before a particular subsidiary came into existence and written into its articles of association.

15 *Company Organization*

International company organizations take a number of forms that derive from upheavals within the company, changing strategies, dominating personalities, the influence of consultants and many other pressures, including the struggle of the subsidiaries for independence. It is possible to frame a decentralized structure, as was shown in the discussion on corporate planning, by ensuring that suitable expertise is available at the subsidiary level, but the structure is not often framed that way. Some hold that strategy has a major influence on structure (while the reverse is also suggested, that the structure has helped to determine the strategy), some that personality has. No doubt there are many factors, but a coherent theory of change in international companies has been built around the conflicts that appear in the decision-making, which will not be unrelated either to strategic or personality change. This conflict has already been introduced (in Chapter 12) and the three principal projections of management identified. From this it seems logical to outline organization types, each of which takes its title from the projection which has priority.[1]

15.1 THE ORGANIZATION TYPES AND INTERNATIONAL COMMUNICATIONS

International company organization can be classified into five main groups, with many sub-classes, of which the first are directly related to the management projections. These are:

Type A, where the most senior staff of the company have a direct relationship with the foreign subsidiary—the *direct* type.

Type B, where this relationship is mediated through managers of the geographical projection, whether with international, regional or national titles—the *geographical* type.

Type C, where product group managers have direct control over the subsidiaries operating in their products—the *product* type.

The other two types are a mixture of projections, in fact, conscious attempts to weld together the conflicting elements in the decision-making. They are:

Type D, nowadays usually called matrix, in which the subsidiary managers report along both the product group and geographical lines, sometimes even functional lines as well—the *matrix* type.

Type E, the application to the total organization of the project organization devised for large-scale assembly operations like aircraft building. The company is organized into a series of project groups which bring together staff drawn from any relevant projection and are constantly changing—the *project* type.

The general scheme is illustrated in Figure 15.1.

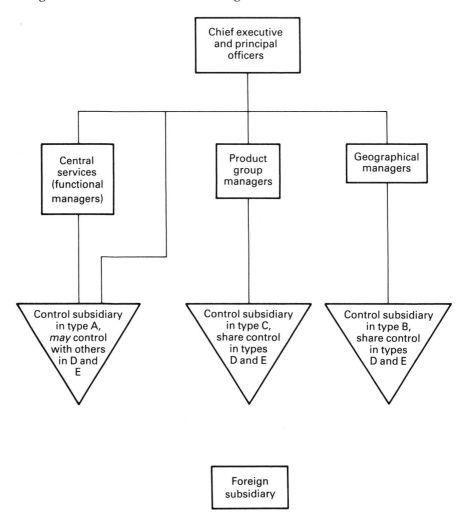

Figure 15.1 The organization types

Each type has its centralized and decentralized sub-types, but some are much more common than others in situations that are anyway fluid. The organizations and the sub-types change frequently. In general, the B type (geographical) is more frequently decentralized, the C type (product) more usually centralized

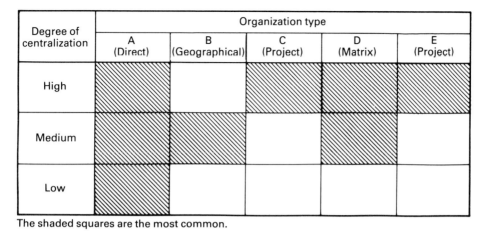

Degree of centralization	Organization type				
	A (Direct)	B (Geographical)	C (Project)	D (Matrix)	E (Project)
High	▨		▨	▨	▨
Medium	▨	▨		▨	▨
Low	▨				

The shaded squares are the most common.

Figure 15.2 Relationships between organization and centralization—some indications

and the E type (project) almost always centralized, while A (direct) and D (matrix) may be either. Figure 15.2 illustrates the position.

A source of confusion in investigating the different organizations is that executives at head office will be unclear about the unit of centralization. Thus, top management in companies that possess product group divisions will describe their firms as decentralized, and affirm that they have delegated a wide range of decisions—but the delegation will have been to the division, not to the foreign operation, a fact which seems to have been missed by some writers on the subject. Subsidiaries in the product organization usually report a higher degree of centralization than those in the geographical. There is, indeed, a correspondence with the industry sector, since consumer goods companies more frequently use either international or regional divisions and incline to decentralization; those in industrial goods are more likely to operate through product groups worldwide and be centralized.

Subsidiaries in these products (type C) organizations register a much greater number of complaints about communication problems than in the B type (geographical). In fact one reason for change between the two types is the discovery of damaging blocks in the communications. In the geographical the block occurs within head office; the product division fails to give the international division adequate support in supplying technical or other information for the foreign operations. This is an argument frequently used for reorganization along the product group worldwide lines. What happens after the reorganization is that the communications problems are transferred from inside head office, between divisions, to the parent–subsidiary relationship. The international, or other geographical, department is more likely to be skilled in the overseas business. Managers in such a division will have been recruited because of their expertise or interest in foreign operations, they will be constantly in touch with subsidiary management, and their performance will be appraised on that of the affiliates. As a result, they will know the policies that cause problems abroad, and are less likely to issue damaging instructions. This built-in sensitivity is itself a safeguard against unwise instructions which appear harmless at home, but arbitrary and unhelpful in the eyes of the subsidiary. This is one reason why the difference between head office and subsidiary responses to questions about centralization is sometimes unexpectedly large. Executives at the centre simply do not realize the implications of their instructions, and this situation is frequently uncovered in product division organizations. Unless these divisions are very large, they do not hire international specialists and the management is carried out by executives who are domestically orientated.

The question of size is, of course, important and accounts for some of the discrepancies in the evidence. A large company (with sales of over £1000 million in 1984 prices) is likely to have divisions each of which is a large concern in its own right. Such divisions can afford to carry their own geographical projection, although not all do. If they do, each division grows into a geographical company in itself and the communications problems with the subsidiaries would not be expected to arise. The need to grow along these lines is one reason for the emergence of larger divisions in the product type firm. The communications block in most of these companies has a further implication, that for government relations. Any international company, especially one with high political visibility, can come into conflict with some branch of government, but the evidence assembled in the *first method of research*[2] was that product type companies were more prone to problems than others.

It would seem, therefore, that special vigilance is needed in such companies. They have a tendency towards centralization in the first place: they are subject to problems (both internal and external) which are of a kind that are frequently solved by increasing centralization. Hence, there exists a self-reinforcing process in which the discretion of the subsidiary is gradually reduced. This is confirmed by the further finding that one reason for the change from product to geographical types is a growing lobby from the subsidiaries voicing dissatisfaction with the system.

There is, it should be noted, one group of companies which is an exception to the generally high level of centralization within the product type, that is, the holding companies—those conglomerates that treat their subsidiaries as investments with little interference, frequently only the requirement for financial information. The number of companies managed in this way appears to be growing less, and one recent takeover[3] suggests that institutional investors prefer those with a more proactive management. The threat of takeover by a more tightly controlled concern is one of the pressures towards the normal line.

The A (direct) and D (matrix) types display more variations than the B (geographical) and C (product). The direct type includes most small international companies who frequently do not have the resources required for central decision-making. There are many exceptions, but this type includes the whole range of possibilities from the most centralized to the most autonomous. The matrix type, on the other hand, includes a limited number of very large companies where the pressures for and against decentralization are both strong. The pressures against decentralization are usually connected with the size of the business and its industry sector, while those for are more personal. The matrix type company is able to employ able managers and place them in situations where a certain degree of autonomy is almost inevitable—the nature of the matrix is that the subsidiary manager has to serve a number of superiors and is not wholly answerable to any one of them. This may enhance local autonomy but may also produce a version of inverted centralization. The concept of organization care also operates especially in companies with considerable head office expertise, and ensure that they are not as decentralized as might be expected.

The question about how far the serving of two or more superiors in the matrix structure allows personal autonomy depends on a number of factors including:

(a)   the personal ability of the manager to play off one superior against another;
(b)   the effect of report writing on the decision-making;
(c)   the amount of interference the superiors themselves undertake;
(d)   the importance of the results of the particular unit for the divisions served.

The evidence points to strong pressures and counter-pressures in the matrix organization, but with local managers often able to work the system so as to ensure maximum autonomy. The E (project) type, on the other hand, is much more centralized in the limited number of cases where it exists. The essence of flexible, short-term arrangements is that there must be a firm central authority to make them work. The project groups, even when registered as subsidiaries, do not have sufficient permanence to become autonomous. In general, the connection between centralization and organization types turns out to be slight although, from the point of view of the foreign subsidiary, type C (product) appears the more centralized and the geographical less so.

A note on levels of management and the regional centre

Any introduction of an extra tier of management between the foreign subsidiary and the top management of the parent company is likely to be represented as centralization by the former and the reverse by the latter. The top management has, indeed, delegated some of its authority, but the new tier may well reduce that of the subordinate, as is shown in Figure 15.3 where a number of examples demonstrate both how the status quo can be maintained and (as is more likely) how the authority of the subsidiary is reduced. Any such reduction will be exaggerated in the eyes of the subsidiary because the introduction of the new level already appears as a demotion, and the cutting of links with the top as reducing the opportunity for clearing up problems and influencing policy formation. The switch from A to B or to C always involves an extra level, although sometimes a transitional arrangement is made so that a subsidiary is allowed to continue along established lines during the tenure of the existing chief executive. This has been brought out in other researches, like one on subsidiaries in Australia where over half the sample reported to subordinate executives at head office, but there were other informal links as well.

In circumstances where the transitional arrangements are not made, the new organization may be discredited in the eyes of the subsidiary management, who will become part of a lobby against it; whether it is B (geographical) or C (product), it will be their first experience of a system which appears to demote

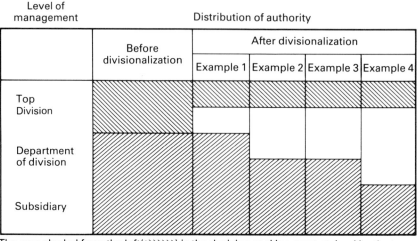

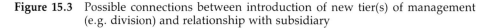

The area shaded from the left(＼＼＼＼) is the decision-making area retained by the top management. The white area is that retained by the division. The area shaded from the right(／／／) is that available to the subsidiary.

Figure 15.3 Possible connections between introduction of new tier(s) of management (e.g. division) and relationship with subsidiary

them. The fact that a change to another type leaves them in a similar position does not prevent a pressure towards continuing change. It is not uncommon for even more levels to be inserted. In the product (type C) organization appear sub-product groups which are introduced as a result of a misunderstanding of the problems with the subsidiary—when a further level of the organization is regarded as providing a unit that can concentrate more attention on subsidiary affairs. The increased centralization that can result is shown on Figure 15.3 (example 4). When an extra level is added to the geographical organization, it is usually a regional department, although it is not unusual for a regional division to replace the international division altogether, in which case the single level is restored unless the region is subdivided.

Regional organizations can themselves be divided into four types,[4] each with different amounts of authority. The first is a national subsidiary with a remit to develop a market plan for a number of countries which have geographical or other links with its own—the term 'region' is often misleading; companies class countries together because of links produced by language, tradition, culture, the history of the particular business or administrative convenience, as well as geography. The national subsidiary with a regional responsibility is frequently found in companies with limited foreign investment either in the world as a whole or in a particular region. The operations which are overseen by this subsidiary are small, and may be agents or licensees. Where they are subsidiaries, they are likely to be sales offices having little independence.

The other types of regional centre are usually incorporated in their own right, separated from the local country organization, sometimes situated in a small country which does not have its own national organization. One type is intended to be highly centralized, that is, the regional centre with direct line responsibilities for all subsidiaries in its area which is, on principle, run as an integrated concern. The intention may not be carried out in practice because, as with other forms of geographical organization, there is likely to be a built-in sensitivity to local needs and expectations. Nevertheless, the intention in setting up this type of centre, within geographical and matrix organizations and mainly in American firms, is to produce a coordinated drive in purchasing, production and marketing. It has been suggested that one way of identifying the degree of centralization of such an organization is by the nationality of the staff. If, whatever the appearance, the senior executives of the national subsidiaries do not regard the regional centre as a genuine authority, they will not apply for jobs there. As a result, the centre will be mainly staffed by head office nationals, usually on short-term assignments and playing an uneasy role between head office and the subsidiaries. It may be argued that nothing changed when the regional centre was established, that the managers were already holding the same offices but located in a different country; but the internal political situation will have changed, and the national subsidiaries will be probing the strength of the new links.

The third type of centre is decentralizing by intention. It occupies a staff position, providing advice and support, especially technical and planning, to the companies in the region. This type of centre appears to be the most common and yet the shortest lived. The intention in setting one up is to sharpen the thrust in the particular area, the reality that it easily becomes an expense bringing little benefit. It may prove, in spite of the intention, to be a centralizing influence for the reason that staff functions often do wield authority even if that is not intended. If it is intended, then this type is moving into the fourth and last category, a combination of the second and third types where the centre has line authority for subsidiaries that are in difficulties and fulfils an advisory role for others.

This brief note on regional centres has concentrated on their authority; in their companies they fulfil many other functions besides those discussed here, like negotiating with supra-national bodies, arranging deals with suppliers or customers who are also regionally organized and providing a training ground for international managers.

15.2 THE COMMUNICATION OF CONTROL

The company which featured in the *communications survey*[5] was a successful, middle-sized company with apparently autonomous subsidiaries, one dominant product which was well-known for its trademark and an A type (direct) organization with an international division. Intensive interviews produced predictable results. The staff of the international division regarded the system as decentralized, with a minimum of mandatory orders sent to the subsidiaries. It was also said that the subsidiaries in developing countries and those that had been started from scratch (usually known as 'green field' operations) had less discretion than those in industrialized countries or which had been formed by the takeover of existing firms. Subsidiary managers from the industrialized countries, on the other hand, considered the system centralized and were particularly resentful of the way that executives below the top of the international division were able to issue instructions to them. After the interviews opportunity was given for a researcher to conduct a detailed analysis of the correspondence. This was easier with this company than with most as almost all communications with the foreign subsidiary passed through the international division, and even those that did not were filed in the central filing system by subsidiary; the files contained letters, telexes and notes on telephone conversations the results of which, with face-to-face talks as well, were normally confirmed in writing. Most messages that had gone through the system were on file.

The correspondence from head office over a four-year period was analysed into eight categories—mandatory orders, suggestions, advice, queries, apologies, information, requests and unrequested comments. The reverse correspondence was looked at with a view to assessing the part the subsidiary played in the decision-making. One measure used as a proxy for centralization was the proportion of the correspondence that consisted of mandatory orders. This novel method of detecting the exercise of authority proved a useful corrective to others, especially the perceptions of the managers themselves. In a large volume of messages a figure of over 20 per cent (the figure is arbitrary, but represents a steady flow of instructions) must surely be a sign of centralization, while a smaller figure would need further investigation before it could be said to demonstrate decentralization. One requirement of this research was an adequate method of distinguishing mandatory orders. There are at least two reasons why companies must not be seen to be issuing instructions to foreign subsidiaries. One is for tax reasons. The foreign subsidiary can be regarded as a branch not a subsidiary for tax assessment in the home country, and in a different category of firm to that in which it is registered by the host country authorities, if head office is found to be issuing direct instructions. Where double taxation agreements operate, the tax difference may not be great unless one country has a markedly different tax rate from the other. The other problem concerns liabilities; if the subsidiary is treated legally as a branch, the parent company may be held liable for its debts and for any legal actions against it. It has already been pointed out that the emerging codes of conduct have clauses making the subsidiary liable in any case but these are not, of course, legally enforceable. Whether or not the problem is exaggerated, the company in question was well aware of it and so, as is usual, the instructions were coded in terms that the subsidiaries well understood,[6] but which were ambiguous to the outsider.

The difficulty was overcome by the researcher's using the definition of mandatory orders used by the international division staff, and checking back on a number of items to make sure that they came within the definition. This method should, at least, ensure that the number of such orders was not exaggerated, which makes the evidence that the system was more centralized than was realized the more convincing. Table 15.1 shows the perceived and actual proportions of mandatory orders in the correspondence sent to the subsidiaries by the three managers who formed the top two levels of

Table 15.1 The perceived and actual percentages of mandatory orders in the correspondence between head office and the foreign subsidiary of the senior managers in one specimen year

Mandatory orders (percentage of total correspondence):	Subsidiaries			
	(1)	(2)	(3)	(4)
As perceived by managing director of international division	10	5	20	5
As perceived by two senior executives	5	1	10	10
As found in the correspondence of the three managers	17	14	32	37

Source: derived from figures published in Brooke and Dorrell (1976) p. 158.

administration in the international division. The table contains a number of implications. It casts doubt on research that rests on managers' perceptions, although this does not invalidate the point that perceptions on the part of *subsidiary* managers are important where conclusions are drawn about the effect of centralization on their behaviour. In the present case, the executives recognized the errors in their own estimates and changed them in the last year, an example of the influence of the researcher on respondents. In spite of this, the figures for subsequent years did tend to confirm that there was a process of decentralization taking place as the subsidiaries became more experienced. The difference between the subsidiaries also confirmed this statement, since numbers (1) and (2) were long-established and (3) and (4) were started more recently. Other beliefs, however, were not confirmed. The differences between the subsidiaries in the developing countries and those in the industrialized countries were less than expected, as were the differences between those taken over and those established from scratch. Over the years, too, the small reduction in mandatory orders was accompanied by an increase in unrequested suggestions—the very borderline messages which were the hardest to classify. The evidence of Table 15.1 is amplified by a chart (Figure 15.4) of one subsidiary, number (3) on the table, that had recently been formed from scratch. On this chart the various categories message are listed and the proportions shown.

The in-depth study of one company provides evidence of the danger of accepting perceptions collected at head office that claim decentralization; it also shows how some statements about different treatment of different types of subsidiary, which appear to conform to common sense, should be treated with caution. Apart from these negative warnings, there is the demonstration that a conscious policy of decentralization can work, even if it is so slow as to be hardly detectable from the subsidiary's point of view.

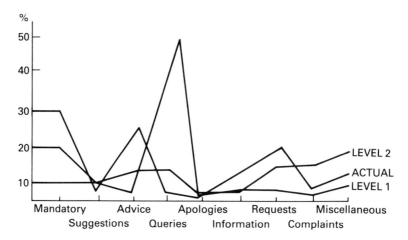

Figure 15.4 Proportion of different kinds of message passed to a subsidiary started from scratch

15.3 CENTRALIZATION AND THE FUNCTIONAL DEPARTMENTS

An accepted view is that the degree of centralization varies according to the function. Finance, production and research are expected to be centralized while marketing and personnel are not. This view is echoed by many managers and is reported in some academic studies, one of which emphasized the difficulty of producing a unified centralization index.[7] The correlations between decision levels in different functions were not normally high and so the conclusion was drawn that a company index was impossible, but this assumes that different functions can be compared. It may be true that a greater number of important decisions in finance are taken centrally than in personnel, but how do you rate one against another? Comparisons made between companies, parts of companies or over time will not be influenced by differences between functions so long as the same questions are asked of each company. The units being compared each have a range of functions; hence, the relationships being measured are not between functions but between units. The experience of the studies reported here was that companies are normally all of a piece when it comes to parent–subsidiary relationships—those more centralized in one department are also more centralized in another—although naturally there are exceptions.

In the *first method of research*, this proposition (that companies more centralized in one function were more so in others) came out clearly. It would still be possible for managers in, for instance, a personnel department to declare that they had relative independence while they had, in fact, less discretion than was usual in such departments. One problem about relying on perceptions of independence among subsidiary managers is that replies to questions depend partly on a person's previous experience. It is also necessary to probe for exact responses and examine decisions taken. A European subsidiary of an American manufacturing company provided yet another example of the difference between perception and reality. The personnel manager rated his independence high in an otherwise centralized firm, and yet it came to light that he had been refused permission by head office to adhere to a national agreement for the wages department to handle union dues. His chief executive considered this the issue which had caused most problems in relations with head office in the year in which it happened.

The notion of a general index of centralization for a company is also open to criticism on the grounds that there are different relationships with different subsidiaries. This is a more substantial criticism, as was evident in both the *communications study* and the *study of British companies in Europe*. Taking one decision (spending discretion limits) and two elements of control (reporting and personal contact), there were differences between functions and between countries. The results are summarized in Table 15.2; where there are discrepancies between the figures these are the result of the exclusion of ambiguous or contradictory responses, which also account for the limited evidence in some functions and some countries. The limitations themselves demonstrate how much easier it is to get clear-cut answers in finance than the other functions, and the difference between monitoring exact figures and the use of more impressionistic data may itself account for some of the apparent differences between the functions.

That particular group of companies had few expatriate managers, including only one in the finance function, where expatriates are most frequently found. Partly as a result, no doubt, language and cultural differences were often mentioned. In particular these differences were held to detract from the usefulness of the visits which were generally unpopular with the subsidiaries and were, as the table shows, infrequent and spread across the countries. The visits were defended by head office on the grounds that the subsidiaries were not competent at planning and all the companies were working on continually updated translation planning in time scales of three to seven years. In this group of companies much was heard about centralized planning for lack of skill in the subsidiaries, and a self-reinforcing trend was evident here with poor planning skills leading to more intervention. But there was also visiting as a direct part of the control system.

Decisions related to loans, where a parent company guarantee was involved, and to dividend payments were usually reserved to head office, while tax questions were not. The subsidiary always had to negotiate its own tax problems. Transfer prices usually, although only in one country invariably, had to be agreed by head office. The practice of circulating comparative figures between the subsidiaries only occurred in one company; the information from head office passed in straight instructions or suggestions (according to the code used in each company).

Table 15.2 supports the view that in international companies frequent reporting and a high level of centralization go together, whatever may be the case in domestic firms. This small group of companies contained examples of every possible reporting frequency from once a week to once every two years, but the lower discretion limits almost always accompanied the frequent reporting not the opposite as might be expected. This is another demonstration

Table 15.2   Control and discretion

| | Company–subsidiary relationships | | | | | | | | | | | | |
| | By function | | | | | | By country | | | | | | |
	Finance	Marketing	Production	Personnel	Purchasing	Total	(1)	(2)	(3)	(4)	(5)	(6)	Total
Monthly reporting (or more often)	10	2	4	0	2	18	4	7	2	0	1	3	17
Reporting less than once a month	3	4	4	4	0	15	1	9	0	1	2	1	14
Personal contact ten or more working days a year	3	0	5	0	2	10	3	3	0	1	2	1	10
Personal contact less than ten working days a year	9	6	4	4	0	23	2	14	2	1	1	3	23
Discretion limits*													
High*	3	3	1	0	0	7	0	5	1	1	0	0	7
Low	7	2	6	0	2	17	3	8	–	2	2	2	17
Low officially but higher permitted	0	1	1	4	0	6	2	3	1	0	0	0	6

*High discretion was defined as spending over £250 000

of the way in which firms behave with some consistency, and that care shown in one activity is also shown in another.

The information on the marketing departments was fragmentary, but probing showed more centralization than appeared in the initial answers. As with the other researches, the study of British companies in Europe found that while discretion limits were generally high in marketing, new techniques were a pressure to centralization. Officially, the service that provides these techniques is advisory only, but considerable uniformity results from the advice. If the marketing department is ambitious and successful, it will find means of enforcing new techniques on the subsidiary and thus reduce its discretion. But the issue is not just over techniques. The opportunities for standardized marketing have long been apparent.[8] It remains, however, that if the subsidiaries assert their independence and their results are satisfactory, the purpose of having a central marketing department is called in question. Only one company of this particular group had actually abolished central marketing, but the other projects produced examples.

Production and technical departments had lower discretion limits but less frequent reporting than finance, and the reporting was a mixture of figures and narrative. One company insisted on weekly production figures, and one had a foreign technical centre which sent in quarterly reports on progress but no production reports. On the other hand, face-to-face meetings were common in all but one of the firms, in the form of conferences and courses. These were centrally organized and designed to improve the technical competence of the affiliates.

Research and development is a department which is, as a rule, centralized and so it was in the companies in the projects included in the research reported here. The exceptions were single companies here and there which provided no general principles.

However, there is evidence of a change related to both the closer investigation of the costs and benefits of corporate research and the changing location policies of international companies. The progress of a new product, from the germ of an idea to the start of manufacture for the customer, can be a long process with costs rising steeply as the equipment is itself developed and declining only when the commercial manufacturing stage is drawing near. The exact process will vary from product to product, and may include a long series of safety tests (as with drugs) or usage tests (as in basic chemicals or metals) but the beginning will be relatively inexpensive. The idea will start with an engineer or scientist producing the basic principles and ideas and lobbying management for permission to go ahead. Although not as costly as the later stages, the degree of expertise and specialization is always increasing, and the research is increasingly carried out in collaboration with universities or other technical institutions, or even subcontracted to them. This itself has implications for siting policies, summed up in current phrases like 'silicon valley' and 'science parks'. As premises, equipment and perhaps even pilot plants are required, the decision has to be taken as to whether they will be located with the research department, near to head office or near to the plant that is the most likely production centre when the development is complete.

The process just described, in a shortened and simplified form, opens up the possibility of new relations between head office and subsidiaries. It has traditionally been maintained that research is entirely centralized, that the need to contain expenses requires that all research and development takes place in the home country. This has, indeed, been one of the subjects of political opposition to the multinational. Now research is increasingly conducted near to the sources of knowledge and development near to the site of manufacture—in some cases the two may be the same, but not necessarily. As with other functions, a number of methods of organization are possible. Research and development can be conducted in different countries, but coordinated at head office with minimal links between the local research and the local subsidiary. In this case (as in central planning) the department remains centralized although its activities are dispersed. On-line computer links make possible the international management of research from one centre. There are problems in this, and a more decentralized system is where the research and development package is split into viable units each allocated to a separate part of the company, but with the necessary control coordination and exchange of staff. Both arrangements are unusual, however well established in a few companies; but the appearances are that research and development will remain closely coordinated if not completely centralized, and this is likely to make the company unresponsive to innovation from the subsidiary, and especially the subsidiary's need for simple equipment. The failure of many multinationals to move into intermediate technology is partly a consequence of centralized research and development.

A further influence likely to become more important in the future is the link between marketing and research. For many years now, speakers at conferences have emphasized the need for closer links (personal and organizational) between the two departments—especially when it comes to design, the most geographically-based research issue. The emphasis has implications for both since one is regarded as a decentralizing and the other as a centralizing function. The closer links have been found difficult to establish on personal grounds; it is likely that the difficulties will be reduced only when a match develops between the style of management in the two functions.

In the personnel function there was no regular reporting in any of the companies among the *British companies in Europe*. In some there was an absence of policies or guidelines. The beginnings of inverted centralization appeared in three of them where the lack of policies was considered a grievance. Additionally, personnel staff were not involved in the planning process. This information contrasts with the findings of two of the other projects. The *personnel policies study*, which investigated foreign companies in Britain, found more involvement in the planning process as did the *first method of research*. There is a possibility, therefore, that the position of the personnel department is affected by nationality; there is also a certainty that, as with other issues, publicity (visibility) will also be an influence. Companies are being forced to interest themselves in local labour conditions when, for instance, they have subsidiaries in South Africa. Two other facts about personnel were established in other research projects. One was that, like marketing, the use of techniques—especially in this case for selection and training—is a force for centralization. The other was that the degree of centralization of personnel increases with the status of the department. This was discovered in a number of companies and leads to the presumption that the particular selection investigated in the *British companies in Europe* consisted of firms where the function had a low status.

The final function mentioned in Table 15.2 was purchasing, shown as largely centralized, but the information was too limited for generalization. Normally, central purchasing is brought into existence to deal with large orders and especially for capital goods. Other reasons are where transport costs are low in relation to price (making international purchasing viable), where several subsidiaries use the same products or the supplies are interdependent and where large suppliers are available. If these conditions do not apply, decentralized purchasing is probable.[9]

In general, then, the functions do operate differently, but consistency within a company implies that the increase, or decrease, of centralization in one function is likely to be followed in another. Two other comments should be added. One is that international companies face considerable problems of logistics, and these may appear in any function. Distribution, in particular, can add considerably to the cost of the product and central masterminding can be essential. The other comment is that each function has its own culture which is likely to produce characteristic relations across frontiers.

15.4 STAFFING AND INDIGENIZATION

Two partially contradictory trends have been noted in senior staff appointments in foreign subsidiaries over the last twenty or thirty years. One is towards indigenous management and the other towards international management development programmes. In almost all companies, the most senior appointments are decided centrally, although they need to be ratified by the local board. Sometimes local discretion is increased by laws protecting local interests or professions, and sometimes these are circumvented by such devices as distinguishing between a titular and an actual head. A number of propositions about staffing have been drafted in the process of research and are listed in the following paragraphs.

(1) That the widespread use of expatriate managers is a sign of centralization; this stems from the view that such managers are inserted in key positions for control purposes,[10] but some of the evidence suggests the opposite. The expatriate can strengthen the subsidiary and establish its independence of head office simply by knowledge of the company. A high degree of identification has sometimes been achieved; this is not always popular with head office, where it may be described as 'going native', a phrase which expresses the power of identification but not the prestige that often goes with it.

(2) That as selection decisions are often made on the basis of personal knowledge, more local nationals will attain the top subsidiary positions or be brought to head office in a company which is centralized. This is because local staff become better known at head office in such companies.

(3)   The provision of training for senior executives from host countries affects the way centralization is perceived abroad and influences the use of local nationals or expatriates. Training the local manager into the ways of the company, both formally by courses and informally through meetings and correspondence, is a means of socialization by which the demands of the company become internalized. This 'socialization' can be a substitute for the formal exercise of authority, and so can produce an apparent autonomy where there is actual centralization.

(4)   The behavioural implications of staffing decisions are of consequence, but difficult to pin-point. The argument about centralization is often conducted in terms of the motivation of managers: that centralization results in a loss of talent in the subsidiaries and a waste of skills, and that there is difficulty in recruiting and retaining high level staff. Yet it is often hard to see, from the direct evidence, whether a centralization or a decentralization of the personnel function motivates managers more. A decentralized personnel policy can limit the ability of the host country managers to move beyond the top of the individual subsidiary. A centralized policy, on the other hand, can be just as demoralizing, since it may create a primarily expatriate subsidiary management structure. This can be overcome by the greater use of third country nationals combined with an international management development programme. Such a scheme is essentially centralized and allows, within certain commonsense limitations, promotion from any part of the company to any other.

(5)   The issue of indigenization causes special difficulties, limiting international management development programmes for countries where the rules are strictly enforced, but there is usually some scope for bargaining, especially where promotion abroad is possible for local managers in return for bringing in foreigners.

15.5   CONCLUSIONS

Conformity of the subsidiary to head office methods rather than to those usual in its own country has already been noted as a sign of centralization. In the case of organization, a mirror effect has been observed where the subsidiary's own structure resembles that of the parent company more closely than similar businesses in its own environment. Usually, the mirror effect develops gradually and is not noticed or commented upon. Sometimes it comes about as the result of a policy; for instance, speaking at a conference, an executive justified such a development in his own company in terms of experience: '. . . we have found that cooperation and exchange of knowhow are made easier . . . if they [subsidiary managers] are all accustomed to using the same methods, systems and management procedures.'

The mirror effect does not necessarily stem from instructions or intentions, it is the way in which other factors like the reporting system penetrate the organization. Appointments are made to match the demands of head office and so the effect emerges. Even in companies which claimed to encourage autonomous subsidiaries, the mirror effect was observed. For senior managers, the results were offset by contacts with head office and a general understanding of the corporate system, but this did not apply to their subordinates, who grew impatient with an organization which appeared to place them at a disadvantage beside their local competitors.

This review of the connections between organization procedures and centralization is summarized in Figure 15.5. Along each side are listed the pressures towards and indications of centralization and decentralization. In the middle are factors which can operate in either direction according to the circumstances. In general, the degree of centralization arises from separate factors from those which produce the structures, but some connections have been noted, like consumer goods—geographical organization—decentralization; and the reverse, heavy equipment—product group organization—centralization.

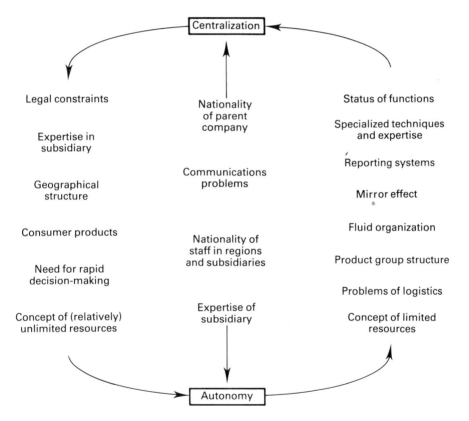

Figure 15.5   Pressures in the organization and communications system

16 *Ownership, Time, Nationality and other Issues*

The links between centralization-autonomy and conflict, effectiveness, government relations, corporate planning and organization have now been explained. This chapter is designed to look at other connections before the results of all the investigations are brought together in Chapter 17. The issues considered here are: ownership, time and size, industry sector and technology, location and nationality, and legal and other issues.

16.1 OWNERSHIP, METHOD OF ACQUISITION AND THE BOUNDARIES OF THE ORGANIZATION

Ownership is a subject on which belief and reality are often in contradiction. On the one hand joint ventures are condemned on the grounds that 100 per cent of the equity is needed to instal the control system without which, it is believed, the project will fail; on the other hand companies are exercising their systems in affiliates, in which they have little or no equity. The belief can be reversed. Companies with 100 per cent ownership have to be circumspect about sending instructions to their subsidiaries, while those with limited equity but a management contract can legally give orders, they may be obliged to by the terms of the contract.[1] The exercise of control, in the sense of installing agreed budgets and a monitoring system, has been uncovered in other partnership agreements like those with agents and licensees. There is evidence that the more successful arrangements are those where the principal negotiates such a role in the foreign partner's business.

The control system can, then, be installed in a joint venture, which does not mean that it always is. Many companies do have a different relationship with foreign subsidiaries that are not wholly owned, and the local management is in a stronger bargaining position when there are other shareholders to be considered. The bargaining strength will apply whether the other shares are owned by one or two other companies or are sold on the local money market to ordinary investors. In the former case the company will be involved in two continuing sets of negotiations, with the partners as well as the management of the joint venture. In either case the local company is likely to have a certain independence and will not reflect head office policies as closely as those that are wholly owned. The same considerations apply to joint ventures with government enterprises, which are becoming increasingly common. In these cases the multinational may be granted control by contract; one motive for bringing or allowing it in is to tap its management expertise. The more serious problem in the developing countries is that of funding; where the law states that the foreign company can only hold a limited proportion of the equity, the government share may not be available. Deals have fallen through because the equity capital was not forthcoming, but special arrangements are usually made where the country considers the investment vital, leaving the company in effective control. Whatever the nature of the partnership, whether with government, private company or wider shareholding, the pressure to local participation is already enshrined in the laws of most countries; there are pressures in this direction in the limited number of industrial countries that do not have such laws.

Evidence does exist that joint venture operations pursue policies that are different from those of wholly owned subsidiaries. This was shown by the financial structures of a sample of foreign owned companies in Britain. Their indebtedness was lower as was their debt-equity ratio at 0.74 compared to 1.14 for wholly owned subsidiaries, with domestic companies having a ratio of 0.91. These were average figures and the number of joint ventures was not large, but they do show that different decisions were being taken in the joint ventures which were behaving more like domestic firms. The high indebtedness of the wholly owned subsidiary has been noted in other countries as well; foreign companies in France, for instance, have been accused of buying local industry with French money.

The difference between joint ventures and wholly owned subsidiaries was even more dramatically demonstrated when the dividend policies were compared. The joint ventures recorded dividends that were either stable or showing small annual increases as is normal with domestic firms where dividends are related to expected long-term profits. For wholly owned subsidiaries, in constrast, the dividends fluctuated considerably between zero and 1521.5 per cent of issued capital. Over an eight-year period 15 per cent of a sample of 115 wholly owned foreign subsidiaries paid no dividend at all, while most of them paid dividends that fluctuated from year to year. Although there was some relationship between short-term profits and dividends, stable profits were over twice as common as stable dividends. Clearly, these erratic payments reflected policies for using funds which were being determined outside the subsidiary. The parent company would require a high dividend when money was needed for developments elsewhere, but a zero pay-out when new investment was planned in the host country. Money was also, of course, being transferred in other ways—royalties, fees, loans, interest and payments for goods—and a general policy for financial resources is easier to manage when an affiliate is wholly owned. A subsidiary can assert its own policies more frequently when the interests of other shareholders do not have to be considered, although there have been instances where the interests of the local shareholders are ignored; in a few cases they would seem to have been ignored for a considerable period of time when the company was able to move money by other means than dividends. Equally rare are instances in which a wholly owned and profitable subsidiary has refused to pay a dividend. The present writer has only heard of three examples of this, but each illustrated how a subsidiary can increase its bargaining power. All three were, in fact, in C type (product group worldwide) companies—again such a small number provides no general principles but adds to other evidence of ineptitude when product divisions operate in foreign countries. In one of these instances, the division was part of a large and well-known company in which other divisions were implementing more sophisticated policies, and shows the kind of factors which, when brought together, increase the bargaining power of the subsidiary. The affiliate in question was led by a strong-minded local national, was in a country which offered some employment protection, and was highly profitable. The articles of association provided that dividends would be paid after adequate provision had been made for the needs of the affiliate. Each year representatives of the proprietors (ownership was 100 per cent) proposed a dividend, and each year the local chief executive blocked payment on the grounds that 'adequate provision' required all the profits to be ploughed back into the subsidiary. The parent division persevered with the situation for many years and retained the chief executive on the grounds that dismissal would be too dangerous. It was likely to destroy the profitability of the company and sure to produce a lawsuit the outcome of which was uncertain, and which could affect the business of other divisions in a high-profile company. Since dividend decisions are virtually always reserved to head office, that situation was one of extreme autonomy achieved by a wholly owned subsidiary using a combination of circumstances none of which would be likely to produce such a result in isolation. Ironically, the combination might have been less effective if the ownership had not been 100 per cent, the partners would also be pressing for a dividend. Nevertheless, the bargaining power of the subsidiary which seeks to follow independent policies is normally increased when the shares are partly owned.

The discussion on joint ventures also raises the problem of organization boundaries, how to determine whether a particular unit is inside or out. For legal and accounting purposes there are rules, but they differ from country to country, and their elasticity is demonstrated when the status of a subsidiary can be altered for tax or liability purposes. Companies distinguish in their published figures between subsidiaries whose accounts are consolidated, and trade investments where the income only is included, but the distinction is an artificial one and does not necessarily coincide with the management system. More complex is the relationship in which no ownership is involved—that with an agent, a licensee, a turnkey venture or a management contract. Research has demonstrated that companies find themselves able to manage many relationships with related companies in the same way as they manage subsidiaries. This is seldom stated publicly—the subject is a delicate one—but many instances were picked up in the research projects reported here where companies had discovered that the most profitable relationships were those in which a high degree of management control was exercised over partners. In management contracts this is to be expected—the contractual arrangement is to provide management services—but the observation still provides an example of centralization without ownership. The dependence of the company being managed on the contractor for technology, and perhaps for supplies, provides just as strong a base for the exercise of authority as shareholding. The difference is that a contract normally has a termination date, whereas a shareholding does not, although in some parts of the world that does not necessarily make the shareholding more secure. Other instances of management without ownership were found in agents, where a similar dependence exists. No one doubts that the agent is an independent company, selling a firm's products in another country; but if working capital, staff training (and selection), instructions about markets and marketing and the operation of a complete reporting system exist as in subsidiaries, then the question arises whether such a firm is or is not within the boundaries of the partner's organization. Certainly the agent will be more integrated, even if the relationship contains none of the items listed, than most of the shareholders; and no one doubts that they must somehow be considered a part of an organization they own. Whatever the opinion about how organization boundaries are drawn in international companies, and a measure of interference in no way corresponds with a measure of ownership, many of the means of identifying centralization and decentralization apply across what are currently considered to be boundaries and do this successfully.[2]

16.2   TIME AND SIZE

The pressures for and against centralization are so strong in both directions that it is hardly surprising that continuous change in headquarters–subsidiary relationships is taking place. Since the measurement of the level of centralization *at any one time* is by its nature subjective and prone to difficulties of definition, it must follow that the relationship *over time* will be even more complex. A process of organization learning is determining which of the pressures from the subsidiary to head office is dominant at any particular time, and vice versa. There are two common ways in which the time pressures are translated into changes in the organization structure. One is by changes at the top of the subsidiary or the head office. This may simply be the result of a new manager wishing to make a distinct mark by shaking things up, or it may result from newly promoted staff being more in touch with company opinion at a lower level. The other influence for change exists where there is evidence of wasted opportunity at any levels expressed, for instance, in declining profitability and morale. Companies recorded examples of missed opportunities which speedily produced greater or less autonomy for the subsidiary management, depending on who was deemed to be responsible. It has been said that the instinct of newly appointed managers is to centralize, and then to relax as they become more confident. There is also a suggestion, to put it no more strongly, that geographical managers work to longer time scales for the foreign operations than the product group. The former see foreign investment as an end, the latter as a means.

In general, the extent to which autonomy declines or increases over time is often difficult to assess since the belief that decentralization has taken place is sometimes found to be mistaken. It has been noted that a statement like: 'we decentralized because opportunities were being lost in the subsidiaries due to slow decision-making at the centre', can mask increased interference. The wasted opportunity problem, in fact, illustrates the difficulties that arise for multinationals between head office and the subsidiary. By and large the subsidiary is concerned with the immediate problems of running a plant, disposing of produce and meeting head office demands. In contrast head-quarters has a wider view of the company's progress and will probably be thinking in a longer time perspective. Lost opportunities for a subsidiary manager may mean a lost order, a production problem or the failure of head office to provide investments to expand into areas deemed by the subsidiary staff to have potential. Parent executives, on the other hand, discern slack decision-making on the part of the subsidiary rather than wasted opportunities. Their view of wasted opportunities will consist of potential markets lost as a result of inadequate research and development three years previously. The time scale is different, so it is not difficult to see how confusions on the nature of centralization come about. A number of other reasons have been identified for this, including:

(1) Inverted centralization.
(2) The centralizing pressure of functional experts. Instructions for greater discretion to be left to the subsidiaries may indeed have been given, but these instructions are thwarted in practice by actions taken by the specialist managers.
(3) Straight misunderstanding as to what the difficulties are, what constitutes simple reporting of fact and what consultation, and who really holds the responsibility.

In spite of these difficulties a process of change over time was identified in the research projects, even though its nature appeared to have been widely misunderstood. The main feature of the change was that centralization could be produced by an accidental and often unconscious process, while the opposite usually involved conscious effort. This effort included a reappraisal of key decisions at head office, as well as strong moves in the subsidiary to use the discretion they believed themselves to have. The facilities to check long-term changes were limited,[3] but it was established through the *first method of research* that a cyclical process was involved. Various factors influence this cycle, but the one most closely related to time is size. The small company does not have the resources to support a foreign subsidiary over a long period of unprofitability, whatever other contributions the affiliate may be making to the company as a whole in market testing or new product development. The credit-worthiness is less and the parent concern may not survive the calling-in of the bank guarantees by which the high indebtedness of the subsidiary has been made possible. The fact that the small firm also lacks the resources to run a centralized system poses a dilemma which is met by using every means of influencing the subsidiary that does not require large resources, including personal contact. The alternative is to abandon any attempt at centralization. This dilemma is the reason why small firms are to be found more frequently towards either end of the centralization–autonomy spectrum than large ones. A special threat, like insolvency in one of the affiliates, is likely to cause a sudden change in control policies. Other pressures towards centralization, like the growth of services at head office, are less likely to apply to a small firm than a large one. A lure to centralization has been noticed in companies of all sizes, a drift in the reverse direction only in smaller companies. If a large firm embraces decentralization it is as a result of a policy decision. The size of the subsidiary is also a consideration. The perceptions of head office staff are more ambiguous. The numbers who claimed that large subsidiaries were more autonomous (on the grounds that they were more able to look after themselves) were almost balanced by those who affirmed that greater authority was exerted over affiliates whose size meant that they had a large share of the overall investment; they had more power to harm the company if their results were bad. The clearest examples of autonomous subsidiaries were found among the larger ones which possessed their own functional staff.

16.3   INDUSTRY SECTOR AND TECHNOLOGY

There is some evidence to support the view that the degree of autonomy is related to industry sector. Consumer product companies are expected to be less centralized than those manufacturing industrial goods, while high capital investment also leads to centralized, global decision-making. This view appeals to common sense, but gives rise to some problems. For instance, many of the large multinationals operate in several industry sectors at the same time. The present investigations evoked replies to show that technology and quality are more important than industry group as such. In the study of the *British companies in Europe,* the four consumer goods companies were concerned with the quality of their products and exercised central control over quality and the purchasing of raw materials. This proved a considerable constraint on the subsidiaries and caused much dissension in one company. The control of supplies also influenced pricing policies, and in two of the companies samples were sent to head office at predetermined intervals of either two or four weeks. Disagreements within companies developed over advertising and brand names, especially in a country used as a test market for Europe. In one company head office imposed a product which was substantially different from any formerly produced and from those of competitors. It just did not suit the local market and the subsidiary managers were led to wonder what the parent company's objective in acquiring them had been. Differences arose in the consumer products companies over head office attitude to lateral contacts between subsidiaries. In one company these were limited; in another they were based on personal contacts and were felt to be useful; in a third company contacts existed but complaints were made about mismanagement in other subsidiaries which hindered cooperation.

Two of the capital goods companies had looser control exercised from head office although there were special circumstances. In one case the subsidiary's products were different from those of the parent; in another the customers were used to and expected individual treatment. In one of these companies a small subsidiary was pressing for a closer relationship with head office and argued for a coordinated policy for the purchase of products made within the group. The more open relationship in these engineering companies between the parent company and the subsidiary did not lead to a more harmonious relationship than existed in the consumer goods companies referred to above; there was much criticism of the other from each side.

From the other studies it became apparent that advanced technology and tied sources of supply both limited the autonomy of the subsidiary. In the case of advanced technology this was associated with a rapid rate of change which left little scope for the subsidiary to be deeply involved in the decision-making. With the tied sources of supply there was the obvious limitation on the discretion of the subsidiary. One other miscellaneous issue came to light when it was noticed that certain industry groups had fixed international standards for specific issues. For instance, the *personnel policies* study discovered that however decentralized the personnel function might be in a particular chemical firm, safety measures were still likely to be enforced internationally. Special considerations relevant to specific industry sectors were observed in all the researches. Unexpected issues, like safety or quality control, as well as unexpected measures of performance, meant that different decisions were indicators of centralization or autonomy in different sectors.

The length of the product life-cycle, and of the period required for the development of new products, differs markedly from industry to industry, being short in clothing and food processing and very long in pharmaceuticals or mining. The longer cycle implies more emphasis on the central allocation of resources, and the company with fewer and more long-lived products will need to supervise their introduction in the subsidiaries more closely. A frequent cause of dissension is when subsidiaries are compelled to take products no longer saleable in the domestic market in the hope that the life of the product can be extended. Such compulsion is one of the measures of centralization that sabotages appraisal schemes.

Another influence is the competition, which is more severe in some sectors than others. Where it is particularly severe, the debate over autonomy also becomes more open. Where the competitors are themselves international, head office will wish to mastermind the corporate response. The founding of regional centres, especially in rapidly growing markets like the Far East, is part of that response and reduces the autonomy of subsidiaries in the region, while representing a geographical devolution on the part of the company.

16.4 LOCATION AND NATIONALITY

A number of propositions have been suggested that relate the degree of centralization to the location of the subsidiary. One is that subsidiaries in countries wealthier than that of the parent company are thought to be more autonomous; this opinion has been particularly mentioned in connection with subsidiaries in Germany or the United States. By the same token, affiliates in poorer, and especially developing, countries are presumed to be less autonomous. Distance from head office is also regarded as a factor. For the first of these propositions there is some positive and little negative evidence. Indeed there is widespread agreement among European companies that their United States offshoots assert their independence. Questioned about problems with American subsidiary managers, European executives will often cite the difficulty of fitting them into the decision-making process, and gaining their cooperation.[4] 'We suffer a lot from insubordination in what is supposed to be our property on the other side of the Atlantic', as one manager said.

The *British companies in Europe* project uncovered problems between head office in five out of the seven subsidiaries in Germany and two examples of inverted centralization. The controversial issues were over budgets, marketing plans, recruitment and (on the part of the subsidiary) slow decision-making. The local managers used their knowledge of law and the market to improve their bargaining power. The legal position is complicated by an ambiguity which will be examined in the next section.

16.5   LEGAL AND OTHER ISSUES

The legal ambiguity can be summarized by two contradictory propositions—*the subsidiary is an independent legal entity with which the parent company must deal at arm's length,* and *so long as the law is not broken, the parent company is entitled to manage the subsidiary as if it were a domestic unit.* The contradiction is normally resolved in the spirit of the latter statement. The law provides a minimum standard and is only invoked when there is a disagreement between the parties. In earlier pages, the law has been mentioned as providing an *extra* bargaining counter if the subsidiary is trying to assert its independence. Such an assertion need not only apply to company law, the articles of association and regulations about the conduct of business; it will also apply to other legal issues like health and safety, employment and consumer protection as well as special constraints on industries like banking. Patent and trade-mark protection, advertising and packaging are just some of the subjects on which global policies are constrained by variations in legislation from country to country.

Normally, the law will not be a serious constraint on centralization except in support of a local management which is successful and which is seeking to free itself from corporate policies. There are, however, exceptions. For instance, it is impossible to dismiss a supervisory board in Germany because the shareholders do not have votes in proportion to their holding. This rule is likely to be carried into the European Community regulations. In other instances the effects of international regulations, like those operating within the Community and other regional organizations, are more uncertain still. The growth of a new body of law, with a complex relationship with existing legislation, can be expected to increase the need for the specialists who form a centralizing pressure. Corporate regional organizations are also likely to gain extra authority when, for instance, the European Community eventually provides facilities for the registration of companies direct to the Community. On the other hand the aim of much international action, like the codes of conduct, is to strengthen national governments in their dealing with companies. Ultimately, larger economic units are likely to favour centralization, or at least fresh units of decentralization, as cross-frontier policies become more profitable.

17 Relationships between Head Office and the Foreign Subsidiary: The Present and the Future

The head office and foreign subsidiary relationship fits most of the general concepts developed for the study of centralization and autonomy. The idea of the normal line and the bargaining process through a built-in network of conflicts are, for instance, relevant. Classifying the relationship in terms of the types listed in Chapter 10 is more difficult, however, and there is the additional dimension of autonomy to be considered—autonomy within the subsidiary's own environment.

There are a number of reasons why the relationship is hard to classify. One is that the range of decisions which can be remitted to the subsidiary is wider than is the case in most organizations, and another that the external influences are more significant. For both these reasons the word 'delegation' is hardly as appropriate as it is in more typical instances.

Take two statements that suggest very different relationships: (1) 'We are only shareholders in the subsidiary and our intervention is confined to exercising the rights of shareholders'; (2) 'we manage our subsidiaries just as we do other operating units of our company.' Further investigation may show that neither of those actually happens, although they represent thought-out positions. The discrepancies demand explanation.

The present author came across another discrepancy along with the germ of an explanation on a routine research visit to the Italian subsidiary of a British company. He had been told at head office that this was the outstanding subsidiary in the group in performance and managerial effectiveness. This was the subsidiary where the corporate system could be seen at its best. He was further assured that this subsidiary was more decentralized than others in the group because of its size and success. Visits to the other subsidiaries would show less autonomy. The Italian managers presented a totally contrasting picture. They spoke bitterly of the minimal discretion left to them in spite of their success, and wondered how head office had such a poor opinion of them that they were supervised so closely. Some discrepancy between the perceptions held at head office and those in the subsidiary is normal, but the complete contradiction of views expressed in this instance was unprecedented.

The search for an explanation led to the discovery that more than one group of managers was involved. The most senior level at head office included those who had claimed that the Italian subsidiary was decentralized, and they were refraining from passing instructions which would limit its authority. The next level of managers, however, including the functional chiefs supposed to be occupying a staff role, were using a number of devices to bring pressure to bear on the subsidiary. A stream of demands and requests were being interpreted in Italy as instructions. This example shows the difficulty of identifying centralization, a theme which will be summarized later along with the characteristics which can be used to make the identification. In the process, the discrepancy with which this chapter began will become understandable.

17.1 THE CHARACTERISTICS

A number of characteristic head office to subsidiary relationships in the multinational firm, some of them little suspected, have been identified, of which the most significant are summarized below.

Corporate relations with foreign subsidiaries are more centralized than head office managers recognize
This was already known, and indeed could be considered the starting-point for the current project. The extent of the gap between perception and reality was not understood, however, nor were some of the implications. It has now been possible to put together evidence, collected at head office and in the subsidiary, of the perceptions of managers as well as of other signs of centralization which might be considered more objective. Both types of data confirm the lure to greater control from the centre, but the reliability of each type merits examination. The so-called objective evidence, which depends on the researcher's interpretation of documents, is not necessarily more reliable than the views of managers who know their constituency. The documentary evidence used by the researcher may not always mean what appears on the surface. The need to weigh against one another the two different kinds of data has made the search for a convincing single measurement of centralization even more elusive than anticipated.

Superficial signs of either centralization or decentralization can sometimes be detected which, on closer examination, demonstrate the opposite, as the example of the Italian subsidiary has demonstrated. The most reliable indications can be found either from correspondence relating to certain key decisions, or by locating the place in the hierarchy where these have been taken. Owing to the difficulties of obtaining the former, or of adequately defining the latter, it may be necessary to fall back on estimates of the influence exerted by the various parties. Some authorities prefer this method, but it makes precise statements more difficult.[1] An alternative approach is to identify in theory the probable pressures on the head office subsidiary relationship and then look for evidence of these pressures in practice.

One consequence of the general finding that the degree of centralization is greater than expected is to emphasize the difference between the legal and the actual situation. Legally, the subsidiary is an independent unit, entirely bound by the laws of the country in which it operates and answerable to head office only at a shareholders' meeting. Laws of the home and the host countries, such as those concerned with taxation, may insist on an arm's length relationship that dealings between the two companies should be similar to those between buyer and supplier rather than to those between units of the same organization; but the arm's length relationship often turns out to be a myth, and the exercise of management controls not to correspond with the legal position. This has also been demonstrated on occasions when the parent company is not the only shareholder in the foreign affiliate. Some companies exercise considerable authority over foreign concerns in which they have a minority holding or none at all; in some cases this authority includes a control system similar to that used in other, wholly owned subsidiaries. A company holding a small amount of stock, even none at all, but with a clear control policy and technical expertise, can dominate a partner, especially if the remaining share-ownership is fragmented.

Three main reasons have been given for the misunderstanding about the level of centralization. In addition to the existence of different groups of managers identified earlier in this chapter, there is the difference of viewpoint and the straight misunderstanding. In this latter case head office fails to understand the extent to which the control system and other demands, especially those of head office experts, reduce the autonomy that is intended for the subsidiary. One guide to this is when complaints are made about lack of initiative in the subsidiary. The system may be stifling the initiative.

Some of the ways in which attempts at decentralization can be reversed and thus increase the lure in the opposite direction are mentioned later, but there are a number of effects that are minor in themselves but add up to a considerable pressure. One example is that an official attempt at promoting autonomy is often accompanied by measures designed to enforce the policy, like banning travel by head office executives. This is designed to prevent their exerting undue pressure on the affiliates, but can have the opposite effect if correspondence is substituted for visits. The personal conversation clears up a point which appears to be an instruction in a letter.

The identification of centralization and autonomy
Little credence can be given to statements at head office that theirs is a decentralized company unless these are confirmed in the subsidiary. If they are confirmed there is likely to be a considerable degree of autonomy; local managers exaggerate their dependence as much as head office executives emphasize the reverse. In questioning it has to be remembered, however, that previous experience will colour the answer even to such questions as: 'in which unit was this decision last taken?' Managers' replies are likely to be biased if they have encountered a different style of management before. This is one reason why postal questionnaires are unreliable in the study of this subject.

It has been argued that perceptions are all-important, since any beneficial effects could hardly be a consequence of an autonomy that was not recognized. There are, however, some indicators of decentralization that can provide a reasonable guide to correct the vagaries of perception. One is the staffing position at head office. Where the staff is confined to a few senior experts with no subordinates available to carry out routine supervision, autonomy is likely whatever the rules say. The rules themselves may be some guide, if they are known by the participants—a fact that cannot be taken for granted. Large spending limits at least suggest an intention of decentralization, although this has to be read in the light of the budgeting process, where all spending will be considered. If the budget is initiated from the subsidiary and accepted without mandatory amendments, and the discretionary limits are high, there is evidence for decentralization.

The organization of the corporate planning system is another sign. Where the decision preparation stage is carried out at subsidiary level, this means that that function is decentralized, as to a lesser degree does the translation. The method of examining which stages of the planning are carried out at the subsidiary is reasonably reliable. Most subsidiaries only operate the implementation stage; if this is the case other evidence is required to determine the amount of centralization. The higher stages are a clear sign of autonomy; the other approach, planning from the top downwards or the bottom upwards, is more difficult to assess. An exercise in which the subsidiary is in fact feeding head office with planning data has been described as decentralized planning.

Another indication of centralization is the organization of the subsidiary. If this resembles similar businesses in the host country, that is a convincing sign of decentralization. The pressures to centralization produce a mirror effect, whereby the subsidiary reflects head office organization. This means that executives are hired with skills that match up to the requirements of head office, rather than those which fit the opportunities of the local market. Responding to demands from the centre easily becomes more important than sensitivity to the customer.

In addition to the signs of autonomy there are a number of measures which are taken to monitor decentralized subsidiaries. These can also be used for centralized ones, so they do not by themselves demonstrate the level of autonomy; they supplement other evidence, and include the positioning of one experienced official from head office (sometimes in charge of finance, but he can be in a number of different posts),[2] the use by the subsidiary of the parent company's internal auditors and the circularization of comparative figures. This last is also a cost-effective means of stimulating thought about productivity, except in cases where more time is spent dressing up figures than correcting faults. The measures described take the panic out of decentralization without constraining the discretion of the subsidiary unduly.

At the same time the subsidiary itself has a number of means of increasing its independence. The strongest is the control of information. Head office normally relies on the local companies for its information on the local market and business conditions in the country as well as on the progress of the subsidiary itself. The way in which the information is presented can strongly influence policies.

The lure to centralization remains active in spite of a hostile climate of opinion and hostile legislation in many countries

The pressures for centralization include the increasingly hostile climate of opinion in which the company operates. This finding was unexpected, since an important element in that climate is the view that foreign companies should not exercise authority over their subsidiaries, and that they should respect the arm's length relationship. In spite of this, a common consequence of increasing hostility is that companies consider it unwise to allow too much discretion to subsidiaries which operate in a difficult political environment. The fear is that a tactless or unsophisticated management may increase the hostility if political initiatives are allowed. There may also be a lack of appreciation of the pressures to which the subsidiary managers are subject. Their political intervention itself may be spurred by the head office drive for profits, while the legal, and the extra-legal, environment remains incomprehensible to their superiors. The subject of corruption is relevant at this point, a subject which head office seldom seems able to see through the subsidiary's eyes. The parent company managers either exaggerate the corruption and insist in joining in, thus insulting the patriotism of the subsidiary; or they refuse to accept that money must be paid to civil servants whose salaries are adjusted to allow for the tips just as surely as are those of waiters or taxi-drivers. Nevertheless, direct intervention in local affairs is not usually ordered from the centre and, where it occurs, may have been provoked by the damage done to the organization's reputation by the subsidiary management. Head office executives, at least in larger companies, are likely to be in touch with supra-national agencies and in general to recruit people with broader political outlooks. They are the ones concerned to improve the international image of the company.

The lure to centralization may be compared to the lure to undivided ownership which has been identified by others.[3] At the same time as political and commercial considerations have made it more likely that a company will not own all the shares in its foreign subsidiaries, it has been discovered that a centralized system is possible even with a minority holding. Of course there have to be compromises and some specific policies may be excepted, but there is no doubt that a company with clearly defined policies, a detailed control system and a successful record, can adopt a centralized policy with regard to associates in which the equity proportion is small. It is now possible to go even further: the research carried out on management contracts demonstrates the possibility of a centralized authority with no ownership at all. A company that has signed a contract stipulating that its management skills will be introduced into the contract venture and fully implemented there has, indeed, an obligation to assert its authority and install its control system. The management contracts study[4] showed many examples of both; the assertion of authority was seen in the introduction of credit control, progress chasing and other procedures, many of them elementary but necessary for the client venture.

This discovery that centralization and ownership do not necessarily go together has implications for the future. On the one hand it will reduce the objections that companies have to partners or local shareholders while, on the other, it will intensify the pressures for central control across all areas of decision-making. Small, highly integrated companies will be able to compete among the giants. There is no evidence that decentralization increases effectiveness of itself; in situations where quick decisions are required at the centre, or where a substantial volume of business information is required there, greater head office authority may be needed. Equally, quick decision-making in the subsidiary may mean more local autonomy. The reduction in the size of companies is likely, in its turn, to reduce the political problems of centralization. These concern power rather than authority and the smaller company will not appear as a threat to the host country in the way that the large multinational does. There is sufficient evidence that most countries are likely to encourage foreign investment where it is unaccompanied by domination; for the conflict of interest between companies and countries is partly related to size.

Other elements of the lure to centralization must not be underestimated. Increasing capital costs and the need for higher standards of technical expertise are an inescapable part of this lure. But there are more subtle implications, like the expectations built up in an autonomous subsidiary that can never be fulfilled. The parent company continues to control the resources, and if these do not produce satisfactory results the firm is likely to be taken over and the system changed. Centralization is seen positively as a means of using limited resources to the best advantage, but the negative view may be the most powerful of all. Over-centralization can damage the company; the abuse of decentralization can destroy it.

Corporate relations are usually compatible throughout the system
The myths and stereotypes about multinational companies, both those held within the companies themselves and those held by outsiders, have been examined and the implications explained. There are differences by function, by type of subsidiary, and according to age, size and other variables, but the differences within a firm are not as large as is often anticipated. One finding is that companies are of a piece—one function may appear more centralized than another, but not when compared to other firms. Corporate relations between parent and subsidiary are usually found to be more compatible with one another than expected. Looking to the future, it would seem that compatibility is a trend that is likely to increase. This is illustrated by the personal problems caused to subsidiary executives by a high degree of centralization which are met, in some cases, not by reducing the exercise of authority from the centre, but by taking other measures to compensate, like higher salaries or greater opportunities.

The problems include the loss or demoralization of able personnel because the limit of their promotion is to the top of the subsidiary, which becomes a more junior position as the company becomes more centralized. The position is analogous to that of the able executive in the family firm finding all promotion channels blocked by members of the family. Subsidiary managers frequently express this difficulty, to overcome which some companies have developed international staffing policies offering opportunities outside their country of origin for executives in any part of the company. In practice there may be some limitations, such as immigration problems, to the policy; but the principle remains, the individual's opportunity is in a company, not in a country. This is different from conventional expatriate policies because managers in all the operating companies are eligible, but a considerable degree of centralization and standardization of staffing policies is clearly involved. A number of the more successful international companies have been operating such policies for many years, but when they are adopted some personnel policies become centralized. International management development cannot occur in a company which leaves all local appointments in local hands, and the system requires centralized records to work effectively. Further, if personnel, which is normally regarded as a decentralized function, is centralized in this way, by the process of providing management incentives, other functions will clearly be affected. Where autonomy of decision-making is eroded in any department, there will be a compound effect on others. Policies partly designed to mitigate the human consequences of centralization produce a more centralized system throughout the company.

The discovery of phenomena like inverted centralization brings a new perspective to the discussion

Conferences and discussions on management style tend to start from the assumption that decentralization is virtuous, while centralization is regarded as a regrettable necessity. A further assumption is that subsidiaries will strive for greater independence, with a result that centralization produces tensions which unnecessarily hamper the decision-making. It is clear from the evidence assembled for this study that centralization is widely practised and that virtue is not all on one side. Failure to use resources to the best advantage in a decentralized system is hardly virtuous, however wasteful some centralized systems can be. Evidence has also been collected to show that not all subsidiary managers seek autonomy for their unit. Over-dependence and lack of initiative are complaints heard at head offices—'we have to force them to take their own decisions'—and reactions that are based on assumed requirements at the centre are often found in the affiliate. These reactions exist where a policy is supposed to be acceptable to head office and is taken in preference to one that would otherwise appear more immediately profitable in the local situation.

Another example is the inverted centralization already discussed.[5] This occurs where managers or specialists in operating units, increase their independence of their subsidiary headquarters by direct reference to head office. In a matrix organization, inverted centralization is virtually built into the system, but it occurs in other organizations as well where the subsidiary is decentralized and the operating units employ specialists who are not found in the higher levels of the subsidiary. This and the other examples of pressures for centralization from below bring a new perspective to a discussion which can otherwise become exclusively concerned with the way frustrated executives struggle to free themselves from allegedly insensitive instructions from abroad. The system has need to cope with managers faced with a continuing and steep growth in requirements for expertise and information.

A new alignment of forces

Simple assumptions, either on a division of centralization by function or indeed of a definition of centralization by function become improbable when they ignore the paradoxes of inverted centralization or of mandatory orders given in the guise of advice. The problem of producing a once-and-for-all definition encounters a level of subjective misunderstanding familiar to those who work with the concepts of power, influence and locus of decision. However, this study shows not merely the definitional difficulties of the subject but, more importantly, the areas of multinational management where it is both sensible and useful to use the concepts. There are many varieties in the organization of the relationship between head office and the subsidiary, and these become apparent in the instinctive responses of managers. These chapters have outlined the areas in which these occur and the symptoms that reveal them. A move to an examination at a deeper level of the relationship in individual companies or industries is then possible.

The search for a comparatively simple measure of the parent–subsidiary relationship which could enable straightforward comparisons to be made within and between companies has been shown to be illusory. Judgement has to be used to inform the measures employed, and the relationship between a subsidiary and its parent company placed along a predetermined scale. Some indicators exist for doing this and are listed in Table 17.1; sometimes the situation can be seen to be beyond doubt. All parties have agreed to the answer given or the correspondence has shown a certain situation to be the case, in comparison with other companies. Even when the evidence of management is overwhelmingly in support of the view that the company is centralized, comparison with other companies in similar situations may reveal discrepancies. Individual managers have to possess a wide experience of different international companies to rate objectively the one to which they belong at the time of the interview. Even where a positive identification has been made there have sometimes been reasons for caution. Significant decisions, by their nature, are not taken frequently and so the last time a particular decision was taken may not have been representative. Nevertheless, when all the difficulties have been pondered, it is usually possible to make a well-informed judgement on the degree of centralization shown in a particular case. The use of this judgement can justify a number of generalizations about the effects of centralization which are considered later.

Conflict theory still holds

The conflict theory states that organization structures and policies emerge through a series of inescapable conflicts. These conflicts are both within the company, between different groups of managers, and between the company and outside interests. The different areas of dispute overlap, and external influences like political opposition affect internal arrangments; but the different projections around which appointments are grouped are intended to ensure that various elements in the decision process are represented. The role of the

Table 17.1 Aids to the identification of centralization and autonomy

General:
(a) perceptions;
(b) correspondence and other documentation;
(c) identification of position in hierarchy where decisions are normally taken;
(d) identification of pressures being exerted on the head office—subsidiary relationship.

Decentralization:
(a) small staff at head office;
(b) high spending limits in subsidiary;
(c) strategy decisions made in subsidiary, and the longer-term stages of corporate planning;
(d) subsidiary organization is local in character, not reflecting head office;
(e) resources available to the subsidiary (but it may be over-resourced);
(f) subsidiary consistently purchases supplies outside the company.

Centralization:
(a) large staff at head office;
(b) low spending limits in subsidiary;
(c) the subsidiary reflects head office rather than resembling other organizations in the host country;
(d) international management development policies;
(e) the existence of inverted centralization—lines of communication and authority which are different from the official links;
(f) restrictions on trading areas.

---

affiliates should not be exaggerated. Inverted centralization and over-dependent subsidiaries provide a warning that subsidiary managers are not always dedicated to a single-minded struggle for autonomy.

The complication is explained by identifying two groups in the subsidiary. Numerous observations have shown that it is the top group which is critical of head office, and the next level who are less interested in decentralization. This ties up with an earlier explanation for contradictory points of view and is summarized in Table 17.2. This table presents a straightforward reason why claims are made for autonomy when the reality is more centralized.

Table 17.2 Centralizing and decentralizing influences in the organization

Head Office	Level one managers	Support autonomy
	Level two managers	Produce centralization
Subsidiary	Level one managers	Strive for autonomy
	Level two managers	Some support centralization

The position of the senior managers in the subsidiary has been compared to that of a buffer or a cushion between the foreign head office and their own staff.[6] Whatever their nationality, they have, to change the metaphor, to filter messages from above to make them more acceptable to their subordinates, on whose behalf they also have to argue with head office; at the same time upward messages have to be doctored to suit the policies of head office. This situation has been shown to be a particularly difficult one in an international company and to account for many of the problems of cross-frontier communication.

Recognizing the situation modifies the presentation of the interlocking conflicts; it also qualifies earlier statements on the unit of centralization. The parent–subsidiary relationship is still to be regarded as an organization on one side of a frontier which manages that on another, but the division is not straightforward. There is more than one interest group on each side. The pressures and counter-pressures are listed in Table 17.3; meanwhile, the connection with the various phases in a company's development will be examined.

Table 17.3 Factors influencing centralization and autonomy

Moves to centralization can be expected when:
(a)   the company is primarily in industrial goods;
(b)   the company is growing;
(c)   there is a high degree of international integration;
(d)   central services in head office have a world remit;
(e)   an elaborate control system exists;
(f)   the political climate is hostile;
(g)   there are high capital costs;
(h)   scarce and expensive expertise is required;
(i)   international management development policies exist;
(j)   lack of initiative in subsidiaries is a problem;
(k)   expertise in lower levels of subsidiary is not available at the top;
(l)   lack of resources in subsidiary are a problem;
(m)   risk avoidance or the fear of disaster dominates policies;
(n)   a need to take a global view of resources or to use managerial techniques worldwide exists;
(o)   the customers are few in number or large in size (this is reinforced when they are international, the same is true of suppliers).

Moves to decentralization can be expected when:
(a)   the company is primarily in consumer goods;
(b)   governments are large customers;
(c)   the company is small;
(d)   there is little international integration;
(e)   legal powers of subsidiary or in host country are used effectively;
(f)   there is divided ownership (note the reservations in the text concerning the extent to which this does produce decentralization);
(g)   subsidiary staff are leaving or are hard to recruit;
(h)   communications problems are identified;
(i)   the market is fragmented.

There are a number of phases in the decision-making

Several methods have been proposed for determining the area of decision-making appropriate to different units. Among them the time factor should not be overlooked. The method employed for corporate planning was into long-term (strategic decision-making), medium-term (tactical) and short-term (implementation, including budgeting). The exact term placed beside each must depend on the industry sector, but a subsidiary which lacks the ability to take strategic decisions will not require the resources to take these decisions. This apparently obvious statement in fact accounts for a common confusion, the lack of correspondence between resources and responsibilities. A subsidiary which is over-resourced will appear more decentralized than it is, and vice versa. A subsidiary that cannot cope with the supposed autonomy because one or more vital requirement—in staff skills or capital, for instance—will appear much more centralized than intended. This latter condition is one of the reasons for the contrast in perceptions between head office and the affiliate. The right to strategic, or at least medium-term, planning has been given but the budget to carry out these functions effectively has not.

On the other hand, a carefully defined restriction to implementation with the support needed can provide the controlled independence described under the heading of *isolated*.[7]

The classification used implies some understanding of a cycle of increasing centralization and autonomy around a normal line, and this also accounts for changes. The relationship to time, organization structure and other factors has been examined. In terms of the types of relationship listed in Table 10.2, the business organization starts as a *personal* type, dominated by the founder or founding family, and may remain so. A world company like Michelin is reported to be still in that position. The family firm often develops imperceptibly into a *close bureaucratic* type which becomes more *open* as the founding family gives place to professional management. The intermediate type results from thought about the organization as such and is frequently found with a matrix structure. However, the *isolated* type is common for at least some relationships in companies which are otherwise classified under one of the other heads, and the main evidence to identify this is that of limited powers over implementation—control over budgets but little control over the resources that make the budgets plausible.

Autonomy can be viewed as multidimensional

Most of the discussion has concentrated on the one dimension of autonomy: the relationship between a unit, in these chapters the foreign subsidiary of a multinational company, and its parent body. There have been a number of suggestions that for this kind of organization there are more kinds of dependence. In particular, governments are trying to increase their control of companies operating within their jurisdiction, by legislation and negotiation on their own account and through international organizations. The addition of an extra dimension always produces complications, as with a matrix organization when first installed or with a growing international investment. In the case of the foreign subsidiary it is even difficult to interpret the complications. It would be naïve to suggest that the exercise of authority by head office be added to that of the local government to make a measure of the lack of autonomy for the subsidiary, although that might just represent the situation. Equally implausible, but equally possible, would be the opposite formula, whereby it is assumed that the action of government liberates the subsidiary from foreign control. This is often the intention of government when the reverse effect actually occurs. Companies tighten their central authority for fear that subsidiaries will embroil them in political troubles. Against this is the reality that subsidiaries can use their knowledge of local affairs to assert their independence, that they can frequently quote legislation to support such a stand, including employment protection in some countries for executives who step out of line, and that they select the information about their market that goes to headquarters.

Another dimension is that between subsidiaries. The consequences of decisions in one subsidiary for those in another, especially in a company with integrated production or other activities, is a reason for increasing authority at head office; but there still remains the limitation on autonomy caused when, for instance, one subsidiary buys its raw materials or components from another. Such a limitation is mitigated in some companies by permission to purchase outside the company, although the affiliate which takes advantage of such permission is placing itself at risk if anything goes wrong with the supplies. When a subsidiary persistently buys outside goods available within the company, this is certainly a sign of decentralization.

Constraints on autonomy, then, can come from a number of directions. Other subsidiaries and national governments have been added to head office as rival centres of authority. In as much as they are rivals, they may cancel one another out; added together they may be expected to paralyse the subsidiary. The relevance of this insight depends on the expectations of the various parties. A head office which aims to provide scope to the subsidiary, believing and intending that this is the route to long-term growth and profitability, needs to ensure that the autonomy granted in one dimension is not removed in another.

17.2 AUTONOMY AND CENTRALIZATION IN THE MULTINATIONAL: THE ADVANTAGES AND DISADVANTAGES

The evidence accumulated on these pages suggests that the advantages and disadvantages of any style of management are related to a subtle mixture of circumstances. In theory and practice the need for a contingency approach has been established. The ordering of the variables is not easy. Statements have been quoted that assume that autonomy is necessary for personal considerations while at the same time being wasteful of material resources. The distinction itself needs some qualification; it is hard to balance motivation needs against those of financing, for instance, while motivation is itself a complex theme. No one suggests that the inefficient allocation of material resources stimulates more effective management, nor is the improved allocation of those resources the only advantage to be gained from centralization. Various options are outlined below; each relevant consideration is arranged in alphabetical order with an attempt to demonstrate the appropriate decisions in each case.

Accountability

Much of the effort aimed at decentralization is about defining accountability more closely, removing the alibis for poor performance and hopefully improving motivation by a convincing display of results in each area of management. Research has shown the problems of achieving a desired level of responsibility. If this is considered a priority, sacrifices have to be made in other directions. Accountability is meaningless if there is little control over major areas like sources of funds, raw materials, or markets; but the nature of the business may demand that such items are centrally controlled. Accountability is convincing where the subjects to which it is attached are closely delimited and where some sacrifice is made of a theoretical best use of resources to improve their local use. Otherwise, accountability becomes an incentive to distort information and to adopt a legalistic approach which effectively sabotages the intentions.

Decision-making

The speed and relevance of the decision-making have been quoted as arguments for both centralization and autonomy. The vicious spiral which over-centralization can produce has been particularly noted as a problem. This spiral occurs when the consequences of too much authority produce unwelcome and unexpected reactions in the subsidiary, and the results lead to fresh but irrelevant instructions; the irrelevance is partly a product of the lack of upward communication. The problems of centralization have a tendency to reinforce themselves (see also planning), but speed is a factor as well. Centralization, it has been claimed, produces greater flexibility. Assets can be redeployed; but this redeployment is never easy and can be blocked by a subsidiary which has been overridden. In the foreign market, too, the result can be a loss of flexibility if the subsidiary lacks the autonomy to react quickly to moves on the part of competitors. Research has uncovered many instances in which slow decision-making at head office caused lost opportunities in the local market. If risk avoidance is considered more important than market gains, this becomes reasonable; risk avoidance is another centralizing pressure. The merits of central or local decision-making will partly depend on the nature of the competition and of the customer. Where a few large companies are competing for a few large customers decentralization is likely to make little sense.

Finance

That funding must be centrally determined is a deeply ingrained belief; countless articles on money management start with this assumption, but some of the arguments have lost their force since floating exchange rates became normal in the early 1970s. One of the responses to this has been to encourage borrowing in the same currency as the operation which it is to fund. The floating exchange rates were themselves a response to the first oil crisis, of which another consequence has been balance of payments problems even more sustained than those felt before. The reaction to these crises has been more regulations about remittances, which make it necessary for companies to use as many different routes as possible for transferring funds. Both local borrowing and remittance methods, which take advantage of the particular mixture of constraints and incentives to be found in a given country, suggest an emphasis on local control of financing arrangements. If this is permitted, one consequence is a role problem for the subsidiary executives. Any zeal they show for transferring funds, and thinking up ever more ingenious schemes for so doing, can be seen as weakening their own operation and the economy of their country.

Industry sector
Manufacturers of industrial goods are more likely to be centralized than those of consumer goods. They are likely to have long-term relations with both suppliers and customers,[8] to which the subsidiaries can contribute little. The exception is where a government is an important customer. In this case the local subsidiary will require as much local colouring as possible, whatever the policies at head office. If, in addition, defence contracts are involved the subsidiary may possess manufacturing secrets which cannot be passed to head office. Where a company is in both consumer and industrial products, there is usually a higher degree of centralization throughout than is normal in similar companies which are exclusively in consumer goods; there may be exceptions in, for instance, pharmaceutical divisions of chemical companies. One of the factors that predisposes industrial goods companies to centralization is that they have fewer customers. Small numbers of large customers produce a centralized marketing effort, as the capital-intensive company is more likely to have centralized financing.

Marketing
This supposedly decentralized function produces a number of examples of the reverse, including the restrictions on exports by subsidiaries to avoid competition within the company. Such restrictions not only produce bitter reactions on the part of governments, they are hard to bargain over. Countries are reacting to an infringement of national policies by a local concern but as a result of instructions from abroad. While multinational companies are often good exporters, the takeover of local companies can block all exports for those taken over if the parent company already possesses adequate sources of supply for its other foreign markets. The companies, for their part, are reacting to the harm done to their reputation with customers when different units are offering varying terms for the same product. The harm can turn into disaster when the rival subsidiaries aim at different market segments and destroy one another's images in the process. Some companies allows inter-subsidiary competition, but only around 5 per cent in one sample allowed this when not compelled by law.

The compulsion itself produces other effects which are disliked by governments. One is that transfer prices, the other principal subject of controversy along with control of exports, are manipulated to minimize the competition.

Apart from those two controversial subjects, centralization or autonomy in marketing departments partly depends on the techniques available at head office. If these are not employed by the subsidiaries. attempts will be made to compel their use. Otherwise there will be a degree of autonomy, limited sometimes by the consequences of an elaborate reporting system, and at others by a close relationship between head office and customers when these are few and international.

Motivation

Conscious efforts towards greater autonomy usually stem from problems that are taken to be evidence of loss of morale or motivation in the subsidiary. These include complaints of neglect or of too much reporting, but they also include loss of managers and of the inability to recruit staff of the required calibre. Such pressures are unquantifiable and are part of the experience which makes up the personal skill of the individual decision-maker. They need to be present in strength to counter demonstrations of savings that can be produced for limiting local discretion. How much is high morale worth? Is it worth the sacrifice of a possible £x loss by bulk purchasing, or of a £y loss by raising funds in the local currency which could more advantageously have been raised elsewhere, or a £z loss by allowing competition with another subsidiary? There are several possible answers, including those listed below.

(1) In view of the evidence that the degree of centralization is usually higher than is thought at head office, the encouragement of more initiative at the subsidiary level might well be considered an acceptable risk.

(2) If the business requires centralization, efforts can be made to mitigate the consequences.

(3) The effectiveness of local management should be measured against the potential for improving or damaging the performance (as some incentive schemes attempt to do). This would accumulate internal evidence on whether priority should be given to personal motivation or other resources. Naturally, the influence of the environment has to be considered along with the lack of autonomy inside the company.

(4) In some cases it should be possible (and commercially profitable) to attempt to calculate answers to questions about the value of managers' services against, for instance, the cost of supplies (itself not unambiguous, see *Purchasing*). Of course the calculations can be wrong. The cost of a manager ranges between the highest profit or the highest loss he or she can achieve with the powers available; but a weighted actual cost (equal to capital costs (notional interest on expenses of recruitment, training, acclimatization and assets allocated to the manager's office) + salary + benefits + secretarial and other assistance + office maintenance and supplies + expenses ÷ a notional weighting calculated on potential for good or harm) can be used. So long as the assumption about motivation is made, this calculation can be

a useful corrective to apparently more conclusive figures on funding and other factors. The costs of an alternative arrangement can be similarly calculated.

Nationalism and politics

The arguments under this heading were rehearsed in Chapter 13. In brief, there is increasing pressure on companies to restrict the instructions given to their subsidiaries, especially where national economic policies are affected; however, the hostile environment has made companies centralize for fear of local managers blundering in delicate situations. The centralizing pressure is likely to be increased by another factor—the desire of governments for the greatest possible immediate benefits, which causes them to compromise. This goes along with some disillusionment with small international operators which has resulted in a desire to deal with companies which have a reputation to lose, and to make sure that these dealings have the support of head office. In a position of strong competition and general recession, the company that produces an international officer at the negotiating table is usually better placed than one that uses the local management, however much the government in question may favour local authority and indigenization. The insight that company decision-making is strongly influenced by the different priorities of different groups of managers also applies to governments. Thus, the conflict diagram (Figure 12.1) can be refined to allow for conflicts within government between those who favour new investment as the highest priority and those who place other economic and social policies first. Some governments are likely to accept a more centralized regime as a part of the price for the funds and the knowhow, and be content to bargain for more local autonomy later; but if the policy changes, the company may have to take drastic action to protect staff, particularly expatriate employees who are sometimes refused exit visas although work on a project has ceased for lack of payment.

Planning

Central planning should be able to take a global view, but is usually dependent on information supplied by the subsidiaries.[9] This has been shown to be one of the areas where centralization easily leads into a self-perpetuating exaggeration, giving the company the worst of both worlds, and is linked to two other disadvantages of centralization. One of the difficulties is that of achieving the high degree of cooperation required for adequate global planning in a centralized system; another is that lack of adequate contact leads to centralization. Autonomy requires adequate communication in order to build up the relationship in which confidence exists, and this means personal contact.

Production

The growth of a single production process across frontiers is almost certain to be a centralizing force, although it sometimes occurs as a result of local regulations about imports. Part manufacture locally may be required or encouraged by tax or tariff concessions. The newly industrializing countries, with subtle rules to encourage local industry, are likely also to provide expanding markets. This is another instance of government intervention producing centralization whatever the intention.

Purchasing

The costs and benefits of purchasing depend on the industry sector. There are many products where a central buying system can obtain a lower price; there are others, especially in primary products, where a central buyer faces higher prices. Some commodities go up when a large company purchasing agent is known to be in the market. In either case large-scale buying can be insensitive to the needs of a particular factory or sub-product. Purchasing is a function which is often of low prestige in a company, and centralization is a sign of increasing status, it is also a function where local initiative can be fostered usefully. There can be a small central buying system which can move into action when alerted by a subsidiary organization that large-scale buying would be advantageous. The problem about this suggestion is the evidence that purchaser–seller relationships for industrial goods are usually long-term.[8] This means that it would be unlikely for many subsidiaries to assign their purchases of the same goods to the centre at the same time. A more plausible arrangement would be to develop centralized buying within a bargaining process about which items are most effectively handled at the centre and which are not. Such a policy would have to be modified according to the costs of buying services at different locations and would need vigilance, otherwise it would become a recipe for centralization.

Research and development

Technical innovation has been recorded as a recipe for success in a number of studies of multinationals, and one that is difficult to manage. The arguments for centralization have already been rehearsed, including the possibility of geographical decentralization without managerial autonomy. A further point is that decentralized developments can distort the costs of a subsidiary, since it will be paying for the most expensive part of the innovation process. Ensuring that this is allowed for in the appraisal scheme proves even more difficult than ensuring that head office overheads are met. The result is that the subsidiary accounts show high costs and apparently low productivity. The expense can mean that the subsidiaries do not strongly compete for the business unless development brings with it the option of local manufacture for other markets outside the local one.

Staffing and expertise

Staff costs were mentioned under 'Motivation', but raise questions in their own right. If a single piece of expertise, whether it be for new product development or market analysis or whatever, can be provided from one source for the whole company, that saves staff costs against the expertise being provided in each subsidiary; but the expertise becomes a head office overhead. The expansion of such overhead charges is disliked in the subsidiaries, and may well be hard to recover if there are laws or tax rules limiting remittances. The result is that the cost savings of a centralized system may be much less than appears. Otherwise the allocation of expertise will follow the general policies of the company. A reappraisal of the need for expertise, and whether it should be located at home or abroad, is possible without any clear policies on centralization and autonomy, which will be partly determined as a result of the appraisal.

The type and record of the subsidiary

In answer to questions, companies often assert that large subsidiaries with a proven track record are more autonomous than smaller or less successful affiliates. Subsidiaries in industrialized countries are said to be more autonomous than those in the less developed. The evidence does not always support these statements, although most companies have mechanisms for taking over the administration of less successful subsidiaries. Otherwise, larger units may be more centralized in practice because more of the business depends on them.

It can be seen that there is no single factor which determines the degree of centralization. This is highest in capital-intensive firms with small numbers of customers and in industrial goods sectors. The pressure for centralization is increased by the difficulties of decentralizing. Over-centralization may have produced subsidiaries which have not the capacity to take initiatives, and this may take a long time to reverse. Hence, management is easily convinced that decentralization does not work. This is considered by companies to be a more potent reason than any resistance to centralization. There is considerable scope for constant reappraisal of key decisions to determine where they may be most effectively taken. Companies sometimes change the rules to suit special circumstances but changes in the rules are not always accompanied by changes in the practices. Centralized companies are commonly those which are well managed in any case. Much thought is given to management methods and techniques through the organization, together with care and attention to recruitment and training.

Hence, a centralized company may appear successful under circumstances where greater delegation would prove even more successful, another argument for the reappraisal process mentioned in the previous chapter. At the same time decentralization *can* arise through negligence—laxity in monitoring the subsidiary—where centralization is produced by the lures and pressures mentioned. Both, whether produced by intention or not, correlate with other organizational features. Those companies where product divisions control the foreign subsidiaries are usually the most centralized in any industry sector—research has discovered a limited number of exceptions to this, invariably connected with some ineptness on the part of the divisional management. The matrix form of organization, which was first developed in the chemical industry and is still more common there than in other sectors, provides a means for allocating responsibilities and decision-making which offers the maximum autonomy with overall control. This form of organization involves making each product division and each national organization a profit centre. There are many variations, but if the controls are not exercised both ways there is no true matrix. The system may involve some extra complexity in the organization, but it works because it matches the realities of the decision-making.

The success or failure of a centralized (or decentralized) system depends on factors like the control system, the staffing policies, the general attention given to management techniques and innovation, and the frequency of face-to-face meetings throughout the organization.

Some companies report that the greatest difficulty is in forcing subsidiaries to take decisions and stand on their own feet, not in limiting their discretion.

The position may change when shares are sold in local subsidiaries. Already this is obligatory in most developing countries and the pressures are likely to increase in the industrialized nations. Such action limits the amount of central decision-making, at least in relation to financial and probably with regard to trading policies. However, companies have shown considerable skill in retaining close control even where they only have a minority holding. One study of foreign investment in Australia suggested that Japanese companies operating in that country were more centralized because they had local shareholders. Nevertheless, central control is more difficult in partly owned companies, and there are also instances of local management exercising considerable ingenuity in avoiding central regulation. Since local shareholding is likely to become more common, companies which need integrated international policies will need to make plans for this.

17.3   THE FUTURE

Words like 'lure', 'drift' and 'pressure' have been used freely in this discussion. They give expression to the observation that a given state, whether centralized or decentralized, has come about through a process of natural development rather than planning. An intentional development has been described as conscious which is not, in this context, the opposite of unconscious—that would not be an appropriate adjective in a discussion on international management. Relationships between head office and the foreign subsidiary fluctuate as a result of reactions to problems rather than the pursuit of policies. There are a number of reasons why an intention to decentralize leads to an opposite result. One is that a number of commercial reasons press in the opposite direction, another is a misunderstanding about the reactions of the subsidiary, and another arises because different groups of managers have different intentions. The result is commonly described as a series of lurches, which are apparent to those in the organization who are apt to exaggerate their extent as well as their chancy nature. In fact, they are usually limited in scope and take place around a relationship, here called the normal line, which is likely to be on the centralized side of the spectrum but varies from company to company according to industry sector, size, number of customers and the many other factors listed on earlier pages.

Small companies may take risks; the larger companies are usually interested in reducing the dangers to a minimum. They do this in a number of ways, including the bringing of large resources to every fresh operation; other evidence for the emphasis on risk-reduction includes the observation that most foreign investment is undertaken for defensive reasons.[10] Risk-reduction points to centralization because decentralization carries the ultimate danger of liquidation. Against this, strong pressures for autonomy have been identified. Within the companies there is an almost fatalistic acceptance that changes will take place and that the movements backwards and forwards seem to occur by chance. The wastefulness of haphazard lurches from a centralized condition to an autonomous one and back again is leading to efforts to find out how more stable conditions can be achieved. The discussion shows that stability arises from understanding the interplay of pressures and their effects. There may still be an element of hit and miss, but the requirements can be specified and the risks reduced. The style of management that is developed by intention to suit a particular industry sector, competitive position, size of company, expertise required and all the other factors identified on these pages is likely to produce a greater variety of responses and more individuality. It is drift that leads to standardized situations, not planning. This has implications for researchers and consultants as well as managers. Research can be concentrated on examples of particular relationships as they develop with attempts to identify the reasons for success and failure, and how the problems are resolved or contained.

Although the subject remains a comparative one, the researcher is likely to have to be content to use a comparison with a theoretical model or standard rather than with a convincing sample of companies. The innovator is lost in a sample. An attempt to sketch the possibilities is set out in Figure 17.1.

As the more centralized end there is emerging an integrated company, usually with production in several countries and with international suppliers or

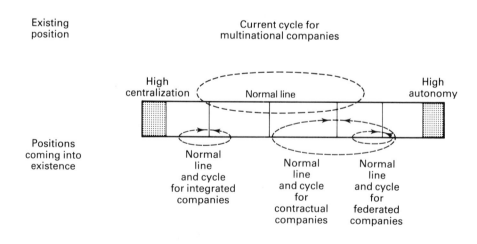

Figure 17.1 The centralization–autonomy scale for multinational companies

customers or both. This company will be as centralized as the laws allow and on principle will make all its plans on a global scale. The local subsidiaries will be treated as if they were units of a domestic company, with essential modifications. Care of the organization is usually emphasized and includes efforts to mitigate the consequences of centralization in a number of ways, including management development programmes and concessions to the policies of host country governments. Great emphasis will be placed on public relations, in particular by emphasizing the benefits for all concerned of the efficiency and profitability of this type of company; the products will usually be machinery, electronics and chemicals, although some service industries like banks are moving in this direction.

The federal system, at the other end of the spectrum, will be used by companies or consortia which are held together by a common interest, a common shareholding, a common market and perhaps a common technology—at least complementary systems. The contractual type occurs where companies are held together by contracts, whatever the nature of the shareholding or the business, and is another way of answering the questions which produce either of the other two arrangements. The contracts provide a means of producing the integration and allowing the local initiative where appropriate.

Both the more decentralized systems have a legal handicap, the possibility of falling foul of competition laws. These have been mentioned by American companies as one reason for being cautious about joint ventures—the laws in their country are stronger than elsewhere—and the degree of collaboration possible may have to be modified where the contracts or the federal system bring together units which would otherwise be in competition. Apart from that problem, and the difficulties over tax and other local policies for the integrated, the three types listed provide outcomes to which some companies have been reaching for a long time.

Part III
Concluding Statements

The final chapters bring together the ideas and facts assembled on these pages and present a coherent statement on the meaning of centralization and autonomy. The ingredients of a theory are proposed with the explanations, the influencing and conditional factors, the analytical considerations and a conclusion which includes prescriptions. The final chapter re-examines the subject from a fresh perspective and questions how organizations can be made more habitable.

18 *Centralization and Autonomy: The Beliefs*

'A decentralizing ideology masks a centralizing reality', wrote the present author some years ago in a statement that now appears both culture- and time-bound. The multinational companies described in these words must appear highly decentralized in reality as well as ideology if your frame of reference is a small tribe struggling to retain its integrity or a country accustomed to authoritarian regimes, or a religious brotherhood, or even the self-same firm when it first came into existence and was staffed by the founding family. The possibility of interest in decentralization only arises, after all, as an organization grows. In some cases size will make delegation possible, and in many dispersal (geographical decentralization) will make some form of authority chain essential. It can be taken for granted that every approach starts from some reference point. The completely natural condition is presumably centralized. The lure to centralization must be seen in this context.

Various frames of reference and approaches to the subject have been examined in an attempt to unravel the truths and fictions that underlie the myths and legends, the pressures and counter-pressures, which include the safeguarding of treasured secrets and group identities, through the mixture of belief in autonomy and administrative convenience which has produced the dialectical process, the see-saws discerned on these pages. The historical analysis could have been traced further through attempts to ensure central authority when the transport and communications were inadequate to the modern attempts to preserve autonomy in the face of a technology which has become over-adequate to run a centralized system.

Which of the two opposites is preferred by a particular person, group, culture or nation depends upon their several aims and expectations; which they will get depends upon the complex interplay of pressures identified on these pages. The options open to an organization may be infinite, but the resulting patterns are limited in number and are definable. In this chapter and the next the patterns are outlined and an attempt is made to carry out the intention of confronting the beliefs and legends with a body of theory that has explanatory and predictive power. The two chapters follow a logical order from explanations through influencing and conditional factors to analytical considerations and, finally, to predictions. The distinctions are not watertight and the explanations provide tools for analysis, while furnishing a suitable opening for this final review.

18.1 EXPLANATIONS

A century and a half ago Le Play wrote that coal mined in the Donetz valley of Russia and transported by pack horse less than a hundred miles was more expensive in the Black Sea port of Odessa than coal mined in South Wales and transported 3000 miles by sea.[1] He gave this as an illustration that free labour was cheaper than that of serfs. He could also have used it as evidence of another theme about which he wrote, decentralization. The Donetz industry was managed from an office in Paris, whereas, in those days, the Welsh coal was mined by local proprietors. In the course of history both the local proprietors and the absentee landlords have disappeared but centralization remains as controversial as ever, and the controversy is heightened by paradoxes, dilemmas and dichotomies. One of these is about subjectivity and objectivity. Is the discussion about an objective condition or is it about a perception which produces certain patterns of behaviour regardless of its factual basis? This dilemma has been evident on these pages and is resolved by answering yes to both halves of the question. The disadvantages of centralization (or autonomy) are seen in terms of perception when words like 'motivation' and 'morale' are introduced; they are seen also in terms of objective reality when the costs and benefits are assessed in terms of the expenses of central staff in a company, or in communicating with members in a voluntary organization. There may appear to be two kinds of argument here, but it is seldom easy to distinguish the two in considering a particular proposition. To suggest that the costs can be assessed without considering the human factor is to invite ridicule. Nevertheless, such calculations are being made all the time. A charity will say that it needs x extra subscriptions or a y increase in the subscription rate so that local branches will be more involved. Frequently, the costs are understated, rather than the reverse, because the extra staff required is not allowed for. Equally, a company will estimate the staff and other expenses as between a centralized and a decentralized system. The problem is to relate the two discussions sufficiently. Decentralization is the subject of emotional debate: 'you cannot leave the subsidiaries to take decisions on which the centre has such a wealth of hard-won experience', or ' it is scandalous that matters affecting the vital interests of this country are decided by a group of businessmen 3000 miles away'. If actual decision-making overlooks the distinction between the two, how much more does research? It would be interesting to know, for instance, the conditions under which an organization which has decentralized funding and staffing arrangements can yet appear centralized to the sub-units. Whatever the answer, the first step in drafting a formula for understanding the subject is the statement that both the material conditions and the subjective reactions are to be included.

The words 'subjective' and 'objective' have also been used in another sense, the frame of reference which was mentioned in introducing this chapter to emphasize the difficulty of determining how objective any statement can be. The anarchist and the supporter of dictatorship will hold different views on desirable degrees of centralization and the difference will influence their interpretation of facts about the organization as well as their perceptions of the situation. The conventional answer to the problem is in terms of the organization's objectives. Analysis and prescription are carried out with the needs of the institution in view and the conscientious observer allows for bias. But centralization and autonomy are not usually objectives, although in some circumstances autonomy may be closely related to aims like independence. The dilemma has been resolved on these pages by the use of the continuum approach, the understanding of centralization and autonomy as opposite poles on a line that runs between the two. This approach has been shown to have two difficulties. One is how to cope with the fluctuations; organizations do not stay in one position. This problem has been overcome by the concept of the normal line, a notional mark along the measuring line near to which the pressures and counter-pressures produce the cycle of change. This view answers the problem that different types of organization have different limits within which the cycles occur; also answered is the problem of bias; comparisons can be made by adjusting the normal line.

The other difficulty of the linear approach is the finding that the subject is not unidimensional. Two considerations are brought together by this difficulty. One is whether the words 'centralization' and 'autonomy' have any meaning across the frontiers of an organization and, if so, is it possible to find a unified measure of autonomy?

The effects of the first consideration can be varied by different definitions of the organization, for the other dimensions of centralization arise because the owners or other central authority are not the only influences that limit the autonomy of the sub-unit. Some writers have distinguished between decentralization, which is a measure of independence within the organization, and autonomy, which concerns the unit's relation with its environment.[2] The two words are used synonymously here, but the distinction has been accepted and the problem of relating different dimensions of autonomy considered in the study of multinationals. It was shown that government authority over a subsidiary could effectively increase autonomy against the parent company and was often intended to do so, although at the same time a hostile political climate had the opposite effect. There are other dimensions of autonomy as well. The subsidiary has a horizontal relationship, which may include the exercise of authority with other subsidiaries, while the charity has a line of authority to employee sub-units and to membership groups. The straight-line relationship (of Figures 10.1 and 17.1) should then be replaced by a number of intersecting lines. This would provide a more accurate picture of the position of a sub-unit and would avoid the error of perceiving autonomy as entirely an internal affair. For analytical purposes, however, each dimension should be taken separately and the unit's position on another axis taken to provide it with bargaining power for the one being examined. At that point the linear analogy breaks down, but is a useful means of identifying what has to be measured and how.

The continuum between centralization and autonomy, albeit allowing for more than one dimension, has been found to be relevant to every kind of organization; in Chapter 2 there was a reference to the 'uncanny resemblances' in the way that different disciplines approached the subject. Similar questions are being asked, similar phenomena addressed; but there are notable differences in practice, in the way that organizations respond or are impelled by the various pressures, as was seen in Chapter 8. For instance, the business organization is worried by the costs of centralization, while many non-commercial organizations, including governments and charities, find autonomy too expensive. A comprehensive theory of centralization must take account of such contradictions and must not make assumptions about the transferability of skills. This issue will be considered under prescriptions; meanwhile, attention will be turned to the unit of autonomy, which provides another example of varying problems within phenomena which resemble one another.

18.2   CONSTRAINTS: THE UNIT OF AUTONOMY AND THE BOUNDARIES OF ORGANIZATION

The need to identify the unit of autonomy has been emphasized more than once, but this identification is not straightforward. The boundaries are blurred inside the organization as well as at its boundaries with related institutions. Executives of the international company may occupy several units at once. The board of the parent company, the board of the subsidiary and the senior management of the subsidiary make three: others exist. If executives are host country nationals, they may also belong to other bodies which will influence their decisions as managers. Examples are a professional institute in their own country or membership of a government advisory body. This blurring of distinctions is well understood and is expressed by phrases like 'the need to avoid conflicts of interest'. For present purposes, the significance is that centralization must not be assumed to rest on ownership, which is, in any case, only applicable to business organizations. Governmental and voluntary organizations possess their own characteristic bonds. The rewards of ownership, the dividends and other payments to head office, have no exact equivalent in non-commercial bodies; so different criteria apply although another consideration, the multiple centres of power which provide multiple sources of authority, does apply to most organizations. Local authorities in government, like local branches in many organizations, derive authority both from delegation and election. The most pressing conflict for members of councils or branch committees is that dual authority. In international companies a similar conflict arises between delegation and the legal and social standing of the subsidiary. Governments, as noted in Chapter 13, are attempting to heighten that conflict through the agency of international and regional institutions set up by treaty.

The individual executive who has appointments in a number of different units is an example of overlapping which recurs in various ways. Any representative or decision-making body contains overlapping representation and the centralization–autonomy formula has to take account of this. At least the concepts apply in areas where authority is meaningful whether derived from ownership, contract tradition or whatever source; the blurring and the rival centres of power are constraints on the economy. Where there are benefits in centralization, the pursuit of these will require the overcoming of difficulties posed by the blurring, but their usefulness can be extended across the normally accepted boundaries of the organization.

18.3   TYPES OF AUTONOMY

A preliminary typology of the relationship between units of an organization (Table 10.2) identified ten varieties each with its distinctive characteristics. A number of bases for autonomy were listed, including delegation, custom and bargaining. In considering the data for multinational companies two more types have been added. One is the integrated, an updated version of the close bureaucratic, and the other the contractual, which is likely to be of increasing importance to non-commercial organizations as well. Table 18.1 restates the typology, while elaborating the characteristics. To examine a particular organization in the light of the types is to see an answer to the puzzling inconsistencies for which a theory of centralization and autonomy must account. As an organization moves from one type of relationship to another, it does so in response to problems, personalities and any of the numerous pressures listed on these pages. In the process there is no clean break with the old system and an embracing of the new; some parts of the old are retained. The types are abstractions drawn from the results of observations. They do not constitute ready-made options to be taken off the peg; they represent phases in an ever-changing relationship.

There is also no suggestion of an evolutionary process in a scheme where all twelve options are open to any organization at any time.[3] The order of the first five does represent some historical progression, but changes can occur in any direction throughout the list. The anarchic relationship, if unsuccessful, can be usurped by the personal and almost any change can take place from one relationship to another, although some are more common. The traditional easily gives place to the bureaucratic and is hard to restore even in an age in which tradition is valued. The contractual appears to have special relevance to a time when size is questioned, and smallness is considered an advantage, in possessing the ability to combine the advantages of central authority with the maximum of delegation.

Some of the types, like the professional and the isolated, can exist within organizations most of whose units are bound by a different relationship; in addition, some remains of a previous type will usually exist and be a cause of misunderstandings, inconsistencies and sudden changes. These can be of the direct kind as when custom and practice, derived from a tradition-bound society, are quoted against the rules of a bureaucratic organization. They can also be of an inverted kind as when an organization conscientiously changes from personal rule to a bureaucracy and some of the sub-units continue to behave as if the change had never taken place. This is frequently noticed in companies, a change from an autocratic to a constitutional rule in a country can provide other examples.

Table 18.1 The types of relationship within which centralization and autonomy have meaning

Type	Characteristics	Examples
1. Personal	Domination by leader, organization informal. Centralized with pressure to decentralization with growth.	Tribe Recently founded firm Recently founded religious, political or other voluntary organization
2. Traditional	Authority stems from accepted customs and practices. Small impetus to change unless environment changes radically.	Tribe Government Church Some armies
3. Bureaucratic —close	Structured organization with tight controls.	Some armies Government Church Company Some voluntary organizations
4. Bureaucratic —open	Structured organization loosely controlled. This develops from the close bureaucratic and often contains pressures to tighter controls and structure.	Company Government Church Some voluntary organizations Some trade unions
5. Intermediate	Semi-structured organization—a repersonalized bureaucracy.	Some companies (especially multinationals)
6. Professional	Framework of rules rather than organization.	Professional institutes
7. Isolated	Individual units within companies with considerable discretion within tightly drawn restrictions.	Military unit Aircraft crew Some company subsidiaries
8. Dual	Two centres of power within organizations otherwise belonging to one of preceding types. A different form to duality occurs where the organization is subject to authority from outside which conflicts with its policies.	Trade unions within companies Membership organizations within voluntary societies
9. Federal	Some *ad hoc* controls within an organization which represents the utmost decentralization in an otherwise recognizable organization.	In the future, but some business organizations moving in this direction—e.g. consortia
10. Contractual	Similar to federal in intention, but can be more centralized.	Multinational companies with joint ventures or management contracts
11. Integrated	Companies managed across frontiers on a highly centralized basis, an updated form of the close bureaucratic but with special provisions to mitigate the centralization.	A few multinational companies
12. Anarchic	Complete decentralization with government on principle by consent.	Some experimental communities and cooperatives

From the cultural standpoint of an industrialized society with universal education numbers 1.–5. on the table (the personal, traditional, the open and close bureaucratic and the intermediate) will all appear to have their place. Numbers 6.–8. (the professional, the isolated and the dual) will be recognized as elements to be found in conjunction with other kinds while the last four (federal, contractual, integrated and anarchic) are to be considered more experimental. Most kinds of organization can be found in more than one type and some (like societies set up to further a cause or belief) in any of the twelve. The pressures which influence organizations to formulate rules and informal proceedings which characterize each type, including culture, have been considered in some detail—but as pressures for and against autonomy, rather than for and against a particular relationship. The purpose now is to summarize the conditions under which both the type and the degree of autonomy can be expected to change.

The personal and the traditional organizations are the subject of much folklore and show strong survival power. In some countries, most local businesses are of the personal type (family owned) and a pressing economic problem is to marshal funds for the support of indigenous entrepreneurs. Financial instruments, like regional development banks, are being put together to overcome this problem in both the public and the private sectors, and some have been founded specifically to overcome weaknesses in those that already exist. The family firm might be expected to be centralized, certainly statements are frequently made to suggest this, but research has found exceptions.[4] The family firm does not have the resources, even if it has the will, for centralization once it is dispersed. A number of statements by managers who have taken over such firms or replaced the members of the family suggest that a fairly loose control is considered normal.

The two bureaucratic types are the most common, and between them form the limits within which the cycle of centralization and autonomy usually takes place. Seen from the standpoint of the personal or traditional types, the significant innovation brought about by the emergence of bureaucratic organizations was that they provided a reasonably safe and reliable means of decentralization which, in its turn, had been made necessary by growth. Efficient organization was expected to be predictable in its operation with promotion by merit and qualifications to an office which had its own duties and privileges to which the holder had to fit. Around this familiar model also developed appropriate norms or guidelines. Earlier modes of succession were condemned by words like 'nepotism', while attempts to minimize the routine were described as maladministration. From the same developments which produced these beliefs has come support for decentralization, and the widespread opinion that centralization was a vice, however necessary. The predictable organization, in which decisions were not just taken at the whim of the leader but in accordance with predetermined rules, makes autonomy meaningful in a way that transcends the distinction between the expressive and the instrumental. It becomes a part of what is described as good administration, which is more than serving an instrumental purpose; rights as well as obligations are conferred.

The lure to centralization, so frequently mentioned on these pages, can now be seen to·consist of a number of component parts which include residual influences from personal and traditional structures as well as material facts which pull against the belief in autonomy. The bureaucratic relationship has been split into three types—the close, the open and the intermediate—representing three different approaches which can be expected to produce different normal lines around which the cycles take place. The close bureaucratic fits the society in which the decentralizing resources, including education and supportive institutions, are not sufficient to maintain a more open system. It also fits the company or organ of government which is emerging from an earlier type. The centralizing lures are strong and the decentralizing attitudes weak in this type, which turns into an open bureaucratic system when suitable conditions develop. The pressures for this change were demonstrated in the study of multinational companies and include the apparent costs and wastefulness of the older system and the need to improve motivation in the sub-units. The change to the more open system exposes dangers that have also been discussed earlier and the threat of disaster; renewed pressure towards centralization forms and is fed by any inefficiencies and incompetencies that the open system has revealed. When the system works well it may accept further experiments in autonomy.

These further experiments lead to one of the intermediate types where some of the most cherished rules of administration are set aside. A repersonalized organization is one in which the job is fitted to the person rather than the person to the job.[5] In a matrix organization, which is frequently of this type, there is the abolition of the direct line of authority and at least the potentially greater opportunity for decentralization. In this type the resources of autonomy become even more essential. It cannot survive without them, a reason why some large companies have tried a matrix organization and declared it a failure. The experiment proved too demanding.

These five relationships, the usual ones for whole organizations as opposed to those within units, do show some historical progression, but this can be reversed. The open bureaucratic or the intermediate types can swing back to a previous (close) condition if unsuccessful, while the personal ruler can take over from any type. There is no inevitable process at work, but most problems seem to occur when the change is too great. Disillusionment is likely to follow a jump from the personal or traditional to an open bureaucratic or intermediate. Many types of organization furnish examples of strong reactions to changes that by-passed intermediate stages. The usual and less risky changes are of an incremental type where the organization adapts to increasing autonomy.

The fifth, sixth and seventh types in Table 18.1 (the professional, the isolated and the dual) have their own links with each of the others, and cause their own characteristic contradictions which have to be coped with. The professional body is a membership association and as such not very different in structure from other voluntary bodies, except that the specialized knowledge is dispersed among the members; a strong centre is needed to enforce the norms and codes of practice. The professional body exercises authority over its members while they are employed by other organizations, with the result that institutes are formed that are centralized themselves while being agents of decentralization. The dual type of relationship derives from such situations and can occur inside most organizations, although it is strongly resisted in voluntary societies and political associations where undivided allegiance is demanded, not always successfully. The dual type occurs both where groups inside an organization accept authority from outside—like members of a professional association or trade union—or where there exists some source of authority which applies to one unit and not to another. The effect of host government regulations on subsidiaries in the multinational firm is an example of this, where the regulations compel the parent company to modify its policies.

The isolated type has a special importance in that it provides a model for combining centralization and autonomy. The unlimited discretion within tightly drawn limits, which is the only option in some cases, is a means of testing the effects of decentralization in others. In fact companies do this whatever degree of decentralization exists. There are always some decisions reserved to head office—the cycle of centralization and autonomy seldom reaches the extremes of the continuum.

The last four relationships (the federal, the contractual, the integrated and the anarchic) represent attempts to clarify, sometimes in an extreme way, the centralization–autonomy divide. The integrated is as completely centralized as is possible, while the federal and the anarchic are both decentralized, the anarchic totally. The contractual is nearer to the centre of the continuum and is, by its nature, more closely defined than the others. All these types are experimental and few examples of the extremes exist although the case for them is often urged, and there is a suggestion that organizations in the future will be framed to allow more relationships with defined and predetermined conditions to come into existence. Where success or failure have immediate and dramatic consequences, the threat of bankruptcy or military disaster, the more decentralized arrangements are likely to remain experimental and subject to sudden change. Otherwise, the thought-out positions, if designed to fit available and necessary resources, can be expected to be more stable than those where there is a mismatch of factors, particularly between attitudes and needs.

Within the conflicting pressures a number of constraints on autonomy have appeared on these pages. The one most frequently mentioned has been the threat of disaster, but the effects of special expertise of definitive knowledge have presented themselves, as have personalities and general principles. Some of the constraints have been built into the organizations, some hold back change and some are formed out of the remains of earlier stages in the relationship. Given the constraints, the preferred arrangement will depend on the influencing factors outlined in the next chapter.

18.4   SUMMARY

The conclusions specified in this chapter are as follows.

Explanations
There is a relationship within organizations which includes regulations and arrangements as well as perceptions. The relationship can be multidimensional

where one dimension is likely to reduce rather than reinforce the other. The costs and benefits vary according to the purposes.

Constraints

Rival centres of power and blurred boundaries inside an organization, and with its environment, have to be taken into account; while the fact that ownership is not the only boundary extends the concept.

Types

Twelve types of relationship have been identified, and are listed in Table 18.1. Of these the first five are commonly found for whole organizations, the next three for parts of organizations where one of the other five is normal, and the other four are less common and more experimental. Of all the types it is claimed that:

(a)   The change from one to another is incremental—problems are caused by over-ambitious changes between the personal, traditional, close bureaucratic, open bureaucratic and intermediate.

(b)   In the process of change, residual parts of other types are retained and cause problems.

(c)   The appropriate type for any particular organization depends on cultural background, purpose and a number of other factors summarized in the next chapter. Failure to find the appropriate type is another source of problems.

(d)   Characteristic of the problems referred to in the previous paragraphs is the organization which lurches between centralization and decentralization in an apparently haphazard fashion.

19 Centralization and Autonomy: Resources and Influencing Factors

'The movement away from simple centralized administration to the extent that it is occurring does not so much reflect the demand for efficiency as the trend towards incorporating other values into organizations. There is an increasing insistence that organizations act responsibly in dealing with their members, clients and public.'[1]

The contrast between efficiency and values summarizes a recurring myth in the debate on centralization and autonomy, one of the myths that provided a starting-point for this study. The equation of efficiency with centralization carries a persistent assumption that resources are most effectively allocated at the top of an organization, while the use of the word 'values' in this quotation reflects the view that there are cultural issues at stake. The influencing factors and those that provide a means of analysis together with some prescriptions that emerge from the discussion form the contents of this chapter.

19.1 THE DIALECTICAL PROCESS—INFLUENCING FACTORS

Besides the equation of centralization with efficiency, another myth is that the relationship within companies or other organizations undergoes an inexplicable sequence of changes. These may be sudden lurches or a gradual transformation; they are habitually viewed with a resigned fatalism. If reasons are given, they commonly echo the personal preferences of a newly appointed chief executive or an inadequacy in a decentralized unit. The confident executive who says 'if we centralize (or decentralize) all will be well', and has the flair or charisma to carry his point of view, acts as a change agent; but the change is not irreversible. Bad results, whether connected with the change or not, can produce a reaction, and send the company back into the cycle of changes. A purpose of analysis is to understand and to break this cycle starting with the factors that have been identified; of these allocating resources is the most intransigent.

Resources

The reason for the intransigence is clear enough. Resource allocation gives rise to a dialectical process because it contains contradictions, and contradictions caused by conditions that become stronger as an organization grows. Consider the argument for central efficiency. This envisages a body of expertise which oversees the well-being of the organization by taking an objective view of all the requirements and the means available for satisfying them. It is the realist view that the sum is greater than the parts and it is reinforced by modern technology which enables the centre to argue that it is best informed as well as objective and fitted to rule. Consider similarly the decentralizing view that resource allocation is entirely in the hands of human beings; the machinery merely copes with some intervening states and people are themselves the main resource. Further, it is argued, that the very technology which makes centralization possible only comes into existence as a result of a rising level of education which makes greater autonomy necessary if it is not to be wasted. The technology can make the information available at any point in the organization's chain; but to create a structure in which most of the levels possess under-utilized expertise and are additionally frustrated by slow reactions from an over-burdened centre is a curious view of efficiency. The taking of a major decision is, after all, not just a matter of moving pieces of paper across a desk. It involves a bringing together of experts and evidence, which is time-consuming and wasteful when the expertise already exists in the sub-unit.

Some divisions in current political outlooks can be seen in terms of the argument in the last paragraph, but there is another complicating factor in that case—another theme of this book, that of determining the unit of decentralization. The political division between left and right could be seen as an argument between priorities in the central or local allocation of resources; it could also be seen as an argument over the unit of autonomy in a decentralizing society, an answer to a question about whether the private sector or public local institutions are to be preferred. Whatever the answer, the inherent contradiction exists: education makes possible a technology which, in its turn, permits a degree of centralization unacceptable to many educated people.

The case of the multinational company illustrates this most clearly because of the juxtaposition of centre and unit where movement between the two is rare. The effort to encourage such movement in a limited number of firms has been represented as an attempt to mitigate the effects of a centralization considered necessary on other grounds, including the scarcity of resources. It is unlikely, for instance, that a mining company would decentralize the search for a mineral like uranium. The arguments for and against further exploration in any particular country could only be resolved at the centre, but the scarcity of resources is an argument which has less application in a world where international advantages are changing, as some newly industrializing countries have been able to show. Education and training can compensate for historical disadvantages; the relationship between raw materials and manufacture has never been straightforward and is becoming less so. In the same way marketing skills can compensate for lack of other resources in increasing the market share of a firm or the exports of a country.

In effect, then, resources exercise a reciprocal influence which only makes centralization necessary under conditions of scarcity, but improved allocation can mitigate the effects of loss of autonomy; and the mitigation is likely to be the option exercised in cases where the balance appears in favour of centralization. Decentralization will be preferred where motivation and other personal resources appear to be damaged by lack of autonomy, but the discussion is often bedevilled by misunderstandings or disagreements about the unit of decentralization.

Other factors

Motivation has been treated as a resource, and one that is assumed to suggest decentralization but not at the expense of efficiency. Other factors are size, time and the division of powers, sometimes seen as a leakage of authority. Size is the factor that makes the subject meaningful in the first place, but the relationship between size and centralization is not straightforward. A theoretical statement of the likely relationship between the two is shown in Figure 19.1; that there is some evidence that this occurs in practice has already been explained (Chapter 10), but the evidence is bedevilled by the difficulty of defining 'middle-sized'. Most research has been carried out on commercial organizations and others could follow a different route. But, assuming the countervailing pressures, the figure shows declining centralization as organizations begin to grow. The pressures for decentralization in an overloaded centre, lacking the resources for a strong exercise of authority, mean that added units increase their autonomy. With the continuing growth of the whole organization, the pressures change. The resources at the centre increase when the dangers of loss of control become more obvious. Over time some of the dangers, like the threat of disaster, are likely to come onto an organization's agenda, and recentralization will take place. At this time the cycle shows an overall improvement that may then decline again. While the overall measure of centralization becomes less meaningful— although it may be valuable to note the trend—and different units will hold different relationships with the centre. The figure (19.1) presents a course that can be expected within the continual changes. It must not be overlooked that once an organization becomes large enough to have a number of sub-units, the measure of centralization will also vary from level to level.

The other issue to be emphasized is that of rival power centres and in particular the leakage of authority that occurs. These power centres may be built into the organization, as with constitutional government. In this case there is a double division of powers: that between the executive, the legislative and the judiciary and that between the different offices of state supervised by the executive. These divisions are recognized and intended as well as being the subject of a wealth of constitutional theory. Their very existence constrains centralization at one level, but not necessarily at others. Some organizations have official divisions of powers which produce restraints on the central authority; most organizations have unofficial power centres which may be recognized under certain conditions—like the trade union members and the

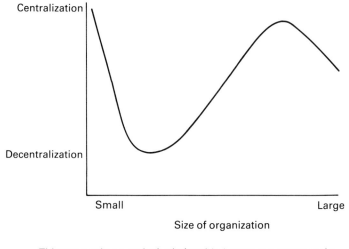

This curve takes a typical relationship between a centre and a unit. It does not take account of the cycle of change which is continuous, nor of the different relationships between different units which will also appear.

Figure 19.1 A theoretical curve of centralization related to size

professionals. This can lead to decentralization although, with one of the many ironies observed on these pages, the trade unions may be instruments of the very centralization they are attacking. This occurs when they prefer negotiating on a central rather than a local basis because the centre is where their bargaining strengths lie. In the case of a recognized union, the dual centre of authority is official and accepted. The extent of its authority depends upon bargaining and lobbying as well as the industrial relations laws of the country. Unofficial power centres may not be recognized, but a picture of a centralized monolith is usually incorrect whether it is an authoritarian government or a tightly controlled company. It would be illuminating, though oversimplified, to suggest that the perceptions of the outsider often indicate more centralization than actually exists. While, as has been demonstrated, the insider is apt to imagine the reverse.

19.2 CONDITIONING FACTORS

Factors that condition the relationship between the centre and the sub-unit have recurred in a number of different contexts. Particularly relevant is the possession of special information; from the sacred knowledge of religion to expertise on global financing in the multinational company, the holding of specialized knowledge is a pressure for centralization. Autonomy becomes real and permanent when the knowledge is widely available and spread. Where this is not possible, decentralization can be dangerous to the organization. A similar centralizing factor is the need to instil loyalty. This is the reverse of the frequently-stated belief that autonomy raises morale. Under some conditions allegiance and loyalty are more important. A high morale combined with disloyalty can be divisive and produce disaster in political and voluntary institutions, even in commercial bodies under some circumstances—another example of centralization being required to avoid disaster, however much autonomy is considered an improvement. Under threat, high morale in a smooth-running organization with high work satisfaction can produce complacency. Wherever disaster threatens or scarce information is in jeopardy, centralizing conditions exist. Predisposing to autonomy is an infrastructure which can support the autonomous institutions—in particular education for expertise and leadership and a communications system which provides at least a minimum reassurance that the sub-unit is viable and effective. The role of communications in the relationship is a factor which has appeared in a number of lights. There is the historical question about how far-flung units of countries, empires, churches or companies could have been centralized before the days of air travel and telephones. The answer is that many devices were used to ensure central authority although, naturally, an *isolated* relationship existed where local authority was exercised within circumscribed boundaries and there were opportunities for rebellion. The devices included regular visits, high insecurity of tenure, promotion and transfer policies and the dependence of the units on resources from the centre.[2]

The historical question about how centralization was possible without rapid communications is accompanied by the contemporary reassurance about the way in which the communications revolution has influenced the centre–unit relationship. The reassurance has been noted, so has the centralizing effect of a burdensome control system, and so has the expense of communicating with members in a voluntary organization. It is clear that communications can provide part of the infrastructure for devolution, especially where cost is not a problem, but can also be manipulated in the cause of central authority. The attitudes which help to determine how the system works will include dissatisfaction and high expectations drawn from education or the local culture. All the demoralizing effects of over-centralized authority can be reversed in a culture antagonistic to autonomy. Further, a society formed from the absorption of differing traditions may value loyalty more highly than local initiatives. The acceptance of large-scale organizations also appears to come more easily in some cultures than others and will influence views on centralization. Meanwhile, we turn from the conditioning factors to the concepts available for analysis.

19.3   ANALYTICAL CONSIDERATIONS

The tools for analysis assembled on these pages have been of two kinds: those that assist an understanding of the concepts and those that are relevant to questions about the effects of centralization or of autonomy in specific situations. The concepts are comprehended in a series of contrasts while the effects are assessed by measurement and by qualitative assessments.

Contrasts

One contrast is that between the *expressive* and the *instrumental* approach to autonomy. The distinction is between a position where the delegation is guaranteed by external forces, like tradition, or is considered to be in the best interests of the autonomous unit, and that where the delegation is understood as a technique. Instrumental decentralization can be seen as a tool of central authority, an alternative route to its own opposite; but this will not necessarily show when the effects are assessed. Pressures towards inverted centralization are likely to be more common in an instrumental relationship, an insight that produces the second pair of contrasts—the *formal* and the *informal,* where inverted centralization is one example of the informal. The distinction is not absolute, but is useful in assessing the degree of centralization where the actual state of affairs differs from the official. Operating manuals may be particularly misleading on this subject if they specify a degree of autonomy which is known not to exist. It has been demonstrated that the contrast between the formal (official) system and the informal needs supplementing. In a number of organizations, including multinational companies, there exists a system which does not fit either category. This has been called the *recognized informal*[3] and is present where informal relationships are officially encouraged to supplement or even replace the official arrangements. In a commercial organization, given the appropriate infrastructure, the recognized informal can be less expensive than the official procedures; it is also a means of decentralization in as much as the local procedures are the ones recognized.

A contrast that looks at similar characteristics is that between the *rational* and *natural* systems. This may be a more precise distinction, with the former those that have been produced by official rules and guidelines and the latter those that have developed to meet problems as they have arisen. Attention should also be given to *exchange theory*[4] which hypothesizes that the natural systems will develop where the rational provide an inadequate return for one group of participants in terms of their own values. Any transaction between two parties where cultural differences exist is likely to produce such problems. These differences can be between occupational groups, classes or regions within a country as well as between different nationalities; they include a difference in outlook which causes one person not to receive the value that the other thinks he is giving. In industrial relations, for instance, one example is provided by attitudes to change. A manager may genuinely believe that a change in working practices has been carried through without anyone 'being worse off'. In terms of the manager's values, change has come to have a favourable image—it has been connected with promotion. To the person on the shop floor the change may be unpleasant. The loss of established working arrangements, including hours (especially if shift work is involved) and of mutual support within an established group, may all appear to be a high price—a price that is no way compensated even by an increase in wages. An exchange which appears favourable to the manager, therefore, presents itself in a very different light to the operative, and the difference is to be found in the informal rather than the formal system. Similarly, decentralization may appear as a sham to some units and a cause of resentment to others. The facts are the same: the values are different.

Another contrast is that between realism and nominalism and this is especially relevant to centralization when the organization is regarded as something more than the sum of its parts. The centralizing view is not necessarily realist in the sense of treating the organization as an entity in its own right, but support for centralization is often couched in realistic language, even in a culture which accepts nominalism as an integral part of a liberal tradition. This contrast is related to the others of which account has been taken—those between authority and participation and between the unitary and the pluralist views. These have been adequately discussed in earlier chapters, and a simple distinction between unitary and authoritarian opinions which favour centralization and the opposite beliefs that uphold autonomy has not been supported, although some connection has been traced. A profile of centralization does include many of the features mentioned, but the exceptions are of special interest. For instance, the contrast between authority and participation needs to be examined in the light of the unit of autonomy. There are international companies that are participative at home but authoritarian in their relations with foreign subsidiaries.[5]

The unitary view of society is in contrast with the pluralist, which allows for a divergence of interests and sees problems as a consequence of that divergence and not as simply due to misunderstandings or bad communications. The unitary view is part of a centralizing outlook, but again the exceptions are interesting. Where, for instance, a considerable identity of interest does occur, a condition for autonomy also exists; the sub-unit can be trusted to identify with the objectives of the whole organization, but the attitudes and ideology are more likely to produce centralization. Through all the dichotomies listed there runs this common thread; the scene is sometimes set for a degree of autonomy or centralization that is not congenial to accepted attitudes, life-styles or management styles. With this insight as a caution against simplistic assumptions, the distinctions can assist in identifying the characteristics of the centralization–autonomy relationship and the routes along which it changes.

The measuring instruments

The measuring line of relationships running from the centralized to the autonomous has been presented as a valuable instrument for conceiving the degree of either; difficulties arise in finding a place for a particular organization along this line. Just as companies find themselves limiting risk as far as possible, never abolishing it, so investigators have to reduce the inaccuracies in their measurements to a minimum. Appropriate cautions—'in the present state of our knowledge' and 'with the tools we have'—must be written into any generalizations drawn from the measurement and the method necessarily involves using judgement and using it at two stages. The first is to determine whether an overall measurement is necessary or viable for a particular organization, and, if it is, the second stage is to compile the measure from the sum of the individual relationships. However, most hypotheses can be tested by individual relationships—the degree of centralization found according to nationality, age or size of a unit, for instance. Where an overall measurement is required, it has to be derived from an averaging process. This in its turn must be closely related to the objects being compared. It is not relevant to examine the different amounts of centralization alleged to exist in different functions when the object of the exercise is to compare different kinds of subordinate units or different organizations, either of which possess a range of functions. Further, for some purposes the measuring scale has to be redrawn to allow for more than one dimension. The straight line may prove to be misleading unless the unit of centralization is clarified along with the unit of autonomy. The latter is sometimes to be regarded as autonomous in relation to either its own head office or to some rival centre of power—a membership group or trade union. It is a relationship that is being placed on a scale, not an absolute degree of autonomy. There is no absolute either in the relationship or in the autonomy or in the centralization.

It has been argued that, although the various dimensions should be kept separate, they will impinge upon one another when it comes to inviting perceptions from the sub-unit. Those questioned may either regard their dependence within another dimension as reinforcing their lack of freedom (like the foreign subsidiary of the multinational company within its local environment), or they may be able to play off one influence against another and secure greater independence. This understandable confusion of the two dimensions is one of the factors that makes responses to questions unreliable, one that probing is needed to disentangle. An example of an extra complication is an organization like the health service where the administrators see themselves as more centralized than the professionals when referring to the same unit. Perceptions need to be treated with caution and probing is again required, but the findings can be checked against objective criteria. In commercial organizations the number of specialists retained at head office is an example. The final formula will include a weighted average of the responses, after the discriminatory powers of the various decisions have been worked out. The weightings will be adjusted in line with any objective evidence available, and the judgement of the researcher added to give a final tier to a process which runs as follows.

(1) Preliminary placing carried out by scoring key decisions and arrived at after probing questions and then testing of answers by regression and factor analysis.[6]
(2) Examine objective signs: if these contradict the above placing, rework, if not, use to adjust placing in relation to other relationships being studied.
(3) Exercise judgement of researcher on the result: if a contradiction appears, rework, if not use to adjust as in (2).

Comparisons with other variables are now possible for the testing of hypotheses. These may relate the degree of centralization to some measures of performance, which are themselves susceptible to the three-tier treatment, or to some statement about the costs of centralization or of autonomy. Other hypotheses arise from the prescriptions outlined in the next section.

19.4   PRESCRIPTIVE CONSIDERATIONS

A case has been made against universal prescriptions, but it is also clear that some statements possess a wider validity than others. Decentralization will frequently raise the spectre of disaster, while over-centralization is likely to produce the vicious circle of misunderstanding and reframing of policies in organizations of many different types.[7] Even these statements are only general, in the sense that they could apply to almost any type of institution; some proneness, propensity, is required to make them actual. Some propositions will have more limited application. For instance, ownership is an important variable in commercial organizations. It is meaningless in most other forms where few varieties of ownership are possible; charities can choose between different kinds of constitution, but this choice has little relationship to that of the difference between the family-owned, the public company or the nationalized business.

Criteria

Where there are problems connected with the degree of centralization, these can be solved by other means than changing that degree. The lurch from over-centralization to an autonomous relationship is not the only response. The problem can be solved in itself, the disaster overcome and the decision taken that further difficulties are an acceptable risk. If the problems arise from centralization this can be mitigated in one of the ways suggested, like international career structures in centralized firms. What is needed is a set of criteria for judging whether the exercise of authority is correct or one that can be used to determine which of the three kinds of solution is required: changing the system, mitigating the effects or living with existing arrangements and solving the problems by other means.

The criteria for centralization or autonomy will vary according to the level of generality and Figure 19.2 lists relevant variables. Some examples are given for illustration. In this case *all* the examples (in columns (2) and (5)) suggest centralization, unlikely in practice but useful in demonstrating the scheme. The 'other examples' (in column (3)) point to either centralization or autonomy, according to the combination in which they occur. Each variable can be given a weighting to indicate a predicted influence and the result compared to an actual degree of centralization measured by a study of the decision-making. The difference between the predicted and the actual provides a basis for investigating the need for change, containment or mitigation of the existing system. A privately owned consumer goods company with fragmented competition and a large subsidiary much subject to government regulation would be likely to be decentralized. Weightings are not suggested in the figure because they have to be calculated for individual circumstances, but the advantage of this system is that it can be operated to any degree of sophistication required. Thus, a rapidly compiled list of characteristics of the organization, with each weighted according to the degree of centralization or autonomy which is appropriate, provides a more reliable guide than hunch and can help to break the cycle of meaningless and wasteful change. The calculation can then be made more elaborate if a number of people are asked to provide lists and weightings independently and these are then put together in a discussion or brainstorming session. Beyond that, any degree of careful analysis can be applied to each variable to provide more permanent criteria. The criteria, however derived, can then be translated into reallocated responsibilities and controls.

The examples given in Figure 19.2 are likely to produce an organization in which centralization is accepted and efforts made at mitigating the effects or containing any problems that result. Most organizations can be examined in the light of such a scheme. First, the appropriate degree of centralization is determined and then a framework is set for solving the difficulties that arise. A voluntary society, mainly devoted to opinion-forming with all its funds subscribed by members, is likely to require a decentralized constitution; means of containing problems will be preferred to changing the system.

It has been found that some variables, like administrative costs, operate differently with different organizations. The costs of operating the system are treated as a reason for centralization in some charitable societies, and for decentralization in commercial concerns. In each case further assumptions are being made, as in the charity where it is assumed that the costs of disseminating information and servicing decentralized decision units would outweigh the benefits. Another assumption is that autonomy has little value when the membership's main function is to subscribe to funds administered by head office and to support views which can be adequately expressed at the centre. In the commercial concern, two different assumptions are being made: one is that centralization involves unproductive expense and the other that this will appear to be the case even if it is not. Charges for head office overheads are disliked and therefore regarded as excessive, but the relevant distinctions do not end with that between voluntary and commercial organizations. In the case of the voluntary bodies there is the further distinction between those that are primarily into fund-raising, for whom decentralization is regarded as dangerous because it can lead to the alienation of important donors, and those that concentrate on opinion-forming. In this case devolution is regarded as helpful in producing a well-informed and active membership. Hence, it can be assumed that the balance between fund-raising and opinion-forming in a particular organization will help to determine the appropriate degree of centralization. A number of similar distinctions influence commercial organizations. One is industry sector and another geographical spread; the degree of integration in the corporate operations and the nature of the customer have also been noted as factors in the multinational. These are among the considerations comprehended in Figure 19.2.

Other factors

A number of words have been used to indicate factors that affect the degree of centralization or autonomy but which cannot be neatly incorporated in a scheme like the one outlined in Figure 19.2. In particular, there are some which have

PARENT VARIABLE (1)	EXAMPLE (2)	(OTHER EXAMPLES) (3)	UNIT VARIABLE (4)	EXAMPLE (5)
Type of organization	COMMERCIAL	(Government, voluntary)	Ownership	100%
Sub-type	INDUSTRIAL GOODS MANUFACTURER	(Consumer goods, service)	Size	Large
			Nationality	Less developed country
Owner	PUBLIC COMPANY	(Government enterprise, family firm)	Experience (age)	Limited
Customer	SINGLE FIRM	(Government, multiple firms)	Resources	Limited
			Potential for disaster	High
Competition	OLIGOPOLY	(Monopoly, fragmented)	Propensity to vicious circle	Low
Control system	DETAILED, FREQUENT	(General, infrequent)	Government regulations	Light
Administrative costs	LOW	(High, irrelevant)	Competition	Severe

Figure 19.2   Variables used in determining an appropriate degree of centralization

important implications when diagnosing and prescribing organization change. One is *care*, the effect on a company or society of the presence of an individual or department specifically devoted to developing the organization. Care may consist of a set of vaguely formulated ideas about structures that are suitable; or it may cover the use of a set of techniques for producing satisfactory relationships (organization development); or it may mean a cost-benefit analysis of each unit, regularly undertaken. Whatever care means in a particular case, the consequences in commercial concerns are usually centralizing with mitigation. The skills and expertise required are not seen to be of a kind that is readily available to the subsidiary; for the large company an internal consultancy or organization department will be utilizing a body of knowledge for the firm as a whole. The exception is where the expertise is used specifically to build a federal system of autonomous units.

The reverse of *care* is *drift*, when an organization moves into a position which is not intended but arises from instinctive reactions to problems. The side-effects of the solutions produce many of the situations described on these pages. The effect of drift can be either towards centralization, when the structure is responding to the *lures* (another of the abstractions), or to autonomy. The drift and the lures set up the characteristic cycle of change.

The other word employed to describe a relevant influence is *contact*. This is more readily identifiable than care, drift or lure. Given that the unit has adequate resources, both human and material, any problems of decentralization can be overcome by adequate contact. The reverse also holds. Difficulties will be exacerbated when an autonomous unit is unduly isolated. The proneness of high contact to produce centralization has been documented, but if there are integrating factors and a decentralized relationship, contact provides the key to effective operation. Decentralization should not be prescribed without it unless the unit's activities are totally irrelevant to those of its owner or controller.

The other word which has occurred in a number of contexts is *mitigation*, usually employed of efforts to make centralization acceptable in cases where it might arouse resistance. One instance is the highly integrated international company where operations are managed from the centre which oversees complicated international logistics. Such companies often have strong pressures to local autonomy because they employ able and highly educated staff who resent the lack of discretion. The difficulty of recruiting and retaining staff in a centralized system is met by international management development schemes and other arrangements to compensate for the lack of autonomy. Other examples of *mitigation* have been noted, like a voluntary society which makes specific efforts to improve communications to meet the demands of members where decentralized decision-making is regarded as too expensive.[8]

Transferability of skills

The transference of skills between different types of organizations has demonstrated a particularly striking paradox in a subject strewn with paradoxical situations. In the discussion of underlying disciplines (Chapter 2) it was noted that there were 'uncanny resemblances' in approaches to centralization and autonomy from many different starting-points. It was further noted that certain concepts and categories fitted phenomena as diverse as government, religion and commerce. In discussing practices rather than theories, on the other hand, the review of non-commercial organizations showed how misleading some of the resemblances could be. This called in question the attempts, currently fashionable, to transfer skills from (for instance) business to a charity. Business has found a way of identifying units ('profit centres') and clarifying objectives ('key results areas') which enable a viable degree of autonomy to be adopted. This may be expressive or instrumental; it will cause some difficulties in practice (the resources may not match the responsibilities), nevertheless it can be seen to work. Hence, worried ('far-sighted') leaders of voluntary organizations are anxious to use the insights, only to be disappointed when the conditioning factors do not apply and the problems are at best only superficially treated.

The paradox of transferability is a suitable note on which to conclude this discussion. It encapsulates the attempt to identify the underlying forces in a subject which is so much cloaked in unnecessary mystification. There are identifiable, measurable and manageable forces at work; organizations do not have to be seen as at the mercy of uncontrollable forces, lurching between the poles of over-interference and neglectful independence, to which their participants must resign themselves. The understanding is compounded of control, integration and dispersal, which relate to all the skills that human experience has built up from the simplest division of an expanding tribe to the most complex attempts at international organizations.[9] To understand the meaning of centralization and autonomy, it has been shown, a number of factors must be held in tension. These include elusive contrasts, like that between the resemblances of the underlying ideas and the differences of practice. To understand the contradictory forces that influence the cycle at the heart of the subject is to gain control over these forces.

20 Coda: The Autonomous Organization

'The worst thing in this world, next to anarchy, is government.'
(Beecher, H.W. *Proverbs from a Plymouth Pulpit*, 1887)

'Ford, the agrarian decentralist, left as his life's work the River Rouge plant, the most highly centralized and most completely mechanized concentration of industrial power in the world.'
(Drucker, P.F. (1971) *The New Markets*, London: Heinemann)

'The age of unmerger may not be far away.'
(Brooke, M.Z. 'The Age of Unmerger', *Financial Times*, 3 Feb. 1970)

'In former days, men sold themselves to the devil to acquire magical powers. Nowadays they acquire these powers from science, and find themselves compelled to become devils.'
(Russell, B. (1938) *Power*, London: Allen and Unwin)

These quotations, all written before the 1980s, bear a special relevance to the coming debate on the autonomous organization.

20.1   LIVING IN ORGANIZATIONS

Of the three characters introduced in Chapter 1, the fixer, the prophet and the bystander, the bystander has made most of the going so far, but with insights designed to support the fixer. A deeper understanding of the issues has been treated as an aim in its own right, but with a further purpose that the understanding should breed action. With as much detachment as possible, centralization and autonomy have been submitted to a hypothetical inspectorate of weights and measures. Not that the emphasis on judgement and calculation necessarily produces an activity free of emotion. The very process of measurement, for instance, can bring discomfort when facts are revealed which destroy a cosy self-image. The hope enshrined in these pages is that the fresh perspective is sufficient purpose, the bringing together of much piecemeal knowledge to enable those who care to see more clearly and to act more surely. There has been no intention to take a moral stance, rather to explode a few myths in order to glimpse the truth. Centralization is not to be seen as synonymous with efficiency any more than autonomy with humanity; and neither are to be seen as the fruits of a completely random process. Without belittling the free choice that can provide exceptions to any generalization, the pressures and counter-pressures have been tracked and the resultant patterns demonstrated. This, it is hoped, provides a basis for further exploration and prescription in a debate which encapsulates the problems of living in organizations.

The focus now moves nearer to that of the prophet. Turning from the here and now to the hereafter, this chapter aims away from the prosaic to glimpses of the horror and the beauty which lie ahead, an asking of questions about the validity of activities that may still lead nowhere. Throughout the book tensions and paradoxes arise from visions of the tolerable and the intolerable. Autonomy recedes before the threat of disaster; page after page has indicated this straightforward truth; now it is time to be less straightforward and to suggest that the threat of disaster is often less plausible, less truly threatening, than the menace of the pervasive organization which rates its own survival above all other virtues. In most places, at least where this discussion is likely to take place, institutions are not regarded as eternal, however treasured they may be. Short of a holocaust, when no organization will survive, there is always a beyond. The ever-present insult of a centralization which belittles the abilities and ambitions of its subjects will surely become more real than the danger of destroying an entity which is not irreplaceable. The cycle of centralization and autonomy will change as the frame of reference, the context, changes.

20.2   THE CHANGING CONTEXT

A fascinating aspect of organization is to glimpse at the way four themes recur—the need for cohesiveness, the safeguarding of information, the instillation of loyalty and the demarcation of boundaries—and to wonder how the skilled administrator simultaneously harnesses the instincts of the coordinator, the informer, the loyalist and the predator. Underlying the themes is the argument between efficiency and humanity that is not to be understood in terms of a simple contrast. The subject could easily be turned into a kind of intellectual soap opera in which the decentralizing goodies are engaged against the centralizing baddies. To avoid such an exercise is not to overlook that there are tendencies at work which reinforce one another. Authority does produce exaggeration and overzealousness, irrelevant in a context of high expertise and motivation, while the temptations of the decentralized unit to laxity are as in need of remedy; but among the slogans which are used to support various points of view, a centralizing phrase like 'the economies of scale', albeit less fashionable than it used to be, is somehow invested with a greater authority than longer-established and better-documented warnings to the contrary like 'power corrupts'.

Weighting the argument the other way, however, there are confrontations between authority and liberty, control and creativity, suppression and stimulus. An impartial investigation must find any connection between liberty, creativity, stimulus and autonomy is, at the least, unproven. A more partial statement is that those who live in organizations and hold such values usually find that autonomous units help to guarantee the values. They also find that, as with so many centralizing arguments, the exceptions lie outside normal experience. Given a reasonably stable society, the reasoning is, the case for centralization has to be proved where the case for autonomy is that it makes an organization easier to live in.[1]

The use of the preposition 'in' (rather than 'with') is not an accident any more than this chapter is an afterthought. The inhabiting of organizations is integral to the changing context. The problems are seen to move from those of interpretation (understanding the relevant phenomena, the bystander's role) to those of administration (the fixer's job) to those of coping with the results, where the prophet comes into his own. Centralization, in this context, has to be justified, whereas autonomy is seen as an objective in its own right. Certain conditions, like intense rivalry or competition, make it easy to justify centralization, but the results will be understood in the light of a belief in autonomy as a desirable condition, a condition which results from a long historical process which began with the growth and subdivision of the tribe and is made possible by a wider dissemination of vital knowledge. The context is a changing climate in which the various underlying factors, knowledge and beliefs, are gradually acquiring a different emphasis. Along with this goes organization experiment.

20.3   BUREAUCRACY AND EXPERIMENT

Bureaucracy describes the typical organization, at least in the industrial world, an organization in which responsibilities are allocated through a hierarchy of appointments allegedly obtained as result of qualifications and experience. The word 'bureaucracy' itself has become a term of abuse in describing an exaggerated rigidity, but any lowering of bureaucratic standards is also abused as a result of a series of beliefs that have grown up in their support. A more personal system of appointment is described as 'nepotism' as a result of these beliefs, which also lead to cries of 'injustice' if the hierarchy is modified. It was, in fact, bureaucracy that turned autonomy into a system, made possible the allocation of responsibilities according to predetermined routines and enabled large organizations to operate predictably. Appointments could be made on the basis of the knowledge required for their fulfilment rather than according to a tradition (long grown irrelevant) or a personal relationship. Trusties were to be replaced by trainees.

The ability to define units and attach duties to them in a systematic manner has produced the background to our subject. All talk of centralizing lures, like criticisms of bureaucratic rigidity, can only be made as a result of the bureaucratic achievement of causing decentralization to become normal and acceptable, even though the achievement has also included the replacement of old traditions by new superstitions, of family relationships by convoluted networks, and time-honoured institutions by meritocratic elites. The debate has been over the appropriate degree of autonomy for different organizations and different situations, how to understand and respond to the varying lures and pressures. We are now able to look further. Some of the central features of bureaucracy have been eroded by the normal development of its own institutions. Thus, the struggle to produce (train, educate) those who are suitable to hold office in decentralized hierarchies has led to demands for even greater devolution and to questions about the purpose of hierarchy. 'You cannot expect', as a senior industrialist said to a bewildered group of steelworks managers thirty years ago, 'that you can go on managing in ways that were suitable to illiterate newcomers to an industrial system after this country has been spending millions a year on education.'[2] That statement could be updated in a number of ways, all pointing to the need for new forms of organization to make more efficient use of creative talents. The managers might be less bewildered today, but not necessarily less believing.

In fact experimentation within large and thrusting organizations is already demonstrating that conventional principles are not essential to management. The matrix system, used by a growing number of companies, has demolished the belief that unity of command is an essential part of sound administration. A manager in a matrix system does have numerous bosses, and that system has been adopted by successful companies because it matches the requirements of the corporate decision-making more closely. The full acceptance of its viability is still in the future for a number of reasons. One is that there have been failures; too many hard conditions have to be met for its successful operation; another is that, since the word 'matrix' became fashionable, companies are claiming a matrix organization where they only have blurred chains of command. The true matrix is a carefully thought-out method of allocating roles in a decision-making system, the reverse of a blurred operation where no one is quite certain of his or her part. When, however, the matrix system becomes normal, it will already be out of date. It produces, of necessity, sub-units consisting of people whose abilities and qualifications will be matched by high expectations. Those who can rise to the demands of the matrix are not for ever going to be content with hierarchy. A more autonomous framework has to emerge.

The matrix organization is not the only innovation to turn up within the conventional organs of business and government. Another bureaucratic principle, that of predictability, is breached by the project organizations which have also been emerging. These flexible structures, subject to constant change, were originally formulated for large-scale constructions projects and are now being extended to other uses. They carry the germ of an almost endless break-up of large organizations into project groups or working parties each possessing a range of skills and each able to offer its services as independent subcontractors. With these developments the cliché which speaks of management as a resource becomes meaningful; it is seen as a facility to be used as required rather than as an authority system. The independent subcontractors would not be part of a hierarchy, but their autonomy would be limited by the demands made on them, the customer's requirements. The age of the independent contractor is already coming. More and more services are being provided by consultants, agencies, software houses and brokers mainly organized in small units. The microcomputer, the on-line link and the video-phone are already beginning to make the journey to work superfluous, a boring luxury. But the technology is not just breeding new housing arrangements, an office in every home, it is producing new routes for the flow of information and new possibilities for the spread of expertise. The bias of the machine age was towards a hierarchical system; it was logical to hand decisions down when the overall view, so frequently mentioned on these pages, could only be seen from the top. That statement was never so completely true as those at the top liked to think, but the logic changes drastically when the information to back this overall view is instantaneously available anywhere. There are plenty of signs that outlooks are changing to match this new reality. The bureaucratic organization fitted the needs of the now outdated industrial system and developed its own norms—promotion by merit and qualification, salary according to responsibilities, clear statements of duties and the rest; now the norms of the electronic age are appearing with less formality, less respect for rank and privilege and more personal responsibility.

Certainly the new technology can also have disastrous consequences. A new dependence can arise with all the monitors and terminals plugged into a central control. The equality can be confined to a new elite, with efficient means of keeping the rest in their places. The passing of the bureaucratic norms may well be followed by a new jungle law—the devil take the hindmost—of unparalleled ferocity. The trusties may drive out the trainees once more. In any circumstances authority will not readily abandon its treasured secrecy, however meaningless and however much a cause of inefficiency, while new social institutions will be slow to replace the comradeship of the workplace so beloved by some. The day when the last office block will be taken over by a preservation society has not yet arrived, but it is creeping up faster than is sometimes realized. A recent broadcast told how a company had helped redundant staff to set up as independent consultants (on industrial relations, training and forecasting for instance) and was employing their services on a contract basis.

So far the emphasis has been on the effects of experiments and of expectations within the conventional economic order, the possibility of a more decentralized society. Experiments outside the mainstream are also burgeoning in spite of much publicized setbacks; the word 'alternative' is being used to express a widespread search, as well as some more humdrum activities. The institutions of autonomous, individual or cooperative units that form part of a society with new links and coordinating mechanisms, with new criteria for success and failure, are coming into existence; perhaps these will eventually turn out to be less wasteful than current procedures for information and liquidation, the familiar means of economic development and control. At least the intellectual and technical equipment is coming into existence to enable these new units to survive within coordinated frameworks, to ensure that freedom can succeed when it produces high motivation. Now that 1984 has arrived the pessimism that gave currency to the phrase 'big brother' is turning to relief that we can cope. But can we?

Well-signposted divisive forces still exist to turn the experiments sour, to transform the intellectual and technical equipment into instruments of torture.[3] In the optimistic fifties and sixties it was possible to assume that the equipment was producing a more unified and harmonious society; phrases like 'we are all in this together' acquired plausibility. Recession changed all that. When redundancy threatens we are obviously not 'all in this together', or not for long. Sober quotations from city editors have become clearer announcements of class war than any propaganda by revolutionaries. To take one example: 'Norcross decision to shut the Hygena operations after five years of losses and attempts at cost cutting was small comfort to its 640 employees, but the market responded by marking up Norcross shares 5p to 102p.'[4] The fact that these divisive forces can so easily compel the replacing of a creaking system by a tyrannical one makes the question of how the controlling levers in society are really operated all the more urgent; the choice between anarchy and tyranny is for real.

The choice is likely to be made more difficult by a distinction that has been avoided so far—that between autonomy for the unit and for the individual. Sometimes, as has been indicated, the two merge, but the wider question of the autonomous person is the subject of another book, in which the continuum and the normal line will still appear but the pressures will be differently presented. The problem noted here is of the nightmare consequences that could follow if there is a total contradiction between the two, the unit and the individual, where the system, any system, adapts itself to accommodating autonomous parts, but these parts make all-absorbing demands on their members. This is not impossible: the assumption that decentralization is more suitable to the human factor can be turned upside down if the autonomous units become all-demanding in order to survive. Memories of the comparative freedom of the large employer, with demands normally limited to fixing and reducing working hours, could seem like glimpses of heaven beside the total demands of the unit struggling for existence in a society made far more competitive by the great efficiency of its small parts. Small can be very ugly indeed if all the individual's discretion is absorbed in that of the unit—like some tribes and communities and other groups with fierce procedures to safeguard conformity and ensure obedience. There is another contradiction, too, when personal autonomy comes under scrutiny—unemployment. This equals high autonomy, but all too little independence.

The nightmare is enhanced when one ponders the place of the heretic in the highly charged autonomous units which could so easily become the enemy of innovation. It has never been clear that autonomy by itself favoured originality, partly for the reason that unit and individual autonomy are not the same and partly because the conditions for autonomy are needed: the institutions, the beliefs, the power, the education and the rest. A decentralization based narrowly on consensus can be the enemy of those who break the consensus. The dynamic of nonconformity has often sprung from a centralized society, an awkward fact that the autonomous society has to cope with. Meanwhile, organization itself will need to cope with a changing purpose.

20.4   THE CHANGING PURPOSE

One purpose of organization has usually been seen as providing stability, a steady state within which activities can be carried out with a minimum of let and hindrance. Existence and promotion are expected where the rules are kept and the qualifications acquired, although intractable conflicts occur from time to time. Survival is the principal objective, even if not usually stated, and risk is dreaded in spite of statements to the contrary.[5] A persistent and simple-minded myth supposes some Darwinian survival of the fittest. The reality is often the reverse. The business firm with an outstanding new invention goes to the wall (and the invention goes elsewhere), while an inefficient and old-fashioned plant survives because it feeds on a corner of the market from which it manages to repel invaders. There are parallels with the voluntary organization too, both in survival and in failure. Not the ability to survive but the ability to form and reform with changing circumstances, to take account of fresh purposes, is likely to be needed—but to be needed in a fresh context, with different activators from those of bankruptcy or disillusionment.

A kind of autonomous society, with looser links than current upholders of the social fabric like to see, is on the horizon. In the meantime some of the experiments will be played out with the opportunities for improvement and for disaster that are inherent in them. These experiments will not be all one way, and will be conditioned by experience. More centralized institutions, together with more isolated relationships, are as likely as more autonomous; but current beliefs will swing towards autonomy unless this is discredited by a series of disasters.

The subject of transferability of management skills has put in a brief appearance on these pages, in order to question the assumption that commercial insights can readily be placed at the disposal of non-commercial organizations. The answer has been cautious—sometimes and with care. More positively, the forces that affect centralization and autonomy have been seen to operate differently in line with the purposes of the organization, and differences have to be taken into account when making prescriptions that assume the transfer of skills. The transfers are normally one way because companies have been subject to more analysis and because some of them have been more apt to experiment, although the experimenters have not usually been the ones to advise the non-commercial organizations, another problem. The aptness to experiment, however, does highlight an inescapable characteristic, the business person's ability to clarify and limit his or her objectives in a way which others cannot. Problems of blurred objectives are met in governmental and voluntary societies by the dual or multiple centres of authority—for instance, that of the full-time staff and the membership. Maybe there is a principle in this that will be institutionalized into commerce in the future, a reverse transfer. Maybe here lies the route to new forms of ownership for private companies, and a greater participation in public concerns—the acceptance of a membership and a management organization which run in parallel. At least, if more autonomous units are to become common, the problems of ownership and coordination will themselves provide a need for thought and experiment.

A more atomized society, in which the office block only survives thanks to the preservation club and the typical worker is an information processor, has the power to bring together a long (and constantly waxing and waning) tradition of communal and cooperative institutions with relevant technology and education. Whether all this works, and whether for good or ill, still remains to be seen. What will also remain is the need to be vigilant over the levels of centralization and autonomy, and their relationship to the other factors which make for the success of an organization—in achieving its material objects and as a framework for living and working. These will continue to be vital factors in the equation.

Notes

Text references to the bibliography are given by author and date

Chapter 1 Centralization and autonomy: an essay in understanding

1. The list is not, of course, meant to be comprehensive.

2. See Crozier (1964) for an outstanding example of such an arrangement.

3. See Brooke and Remmers (1970), 3–5.

4. For decentralization, *Roget's Thesaurus* gives nonuniformity, decomposition, arrangement, dispersion, laxity and commission!

5. See Thomas, Harford (1982) 'A prize case of what has now come to be called bureaucratic centralism', The *Guardian*, Jan. 30, 18.

Chapter 2 The background: some paradoxes

1. Exodus 18.17–18 (revised version). The following quotation is from *The Anglo–Saxon Chronicle*, trans. E.E.C. Gomme, London: Bell (1909), 246.

2. The socialist party, which won the election, placed decentralization in this sense among its election promises.

3. Douglas (1966), 115.

4. The studies were begun by Evans-Pritchard. See Evans-Pritchard, E.E. (1940) *The Nuer*, Oxford: The Clarendon Press. His interpretations have been criticized and modified in many publications including: Greuel, P.J. (1971) 'The Leopard-Skin Chief: An Examination of Political Power among the Nuer'. *American Anthropologist*, **73,** 115–120, and Haight, B. (1972) 'A Note on the Leopard-Skin Chief'. *American Anthropologist*, **74,** 1313–8. The argument is summarized in Keesing, R.M. (1978) *Cultural Anthropology: A Contemporary Perspective*, New York: Holt, Rinehart and Winston.

5. An example of the process described here is Burma in the early twentieth century. A number of studies of that country are summarized in Mead (1955).

6. See Benedict, Ruth (1934) *Patterns of Culture*, Boston, Mass.: Houghton Mifflin, Chapter 7. The quotation is from page 225.

7. Benedict (see note 6), makes this point strongly.

8. Keesing, see above note 4, uses the words in the way they are used in this text.

9. Trevelyan, G.M. (1926) *History of England*, London: Longman, 146.

10. The figure is an estimate by C.R. Conder in Hastings, J. (1899) *A Dictionary of the Bible*, Edinburgh: T. and T. Clarke, **II**, 589. The author's estimate may not be unrelated to the fact that 30 000 was the population also at the end of the nineteenth century. He points out that during the siege of Jerusalem Roman writers gave much higher figures, but suggests that these were inflated partly by pilgrims and partly by exaggeration. The general theme of the growth of the city as an institution is set out in Mumford, L. (1961) *The City in History*, London: Secker and Warburg.

11. A document called the *False Decretals*, because its origins were unknown, was circulating in the eleventh century and provided a succession of popes with the justification for centralizing the Church. The moves towards centralization are outlined in Brooke, Z.N. (1931) *The English Church and The Papacy*, Cambridge: Cambridge University Press. Note especially pages 28–30 ('coincidentally, and consequently, was gradually being created the centralization of the church under papal headship.' page 28) and 90–1. The most recent edition of the Constitutions of Clarendon and commentary upon them is Whitelock, D. and others (eds.) (1981) *Councils and Synods*, **I, ii**, 852–893.

12. The quotation is from Brooke, C.N.L. (1969), 55. The centralization of learning is discussed on p. 23 of the same book, while the centralization of the burgh is illustrated on p. 55 by a picture of the layout of Old Sarum.

13. The story has been told a number of times. See, for example, Blair (1972), 576–587.

14. See Le Play, F. (1864) *La réforme sociale en France*, 2 vols. Paris.

15. See Brooke, C.N.L. (1969), 53–64 where John of Salisbury's work is summarized and he is described as 'an Englishman, and yet also at home, very much at home, in Paris, Reims and Rome'.

16. See Burke, Edmund (1972) *Appeal from the New to the Old Whigs*, London: J. Dodsley.

17. See Locke, John, *Second Treatise of Government* first published 1779 and reprinted numerous times and Rousseau, J-J. *Du contrat social* (1962) trans. Cole, G.D.H. (1973) *The Social Contract*, London: Dent.

18. See Gerth and Mills (1948). Their translation of Weber is used in this book.

19. See, for instance, Catlin (1962), 298–304.

20. See Apter (1977) for a general discussion of this subject.

21. Immanuel Kant (1724 to 1804) published his *Zum ewigen Frieden* in 1795. See Kant, I. (1957) *Perpetual Peace*, trans. Beck, L.W., Indianapolis, N.Y: Bobbs Merrill.

22. Benedict (see above note 6), 231.

23. 'Positivism. The view that all the knowledge is scientific, in the sense of describing the coexistence and succession of observable phenomena.' (*The Fontana Dictionary of Modern Thought*, 488). Nominalism and realism are explained in the text; the reader may like to refer to Stark, Werner (1962), *The Fundamental Forms of Social Thought*, London: Routledge and Kegan Paul, ch. 1.

24. Durkeim (1965), 102–3.

25. See Goodman, Nelson (1973) *Fact, Fiction and Forecast*, Indianapolis, New York: Bobbs-Merrill, 3–27 and 34–40.

26. This was pointed out by Mr David

Bell of the University of Glasgow to whom the author is indebted for many stimulating suggestions. Bell's phrase is the *conditional counterfactual*.

27. Compare Emery (1969), 86–103 where the analogy with nature is carried to extremes with Wiener, 1961 c. 4 where systems theory is expressed in mathematical terms.

28. Tillich, P. (1951) *The Protestant Era*, London: Nisbet, 203.

29. This phrase is quoted from a conversation with Professor Bowker to whom I am indebted for many suggestions.

30. See Tillich, as in note 28, 51–3.

31. Rauschenbusch, Walter (1919) *A Theology for the Social Gospel*, New York: Macmillan, 7.

32. A brief overview of the theories of the firm is to be found in Curwen (1976).

33. See Morris (1964), c. 7.

34. See Penrose (1959), 26–30.

35. See March and Simon (1958), 138–9.

36. The choice of words can be criticized, as it is elsewhere in this book, but they express in this context a valid distinction and are quoted from Gouldner, A. (1959), 'Organizational Analysis', c. 18 in Merton et al. 1959 (vol. II).

37. See Kay (1979), 13–17 and cross-references; this paragraph draws on both the pages and the cross-references.

38. For a statement of exchange theory see Parsons (1951), 70–2, 122–130, 243–8.

39. This so-called vicious circle or spiral is discussed in c. 4 (see also note 19) where reference is made to Crozier (1964), 183–194.

40. The phrase is quoted from a conversation with Professor H. Street of the Faculty of Law, Manchester University, to whom the author is indebted for suggestions and comments relevant to this section.

41. There are two kinds of agent—the subsidiary considered here, and the collaborator. The latter case is not considered in this book, but the present author hopes to consider it in a forthcoming work on the boundaries of organization.

42. The story is told briefly in Brooke, M.Z. and Remmers, H.L. (1970) *The Strategy of Multinational Enterprise* First Edition, Harlow: Longman, 255. A list of press cuttings can be found in note 25 on p. 360 of that book.

43. For fuller details, see below c. 13. The story is told in Blanpain, R. (1977) *The Badger Case and the OECD Guidelines for Multinational Enterprises*, Deventer: Kluwer.

44. See Carsberg (1975), 245–261, for a brief account of the history of the profession.

45. See Shillinglaw (1972), 527. Five different methods of reporting divisional income are shown in the following table reproduced from Anthony & Dearden (1980), 222.

Income statement showing five different methods of calculating income from a profit centre

Revenue		$1000
Cost of Sales		600
Gross margin		$ 400
Variable expenses		180
(1) Contribution margin		$ 200
Other divisional expenses	$60	
Charges from other divisions	30	90
(2) Direct divisional profit		$ 130
Controllable corporate allocations		10

(3) Controllable divisional
profit $ 120
Other corporate allocations   20

(4) Income before taxes $ 100
Taxes   50

(5) Net income $ 50

Copyright Richard D. Irwin Inc. 1965, 1972, 1976 and 1980, reproduced by permission.

46. See Dearden, J. (1969) 'The Case against R & D Control.' *Harvard Business Review*, May-June, reprinted in *Harvard Business Review Reprint of selected articles*: Control part III, 1974.

47. See Shillinglaw (1972), 523–528. For drawing his attention to some of the literature considered here the author is indebted to Jennergren (1974).

48. This was first proposed by Hirschleifer (see Hirschleifer, J. (1956) 'On the economics of transfer pricing.' *Journal of Business*, **29**, 172–184.

49. See Shillinglaw (1972), 598–600.

50. See, for example Danert, G. et al. (1973) *Verrechnungspreise*, Opladen: Westdeutscher Verlag.

Chapter 3   Decision and theory

1. Tuchman, B.W. Of August 1914, c. 9.

2. A summary of social Darwinism can be found in Stark (1958), 50–1 and 170–1.

3. These biological analogies for change in social institutions are expounded in Burns, L.S. (1959) 'Recent theories of the behaviour of business firms' *University of Washington Business Review*, Oct. See also Hayley, B. (1952) *A Survey of Contemporary Economies*, Irwin, 212. These views are summarized in Curwen (1976), 123–6.

A resounding retort, which has not stopped the growing use of these analogies, is to be found in Penrose, E.T. (1952) 'Biological Analogies in the Theory of the Firm.' *American Economic Review*, Dec., 804–9.

4. Outlines of several systems theories can be found in Emery (1969); note especially Chapters 7 and 8.

5. This argument is expanded in Chapter 10. The distinction between formal and informal socialization is discussed in Etzioni (1975), 243–253. For the following passage on elaborate socialization see Rothschild-Witt, J. (1979) 'The collectivist organization: an alternative to rational bureaucratic models.' *American Sociological Review*, **44**, 509–527.

6. See Etzioni (1975) 155–7. Etzioni traces the use of the words 'instrumental' and 'expressive' back to Parsons (1951).

7. See Gellerman (1974), 21–8. For an examination of the cultural effects on organization, see Hajimirzatayeb (1979).

8. See Maslow (1954) and Herzberg (1959). The distinction between universalism and particularism is well discussed in Lupton (1971), especially 98–100 and 124–132. See also Silverman (1970), 81–9.

9. See Blake and Mouton (1964), Macgregor 1967, Likert (1961).

10. The work on organization and technology was originally reported in Woodward (1958) and amplified in Woodward (1965). Some updating of the original reports can be found in Woodward (1970).

11. See for example, Walker and Guest (1965) and Lawrence et al. (1967).

12. For a review of contingency theories see Duncan (1981) and Galbraith (1973) c. 1.

13. See Hage and Aiken (1969). The hypotheses they were investigating are set out in Perrow (1972).

14. See Simon, H.A. (1959) 'Theories of Decision-making in Economics and Behavioural Science.' *American Economic Review*, XLIX, No. 3 (June), reprinted in Greenwood (1965), ch. 17 (the quotation is from 329).

15. See Abell (1976), chapter 1.

16. See Astley, W.G. et al. (1982) 'Complexity and cleavage: dual explanations of strategic decision-making' *Journal of Management Studies*, Oct., 19, No. 4, 357–375.

17. For studies based on the locus of decision-making approach see Pugh and Hickson (1976); for an advocate of measures of influence see Tannenbaum (1966) c. 7. The distinction between power and authority is discussed in the next chapter while issues concerning locus or influence are re-examined in Chapters 9 and 10, and the statements made in the following paragraphs are justified.

18. See Hall (1981), 15–55. The book gives other examples of how decisions have been reached.

19. By the Organizational Analysis Research Unit at the University of Bradford Management Centre. I am indebted to Dr D.C. Wilson of the Centre for this information and several helpful comments on this chapter. For an account of some of the unit's research see the article referenced in note 16 and: Butler, R.J. et al. (1979) 'Strategic Decision-Making: Concepts of Content and Process.' *International Studies of Management and Organization*, IX, No. 4, 5–36. Wilson, D.C. (1982) 'Electricity and Resistance: A Case Study of Innovation and Politics.' *Organization Studies*, 3, 2, 119–140.

20. The distinction is explored in Chapter 4.

21. The two classic statements of this view are March and Simon (1958) (see especially 138–158) and Cyert and March (1963) (esp. 44–66). Many other authors have picked up these ideas and developed them. The paragraphs that follow draw heavily on this train of throught.

22. See Cohen, M.D. et al. (1972) 'A garbage can model of organizational choice' *Administrative Science Quarterly*, No. 1, 1–25.

23. From the Bradford Management Centre. See Astley et al. (1982) referenced above in notes 16 and 19. See also Hickson et al. (1984).

24. This section has been written for this book by Professor Peter Jennergren of Odense University, Denmark. It illustrates the use of mathematical, and in particular linear programming, techniques in interpreting decision-making. Other work by Professor Jennergren, to whom the author is much indebted, is mentioned in the following notes and in the bibliography.

25. The term 'resource-allocation mechanism' is often used rather than 'decision mechanism'. The rationale is that the 'decision' is often one of resource allocation (as in the following discussion). Yet another term which is sometimes used is 'planning procedure'.

26. An upper index o in a^o_j denotes a specific a_j- or x_j-vector.

27. This terminology is used in, for example Dirickx and Jennergren (1979). 'Adjustment phase' is meant to indicate that HQ starts out with a rather crude approximation to the true resource-allocation problem R; this approximation is improved, or adjusted, with successive iterations of information exchange between HQ and divisions. Some authors use a different terminology. For instance, Obel (1981) uses 'iteration phase' and 'termination and implementation phase'.

28. Incentive design is a huge subject with contributions from the fields of management science, mathematical economics, finance, and accounting. See Jennergren (1980) for a survey.

29. The design of the execution phase has not been an issue here, because it was simply assumed that head office would decide on allocation vectors a^o_j (j = 1, 2 . . . n), and that divisions would then decide on, and implement, production plans, by solving their sub-problems $S_j(a^o_j)$. However, different specifications of the execution phase are possible (see, for example, Ljung and Selmer (1979) on this), so design choices have to be made here as well.

30. One element that is actually missing in the present discussion is an explicit rationale for divisions to cheat in the first place. Suppose head office rewards each division with a lump sum payment totally independent of any actions taken in the adjustment or execution phase. There is nothing in the discussion so far to indicate why divisions would not then cooperate honestly; there is nothing to be gained (or lost) through cheating. In order to provide an explicit rationale for cheating, additional assumptions have to be imposed, for instance, that different production programmes involve more or less effort, and that divisions dislike effort (cf. also Harris et al. (1981)).

31. This is explained in Jennergren (1980), 195.

32. See, for example, Ekern (1979), Loeb and Magat (1978), Snowberger (1977), Weitzman (1976).

33. See Groves and Loeb (1979).

34. See, for example, Atkins (1974), Burton and Obel (1977), Ruefli (1974), Sweeney et al. (1978), and compare Dirickx and Jennergren (1979)

35. It is surveyed in Heal (1973) and Hurwicz (1973).

36. See Ellman (1973), 128–133 and Zauberman (1975). For Soviet surveys of this subject see Ennuste (1972), Mandel (1973) and Martines-Soler (1974).

37. By Christensen and Obel (1978) and by Ljung and Selmer (1975, 1979).

38. In addition to the original sources referenced in the text, see Dirickx and Jennergren (1979) c. 6, Jennergren (1981), 44–46 and Obel (1981), c. 6.

Chapter 4 Power and authority

1. In Scott W.R. (1970), 198. The quotations in the following sentence are from Gross, B.M. (1968), 88 while the discussion in the next paragraph echoes Scott and Mitchell (1976), 270–2.

2. For references see section 8.9, which is dominated by this theme.

3. Bacharach and Lawler (1980), 16–17 print six definitions of power all of which refer to relationships. They print one (by Talcott Parsons) which refers to the system rather than to the relationship, but choose to interpret this as not in conflict with the others.

4. See Etzioni (1975), 14–16. Neither centralization nor decentralization appears in the index of this work.

5. See, for example, Duncan (1981), 217.

6. This statement derives from but stretches Etzioni's presentation since he is concerned with 'lower participants' as opposed to 'elites' or 'representatives' (Etzioni (1975), 5 and 17). The cut-off point between the 'power positions' and the 'subject positions' (the phrases are his) is not clear. All employees have a commitment to an organization.

7. Archimedes, see Pappus, *Collections* 8.10.11.

8. Shapley and Shubik (1954), 787.

9. See Harsanyi, J.D. (1962) 'Measurement of social power . . .' *Behavioural Science*, **7**, 77–9 from which this list is derived. Harsanyi, in his turn, quotes Dahl, R.A. (1957), 'The concept of power', *Behavioural Science*.

10. I am indebted to my former colleague, Niklaus Blattner, for this observation. See Blattner (1972), 54. Some of the comments in the following paragraphs also derive from Blattner's suggestions. The subject is discussed again in Chapter 9.

11. Quoted from March (1955), 445.

12. See below, Chapter 9, for a comment on subjectivity and objectivity in this context.

13. Tannenbaum (1968), 5. The reference in the following sentence is to Tannenbaum, A.S. and Kahn, R.L. (1957) 'Organizational control structure: . . .' *Human Relations*, **10**, 127.

14. Tannenbaum (1966), 97. The implications of Tannenbaum's research for centralization are discussed below in section 9.4.

15. This method is described in March (1955), 446–448. The indirect measure, mentioned in the following paragraph, is described in pages 448–9.

16. See Evan, W.M. (1963) 'Indices of hierarchical structure of industrial organizations', *Management Science*, **9**, 468–477.

17. The ensuing discussion assumes a background of Weberian studies on bureaucracy. See Gerth and Mills (1948), 196–240. The main implications of those pages are not discussed here, only the issues that are important for the present study.

18. See Toffler (1981), 258–9. Toffler frequently emphasizes the movement between centralization and decentralization.

19. See Crozier (1964), 183–194.

20. The phrase is quoted from Crozier (see note 19) who in turn refers to the work of Blau. See Blau and Scott (1962).

21. See Dahrendorf (1964), reprinted in Burns (1969), 143–4.

22. See Taylor, F.W. (1947) *Scientific Management*, New York: Harper and Row (the first edn. was published in 1911).

23. See Richardson, F.L.W. and Walker, C.R. (1948) *Human Relations in an Expanding Company*, New Haven, CT: Yale University Press.

24. See Woodward (1958), 4–40.

25. See Gerth and Mills (1948), 235–9.

26. This is emphasized in Johns (1973), 70–71.

27. Katz (1968), 82.

28. See Gerth and Mills (1948), 196–198 and Brooke and Remmers (1978), 134, 226.

29. Etzioni (1975), 20. The following passage draws on pages 20–21 and 462–4 of this book.

30. Scott (1970), 428.

31. March and Simon (1958), 89.

32. Coke, S. (1982) 'Richer industrial countries: Japan' (p.5.4–13). c. 5.4 in Brooke, M.Z. and Buckley, P.J. (eds.), (1982) *Handbook of International Trade*, Brentford: Kluwer, Vol. II.

   The evidence for the assertions in the following paragraph is contained in a number of unpublished papers of the International Business Unit of the University of Manchester Institute of Science and Technology.

   The present author is working on a comprehensive study of organization boundaries which, it is hoped, will eventually be published as a companion to the present volume. The trend to more dependent companies was forecast in 1970 see Brooke, M.Z. (1970) 'The age of unmerger', *Financial Times*, 3 Feb. 1970, 13.

33. The following paragraph draws on Likert (1967), especially Table 3.1, 14–24.

Chapter 5 Control, communication and planning

1. See Sloan, A. (1964) *My Years with General Motors*, Garden City, N.Y.: Doubleday. Sloan was not, of course, the first person to write about decentralization and control, but his reflective comments make a readable statement of the case by an experienced executive.

2. See MacIntosh, N.B. and Daft, R.L. (1980) 'Management control systems and organizational context', *Report to the Society of Management Accountants (Canada) and the National Association of Accountants (USA)*, Kingston, Ontario; also Daft, R.L., MacIntosh, N.B. and Baysinger, B. (1981) 'The design of management control systems', paper presented at the National Academy of Management Meetings, San Diego, August. The author is grateful to Professor MacIntosh for advice in preparing this chapter.

3. This subject will be developed in the next chapter. The word 'intended', used twice in this sentence, may be disputed. Some will say that there is seldom, if ever, an intention to devolve authority except to relieve head office of burdensome detail; others will maintain, on the contrary, that the most serious problem is to persuade sub-units to accept responsibility.

4. See Dew and Gee (1973), c. 8. Professor Dew has read and commented on this chapter and his

suggestions are gratefully acknowledged. Item (9) on *sense of direction* is based on some notes he prepared. Professor Dew argues that control is a middle-management function which operates within a sense of direction and understanding derived from the top.

5. In this connection the disappointing performance of conglomerates, *on average*, should be noted. The recent hard fought takeover of Tilling by BTR (one British conglomerate absorbing another) is an example of a more directively managed company taking over one that encouraged a higher level of autonomy.

6. See Blau (1955); the 'dysfunctional' controls, as Blau calls them, are a major theme of that book. See Lawler (1971) for the source of the following paragraph. The relevant excerpts from both books are printed in Dunnette (1976), 1254–1278.

7. See Nystrom and Starbuck (1981) vol. 2, c. 2 (by L.P. Jennergren) 47–51 for a survey of the empirical evidence.

8. Job enrichment, or work structuring as it is sometimes called, is reviewed in Maher (1971). Case studies can be found in Buckingham et al. (1975) and Paul and Robertson (1971).

9. This autonomous relationship within strict constraints is known as the *isolated* in Chapter 10, see Table 10.2.

10. The Bol' Shevicka Clothing Company, a case prepared for private circulation by Leonard Wrigley. The facts in the text are either quoted or calculated from the material in that study.

11. 'Economic progress elusive after age of the plan', the *Guardian* (London) 13 Nov. 1982. A further article in the same newspaper (27 July 1983) reported another attempt at decen-

tralization under the heading: 'Industry in Russia gets greater freedom.' The article made it clear that the freedom only applied to a limited sector. A month later the shooting down of a Korean airliner, apparently on the orders of a local commander, gave the impression to the world that considerable autonomy existed within the Soviet armed forces.

12. See Brooke and van Beusekom (1979), 8–9. The three phrases are there called: decision preparation, translation and adjusting to operations.

13. The evidence is summarized in Ezzamel, M.A. and Hilton, K. (1980) 'Divisionalization in British industry: A preliminary study' *Accounting and Business Research*, Spring, 197–211.

14. See Child, J. 'What determines organization performance? The universals versus the it-all-depends', 420–437 in Magnusen (1977).

15. See above, note 4. Since this book went to press a thorough review of control systems and their implications has been published. See Lowe and Machin (1983).

Chapter 6   Conflict and cooperation

1. This sentence echoes the words of Mary Parker Follett. In a paper entitled 'Constructive Conflict' (reprinted in Metcalfe and Urwick (1941), 30) she writes: 'We shall not consider merely the differences between employer and employee, but those between managers, between the directors at the Board meetings, or wherever difference appears.'

2. While these words were being written, there was a much publicized controversy in progress within the Labour Party in Britain. The issue was the attempt of the central

organization to outlaw an organization that existed to promote a certain approach within the party. Along with this went a controversy with constituency organizations over the selection of candidates whose views were not acceptable to the centre—an exact example of the statement in the text. For a brief summary and further references see: Keesings Contemporary Archives (1983), Feb., 3 1983. The controversy continues.

3. By Eric Rhenman. See Rhenman et al. (1970), esp. 71–87. The model is outlined on 74–5.

4. It is not intended on these pages to undertake a discussion of rival views of conflict. On the one hand the subject is reduced to a view of social deviance and phrases like 'adaptation to institutionalized expectations' (Merton (1959), 464) are used. On the other hand, there are emphatic statements that 'social life is full of contradictions' (Lenin (1939), XI. 20). One author who take conflict seriously but without exaggeration is John Rex. On pages 129–130 of Rex (1961), he sets out a model of class conflict which is further generalized on pages 180–185.

5. 'Conflict is resolved by using local rationality, acceptable-level decision rules, and sequential attention to goals.' Cyert and March (1963), 117.

6. Centralization in unions is discussed further in Chapter 8.8 and international industrial relations in Chapter 13.

7. See Bourgeois et al. (1978), 508–9. The authors are not using the words 'mechanistic' and 'organic' in quite the sense intended by Burns and Stalker (1961), 119–122. Yet another definition of 'organic' and 'mechanistic' is given in Weldon (1946), c. 3 where, echoing Hegel, the author declares that 'organic' implies a belief that the state is more impor-

tant than the individual—a centralizing view. The various meanings given to these words could form a study in itself.

8. See Hofstede and Kassem (1976), c. 10. See also Cotta (1973) and (1974).

9. 'Towards a sociological theory of peace' by A.I. Etzioni, pages 267–293 of Gross (1967).

10. Napoleon I, *Maxims* (1804–1815).

11. See, for instance, 'The operation of group standards' by L. Festinger et al. in Cartwright and Zander (1953), 204–222. For a critique of the view that social cohesion rests on consensus see Dahrendorff (1959), 157–164.

Chapter 7   Motivation and alienation

1. See section 3.2 for some comments on these views, including note 8; for a critique of the universalist approaches see Lupton (1971), 99. For a thorough study of alienation see Schacht (1971).

2. For a discussion of this subject see 'Social attitudes and the resolution of motivational conflict' by I. Sarnoff reprinted in Yahoda and Warren (1966), 279–284.

3. The use of psychological categories for social phenomena is an issue which is discussed more fully in connection with international companies, see Chapter 11 including note 20.

4. Frankenberg (1965), 118. The passage occurs in a discussion in Dennis, N. et al. (1957), *Coal is Our Life*, London: Eyre and Spottiswoode.

5. See Southall, A. (1959) 'An operational theory of role'. *Human Relations*, xii. 1.

6. See Child (1973a) 249. Child quotes Aiken and Hage (1966) in support.

7. Sartre (1960), vol. I, 37.

8. Frankenberg (1965), 276–8. The other references are to: Marx, K. and Engels, F. (1957), *The Holy Family*, London; Lawrence and Wishart, 156; Durkheim, E. (1960), *The Division of Labour*, New York; Free Press of Glencoe, 353; Merton (1957), 134. Baran and Sweezy (1968), while taking a generally Marxist view, appear to comprehend all three approaches in postulating increasing alienation. See also Labedz (1962), chapter entitled 'The debate on alienation' by D. Bell. A theological version can be found in Tillich, P. (1957) *Systematic Theology*, London: Nisbet vol. II, 52–86.

9. See c. 4 including notes 19 and 20.

10. See Whyte (1952), 127–144. Whyte also wrote *The Organization Man*, see Whyte (1956).

11. See especially Litterer (1969), c. 19, including the summary on 393, where the requirements of leadership in a decentralized organization are discussed.

12. See Lorsch and Morse (1974), 112–3. Some of the points made are confirmed in other terms by Ezzamel and Hilton (1980).

13. See *Business Week*, 23 Feb. 1981, 62.

14. See Adorno (1950).

Chapter 8   Centralization in non-commercial organization

1. The author acknowledges assistance provided in the writing of this chapter by Mr Bob Foxcroft and Dr Barry Long, both of whom provided useful material.

2. These reports are published by the National Trust. The author acknowledges the assistance of Mr I.F. Blomfield, the secretary of the Trust, in providing some of the material on which these comments are based.

3. See *The Times*, 22 June 1983, 4.

4. The author is indebted to Mr Alan Mattingley—Secretary of the Ramblers' Association, an organization which appoints a representative to the Council of the National Trust—for information on this subject. The information on War on Want is derived from publications, members and Miss Angela Hale, a regional organizer.

5. This passage is based on the publications of the organization and consultation with Miss Janet Johnstone, director of Amnesty International British Section.

6. The state system of education was already coming into existence before Napoleon seized power, the École Polytechnique was founded in 1794. Napoleon's law of 1802 set up a state system of primary and secondary education. The establishment of schools in each local authority area (commune) came later, in 1833, the year in which the *first* government grant to schools was made in England—there had been schools in every parish in Scotland since the seventeenth century.

7. See 'DES should have greater curriculum control', *Times Educational Supplement*, 1 July 1983. See also 'Centralized criteria need checks', *Times Educational Supplement*, 29 July 1983. The author acknowledges the help of Mrs Eileen Smith for drawing his attention to these and other issues discussed in this chapter.

8. The issues involved were summarized in the *Times Educational Supplement*, 14 November 1975.

9. Writers on early university history, naturally, did not concentrate on organization structure. One account of what is known is provided in Leff, G. (1968), *Paris and Oxford in the Thirteenth and Fourteenth Centuries*, New York: Wiley. The contemporary position is discussed in Moodie, G.C. and Eustace, R. (1974) *Power and Authority in British Universities*, London: Allen and Unwin. The authors of this book point out that the rights of property featured as much as academic freedom in traditional arguments for autonomy (27–8) and that this led to the separation between teaching and decision-making.

10. Many writers are concerned with making the universities more responsive to public policy (a phrase which has an intriguing variety of meanings), but with doing so by means of internal reform. See, for example, Carter, C. (1980) *Higher Education for the Future*, Oxford: Blackwell.

    It should be added that, in spite of the emphasis on university autonomy in the text, most of the income is provided from outside and most of the expenditure determined outside (by bodies set up to negotiate staff salaries).

11. The first quotation is from B. Constant (1818–1820) *Cours de politique constitutionnelle* and the other from A. de Tocqueville (1835–9) *Democracy in America*, 2.4.3.

12. Royal decree No. 110 (1982). Some details are supplied in: 'Municipal Finance: in dire straits', (1983) *Weekly Bulletin*, Brussels Kredietbank, 28.20, 20 May.

13. See, for example, Byrne (1981) c. 12, Thornhill (1975), Birch (1980) c. 14, Hill (1974).

14. The evidence for some of the statements in this passage has been provided by Professor R. Hinings of the Institute of Local Government Studies at the University of Birmingham. The following statement of the two views of local government is derived from Hill (1974).

15. The author is indebted to Dr B. Moores of UMIST and to several officers of the Department of Health

and Social Security who provided evidence for the notes on these pages. As this book goes to press the health authorities are suffering cuts in their income and are under pressure from the government on how to implement the cuts. Autonomy ebbs and flows.

16. See *Royal Commission on the National Health Service* (1979) HMSO, command paper No. 7615. The report is usually named after Sir Alex Morrison the chairman of the committee which produced it; the discussion on organization is to be found on pages 310–331 and the recommendations are summarized on pages 375–8.

17. See Hortell, S.M. and Brown, M. (eds.) *Organizational Research* in Hospitals Blue Cross Association (1976), 62–71; *Millbank Memorial Fund Quarterly*, Summer (1974), 315–346; Olofsson, C. and Svalander, P.A., *The Medical Service Change over to a Poor Environment* Linköping University, no date.

18. This restricted decentralization is discussed below in the section on military organizations and again in Chapter 10.

19. See Trevelyan, G.M. (1913) *Clio, A Muse*, Harlow: Longman, 27.

20. Notes on the organization of the Roman army were provided by Dr Barry Long of the Anglian Regional Management Centre. The information is derived from Grimal, E. et al. (1968) *Hellenism and the Rise of Rome*, London: Weidenfeld and Nicolson; Gabba, E. (1976) *Republican Rome*, trans P.J. Cuff, Oxford: Blackwell; Salmon, E.T. (1970) *Roman Colonization under the Republic*, Ithaca, N.Y.: Cornell University Press.

21. Thus the action in Northern Ireland has come to be known as the 'corporal's war' because only the smallest of units are relevant to the fight against urban guerrillas. For much of the information in this part of the chapter, the author is indebted to his friend and former student Major B.C. Mobley of the RAOC.

22. For notes on prison organization, the author is indebted to Dr Barry Long of the Anglian Management Centre.

23. See Etzioni (1975), 28–31 (there are other relevant passages in this book, see the index).

24. See the introductory essay to Schacht (1971). For the following passage see Goffman (1961). He first defined the 'total institution' in *Symposium on preventative and Social Psychiatry* (1957), Walter Reed Army Institution of Research, Washington DC, 45.

25. See McCleery, R.H. 'Policy change in prison management', 383 ff in Etzioni and Lehman (1980).

26. See Moreno, J.L. (1978) *Who shall survive? Foundations of sociometry, group psychotherapy and sociodrama*, Beacon House, new edn. (this book was first published in 1934).

27. From a typewritten paper entitled 'Managing the local Church' by H.L. Gray. The reader is reminded that the paradoxes mentioned later in this paragraph have already been discussed (c. 2.5). Advice on this section is acknowledged from Professor J. Bowker, Canon R. Preston and Dr N. Thornton.

28. The author is aware that there were secular as well as religious charges against the Baha'i (if the two can be distinguished) but the news item that those who recanted would be reprieved suggests that the most damning charges were religious.

29. This has, of course, many parallels. How, for instance, does the British Prime Minister decide which colleagues are to be sacked and which ennobled? Or how did Stalin decide

which ex-friends were to be shot and which to be appointed ambassadors?

30. See *Visible Unity in Life and Mission* (1977), Baptist Union of Great Britain and Ireland, 8–9. The document produced by the British Council of Churches (mentioned in the following paragraph) is *Moving into Unity*, published by the British Council of Churches—Division of Ecumenical Affairs. This report is undated but cites three documents published in 1977. The quotation is from 4. The other quotation is from: *Public Statements on Moral Issues* (1978), A Report from the Liaison Committee of the British Council of Churches and the Roman Catholic Church in England and Wales, 19.

31. *Far Eastern Economic Review*, 21 August 1981, 3. The view expressed has been echoed in Britain as well; see, for instance: 'Leaders of the National Union of Mineworkers today warn their members that plans to decentralize the coal industry threaten the union's very existence.' (The *Guardian*, 8 August 1983); or: 'The general secretary of NUPE, Mr Rodney Bickerstaffe, promised full support and said that decentralization of wage negotiations was an important part of the present Government's anti-union policy.' (The *Guardian*, 18 May 1983).

32. The author is indebted to Professor B.M. Downie of the School of Business, Queen's University, Kingston, Ontario for the notes on which this passage is based.
   For the Michelin case see *Business Week*, 26 July 1976, 57–60.
   For the figures of union membership and strikes see *International Labour Office Statistical Yearbook 1981*. Comparable figures for other countries are France 0.73, Germany 0.02, Italy 0.51, United Kingdom 0.20.

33. On the relevance of this principle to the trade unions see, for instance,

Raskin, A.H. (1962) 'Are union democracy and responsibility compatible?' *Challenge*, 10.5, February.

34. The list is based on Kirkman, F. (1976) *The Professionalisation of Work Study*, unpub. Ph.D. thesis Manchester University. Kirkman, in his turn, acknowledges the work of Greenwood; see Greenwood, E. (1957) 'Attributes of a profession', *Social Work* vol. 2, July. The phrase 'disaster criterion' was first used in Nokes, P. (1967) *The Professional Task in Welfare Practice*, London: Routledge and Kegan Paul. For a review of the structure of a sample of professional institutes see Hickson, D.J. and Thomas, M.W. (1969) 'Professionalization in Britain: a preliminary measurement', *Sociology*, vol. 3, 37–52.

35. See *Engineering our Future: A Report of the Committee of Inquiry into the Engineering Profession*, London: Her Majesty's Stationery Office. The chairman of the committee was Sir Monty Finniston, after whom the report is usually named.

Chapter 9   Empirical studies into centralization and autonomy

1. Simon (1954), 1.

2. Pugh et al. (1968), 67.

3. Price (1972), 43.

4. See Jennergren (1974), 1–8.

5. Simon (1960). For the concept of the normal line mentioned in the following sentence, see c. 11 below.

6. Fayol (1949), 33–4.

7. A problem strongly emphasized in Abell (1976).

8. See Ramsay, H. (1980) *Evolution or Cycle? Worker Participation in the 1970s and 1980s*, c. 10 in Crouch and Heller (1983). See also chapters 1, 2

and 3 in Dunkerley and Salaman (1980b). For a report on the research mentioned in the following paragraph, see Doteuchi 1977, 7–11.

9. Pugh et al. (1969).

10. Child (1973b).

11. Holdaway et al. (1975). The positive relationship between standardization and centralization has also been found in multinational companies, see part II.

12. Mansfield (1973), 478.

13. Fayol (1949), 33–4.

14. Donaldson (1975), 455.

15. Vickers (1965).

16. Pugh et al. (1968), 67.

17. Sloan (1964), 429.

18. Blau (1970).

19. Stopford and Wells (1972), c. 3.

20. Child (1973a), 3.

21. Pugh et al. (1968), 67. The whole questionnaire, together with interview instructions, is printed in Pugh and Hickson (1976), 201–223.

22. Khandwalla (1971).

23. Blau and Schoenherr, (1971), 113; Meyer (1972) and Abell (1976).

24. Ackerman (1970).

25. Tannenbaum (1966), c. 7.

26. Farris and Butterfield (1972), 584–5.

27. Brown (1971), 239. For a discussion of the technique see Jaques (1964).

28. Whisler (1970).

29. See below section 15.2. For the other references see Chorafas (1969) and

Katz and Kahn (1966), Chapters 4 and 10.

30. Conroy (1980), see 50 ff. and, for summary, 101.

31. Whisler et al. (1967).

32. See Hofstede (1977)a, 67.

33. See Hajimirzatayeb (1979), 89, 133–6.

34. See, for example, Drenth, P.J.D. et al. (1979), 'Participative decision-making: a comparative study'. *Industrial Relations*, 18.3, fall, 295–309; and Heller, F.A. (1979) 'Some problems in multinational and crosscultural research on organizations', paper read to the 39th annual meeting of the Academy of Management. Atlanta, Georgia, 7–11 August. The author is grateful to Dr Heller for a number of discussions during the preparation of this book and to drawing his attention to these and other papers.

35. See Weinshall (1977), c. 3 (the chapter on management education) and c. 15 (a study of cultural differences among managers in multinational companies. Action research is mentioned in the latter chapter). See also Hesseling, P. 'The users of auto-observation of interactions in a multinational product centre', 383–405 in Roig (1970). For a general study of action-research see Revans (1971).

Chapter 10 Raw materials for a theory

1. Quoted from Arrow, K.J. (1964), 'Control in large organizations', *Management Science*, April, 397. The following quotation is from Fayol (1949), 33.

2. See Katz (1968), 76.

3. Quoted from the *Financial Times*, 10 July 1981, 1. Imps is an abbreviation for the British Company Imperial

Group p.l.c. (formerly Imperial Tobacco).

4. See Gerth and Mills (1948).

5. See Sorokin (1966), 89.

6. This point is made in Hajimirazatayeb (1979), see 201–2.

7. This was a theme of Perrow (1967) and was confirmed in Hage, J. and Aiken, Michael (1969) 'Routine technology, social structures and organization goals,' *Administrative Science Quarterly*, 14.3 (Sept), 366–376 (reprinted in Hall (1972)).

8. Hofstede and Kassam (1976), 280–1.

9. See Liebling, Barry A. (1981) 'Is it time to (de)centralize?' *Management Review*, Sept.

10. As in earlier chapters, the word 'bureaucratic' is used in a neutral sense of an organization with the characteristics outlined by Weber, and the first three types listed in the text correspond with Weber's charismatic, traditional and bureaucratic modes of organization.

11. See Burns and Stalker (1961), 119–125. Less happily, it might be thought the mechanistic is contrasted with the organic—a name which covers both the bureaucratic (open) and the intermediary types listed here. The use of the words 'organic' and 'mechanistic' is discussed in Chapter 6, note 7.

12. For an emphatic statement along these lines, see Perrow (1972), 58.

13. By the present author in Brooke and Remmers (1978), 226.

14. See back, Chapter 4.

Chapter 11   Studies of the international firm

1. In this book the phrase 'international firm' is used of all firms with any form of business activity outside their countries of origin—the *home* country. The phrase 'multinational firm' is used of those international companies which have *direct* investment abroad—that is, they own (at least partially) and manage companies in foreign, *host*, countries. The word 'multinational' is used sparingly for the reason given in the text that the distinction between investment and other operations abroad is becoming increasingly unreal. Other words purporting to describe some particular type of international company, like 'transnational', are not used except in direct quotation.

2. See Cyert and March (1963) c. 2, discussed above in c. 1 and c. 2.

3. See Dunning (1966), 17.

4. Stopford and Wells (1972) also point out that the expatriate manager can have considerable autonomy (see 20). They do not offer any measurement for this and assess the degree of autonomy by observation.

5. See Mathew (1979), 181. The subsequent reference in this paragraph is to 184, and the references in the following pargraph are to pages 185 and 205.

6. See Robinson (1973), 585–9. It should be said that, like Dunning, Robinson is not looking for a measure of centralization. He also writes cautiously—'The degree to which control is centralized is probably related to: . . .'

7. See Franko (1971), 38–40. The later reference is to Franko (1976), 191–2. The countries of origin of companies discussed in this book are: Belgium, France, Germany, Italy, Netherlands, Sweden, Switzerland.

8. See Servan-Schreiber (1969), 200–205.

9. See Schöllhamer, Hans (1980) 'Decision-making and intra-organizational conflicts in multinational companies;' Garnier, Gérard (1980), 'The dimensions of autonomy in parent company-foreign affiliates relationships within multinational companies;' Ondrak, Daniel A. (1980), 'A longitudinal study of headquarters-subsidiary control relationships;' Kagono, Tadao (1980) 'Structural design of headquarters-division relationships and economic performance: an analysis of Japanese firms'. All four were papers read to a Conference on the Management of Headquarters—Subsidiary Relationships in Transnational Corporations, Stockholm School of Economics.

10. The story has been written up as a case study at INSEAD—The European Institute of Business Administration, Boulevard de Constance, 77305 Fontainebleau-Avon, France. Case study ref. ICH, 9-210-117.

11. A recent example in Britain is that of Dunbee-Combex-Marx, bankrupt as a result of a failure in the United States subsidiary.

12. See F. Slipsager, 'Intra-company problem solving in international business—a case study', Mattson and Wiedersheim-Paul (1979), 208–219. The author does not explain how the investigation was conducted.

13. See below, c. 16.

14. See Salera (1969), 382.

15. See Stopford and Wells (1972), 179–80. In the latter part of the paragraph, the reference is to Holton, R.H. (1981) 'Making International Joint Ventures Work', c. 11 in Otterbeck (1981).

16. See Robock and Simmonds (1973), 424, and Robinson (1973), 585. The study referred to in the next sentence is that of Alsegg (1971).

17. Stopford and Wells (1972), 18–21. See above note 4.

18. Salera (1969), 382–4.

19. See Prahalad, C.K. (1979) 'Strategic choices in diversified MNC's' *Harvard Business Review*, June-July; see also c. 8 of Otterbeck (1981). Prahalad uses the word 'salient' where the present author uses 'visibility' to refer to companies that attract attention.

20. See Perlmutter (1969), (reprinted in Kapoor and Grub (1972), c. 3). Perlmutter is also one of the writers who postulates degrees of multinationality. See the title of Perlmutter and Heenan (1974) 'How multinational should your manager be?' The title also suggests the moral considerations discussed later. A book of case studies which uses Perlmutter's classification to interpret the activities under discussion is Rutenberg (1982).

21. See 307–330 of Ghertman and Leontiades (1978). Hofstede's work is also examined above in Chapters 2 and 9.

22. See 29–43 of Ghertman and Leontiades (1978). See also Neghandi and Prasad (1975), 58–65.

23. These studies have been widely reported, see, for instance, the following publications: Brooke and Remmers (1970 and 1978), c. 3, Brooke and Black (1976).
    See also *Centralization and Decentralization in the Multinational Firm* (1979), a report to the Social Science Research Council by Michael Z. Brooke. The research on which this and the following chapters is based was supported by a grant from the Social Science Research Council.

24. See above c. 10, and especially Figures 10.1 and 10.2.

25. See Blau (1955), 5. Transfer pricing, mentioned in the following paragraph is discussed further in 14.3.

26. The check-list referred to may be summarized thus:
Objectives (in order of priority):
(a) of subsidiary;
(b) of parent company for subsidiary.
Return on investment,
Market share,
Development of new products
Or what?
Is the image intended that of a national company, or part of an international group, or what?
Ownership:
(a) 100 per cent by parent company;
(b) more than one company;
(c) local shareholders.
If established recently, was it by purchase or by starting a new company?
If you were starting afresh what changes would make and why?
Organization:
How are profit responsibilities fixed?
Who reports to whom?
What are the responsibilities of the principal executives?
Do these arrangements reflect those in head office?
Are there significant 'informal' variations?
Are there notable problems in the present arrangements?
What are the main limits to discretion?
How do you know?
What are the main items on which reports are made? And how often?
Corporate planning:
What part does the subsidiary play in the process? The actual decisions examined are listed below; see section 11.4

27. For an outline of this project see Brooke and Dorrell (1976); see also Dorrell (1979), a Ph.D. thesis which resulted from this project. The results are discussed in more detail in Chapter 15.

28. See section 11.4. The reference is to Anthony and Dearden (1976).

29. See Bacharach, P. and Baratz M.P. (1962) 'Two faces of power', *American Political Science Review*, 56, 947–52. Reprinted in Castles (1976) c. 23.

30. The present author has commended this approach before, see Brooke and Remmers (1978), 5, as have Litvak and Maule (1970).

31. See Sachdev (1975) and (1976).

32. An example of this, the case of Badger (Belgium), is discussed in section 13.1.

Chapter 12   Organization conflict and performance appraisal

1. The organizational implications of this paragraph are considered further in Chapter 15. For a full discussion of the projections see Brooke and Remmers (1978), c. 2. Evidence for the statement that geographical managers actually do promote higher growth overseas is shown on 25 of that book.

2. For further details see the next chapter. For a comprehensive report on external affairs departments see Boddewyn (1975).

3. For a fuller discussion of appraisal of subsidiary performance see Brooke and Remmers (1978), 115–124 and 138–144.

4. See *Chlordiazepoxide and Diazepam*, a report of the Monopolies Commission (1973), Her Majesty's Stationery Office. The question of pricing in international companies is discussed in Chapter 14.

5. See Doteuchi (1977). This was one of the pieces of research on which these chapters have been based.

6. The evidence for this statement is explained in Brooke and Dorrell (1976) and Dorrell (1979), and summarized below in section 15.2.

Chapter 13 Company-country relations

1. Especially since the publication of *Small is Beautiful*; see Schumacher (1973).

2. See Ádám (1971).

3. '650 ouvriers français ont failli devenir chômeurs parce que Johnson et Mao ne sont pas d'accord', the story is told briefly with references in Brooke, M.Z. and Remmers, H.L. (1970) *The Strategy of Multinational Enterprise*, 1st edn., Harlow: Longman, 255 and 360.

4. See *Crane Fruehauf Ltd* (1977), London: HMSO, Cmd. 6906. The case was widely reported at the time. See, for instance, 'Freuhauf v. Crane: Anatomy of a take-over', *International Management*, July 1978, 41–45. The action taken over Dresser France and John Brown UK is summarized in *World Gas Report*, 3.17, 16 Aug. 1982, 1–2 and 30 Aug. 1982, 1–2.

5. This instruction was reported in the *Guardian* on 20 March 1982. The controversy is summarized in Dickinson, G.M., Brooke, M.Z. and MacArthur, J.P. (1983) *International Financial Management*, Brentford: Kluwer, c. 8.2. The story up to 1978 is told in *Nestlé and the Infant Food Controversy* (1979), Institut pour l'Etude des Méthodes de Direction de l'Entreprise, Lausanne (Case study OIE-50).

6. This incident is discussed in detail in Blanpain, R. (1977) *The Badger Case and the OECD Guidelines for Multinational Enterprise*, Deventer: Kluwer. There is a summary in the *Journal of the Royal Society of Arts* (1978) vol. CXXVI No. 5262, May, 326–334.

7. This was published in each of the member countries. For the English version see: *International Investment Guidelines for Multinational Enterprises* (Her Majesty's Stationery Office, London, Command 6525, 1976). For a general discussion of the codes of conduct see Mousouris, S.G. 'Codes of conduct facing multinational companies', Chapter 28 of Walter (1982).

8. The United Nations has published a series of papers on the code of conduct and preliminary versions. See, for example, *Transnational Corporations: Issues relevant to the Formulation of a Code of Conduct*, (New York: United Nations, sales No. E77 II A5) or the CIC (Centre for Transnational Corporations) Reporter No. 12 (UN 1982). For a review of the subject see: Mousouris, S.G. 'Codes of Conduct facing multinationals', c. 28 of Walter (1982).

9. See *The International Code of Marketing of Breast Milk Substitutes* (1981), Geneva: Food and Agricultural Organization (FAO).

10. See *The Set of Multilaterally Agreed Equitable Principles and Rules on Restrictive Practices* (1980), Geneva: United Nations Conference on Trade and Development (UNCTAD).

11. *The Tripartite Declaration Concerning Multinational Enterprises and Social Policies* (1981), Geneva: International Labour Office (ILO).

12. See *Towards International Standardization of Corporate Accounting and Reporting* (1980), New York: United Nations.

13. The author is indebted to Dr R.K.D.N. Singh, director of the Information Analysis Division of the United Nations Centre on Transnationals, for this point. For a statement of his views see Otterbeck (1981), c. 2.

14. The first quotation is from Servan-Schreiber, J.-J. (1967) *Le défi américaine*, Paris: Editions Noël, 17 (trans. from the French), and the second from a speech by Anthony

Benn (then a member of the British government) in 1968. The speaker also pointed out that foreign companies in Britain did, in fact, make a contribution to exports out of proportion to their size. The speech was reported in *Weekly Hansard* No. 776, 491.

15. For this information and the use of the phrase 'counteractive response' see Doz, Y.L. and Prahalad, C.K. (1980), 'How MNCs cope with host government intervention', *Harvard Business Review*, March-April, 149–157. The distinction between product differentiation based on marketing considerations and that based on technology is to be found in this article on page 155.

16. See Boddewyn (1975), a thorough review of the reasons for and work of external affairs department together with the problems to be expected. The report was also mentioned in Chapter 12.

17. Vernon (1971), 135 quotes an Australian study which shows that only 19 out of 79 American owned subsidiaries allowed freedom to export, while a New Zealand study gives 57 out of 115. The references are to Brash, D.T. (1966) *American Investment in Australian Industry*, Boston, Mass.: Harvard Business School, 228; and Deane, R.S. (1967) *Foreign Investment in New Zealand Manufacturing*, unpub. Ph.D. dissertation, Victoria University, Wellington, New Zealand, 334.

18. The evidence available is discussed in Gillies, G.I. (1983), 'International Production and Trade', unpub. paper read at Academy of International Business International Convention, Strathclyde University, Glasgow, March. While writing with caution, conclusive evidence being hard to come by, the author finds a steady increase in intra-company trade.

19. This subject has been mainly discus-sed in Canada with its high proportion of foreign investment (around 65 per cent of manufacturing industry is foreign owned). See, for instance: *Multinationals and Industrial Strategy: The Role of World Product Mandates* (1980), Ottawa: Science Council of Canada; and Rugman, A.M. (1981) 'World Product Mandates: Theory and Policy', unpub. paper read at the Queen's University Colloquium on International Business, Kingson, Ontario, May.

Chapter 14 Planning, control and pricing

1. Hall (1981).

2. For a discussion of how this works, see Sasaki (1981), c. 4.

3. See Mathew (1979), 210. Other references to this have already appeared in c. 11; see note 5 to that chapter.

4. See Brooke and Remmers (1978), 86 and the references provided in a note on that page.

5. See *Wilmot Breedon (Holdings) Ltd* (1964) a case study published by the European Institute for Business Administration (INSEAD) No. F-3135.

6. See Brooke and Remmers (1977), c. 10 for evidence relevant to this paragraph.

7. Transfer pricing has been the subject of numerous papers, most of them highly speculative. For brief accounts of the subject see Brooke and Remmers (1978), 119–123, Chown 1974 c. 10, Robock and Simmands (1983), 532–536, Eiteman and Stonehill (1979), 401–427. This last contains many useful cross-references. For a more recent review of current practices see Plasschaert M.R.F. (1983) 'International Transfer Pricing', c. 6.4. in Dickinson et al. (1983).

8. The latter case is reported in Vait-sos, C.V. (1974) *Intercountry Income Distribution and Transnational Enter-prises*, Oxford: Oxford University Press. Most of the other examples listed involved pharmaceutical com-panies, some are also in Eiteman and Stonehill (1979), 404.

9. See Robbins and Stobaugh (1973), 91–2, and Dickinson et al. (1983), c. 6.4.

10. For notes on the procedures in some of the industrialized countries see: *Transfer Pricing and Multinational Enterprises* (1979), Paris: Organiza-tion for Economic Cooperation and Development.

Chapter 15 Company organization

1. The types are explained briefly in this chapter; for a fuller discussion see Brooke and Remmers (1978) c. 2; this explains in more detail the theory behind the typology. Other characteristics, like the communica-tions problems mentioned in a later paragraph, are also discussed in that book.

2. The expression is explained in c. 11, 209; the various parts of the research programme on which this discus-sion is based are listed there and referenced under these titles in the rest of this chapter.

3. That of the Tilling Group by BTR.

4. See Brooke and Remmers (1978), 39–48 for a fuller discussion.

5. This is discussed in more detail in Dorrell (1979) and Brooke and Dor-rell (1976).

6. The problem of sending instructions to foreign subsidiaries may be exaggerated, but is well understood. Right up to the date of finalizing this chapter (August 1983) the author is seeing fresh examples of internal memos from, mainly smaller, com-panies reminding staff that direct instructions in writing must not be sent to foreign subsidiaries.

7. See Abell (1976), 21–6.

8. See Buzzell, R.D. (1968) 'Can you standardize international market-ing?' *Harvard Business Review*, Nov.-Dec., 102–113. An edited version of this article can be found in Thorelli (1973), 325–339.

9. Mattson, L.G. (1972) 'Multinational customers' influence on the indus-trial goods manufacturers' market-ing organization and competitive position', Unpub. paper, University of Linkoping, Sweden. Excerpts are reprinted in Brooke and Remmers (1977), 139–144.

10. This was first suggested long ago (see Shearer (1960)).

Chapter 16 Ownership, time, national-ity and other issues

1. For a discussion of ownership poli-cies see Brooke and Remmers (1978), c. 8 where evidence is pro-vided that joint venture projects do in fact pursue different policies from wholly owned subsidiaries. More detailed data in support of this were published in Brooke and Remmers (1970), 159–161 and 318–339. The present author is preparing a book on management contracts; mean-while, an unpublished review of research can be found in Brooke and others (1983), note especially c. 12. 'Authority and responsibility' and c. 15 'Control and monitoring'.

2. The evidence for the statements in these paragraphs is partly to be found in the research mentioned in note 1 and partly in unpublished research papers of the International Business Unit. See also Brooke and Remmers (1977), 21.

3. The monitoring of change over time is an important requirement for future research.

4. Independent evidence of this is to be found in Franko (1976) c. 7.

Chapter 17   Relationships between head office and the foreign subsidiary: the present and the future

1. See, for instance, De Bodinat, H. (1975) 'Influence in the multinational corporation: the case of manufacturing', typescript paper, Harvard Business School.

2. This came out in several interviews and was sometimes bluntly stated in words like: 'The subsidiaries have all the discretion in the world, more they are always being urged to go their own way; but I have a trusty out there who will alert me if things are going wrong.'

3. See Stopford and Wells (1972), c. 8.

4. See Brooke et al. (1983), 154–8.

5. See c. 12. The organization types are explained in c. 15.

6. The buffer situation, as it is there called, is discussed more fully in Brooke and Remmers (1978), 134–138.

7. See c. 10. The different types of relationship are listed in Table 10.2 and the cycle referred to in the next paragraph is demonstrated in Figure 10.2. In the next chapter (18) the types are re-examined and relisted in Table 18.1.

8. For evidence of this see Håkansson (1982) c. 2.

9. This subject was examined thoroughly in Chapter 14, where the evidence for the statements made here is provided.

10. For evidence of this statement see Brooke and Remmers (1978), c. 6; a number of other writers have corroborated this.

Chapter 18   Centralization and autonomy: the beliefs

1. See Brooke, M.Z. (1970), *Le Play: Engineer and Social Scientist*, Harlow: Longman, 46.

2. See Price (1972), 36–7.

3. For reasons see c. 3(3.1) and notes 2 and 3 to that chapter.

4. See Pugh and Hickson (1976), 56, where one large family firm records low centralization and another (much smaller) records high. This may be a function of size; a subsidiary of a public company also records low centralization. Both municipal and government owned concerns register higher centralization.

5. Lest some readers consider this a light step, the author records a meeting at which he used this phrase and the horrified reaction of some personnel managers present.

Chapter 19   Centralization and autonomy: resources and influencing factors

1. Meyer (1972, 119–120.

2. The author has a number of anecdotes in his files about the way authority was maintained in international firms in the past. These include the company which sent a top executive to the Far Eastern subsidiaries on each alternative P. & O. liner sailing; the local management and staff were expected to be on the docks to welcome the executive and the ensuing meeting looked over the reports for the previous months and worked through in detail all plans for the following period. No deviation was permitted except in a serious emergency—typical of the isolated relationship. An earlier example is Le Play, mentioned in c. 18, note 1, who managed extensive operations in Russia from an office in Paris before the days of railways or telegraphy. Evidence has

been assembled to show that the improved communications were accompanied by a growth in foreign investment, but this may have been a coincidence due to other factors.

2. See Brooke and Remmers (1978), 59–61.

4. See section 2.6 and note 38 to c. 2.

5. For some comments on this subject see Crouch and Heller (1983), especially Part IV. Crouch and Heller was published in August 1983 during the final weeks of the preparation of this book.

6. See Nie (1975) for the appropriate techniques.

7. See c. 5. The work of Crozier (1964) has already been cited as an example of how the vicious circle operates.

8. The role of contact in reducing the problems of autonomy and of mitigation in reducing those of centralization are two issues that merit further research.

9. Apart from international companies with common ownership, international institutions in the sense of treaty organizations (like the United Nations or the European Community) have not been considered on these pages although they raise fascinating questions concerned with the exercise of authority. They are reserved for a further study of the boundaries of organization.

Chapter 20 Coda: the autonomous organization

1. The claim to detachment should be modified to the extent that this assumed preference for decentralization on the part of readers has led throughout the book to an emphasis on the reality of centralization and its necessity given certain conditions and certain objectives, an

emphasis which is not pursued in this chapter.

2. Sir George Schuster speaking to a meeting of steelworkers' managers in 1952.

3. As Bertrand Russell forecast (see the quotation at the beginning of the chapter).

4. *The Times*, 28 Jan. 1982.

5. In spite of beliefs to the contrary; a company manual revealingly states: '. . . no attempt should ever be made to maximize income at the expense of risk or loss of funds invested.' (Quoted in Brooke and Remmers (1978), 88.)

Bibliography

This reading list contains titles that have been used in preparing this text. Other sources are provided in the notes.

Abell, P. (1973) 'Organisations as Bargaining Systems—measuring intraorganisational power', Imperial College: Industrial Sociology Unit working paper.

Abell, P. (1975) *Organizations as Bargaining and Influence Systems*, London: Heinemann.

Abell, P. (1976) 'The task determinants of decentralization between HQ and UK subsidiaries of international corporations', Unpublished research report, Birmingham University.

Abrams, H.J. (1971) 'Optimal pricing of intermediate products', *Chemical Engineer*, **248**, 164–168.

Ackermann, R.W. (1970) 'Influence of Integration and Diversity on the Investment Process', *Administrative Science Quarterly*, **15**, 341–351.

Ádám, G. (1970) Amerika Európában Vállalatbirodalmak a Világgazdaságban. Budapest: Közgazdasági és jogi Könyvkiadó.

Ádám, G. (1971) *The World Corporation: Problematics, Apologetics and Critique.* Budapest: Hungarian Scientific Council for World Economy (Trends in World Economy, No. 5).

Adorno, T.W. et al. (1950) *The Authoritarian Personality.* London: Harper and Row.

Aharoni, Y. (1966) *The Foreign Investment Decision Process*, Boston, Mass.: Harvard Business School.

Aiken, M. and Hage, J. (1966) 'Organizational alienation: a comparative analysis', *American Sociological Review* **31**, 497–507.

Aiken, M. and Hage, J. (1968) 'Organizational Interdependence and Intraorganizational Structure', *American Sociological Review*, **33**, 912–930.

Ajiferuke, M. and Boddewyn, J. (1970) 'Culture and other Explanatory Variables in Comparative Management Studies', *Academy of Management Journal*, **13.2.**, 153–162.

Albers, H. H. (1974) *Principles of Management*, 4th edn., New York: Wiley.

Albrow, M. (1970) *Bureaucracy*, London: Macmillan.

Aldrich, H. (1972) 'Technology and Organization Structure—a Reexamination of the findings of the Aston Group', *Administrative Science Quarterly*, **17.1.**

Allsopp, M. (1979) *Management in the Professions: Guidelines to improved professional performance*, London: Business Books.

Alsegg, J. (1971) *Control Relationships between American Corporations and Their European Subsidiaries*, New York: American Management Association.

Altman, S. and Hodgetts, R.M. (1979) *Readings in Organizational Behavior*, New York: Holt, Rinehart and Winston.

Ames, E. (1971) *A Priceless Planned Economy*, Paris: Université de Paris IX.

Andriaansens, H.P.M. (1980) *Talcott Parsons and the Conceptual Dilemma*, London: Routledge and Kegan Paul.

Ansoff, H. (1968) *Corporate Strategy*, Harmondsworth: Penguin.

Ansoff, H.I. et al. (eds.) (1974) *From Strategic Planning to Strategic Manage-

ment, New York: Wiley.

Anthony, R.N. and Dearden, J. (1980) *Management Control Systems*, 4th edn., Homewood, Ill.: Irwin and Dorsey.

Apter, D.E. (1977) *Introduction to Political Analysis* Cambridge, Mass.: Winthrop.

Archibald, G. (ed.), (1972) *The Theory of the Firm*, Harmondsworth: Penguin.

Argyris, C. (1957) *Personality and Organization*, New York: Harper and Row.

Argyris, C. (1962) *Interpersonal Competence and Organizational Effectiveness*, Homewood, Ill.: Irwin and Dorsey.

Argyris, C. (1970) *Intervention Theory and Method: A behavioural science view*, Reading, Mass.: Addison-Wesley.

Argyris, C. and Schön, D.A. (1978) *Organizational Learning: A Theory of Action Perspective*, Reading, Mass.: Addison-Wesley.

Arrow, K.J. (1964) 'Control in Large Organizations', *Management Science*, Apr. 397–408.

Ashfield, M. (1974) *Methods of Measuring Local Autonomy in International Firms*, Unpublished Research paper, International Business Unit, University of Manchester.

Astley, W.G. et al. (1981) *An Arena Theory of Organizational Decision-Process*, Bradford Management Centre, Unpublished paper.

Atkins, D. (1974) 'Managerial decentralization and decomposition in mathematical programming', *Operational Research Quarterly*, **25**, 615–624.

Attali, J. (1972) *Analyse économique de la vie politique*, Paris: Presses Universitaires de France.

Aylmer, R.J. (1970) 'Who makes the marketing decisions in the multinational firm?' *Journal of Marketing*, Oct., 1–34. Reprinted in Thorelli (1973), c. 30.

Azumi, K. and Hage, J. (1972) *Organizational Systems*, Lexington, Mass.: D.C. Heath.

Bacharach, S.B. (1982) *Research in the Sociology of Organizations*, vol. I, Greenwich, CT: JAI.

Bacharach, S.B. (1983) *Research in the Sociology of Organizations*, vol. II, Greenwich, CT: JAI.

Bacharach, S.B. and Lawler, E.J. (1980) *Power and Politics in Organizations*, San Francisco: Jossey-Bass.

Baran, P.A. and Sweezy, P.M. (1968) *Monopoly Capital*, Harmondsworth: Penguin.

Barkan, J.D. and Okumu, J. (eds.) (1979) *Politics and Public Policy in Kenya and Tanzania*, New York: Praeger.

Barkdull, C.W. (1963) 'Span of Control: A Method of Evaluation', *Michigan Business Review*, 15.

Barreau, J. (1978) *Economie et Organisation de l'Entreprise*, Paris: Editions Sirey.

Baugh, J.G. (1981) *A Study of Decision-making within a Matrix Organization*, Unpub. DBA Thesis, United States International University.

Baumol, W.J. and Fabian, T. (1964) 'Decomposition, pricing for decentralization and external economies' *Management Science*, **11**, 1–32.

Becker, S.W. and Gordon, G. (1966) 'An Entrepreneurial Theory of Formal Organization, 1: Patterns of Formal Organizations', *Administrative Science Quarterly* **3**, 315–344.

Beckhard, R. (1969) *Organization Development: Strategies and Models*, Reading, Mass.: Addison-Wesley.

Beckhard, R. and Harris, R.T. (1977) *Organizational Transitions: Managing complex change*, Reading, Mass.: Addison-Wesley.

Belasco, J.A. et al. (1975) *Management Today: An Experimental Approach*, New York: Wiley.

Bendix, R. (1978) *Max Weber: An Intellectual Portrait*, Berkeley, Cal.: University of California Press.

Bendix, R. (1964) *Nation-Building and Citizenship: Studies of our Changing Social Order*, New York: Wiley.

Bennis, W.G. (1968) *Organization Development: Its Nature, Origins and Prospects*, Reading, Mass.: Addison-Wesley.

Benson, J.K., (ed.) (1978) *Organizational Analysis: Critique and Innovation*, Berkely, Calif.: Sage.

Bensoussan, A. (1972) *Decentralisation in Management*, European Institute for Advanced Studies in Management: Working paper.

Bertrand, A.L. (1972) *Social organizations. A general systems and role theory approach*, Arlington Heights, Ill.: AHM Publishing.

Birch, A.H. (1980) *The British System of Local Government*, 4th edn. London: Allen and Unwin.

Black, D. (1958) *The Theory of Committees and Elections*, Cambridge, Mass.: MIT University Press.

Black, M. and Neville, P. (1976), 'Decision-making processes in Multinationals', Department of Employment Research Project No. 2187.

Blair, J.M. (1972) *Economic Concentration*, New York: Harcourt Brace Jovanovich.

Blake, D.H. (1973) 'Cross-national cooperative strategies: union response to the MNC's in Tudyka, K.P. (ed.), (1973) *Multinational Corporations and Labour Unions Symposium*, Nijmegen: Werkuitgave Sun.

Blake, R.R. and Mouton, J.S. (1964) *The Managerial Grid*, Houston: Gulf Publishing.

Blattner, N. (1972) *Power in Organisations*, Unpub. research paper, University of Manchester Institute of Science and Technology.

Blau, P.M. (1955) *The Dynamics of Bureaucracy*, Chicago: University of Chicago Press.

Blau, P.M. (1970) Decentralization in Bureaucracies' chapter in Zald (1970).

Blau, P.M. (1974) *On the Nature of Organization*, New York: Wiley.

Blau, P.M. and Meyer, M.W. (1971) *Bureaucracy in Modern Society*, 2nd edn., New York: Random House.

Blau, P.M. and Schoenherr, R.A. (1971) *The Structure of Organizations*, New York: Basic Books.

Blau, P.M. and Scott, W.R. (1962) *Formal Organizations*, San Francisco: Chandler.

Boddewyn, J.J. (1975) *International External Affairs*, New York: Business International.

Bonham-Yeaman, D. (ed.), (1982) *Developing Global Corporate Strategies*, Florida: Florida International University.

Boudon, R. (1971) *The Uses of Structuralism*, trans. Vaughan, M., London: Heinemann.

Bourgeois, R.J. et al. (1978) 'The Effects of Different Organizational Environments upon Decisions about Organizational Structure', *Academy of Management Journal* **21.3,** 508–513.

Brandt, F.A. (1976) *A Comparative Analysis of Management and Organizational Processes in Product and Service Organizations*, Unpub. doctoral thesis Arizona State University.

Brandt, W.K. and Hulbert, J.M. (1975) 'Organizational structure and marketing strategy in the multinational subsidiary', *Proceedings of the American Marketing Association*.

Brooke, C.N.L. (1969) *The Twelfth Century Renaissance*, London: Thames and Hudson.

Brooke, M.Z. and Black, M. (1976) 'The Autonomy of the Foreign Subsidiary', *International Studies of Management and Organization* Spring-Summer, 11–26.

Brooke, M.Z. and Buckley, P.J. (1982) *Handbook of International Trade*, Brentford: Kluwer.

Brooke, M.Z. and Dorrell, M.G. (1976) 'The Communication of Control in an International Company: Methods of Investigation', *Omega*, 4.2.

Brooke, M.Z. and Remmers, H.L. (1970 and 1978) *The Strategy of Multinational Enterprise*, 1st edn.; Harlow: Longman (1970), 2nd edn.; London: Pitman (1978).

Brooke, M.Z. and Remmers, H.L. (1972) *The Multinational Enterprise in Europe*, Harlow: Longman.

Brooke, M.Z. and Remmers, H.L. (1977) *The International Firm*, London: Pitman.

Brooke, M.Z. and Van Beusekom, M. (1979) *International Corporate Planning*, London: Pitman.

Brooke, M.Z. et al. (1983) *International Management Contracts*, 2 vols., Unpub. report to the Leverhulme Trust, University of Manchester Institute of Science and Technology.

Brossard, M. and Maurice, M. (1976) 'Is there any Universal Model of Organization Structure?' *International Studies of Management Organization*, 6, 3, 11–45.

Brown, J.A.C. (1965) *The Social Psychology of Industry*, Harmondsworth: Penguin.

Brown, W. (1971) *Organization*, London: Heinemann.

Buchanan, D.A. et al. (1983) *Organizations in the Computer Age*, Farnborough: Gower.

Buchele, R.B. (1979) *The Management of Business and Public Organizations*, New York: McGraw-Hill.

Buckingham, G.L. et al. (1975), *Job Enrichment and Organizational Change*, Farnborough: Gower.

Buckley, P.J. and Casson, M. (1976) *The Future of the Multinational Enterprise*, London: Macmillan.

Burke, W. Warner (ed.), (1977) *Current Issues and Strategies in Organization Development*, New York: Human Sciences Press.

Burns, T. (ed.), (1969) *Industrial Man*, Harmondsworth: Penguin.

Burns, T.R. (1980) *Work and Power: The liberation of work and control of political power*, London: Sage.

Burns, T. and Stalker, G.M. (1961) *The Management of Innovation*, London: Tavistock.

Burton, R.M. and Obel, B. (1977) 'The multilevel approach to organizational issues of the firm . . . a critical review.' *Omega*, **5**, 393–414.

Butler, R.J. et al. (1977) 'Organizational Power, Politicking and Paralysis', *Organization and Administrative Science*, **8.4**, 45–60.

Butler, R.J. et al. (1979) 'Strategic Decision-making in Organizations: Concepts of Content and Process', *International Studies of Management and Organization*, ix, **4**, 5–36.

Byrne, T. (1981) *Local Government in Britain—Everyone's Guide to How it All Works*, Harmondsworth: Penguin.

Cameron, K.S. and Whetten, D.A. (1983) *Organizational Effectiveness*, London: Academic Press.

Carlisle, H.M. (1974) 'A contingency approach to decentralization' *Advanced Management Journal*, July.

Carsberg, B. (1975) *The Economics of Business Decisions*, Harmondsworth: Penguin.

Carsberg, B. and Hope, T. (1977) *Current Issues in Accounting*, Oxford: Philip Allan.

Cartwright, D. and Zander, A. (eds.), (1953) *Group Dynamics, Research and Theory*, Evanston, Ill.: Row, Peterson.

Castles, F.G. et al. (1976) *Decisions, Organizations and Society*, 2nd edn., Harmondsworth: Penguin.

Catlin, G.E.G. (1962) *Systematic Politics*, Toronto: University of Toronto Press.

Chandler, A.D. (1962) *Strategy and Structure*, Cambridge, Mass.: MIT Press.

Channon, D.F. (1973) *The Strategy and Structure of British Enterprise*, Boston, Mass.: Harvard Business School.

Charnes, A. et al. (1967) 'Effective control through coherent decentralization with preemptive goals.' *Econometrica*, **35**, 292–320.

Cheney, P.H. (1977) *Organizational Characteristics and Information Systems*, Unpub. Ph.D. thesis, University of Minnesota.

Cheng, Joseph Lap-Chiu (1977) *Organizational Coordination, Integration Interdependence and their Relevance to Research Unit Effectiveness: A Comparative Study*, Unpub. Ph.D. Thesis, University of Michigan.

Child, J. (1972a) 'Organizational Structure and Strategies of Control—a Replication of the Aston Study' *Administrative Science Quarterly*, 17.2.

Child, J. (1972b) 'Organizational Structure, Environment and Performance—the role of strategic choice', *Sociology*, 6.1.

Child, J. (ed.), (1973a) *Man and Organization*, London: Allen and Unwin.

Child, J. (1973b) 'Strategies of Control and Organizational Behaviour' *Administrative Science Quarterly*, Sept., 1–17.

Child, J. (1973c) 'Predicting and Understanding Organization Structures', *Administrative Science Quarterly*, 18.2.

Child, J. (1973d) 'Organization Structure—a reply to Tyler', *Sociology*, 7.

Child, J. (1974–5) 'Managerial and Organizational Factors Associated with Company Performance', *Journal of Management Studies*, Oct. and Feb.

Child, J. (1977) *Organization: A Guide to Problems and Practices*, London: Harper & Row.

Child, J. and Mansfield, R. (1972) 'Technology, Size and Organization Structure', *Sociology*, 6.

Chorafas, D.N. (1969) *The Communication Barrier in International Management*,

New York: American Management Association.

Chown, J.F. (1974) *Taxation and multinational Enterprise*, Harlow: Longman.

Christensen, J. and Obel, B. (1978) 'Simulation of decentralized planning in two Danish organizations using linear programming decomposition,' *Management Science*, **24**, 1658–1667.

Clarke, P.A. (1972a) *Organizational Design: Theory and Practice*, London: Tavistock.

Clarke, P.A. (1972b) *Action Research and Organizational Change*, London: Harper and Row.

Conroy, R.M. (1980) *Centralization and Formalization of Commercial Banks Located in the Commonwealth of Virginia*. Unpub. Ph.D. thesis Virginia Polytechnic Institute and State University.

Clegg, S. (1975) *Power, Rule and Domination*, London: Routledge and Kegan Paul.

Clegg, S. and Dunkerley, D. (1980) *Organization, Class and Control*, London: Routledge and Kegan Paul.

Cohen, S.I. (1980) 'Incentives, iterative communication, and organizational control.' *Journal of Economic Theory*, **22**, 37–55.

Collins, R. (1977) *Conflict Sociology; Towards an explanatory science*, London: Academic Press

Cooper, C.L., (ed.) (1979) *Behavioural Problems in Organizations*, Hemel Hempstead: Prentice-Hall.

Cortes, F. et al. (1974) *Systems Analysis for Social Scientists*, New York: Wiley.

Cotta, A. (1973) 'La structure du pouvoir dans les organisations' *Revue economique*, 24, Mars.

Cotta, A. (1974) 'La Stratégie du chef dans un système centralisé' *Revue d'économie politique*, 3.

Cray, D. (1980) 'Control in Multinational Corporations', Paper presented at the American Sociological Review meetings 1980.

Crouch, C. and Heller, F.A. (eds.), (1983) *International Yearbook of Organizational Democracy*, vol. I, Chichester: Wiley.

Crozier, M. (1964) *The Bureaucratic Phenomenon*, London: Tavistock.

Crozier, M. (1973) *The Stalled Society*, New York: The Viking Press.

Crozier, M. and Thoenig, J.C. (1976) 'The Regulation of Complex Organized Systems' *Administrative Science Quarterly* **4**, 547–570.

Cummings, L.L. and Schwab, D.P. (1973) *Performance in Organizations*, Glenview, Ill.: Scott Foresman.

Curwen, P.J. (1976) *The Theory of the Firm*, London: Macmillan.

Cyert, Richard M. (1975) *The Management of Nonprofit Organisations*, Farnborough: D.C. Heath.

Cyert, R.M. and March, J.G. (1963) *A Behavioural Theory of the Firm*, Englewood Cliffs, N.J.: 'Prentice Hall.

Dahrendorf, R. (1959) *Class and Class Conflict in Industrial Society*, London: Routledge and Kegan Paul.

Dahrendorf, R. (1964) 'Recent changes in the class structure of European Societies', *Daedalus* **93**, 244–252 (reprinted in Burns (1969), c. 8).

Dalton, G.W. and Lawrence, P.R., (eds.), (1970) *Organizational Change and Development*, Homewood: Ill.: Irwin-Dorsey.

Daniels, J.D. (1972) 'The non-American manager, especially as a third country national in U.S. multinationals: a separate but equal doctrine?' *Journal of International Business Studies*, fall, 25–40.

Dantzig, G.B. and Wolfe, P. (1961) 'The decomposition algorithm for linear programs' *Econometrica*, **29**, 767–778.

Danziger, K. (1971) *Socialization*, Harmondsworth: Penguin.

D'Aprix, R.M. (1976) *In Search of a Corporate Soul*, New York: Amacom.

Davis, L.E. and Cherns, A.R. (1975) *The Quality of Working Life*, 2 vols., New York: Collier-Macmillan.

Davis, M. (1972) *The Future for Decentralization*, London: PA Management Consultants.

Davis, S.M., (ed.) (1971) *Comparative Management: Organizational and Cultural Perspectives*, Englewood Cliffs: Prentice-Hall.

Dew, R.P. and Gee, K. (1973) *Management Control and Information*, London: Macmillan.

Dewar, R. and Hage, J. (1978) 'Size, Technology, Complexity and Structural Differentiation: Toward a Theoretical

Synthesis' *Adminstrative Science Quarterly,* 111–136

Dickinson, G. et al. (1983) *International Financial Management Handbook,* Brentford: Kluwer.

Dill, W. (1958) 'Environment as an Influence on Managerial Autonomy' *Administrative Science Quarterly,* **2,** 409–443.

Dirickx, Y.M.I. and Jennergren, L.P. (1979) *Systems Analysis by Multilevel Methods: With Applications to Economics and Management,* Chichester: Wiley.

Dittman, D.A. (1972) 'Transfer pricing and decentralization' *Management Accounting* 55, 5, Nov., 47 ff.

Donaldson, L. (1973a) 'Forecasting the Future Trend of Bureaucratisation', London Business School paper, presented to the Third World Future Research Conference, Bucharest, Sept.

Donaldson, L. (1973b) 'Woodward, Technology, Organisation Structure and Performance' London Business School working paper.

Donaldson, L. et al. (1975) 'The Aston Findings on Centralization—Further discussion', *Administrative Science Quarterly,* **20,** 453–9.

Dornbusch, S.M. and Scott, R.W. (1975) *Evaluation and the Exercise of Authority*: A theory of control applied to diverse organization, San Francisco: Jossey-Bass.

Dorrell, M.G. (1979) *The communication of control in a multinational company,* Unpublished Ph.D. thesis at University of Manchester Institute of Science and Technology.

Doteuchi, Kiyotsugu (1977) 'An approach to the concept of accounting practices in multinational enterprises,' unpub. research paper, International Business Unit, University of Manchester Institute of Science and Technology.

Douglas, M. (1966) *Purity and Danger,* New York: Praeger.

Drake, B.H. (1976) *An Experimental Study of the effects of vertical and horizontal power on behavioral commitment, satisfaction and involvement in decision-making.* Unpub. Ph.D. thesis University Washington.

Drucker, P.F. (1946) *The Concept of the Corporation,* New York: John Day.

Dubin, R., (ed.), (1976) *Handbook of Work, Organization and Society,* Chicago: Rand McNally.

Dulz, T.H. (1976) *Characteristics of perceived environmental uncertainty, task interdependence and their relationship to subunit power in complex organizations,* Unpub. Ph.D. thesis Michigan State University.

Duncan, R. (1971) *The Effects of Perceived Environmental Uncertainty on Organizational Decision Unit Structure.* Unpub. Dissertation, Yale University.

Duncan, R. (1972) 'Characteristics of Organisational Environments and Perceived Environmental Uncertainty', *Administrative Science Quarterly,* 17.3.

Duncan, R.B. (1973) Multiple Decision-Making Structures in Adapting to Environmental Uncertainty: The Impact on Organizational Effectiveness', *Human Relations,* 26.

Duncan, W.J. (1981) *Organizational Behaviour,* 2nd edn., Boston, Mass.: Houghton Mifflin.

Dunham, R. and Smith, F.J. (1978) *Organizational Surveys*: Internal Assessment of Organizational Health, Glenview, Ill.: Scott Foresman

Dunkerley, D. and Salaman, G. (1980a) *The International Yearbook of Organization Studies 1979,* London: Routledge and Kegan Paul.

Dunkerley, D. and Salaman G. (1980b) *The International Yearbook of Organisation Studies 1980,* London: Routledge and Kegan Paul.

Dunkerley, D. and Salaman G. (1982) *The International Yearbook of Organizational Studies 1981,* London: Routledge and Kegan Paul.

Dunnette, M.D. (ed.), (1976) *Handbook of Industrial and Organizational Psychology,* Chicago: Rand McNally.

Dunning, J.H. (1966) 'U.S. subsidiaries in Britain and their U.K. Competitors—a case study in Business Ratios' *Business Ratios* No. 1.

Dunning, J.H. (1971) *The Multinational Enterprise,* London: Allen and Unwin.

Dunning, J.H. (1972) *International Investment,* Harmondsworth: Penguin.

Dunsire, A. (1978) *The Execution Process*, 2 vols., Oxford: Martin Robertson.

Durkheim, E. (1965) *The Rules of Sociological Method*, 8th edn., trans. S.A. Soloway and J.H. Mueller and ed. G.E.G. Catlin, Free Press (the first edition of this translation was published in 1938 by the University of Chicago Press).

Dymsza, W. (1972) *Multinational Business Strategy*, New York: McGraw-Hill.

Ehrmann, J., (ed.) (1970) *Structuralism*, New York: Anchor Books.

Eiteman, D.K. and Stonehill, A.I. (1979) *Multinational Business Finance*, 2nd edn., Reading, Mass.: Addison-Wesley.

Ekern, S. (1979) 'The new Soviet incentive model: comment', *The Bell Journal of Economics*, **10**, 720–725.

Elbing, A.O., (ed.), (1978) *Behavioral Decisions in Organizations*, 2nd edn., Glenview, Ill.: Scott Foreman.

Elkins, A. and Callaghan, D.W. (1978) *A Managerial Odyssey: Problems in Business and Its Environment*, 2nd edn., Reading, Mass.: Addison-Wesley.

Ellman, M. (1973) *Planning Problems in the USSR*, Cambridge: Cambridge University Press.

Emerson, R.M. (1962) 'Power-Dependence Relations', *American Sociological Review*, **1**, 31–41.

Emery, F.E., (ed.), (1969) *Systems Thinking*, Harmondsworth: Penguin.

Emery, F.E. and Trist, E.L. (1973) *Towards a Social Ecology: Contextual Appreciation of the Future in the Present*, London: Plenum Press.

Ennuste, I.A. (1972) 'Problems of decomposition analysis of optimal planning tasks' (in Russian), *Ekonomika i matematicheskie metody*, **8**, 535–545.

Etzioni, A. (1961) *Complex Organizations: A Sociological Reader*, New York: Holt, Rinehart and Winston.

Etzioni, A. (ed.), (1969) *Readings on Modern Organizations*, Englewood Cliffs, N.J.: Prentice Hall.

Etzioni A. (1975) *A comparative analysis of Complex Organizations*, 2nd edn., Glencoe, Ill.: Free Press.

Etzioni, A. and Lehman, W. (1980) *A Sociological Reader on Complex Organizations*, New York: Holt, Rinehart and Winston.

Etzioni-Halévy, E. (1980) *Political Manipulation and Administrative Power*, London: Routledge and Kegan Paul.

Evan, W.M. (1976) *Interorganizational Relations*, Harmondsworth: Penguin.

Ezzamel, M.A. and Hilton, K. (1980) 'Divisionalisation in British Industry: A preliminary study', *Accounting and Business Research*, Spring, 197–211.

Falk, R. (1978), *The Business of Management*, revised edn. Harmondsworth: Penguin.

Farmer, R.N. and Richman, B.M. (1974) *International Business*, 2nd edn., Bloomington, In.: Cedarwood Press.

Farris, G.F. and Butterfield, D.A. (1972) 'Control Theory in Brazilian Organizations', *Administrative Science Quarterly* **17**, 574–585.

Fayerweather, J. (1960) *Management of International Operations: Texts and Cases*, New York: McGraw-Hill.

Fayol, H. (1949) *General and Industrial Management*, London: Pitman.

Ferguson, S. and Ferguson, S.D. (1981) *Intercom: Readings in Organizational Communication*, New York: Wiley.

Filley, A.C. et al. (1976) *Managerial Process and Organizational Behaviour*, 2nd edn., Glenview, Ill.: Scott Foresman.

Ford, J.D. and Slocum, J.W. (1977) 'Size, Technology, Environment and the Structure of Organizations', *The Academy of Management Review*, **4**, 561–575.

Fouracker, L.E. and Stopford, J.M. (1968) 'Organizational Structure and the Multinational Company', *Administrative Science Quarterly*, **13**, 47–64.

Frankenberg, R. (1965) *Communities in Britain*, Harmondsworth: Penguin.

Franko, L.G. (1971) *European Business Strategies in the United States*, New York: Business International.

Franko, L.G. (1976) *The European Multinationals*, London: Harper and Row.

Freddi, G. (1968) *L'analisi comparata di sistemi burocratici publici*, Milano: Giuffrè.

Freeland, J.R. and Moore, J.H. (1977) 'Implications of resource directive allocation models for organizational design', *Management Science*, **23**, 1050–1059.

Friedmann, W.G. and Kalmanoff, G. (eds.), (1961) *Joint International Busi-*

ness Ventures, New York: Columbia University Press.

Galbraith, J. (1973), *Designing Complex Organizations*, Reading, Mass.: Addison-Wesley.

Galbraith, J. (1977) *Organization Design*, Reading, Mass.: Addison-Wesley.

Galtung, J. (1967) *The Theory and Methods of Social Research*, London: Allen and Unwin.

Gellerman, S.W. (1974) *Behavioural Science in Management*, Harmondsworth: Penguin.

Georgopolous, B.S. and Tannenbaum, A. (1957) 'The Study of Organizational Effectiveness', *American Sociological Review* 22, 534–540.

Gerth, H.H. and Mills, C. Wright (1948) *From Max Weber: Essays in Sociology*, London: Routledge and Kegan Paul.

Ghertman, M. and Leontiades, J. (eds.), (1978) *European Research in International Business*, Amsterdam: North-Holland.

Gilbert, M. (ed.), (1972) *The Modern Business Enterprise*, Harmondsworth: Penguin.

Gluckman, M. (ed.), (1972) *The Allocation of Responsibility*, Manchester: Manchester University Press.

Goffman, E. (1961) *Asylums*, New York: Doubleday.

Goldman, K. and Sjöstedt, G. (1980) *Power, Capabilities, Interdependence*, Beverly Hills, Cal.: Sage.

Goodman, E. (1969) *The Impact of Size*, London: Acton Society Trust.

Goodman, P.S. et al. (1979) *Assessing Organizational Change*, New York: Wiley.

Gouldner, A. (1954) *Patterns of Industrial Bureaucracy*, Glencoe, Ill.: Free Press.

Greenwood, R.G. (1974) *Managerial Decentralization*, Lexington: Lexington Books.

Greenwood, W.T. (1965) *Management and Organization Behavior Theories*, Cincinnatti, Ohio: South-Western.

Greiner, L.E. (1972) 'Evolutions and Revolutions as Organizations Grow', *Harvard Business Review*, July-Aug.

Gross, B.M. (1968) *Organizations and Their Managing*, Glencoe, Ill.: Free Press.

Gross, L. (ed.), (1967) *Sociological Theory: Inquiries and Paradigms*, London: Harper and Row.

Groves, T. and Loeb, M. (1979) 'Incentives in a divisionalized firm', *Management Science*, **25**, 221–230.

Guggenbühl-Craig, A. (1971) *Power and the Helping Professions*, Feltham: Spring Publications.

Guillet de Monthoux, P. (1983) *Action and Existence: Anarchism for Business Administration*, Chichester: Wiley.

Haas, H. van der (1967) *The Enterprise in Transition*, London: Tavistock.

Hage, J. (1980) *Theories of Organizations: Form, Process and Transformation*, New York: Wiley.

Hage, J. and Aiken, M. (1969) 'Routine Technology, Social Structure and Organization Goals', *Administrative Science Quarterly*, 14–3, Sept., 366–376.

Haimann, T. and others (1978) *Managing the Modern Organization*, 3rd edn., Boston, Mass.: Houghton Mifflin.

Haire, M. et al. (1966) *Managerial Thinking: An International Study*, New York: Wiley.

Hajimirzatayeb, M. (1979) *Cultural Determinants of Organizational Behaviour and Responses to Environmental Demands. An Empirical Test in Iranian Culture and Organizations.* Unpub. Thesis, Oxford.

Håkansson, H. (ed.), (1982) *International Marketing and Purchasing of Industrial Goods*, Chichester: Wiley.

Hall, P. (1981) *Great Planning Disasters*, Harmondsworth: Penguin.

Hall, R.H. (1972) *Organizations: Structure and Process*, Englewood Cliffs, N.J.: Prentice-Hall.

Hall, R.H. (1978) 'Conceptual, Methodological and Moral Issues in the Study of Organizational Effectiveness', Working paper, Dept. of Sociology, SUNY-Albany.

Hampton, D.R. and others (1978) *Organizational Behavior and the Practice of Management*, Glenview, Ill.: Scott Foresman.

Handy, C. (1976) *Understanding Organizations*, Harmondsworth: Penguin.

Hanf, K. and Scharpf, F.W. (1978) *Interorganizational Policy-Making*, Beverly Hills, Calif.: Sage.

Harris, M. et al. (1982) 'Asymmetric information incentives and intrafirm resource allocation', *Management Science*, 28.6, June.

Harrison, E.F. (1975) *The Managerial Decision-Making Process*, Boston, Mass.: Houghton-Mifflin.

Harrison, E.F. (1978) *Management and Organizations*, Boston, Mass.: Houghton-Mifflin.

Harsanyi, J.C. (1977) *Rational Behaviour and Bargaining Equilibrium in Games and Social Situations*, Cambridge: Cambridge University Press.

Harvey, E. (1968) 'Technology and Structure of Organizations', *American Sociological Review*, 33, 247–259.

Heal, G.M. (1973) *Theory of Economic Planning*, Amsterdam: North-Holland.

Heenan, D.A. and Perlmutter, H.V. (1979) *Multinational Organization Development: A Social Architectural Perspective*, Reading, Mass.: Addison-Wesley.

Heflebower, B. (1960) 'Observations on decentralization in large enterprises', *Industrial Economics*, 9, Nov., 7–22.

Heller, F. (1972) *The Decision-Process—an analysis of power-sharing at senior organizational levels*. London: Tavistock.

Heller, F.A. et al. (1976) 'Methodology for a Multinational Behaviour: The Use of Contingency Theory', Paper presented at the Third Congress of Cross-Cultural Psychology, Tilburg, Netherlands, July.

Hellriegel, D. and Slocum, J.W. (1978) *Management: Contingency Approaches*, 2nd edn., Reading, Mass.: Addison-Wesley.

Hellriegel, D. and Slocum, J. (1979) *Organizational Behaviour*, 2nd edn., St Paul, Mi.: West Publishing.

Hertzberg, F. et al. (1959) *The Motivation to Work*, New York: Wiley.

Hickson, D.J. et al. (1969a) 'A Strategic Contingencies' Theory of Power', Unpub. paper, University of Alberta, Edmonton.

Hickson, D.J. et al. (1969b) 'Operations Technology and Organization Structure: An Empirical Reappraisal', *Administrative Science Quarterly* 3, 378–397.

Hickson, D.J. et al. (1979) *Grounds for Comparative Organization Theory: Quicksand or Hardcore?*, London: Routledge and Kegan Paul.

Hickson, D.J. et al. (1984) *Top Decisions*, San Francisco: Jossey-Bass.

Hill, D.M. (1974) *Democratic Theory and Local Government*, London: Allen and Unwin.

Hinings, C.R. et al. (1967) 'An approach to the study of bureaucracy', *Sociology*, 1, 61–72.

Hinings, C.R. et al. (1974) 'Structural Conditions of intraorganizational power', *Administrative Science Quarterly*, 19 (March), 22–44.

Ho, S.P.S. (1979) 'Decentralized Industrialized and Rural Development: Evidence from Taiwan', *Economic Development and Cultural Change*, Oct. 28.1, 79 ff.

Hodgetts, R.M. and Altman, S. (1979) *Organizational Behavior*, New York: Holt, Rinehart and Winston.

Hodgetts, R.M. and Wortman, M.S. (1979) *Administration Policy: Text and Cases in the Policy Sciences*, 2nd edn., New York: Wiley.

Hofstede, G. (1976) 'Measuring Hierarchical Power Distance in Thirty-seven Countries', Working paper 76–32, Brussels: European Institute for Advanced Studies in Management, July.

Hofstede, G. (1977a) 'Cultural Determinants of the Exercise of Power in a Hierarchy', Working paper 77–8, Brussels: European Institute for Advanced Studies in Management, Feb.

Hofstede, G. (1977b) 'Cultural Determinants of the Avoidance of Uncertainty in Organizations', Working paper, 77–18, Brussels: European Institute for Advanced Studies in Management, June.

Hofstede, G. and Kassem, M.S. (1976) *European Contributions to Organization Theory*, Amsterdam: Van Gorcum.

Holdaway, E.A. et al. (1975) 'Dimensions of Organizations in Complex Societies', *Administrative Science Quarterly* 20, 37–54.

Horovitz, J.H. (1976) *A cross national study of management control practices: France, Germany, Great Britain*, Unpub. Ph.D. thesis Columbia University.

Huard, P. (1974) *L'objectif et le systéme de guidage de l'entreprise*, Unpub. doctoral thesis Aix-en-provence: Université d'Aix-Marseille II.

Hulbert, J.M. and Brandt, W.K. (1980) *Managing the Multinational Subsidiary*,

New York: Holt, Rinehart and Winston.

Hurwicz, L. (1973) 'The design of mechanisms for resources allocation' *American Economic Review*, **63** (proceedings issue), 1–30.

Hymer, S.H. (1979) *The Multinational Corporation: A Radical Approach*, ed. Cohen, R.B. et al. Cambridge: Cambridge University Press.

Inbar, M. (1979) *Routine Decision-Making: The Future of Bureaucracy*, Beverly Hills, Calif.: Sage.

Jabes, J. (1978) *Individual Processes and organizational behavior*, Arlington Heights, Ill.: AHM Publishing.

Jackson, G.T. (1976) *British Retailers' Expansion into Europe*, Unpub. Ph.D. thesis, University of Manchester.

Jacoby, H. (1973) *The Bureaucratization of the World*, Berkely: University of California Press.

Jacquemin, A. (1972) 'Stratégies d'entreprises, structure de marchés et contrôle optimal', *Revenue d'Economie Politique*, **6**.

Jaques, E. (1964) *Time-span Handbook*, London: Heinemann.

Jaques, E. (1972) 'Grading and Management Organization in the Civil Service', *O & M Bulletin*, Aug.

Jaques, E. (1976) *A General Theory of Bureaucracy*, London: Heinemann.

Jay, A. (1967) *Management and Machiavelli*, Harmondsworth: Penguin.

Jay, A. (1975) *Corporation Man*, Harmondsworth: Penguin.

Jennergren, L.P. (1973) 'A price schedules decomposition algorithm for linear programming problems,' *Econometrica*, **41,** 965–980.

Jennergren, P.L. (1974) *Decentralization in Organizations*, Berlin: Reprint series of the International Institute of Management.

Jennergren, L.P. (1980) 'On the design of incentives in business firms—a survey of some research.' *Management Science*, **26,** 180–201.

Jennergren, L.P. (1981) 'Decentralization in organisations' in Nystrom and Starbuck (1981) vol. 2, c.2.

Johns, E.A. (1973) *The Sociology of Organizational Change*, Oxford: Pergamon.

Jun, J.S. and Storm, W.B. (eds.), (1973) *Tomorrow's Organizations*, Glenview, Ill.: Scott Foresman.

Juster, E.T. and Land, K.C., (eds.) (1981) *Social Accounting Systems*, New York: Academic Press.

Kaplan, N. (1960) 'Theoretical Analysis of the Balance of Power', *Behavioural Science*, 5.

Kapoor, A. and Grub, P.D. (eds), (1972) *The Multinational Enterprise in Transition*, Princeton, N.J.: Darwin.

Karmel, B. (1979) *Point and Counterpoint in Organizational Behavior*, New York: Holt, Rinehart and Winston.

Karpik, L. (ed.), (1977) *Organization and Environment: Theory, Issues and Reality*, Berkely, Cal.: Sage.

Kast, F.E. and Rosenzweig, J.E. (1978) *Organization and Management: A Systems and Contingency Approach*, 3rd edn., New York: McGraw-Hill.

Katz, D. and Kahn, R.L. (1966) *The Social Psychology of Organization*, New York: Wiley.

Katz, F.E. (1968) *Autonomy and Organization: The limits of Social Control*. New York: Random House.

Kaufman, G. and Thomas, H. (eds.), (1977) *Modern Decision Analysis*, Harmondsworth: Penguin.

Kay, N.M. (1979) *The Innovating Firm*, London: Macmillan.

Kempner, T. et al. (1976) *Business and Society*, Harmondsworth: Penguin.

Kempner, T. (1976) *A Handbook of Management*, Harmondsworth: Penguin.

Khandwalla, P.N. (1971) 'The effect of competition and firm size on recentralization of top management decisions', Unpub. working paper, Faculty of Management, McGill University.

Khandwalla, N. (1972) 'Uncertainty and the "Optimal" Design of Organizations', Working paper, Faculty of Management, McGill University.

Khandwalla, P.N. (1973) 'Viable and Effective Organizational Design of Firms', *Academy of Management Journal*, Sept.

Kiesler, S.B. (1978) *Interpersonal Processes in Groups and Organizations*, Arlington Heights, Ill.: AHM Publishing.

Kimberley, J.R. et al. (1980) *The Organizational Life Cycle: Issues in the Creation, Transformation and Decline of Organizations*, San Francisco: Jossey-Bass.

Kindleberger, C.P. (1970) *The International Corporation*, Cambridge, Mass.: MIT Press.

Kingdon, D.R. (1973) *Matrix Organization*, London: Tavistock.

Kircher, P. and Mason, R.O. (1975) *Introduction to Enterprise: A systems approach*. New York: Wiley.

Kircht, J.P. and Dillehay, R.C. (1967) *Dimensions of Authoritarianism*, Lexington: University of Kentucky Press.

Knight, K. (1976) 'Matrix Organization—A Review', *Journal of Management Studies*, May.

Kolb, D.A. et al. (1979) *Organisational Psychology: A book of readings*, Englewood Cliffs, N.J.: Prentice-Hall.

Koontz, H. and O'Donnell, C. *Principles of Management: An Analysis of Managerial Functions*, 4th edn., New York: McGraw-Hill.

Kotter, J.P. (1978) *Organizational Dynamics: Diagnosis and Intervention*, Reading, Mass.: Addison-Wesley.

Krantz, H. (1976) *The Participatory Bureaucracy*, Lexington: Lexington Books.

Kraus, W.A. (1980) *Competition and Collaboration in Organizations*, New York: Human Sciences Press.

Kuhn, A. and Beam, R.D. (1982) *The Logic of Organization*, San Francisco: Jossey-Bass.

Kydland, F. (1975) 'Hierarchical decomposition in linear economic models', *Management Science*, 21, 1029–1039.

Labedz, L. (ed.), (1962) *Revisionism*, London: Allen and Unwin (see c. 14 'The debate on alienation' by D. Bell).

Lammers, C.J. and Hickson, D.J. (1980) *Organizations Alike and Unlike*, London: Routledge and Kegan Paul.

Lanco, P. (1971) *Valeur de certaines formes de communication dans une équipe*, Paris: Université de Paris IX.

Lawler, E.E. (1971) *Pay and Organizational Effectiveness: A Psychological View*, New York: McGraw-Hill. The excerpts quoted in the text are from Dunnette (1976).

Lawler, E.E. et al. (1974) 'Organizational Climate: Relationship to Organizational Structure, Process, and Performance', *Organizational Behaviour and Human Performance*, 11, 139–145.

Lawrence, R. and Lorsch, J.W. (1967) *Organization and Environment*, Boston, Mass.: Harvard Business School.

Lawrence, P.R. and Lorsch, J.W. (1969) *Developing Organizations: Diagnosis and Action*, Reading, Mass.: Addison-Wesley.

Lawrence, P.R. et al. (eds.), (1976) *Organizational Behavior and Administration*, 3rd edn., Homewood, Ill.: Irwin and Dorsey.

Leavitt, H.J. et al. (1973) *The Organizational World*, New York: Harcourt, Brace, Jovanovich.

Leavitt, H.J. et al. (eds) (1974) *Organizations of the Future—Interaction with the External Environment*, New York: Praeger.

Lenin, V.I. (1939) *Selected Works*, vol. 11, London: Lawrence and Wishart.

Leontiades, M. (1979/80) 'Strategic Theory and Management Practice', *Journal of General Management*, 5.2, 23 ff.

Leontief, W. (1977) *Structure, System and Economic Policy*, Cambridge: Cambridge University Press.

Lerner, L.W. (1979) *The Politics of Decision-Making: Cooperation and Conflict*, Beverly Hills, Cal.: Sage.

Levinson, H. (1972) *Organisational Diagnosis*, Boston, Mass.: Harvard Business School.

Levi-Strauss, C. (1963) *Structural Anthropology*, trans. Jacobson, C. and Schoepf, B.G., New York: Basic Books.

Likert, R. (1961) *New Patterns of Management*, New York: McGraw-Hill.

Likert, R. (1967) *The Human Organization*, New York: McGraw-Hill.

Litterer, J.A. (1973) *The Analysis of Organizations*, 2nd edn., New York: Wiley.

Litterer, J.A. (1969) *Organizations*: vol. I—Structure and Behaviour, Vol. II—Systems, Control and Adaptation, New York: Wiley.

Litvak, I.A. and Maule, C.J. (1970) 'The Multinational Corporation: some perspectives', *Canadian Public Administration*, 13.2, Summer.

Ljung, B. and Selmer, J. (1975) *Coordinated Planning in Decentralized Business Firms* (in Swedish), Stockholm: Bonniers.

Ljung, B. and Selmer, J. (1979) 'An experimental test of the Dantzig and Wolfe decomposition algorithm as a planning tool in a business firm', *Scandinavian Journal of Economics* **81,** 415–426.

Loeb, M. and Magat, W. (1978) 'Soviet success indicators and the evaluation of divisional management', *Journal of Accounting Research,* **16,** 103–121.

Lorsch, J.W. and Allen, S.A. (1973) *Managing Diversity and Interdependence,* Boston, Mass.: Harvard Business School.

Lorsch, J.W. and Lawrence, R.R. (eds.), (1970) *Studies in Organizational Design,* Homewood, Ill.: Irwin-Dorsey.

Lorsch, J.W. and Morse, J.J. (1974) *Organizations and their Members: A Contingency Approach,* New York: Harper and Row.

Lowe, T. and Machin, J.L.J. (1983) *New Perspectives in Management Control,* London: Macmillan.

Luce, R.D. and Raiffa, H. (1957) *Games and Decisions,* New York: Wiley.

Lupton, T. (1971) *Management and the Social Sciences,* 2nd edn., Harmondsworth: Penguin.

Lustac, S. (1973) *Essai de formalisation du fonctionnement interne d'une organisation politique par la théorie des messages,* Paris: Université de Paris IX.

McConkey, D.D. (1980) 'Across the hierarchy: a look at the future', *Business Quarterly,* 45.2.

McGregor, D. (1967) *The Professional Manager,* new edn., New York: McGraw-Hill.

Mack, R.P. (1971) *Planning on Uncertainty: Decision-making in business and government administration.* New York: Wiley.

Mackenzie, K.D. (1978) *Organizational Structures,* Arlington Heights, Ill.: AHM Publishing.

Mackenzie, W.J.M. (1978) *Biological Ideas in Politics,* Harmondsworth: Penguin.

Macintosh, N.B. (1981) *Management Control and Organizational Technology,* New York: National Association of Accountants and Hamilton, Ont.: Society of Management Accountants of Canada.

McNaughton, W.L. et al. (1970) *Introduction to Business Enterprise,* 2nd edn., New York: Wiley.

Macrae, D.G. (1979) *Weber,* London: Fontana and Harvester.

Magid, A. (1976) *Men in the Middle: Leadership and Role Conflict in a Nigerian Society.* Manchester: Manchester University Press.

Magnusen, K.O. (ed.), (1977) *Organizational Design, Development and Behavior,* Glenview, Ill: Scott Foresman.

Maher, J.R. (ed.), (1971) *New Perspectives in Job Enrichment,* New York: Van Nostrand Reinhold.

Mandel, A.B. (1973) 'Internal prices in the control of industrial firms' (in Russian) *Ekonomika i matematicheskie metody,* **9,** 500–513.

Mangham, I. (1979) *The Politics of Organization Change,* London: Associated Business Press.

Manners, R.A. and Kaplan, D., (eds.), (1968), *Theory in Anthropology,* London: Routledge and Kegan Paul.

Mansfield, R. (1973) 'Bureaucracy and Centralisation', *Administrative Science Quarterly,* **18,** 477–488.

Mansfield, R. et al. (1978) 'Company structure and market strategy', *Omega,* **6.2.,** 133–8.

March, J.G. (1955) 'An Introduction to the Theory and Measurement of Influence', *American Political Science Review,* 49.

March, J.G. (1965) *Handbook of organizations,* Chicago: Rand McNally.

March, J.G. and Simon, H.A. (1958) *Organizations,* Chichester: Wiley.

Margulies, N. and Wallace, J. (1973) *Organizational Change: Techniques and Applications,* Glenview, Ill.: Scott Foresman.

Marris, R. (1964) *The Economic Theory of Managerial Capitalism,* London: Macmillan.

Marris, R. and Wood, A. (eds.), (1971) *The Corporate Economy,* London: Macmillan.

Marschak, J. (1959) 'Centralization and Decentralization in Economic Organizations', *Econometrica,* **27,** 399–430.

Marschak, J. and Radner, R. (1972) *Economic Theory of Teams,* New Haven, Con.: Yale University Press.

Martines-Soler, R. (1974) 'Mechanisms for guiding processes of working out the plan in systems of optimal planning' (in Russian) In *Matematicheskie metody v ekonomicheskikh issledovaniiakh*, 154–171, Moscow: Nauka.

Maslow, A.H. (1954) *Motivation and personality*, New York: Harper and Row.

Mathew, A.M. (1979) *Recent Direct Investment in Australia by First Time UK Investors*, Unpub. Ph.D. Thesis, University of Bradford.

Mattson, L.G. and Wiedersheim-Paul, F. (eds.), (1979) *Recent Research on the Internationalization of Business*. Proceedings from the Annual Meeting of the European International Business Association, Uppsala Sweden, December 14–17, 1977. Uppsala: Almquvist and Wicksell.

Mead, M. (ed.), (1955) *Cultural Patterns and Technical Change* A manual prepared by the World Federation of Mental Health, and published by the United Nations Educational, Scientific and Cultural Organization.

Merton, R.K. (1957) *Social Theory and Social Structure*, Glencoe, Ill.: Free Press.

Merton, R.K. et al. (eds.), (1959) *Sociology Today*, 2 vols., New York: Harper and Row.

Metcalfe, H.C. and Urwick, L. (1941) *Dynamic Administration*, London: Management Publication Trust.

Meyer, M.W. (1972) *Bureaucratic Structure and Authority*, New York: Harper and Row.

Meyer, M.W. (1978) *Environments and Organizations: Theoretical and Empirical Perspectives*, San Francisco: Jossey-Bass.

Michelman, H.J. (1978) *Organisational Effectiveness in a Multinational Bureaucracy*. London: Saxon House.

Michels, R. (1949) *Political Parties*, Glencoe, Ill.: Free Press.

Miles, R.E. et al. (1974) 'Organization–Environment: Concepts and Issues' *Industrial Relations*, **13**, 244–264.

Miller, E. (1976) *Task and Organization*, Chichester: Wiley.

Millor, W.J. and Butler, H.E. (eds.), and Brooke, C.N.L., revised (1955) *The Letters of John of Salisbury*, Walton-on-Thames: Nelson.

Mintzberg, H. (1978a) 'Patterns in Strategy Formation', *Management Science*, 24.9.

Mintzberg, H. (1978b) *The Structuring of Organizations: a Synthesis of Research*, Englewood Cliffs, N.J.: Prentice-Hall.

Mintzberg, H. et al. (1976) 'The structure of unstructured decision processes', *Administrative Science Quarterly*, 21.2.

Mohan, R.P. (1979) *Management and Complex Organizations in Comparative Perspective*, Westport, CT: Greenwood.

Mohr, L.B. (1971) 'Organizational Technology and Organizational Structure', *Administrative Science Quarterly* **16**, 444–459.

Moore, P.G. et al. (1976) *Case Studies in Decision Analysis*, Harmondsworth: Penguin.

Morrell, J. (1962) *Management Decisions and the Role of Forecasting*, Harmondsworth: Penguin.

Morris, W.T. (1964) *Decentralisation in management systems: an introduction to design*. Columbus, Ohio: Ohio State University Press.

Mouzelis, N. (1967) *Organizations and Bureaucracy*, London: Routledge and Kegan Paul.

Nadler, D.A. (1977) *Feedback and Organization Developing: Using Data-based Methods*, London: Addison-Wesley.

Negandhi, A.R. (1973) *Modern Organizational Theory: Contextual, Environmental, and Socio-Cultural Variables*. Kent, Ohio: Kent State University Press.

Negandhi, A. (ed.), (1980) *Interorganization Theory*, Kent, Ohio: Kent State University Press.

Negandhi, A.R. and Prasad, S.B. (1971) *Comparative Management*, New York: Meredith.

Neghandhi, A.R. and Prasad, S.B. (1975) *The Frightening Angels*, Kent, Ohio: Kent State University Press (a 2nd edn of Neghandi and Prasad, 1971).

Negandhi, A.R. and Reimann, B.C. (1973) 'Task Environment, Decentralization and Organizational Effectiveness', *Human Relations*, 26.

Newcomb, T. and Hartley, E., (eds.), (1947) *Readings in Social Psychology*, New York: Holt, Rinehart and Winston.

Newman, W.H. and Logan, J.P. (1966) *Business Policies and Central Management*. London: Edward Arnold.

Nickell, S.J. (1978) *The Investment Decisions of Firms*, Cambridge: Cambridge University Press.

Nie, N.H. et al. (1975) *SPSS: A Statistical Package for the Social Sciences*, New York: McGraw-Hill.

Nowotny, O.H. (1964) 'American vs European Management Philosophy', *Harvard Business Review*, 42.2, March/April.

Nystrom, P.C. and Starbuck, W.H. (1981) *Handbook of Organizational Design*, Oxford: Oxford University Press.

Nystrom, P.C. and Starbuck, W.H. (eds), (1977) *Prescriptive Models of Organization*, Amsterdam: North Holland.

Obel, B. (1981) *Issues of Organizational Design*, Oxford: Pergamon.

Oleck, H.L. (1974) *Non-Profit Corporations, Organizations and Associations*, Englewood Cliffs, N.J.: Prentice-Hall.

Olsen, M.E. (1968) *The Process of Social Organization*, New York: Holt, Rinehart and Winston.

O'Shaughnessy, J. (1976) *Patterns of Business Organization*, London: Allen and Unwin.

Otterbeck, L-G. (ed.), (1981) *The Management of Headquarters-Subsidiary Relationships in Multinational Corporations*. Aldershot: Gower.

Ouchi, W.G. (1979) 'A conceptual framework for the design of Organizational Control Mechanisms', *Management Science*, 25. 9, Sept.

Ozawa, T. (1979) *Multinationalism, Japanese Style: The political economy of outward dependency*, Princeton, N.J.: Princeton University.

Palumbo, D.J. (1969) 'Power and Role Specificity in Organization Theory', *Public Administration Review*, 29.3; 237–248.

Parsons, T. (1951) *The Social System*, Glencoe, Ill.: Free Press.

Paul, W.J. and Robertson, K.B. (1970) *Job Enrichment and Employee Motivation*, Aldershot: Gower.

Paulson, St. K., et al. (1980) 'A Model for the Measurement of Co-op. Relationships among Health Related Organizations', *Management International Review*, 20.2, 96.

Pennings, J.M. (1975) 'The Relevance of the Structural-Contingency Model for Organizational Effectiveness', *Administrative Science Quarterly*, Sept.

Penrose, E.T. (1959) *The Theory of the Growth of the Firm*, Oxford: Blackwell.

Perlmutter, H.V. (1969) 'The tortuous evolution of the multinational corporation', *Columbia Journal of World Business*, 4.1, Jan.-Feb., 9–18, reprinted in Kapoor and Grub (1972).

Perlmutter, H.V. and Heenan, D.A. (1974) 'How multinational should your managers be?' *Harvard Business Review*, 52.6, Nov.-Dec., 121–132.

Perrow, C. (1967) 'A framework for the comparative analysis of organizations', *American Sociological Review*, **32,** 194–208.

Perrow, C. (1972a) *The Radical Attack on Business*, London: Harcourt, Brace, Jovanovich.

Perrow, C. (1972b) *Complex Organizations*, 2nd edn., Glencoe, Ill.: Scott Foresman.

Pettigrew, A.M. (1975) 'Strategic Aspects of the Management of Specialist Activity', *Personnel Review*, 4.

Pfeffer, J. (1978) *Organizational Design*, Arlington Heights, Ill.: AHM Publishing.

Pfeffer, J. and Leblebici, H. (1973) 'The Effect of Competition on Some Dimensions of Organizational Structure', *Social Forces*, **52,** 268–279.

Pfeffer, J. and Salancik, G.R. (1978) *The External Control of Organizations*, New York: Harper and Row.

Piaget, J. (1971) *Structuralism*, trans. Maschler, C., London: Routledge and Kegan Paul.

Polèse, M. (1980) 'Concentration et déconcentration des administrations publiques: une analyse de la structure spatiale de l'administration fédérale Canadienne', *Annals of Public and Co-op. Economy*, Jan.-June, 123.

Porter, L.W. and Lawler, E.E. (1965) 'Properties of organization structure in Relation to Job Attitudes and Job Behaviour', *Psychological Bulletin*, July.

Porter, L.W. and Roberts, K. (1977) *Communication in Organizations*, Harmondsworth: Penguin.

Prahalad, C.K. (1975) 'Strategic control in

diversified multinational corporations', Conference paper, Academy of International Business Annual meeting, Dallas.

Price, J.L. (1972) *Handbook of Organizational Measurement*, Lexington, Mass.: D.C. Heath.

Przeworski, A. and Teune, H. (1970) *The Logic of Comparative Social Enquiry*, New York: Wiley.

Pugh, D.S. (1969) 'Organisational Behaviour—an approach from psychology', *Human Relations*, 22.

Pugh, D.S. (ed.), (1971) *Organization Theory*, Harmondsworth: Penguin.

Pugh, D.S. and Hickson, D.J. (1972) 'To the Editor – Causal Inference and the Aston Studies', *Administrative Science Quarterly*, 17.2.

Pugh, D.S. and Hickson, D.J. (1976) *Organizational Structure in its Context*, The Aston Programme I, London: Saxon House.

Pugh, D.S. and Hinings, C.R. (1976) *Organizational Structure: Extensions and Replications*, The Aston Programme II, London: Saxon House.

Pugh, D.S. et al. (1963) 'A Conceptual Scheme for Organizational Analysis', *Administrative Science Quarterly*, 8.3.

Pugh, D.S. et al. (1968) 'Dimensions of Organisational Structures', *Administrative Science Quarterly*, **13**, 65–105.

Pugh, D.S. et al. (1969) 'The Context of Organisational Structure', *Administrative Science Quarterly*, **14**, 91–114.

Pugh, D.S. et al. (1971) *Writers on Organizations*, Harmondsworth: Penguin

Pugh, D.S. and Payne, R.L. (eds.), (1977) *Organization Behaviour in its Context*, The Aston Programme III, London: Saxon House.

Pugh, D.S. and Pheysey, D. (1968) 'Some developments in the study of organizations', *Management International Review*, **8**, 97–107.

Redding, S. (1980) 'Cognition as an aspect of culture and its relation to management processes: an explanatory view of the Chinese case', *Journal of Management Studies*, May, **17**, 127.

Reeser, C. and Loper, M. (1978) *The Key to Organizational Effectiveness*, Glenview, Ill.: Scott Foresman.

Reiman, B.C. (1977) 'Dimensions of Organizational Technology and Structure: An Exploratory Study', *Human Relations* **6**, 545–566.

Reitz, H.J. (1977) *Behavior in Organizations*, Homewood, Ill.: Irwin-Dorsey.

Revans, R.W. (1962) 'Myths of decentralisation', *New Society*, 6 Dec., 17–19.

Revans, R.W. (1971) *Developing Effective Managers*, Harlow: Longman.

Rex, J. (1961) *Key Problems of Sociological Theory*, London: Routledge and Kegan Paul.

Rhenman, E. (1972) *Organization Theory for Long-Range Planning*, Chichester: Wiley.

Rhenman, E. et al. (1970) *Conflict and Cooperation in Business Organizations*, Chichester: Wiley.

Rigby, P.H. (1965) *Conceptual Foundations of Business Research*, Chichester: Wiley.

Robbins, S.M. and Stobaugh, R.B. (1973) *Money in the Multinational*, New York: Basic Books.

Roberts, B.C. and May, J. (1974) 'The response to multinational enterprises to international trade union pressures', *British Journal of Industrial Relations*, Nov., 403–416.

Roberts, K.H. et al. (1978) *Developing an Interdisciplinary Science of Organizations*, San Francisco: Jossey-Bass.

Robinson, R.D. (1973) *International Business Management*, Hinsdale, Ill.: Dryden Press.

Robock, S.H. and Simmonds, K. (1973) *International Business and Multinational Enterprise*, Homewood, Ill.: Irwin and Dorsey.

Rodriguez, R.M. and Carter, E.E. (1976) *International Financial Management*, Englewood Cliffs, N.J.: Prentice-Hall.

Roeber, R.J.C. (1973) *The Organization in a Changing Environment*, Reading, Mass.: Addison-Wesley.

Roig, B. (1970) *La Empresa Multinacional*, Barcelona: Ediciones Universidad de Navarra.

Rose, M. (1978) *Industrial Behaviour: Theoretical Development Since Taylor*, Harmondsworth: Penguin.

Ruefli, T.W. (1974) 'Analytic models of resources allocation in hierarchical multi-level systems'. *Socio-Economic Planning Sciences*, **8**, 353–363.

Rumelt, R.P. (1974) *Strategy, Structure and Economic Performance*, Boston, Mass.: Harvard Business School.

Rushing, W.A. and Zald, M.N. (1976) *Organizations and Beyond*, Lexington: Lexington Books (essays by the late James D. Thompson).

Rutenberg, D.P. (1969) 'Planning for a multinational synergy', *Long Range Planning*, 2.2., Dec.

Rutenberg, D.P. (1982) *Multinational Management*, Boston, Mass.: Little Brown.

Sachden, J.C. (1975) 'Disinvestment—corporate strategy or admission of failure?', *Multinational Business*, **4**, 12–19.

Sachden, J.C. (1976a) 'Disinvestment: a new problem in multinational corporation—host government interface', *Management International Review*, **16.3**, 23–36.

Sachden, J.C. (1976b) *A Framework for the Planning of Disinvestment Policies for Multinational Corporations*. Unpub. Ph.D. thesis, University of Manchester.

Sadler, Philip et al. (1974) *Management Style and Organization Structure in the Smaller Enterprise*, Boston, Mass.: Harvard Business School.

Saldich, A.R. (1979) *Electronic Democracy: Television's impact on the American political process*, New York: Praeger.

Salera, V. (1969) *Multinational Business*, Boston, Mass.: Houghton-Mifflin.

Sartre, J.P. (1960) *Critique de la Raison dialectique*, Paris: Gallimard.

Sasaki, N. (1981) *Management and Industrial Structure in Japan*, Oxford: Pergamon.

Schacht, R. (1971) *Alienation*, London: Allen and Unwin.

Schelling, T.C. (1969) *The Strategy of Conflict*, Cambridge, Mass.: Harvard University Press.

Schumaker, E.F. (1963) *Small is Beautiful*, Tunbridge Wells: Abacus.

Schumpeter, J. (1943) *Capitalism, Socialism and Democracy*, London: Allen and Unwin.

Scott, B.R. (1971) *Strategies of Corporate Development*, Boston, Mass.: Harvard Business School.

Scott, W.G. and Mitchell, T.R. (1976) *Organization Theory*, Homewood, Ill.: Irwin-Dorsey.

Scott, W.R. (1970) *Social Processes and Social Structures*, New York: Holt, Rinehart and Winston.

Servan-Schreiber, J-J. (1969) *The American Challenge*, Harmondsworth: Penguin (first edition in English 1968, original edition: *Le défi américain*, Paris: Denoël (1967)).

Sethi, S.P. and Sheth, J.N. (eds.), (1973) *Multinational Business Operations: Long Range Planning, Organization and Management*, Pacific Palisades, Calif.: Goodyear Publishing.

Sfez, L. (1974) *La décision publique*, Paris: Armand Colin.

Shapley, L.S. and Shubik, M. (1954) 'A Method for Evaluating the Distribution of Power in a Committee System', *American Political Science Review*, 48, Sept.

Sharpe, L.J. (ed.), (1980) *Decentralist Tendencies in Western Democracies*, Beverly Hills, Cal.: Sage.

Shearer, J.C. (1960) 'American Overseas Managers—Necessities or Luxuries?', *Management in the Industrial World, an International Analysis*, Princeton, N.J.: Princeton University Press.

Sherrard, W.R. and Steade, R.O. (1966) 'Power comparability—its contribution to a theory of firm behaviour', *Management Science*, 13.

Shillinglaw, G. (1972) *Cost Accounting*, 3rd edn., Homewood, Ill.: Irwin and Dorsey.

Shirley, R.C. et al. (1976) *Strategy and Policy Formulation*, New York: Wiley.

Shonfield, A. and Shonfield, A. (eds.), *The Use of Public Power*, Oxford: Oxford University Press.

Shortell, S.M. (1977) 'The Role of Environment in a Configurational Theory of Organizations', *Human Relations*, **3**, 275–302.

Silverman, D. (1970) *The Theory of Organizations*, London: Heinemann.

Sim, A.B. (1977) 'The Performance of Decentrally Managed International Subsidiaries', *Management International Review*, **17.2** 45–51.

Simmel, G. (1980) *Essays on Interpretation in Social Science*, Manchester: Manchester University Press.

Simmons, R.E. (1978) *Managing Behavioral Processes: Applications of Theory and*

Research, Arlington Heights: AHM Publishing.

Simon, H.A. et al. (1954) *Centralization versus Decentralization in Organizing the Controller's Department*, New York: Controllership Foundation.

Simon, H.A. (1955) 'A behavioural model of rational choice', *Quarterly Journal of Economics*, **69**, 99–118.

Simon, H.A. (1960) *The New Science of Management Decision*, New York: Harper and Row.

Simon, H.A. (1965) *The Shape of Automation for Men and Management*, New York: Harper and Row.

Siu, R.G.H. (1979) *The Craft of Power*, New York: Wiley.

Skinner, C.W. (1968) *American Industry in Developing Economies*, New York: Wiley.

Skinner, R. (1976) 'Technological determinism: a critique of convergence theory', *Comparative Studies in Society and History*, **18**.

Slipsager, F. (1973) *Studier i decentraliseringsproblemet i international afsoetning*. Copenhagen: Nyt Nordisk Forlag, Arnold Busck (in Danish).

Sloan, A. (1964) *My Years with General Motors*, New York: Doubleday.

Smith, et al. (1972) *Renewing the Management Structure*, London: British Institute of Management.

Smith, G. (1979) *Social Work and the Sociology of Knowledge*, London: Routledge and Kegan Paul.

Snowberger, V. (1977) 'The new Soviet incentive model: comment', *The Bell Journal of Economics*, **8**, 591–600.

Sofer, C. (1974) 'Post Bureaucratic Organizations and Managers', *Omega*, **2**.

Sorokin, P.A. (1966) *Sociological Theories of Today*, New York: Harper and Row.

Spulber, N. (1979) *Organizational Alternatives in Soviet-type Economies*, Cambridge: Cambridge University Press.

Stammer, O. (1971) *Max Weber and Sociology Today*, Oxford: Blackwell.

Stanfield, G.G. (1976) 'Technology and Organization Structure as Theoretical Categories', *Administrative Science Quarterly*, **3**, 489–493.

Starbuck, W.H. (ed.), (1971) *Organization Growth and Development*, Harmondsworth: Penguin.

Stark, W. (1958) *The Sociology of Knowledge*, London: Routledge and Kegan Paul.

Stark, W. (1962) *The Fundamental Forms of Social Thought*, London: Routledge and Kegan Paul.

Staw, B.M. and Cummings, L.L. (eds.), (1979–80) *Research in Organizational Behaviour*, Vol. I (1979), Vol. II (1980) Greenwich, CT: JAI Press.

Staw, B.M. (ed.), (1982) *Research in Organizational Behavior*, Greenwich CT: JAI Press.

Staw, B.M. and Salancik, G.R. (eds) (1977) *New Directions in Organizational Behavior*, Chicago: St. Clair Press.

Stieglitz, H. (1962) 'Optimizing Span of Control', *Management Record*, **24**.

Stopford, J.M. and Wells, L.T. (1972) *Managing the Multinational Enterprise*, New York: Basic Books.

Storey, J. (1981) *The Challenge to Management Control*, London: Business Books (originally published London: Kogan Page (1980)).

Sweeney, D.J. et al. (1978) 'Composition vs. decomposition: two approaches to modelling organizational decision process', *Management Science*, **24**, 1491–1499.

Tabatoni, P. (1973) *La dynamique des normes dans l'action stratégique*, Nashville, Tenn.: Vanderbilt University.

Tajfel, H. and Fraser, C. (1978) *Introducing Social Psychology*, Harmondsworth: Penguin.

Tannenbaum, A.S. (1966) *Social Psychology of the Work Organization*, London: Tavistock.

Tannenbaum, A.S. (1968) *Control of Organizations*, New York: McGraw-Hill.

Tannenbaum, A.S. et al. (1974) *Hierarchy in Organizations*, San Francisco: Jossey-Bass.

Ten Kate, A. (1972) 'Decomposition of linear programs by direct distribution', *Econometrica*, **40**, 883–898.

Thierauf, R.J. et al. (1977) *Management Principles and Practices: A Contingency and Questionnaire Approach*, New York: Wiley.

Thomas, H. and Moore, P.G. (1976) *Anatomy of Decisions*, Harmondsworth: Penguin.

Thompson, J.D. (1967) *Organizations in*

Action, New York: McGraw-Hill.

Thorelli, H.B. (ed.), (1973) *International Marketing Strategy*, Harmondsworth: Penguin.

Thornhill, W. (1975) *The Modernisation of British Government*, London: Pitman.

Tillett, A. et al. (1978) *Management Thinkers* (reissue), Harmondsworth: Penguin.

Toffler, A. (1981) *The Third Wave*, London: Bantam (this is the edition quoted here, the book was first published in 1980 by Morrow in New York).

Tomwszewski, L.A. (1972) 'Decentralised development', *Datamation*, 18.11, Nov., 61 ff.

Toronto, R.S. (1975) 'A General Systems Model for the Analysis of Organizational Change', *Behavioural Science*, **20**.

Tuggle, F.D. (1978) *Organizational Process*, Arlington Heights, Ill.: AHM Press.

Tuite, M. et al. (eds.), (1972) *Interorganizational Decision-Making*, Chicago: Aldine.

Turk, H. (1977) *Organizations in Modern Life: Cities and other large networks*, San Francisco: Jossey-Bass.

Van Cauwenbergh, A. and Van Robaeys, N. (1980) 'The Functioning of Management at the Corporate Level', *Journal of General Management* **5.3**, 19 ff.

Van Der Hass, H. (1967) *The Enterprise in Transition*, London: Tavistock.

Van De Ven, A. et al. (1976) 'Determinants of Coordination Modes with Organizations', *American Sociological Review*, April.

Veiga, J. and Yanouzas, J. (1979) *The Dynamics of Organizational Theory: Gaining a Macro Perspective*, St Paul, Mn: West Publishing.

Vernon, R. (1971) *Sovereignty at Bay*, New York: Basic Books.

Vernon, R. and Wells, L.T. (1976) *Manager in the International Economy*, 3rd edn., Englewood Cliffs, NJ: Prentice-Hall.

Vickers, G. (1965) *The Art of Judgment: A Study of Policy-making*, London: Chapman and Hall.

Villiers, R. (1954) 'Control and freedom in a decentralised company', *Harvard Business Review*, 32.2, March–April.

Vroom, V. and Deci, E.L. (1970) *Management and Motivation*, Harmondsworth: Penguin.

Walker, A.H. and Lorsch, J.W. (1968) 'Organizational choice: product vs. function', *Harvard Business Review*, **46.6**, 129–138.

Walker, C.R. and Guest, R. (1965) *The Man on the Assembly Line*, Cambridge, Mass.: Harvard University Press.

Wallerstein, I. (1974) *The Modern World System: Capitalist Agriculture and the Origins of the European World Economy*, London: Academic Press.

Walter, I. (ed.), (1982) *Handbook of International Business*, New York: Wiley.

Warner, M. (ed.), (1977) *Organizational Choice and Constraint*, London: Saxon House.

Weber, M. (1974) *The Theory of Social and Economic Organization*, Trans. and ed. by Henderson, A.M. and Parsons, T., Glencoe, Ill.: Free Press.

Weber, M. (1978) *Economy and Society*, Berkely, Cal.: University of California Press, 3 vols.

Weick, K.E. (1969) *The Social Psychology of Organizing*, Reading, Mass.: Addison-Wesley.

Weinshall, T.D. (ed.), (1977) *Culture and Management*, Harmondsworth: Penguin.

Weinshall, T.D. (ed.), (1979) *Managerial Communication: Concepts, Approaches and Techniques*, London: Academic Press.

Weitzman, M. (1976) 'The new Soviet incentive model', *The Bell Journal of Economics*, **7**, 251–257.

Weldon, J.D. (1946) *States and Morals*, London: Murray.

Whisler, T.L. (1970) *Information Technology and Organizational Change*, Monterey, Calif.: Wadsworth.

Whisler, T.L. et al. (1967) 'Centralization and Organizational Control—an empirical study of its meaning and measurement', *Journal of Business*, **40**, 10–26.

Whitfield, P.R. (1975) *Corporation Man*, Harmondsworth: Penguin.

Whyte, W.H. (1952) *Is Anybody Listening?* New York: Simon and Schuster.

Whyte, W.H. (1956) *The Organization Man*, New York: Simon and Schuster.

Wieland, G.F. and Ullrich, R.A. (1976)

Organizations, Homewood, Ill.: Irwin and Dorsey.

Wiener, N. (1950) *The Human Use of Human Beings*, London: Doubleday.

Wiener, N. (1961) *Cybernetics*, New York: Wiley.

Wilbert, B. and Negandhi, A. (eds.), (1978) *Work Organization*, Kent, Ohio: Kent State University Press.

Williams, J.C. (1978) *Human Behavior in Organizations*, Cincinnati, Ohio: South-Western.

Williamson, O.E. (1975) *Markets and Hierarchies: Analysis and Antitrust Implications*, Glencoe, Ill.: Free Press.

Wilson, D.C. (1982) 'Electricity and resistance: a case study of innovation and politics', *Organization Studies*, **3.2.** 119–140.

Woodward, J. (1958) *Management and Technology*, London: Her Majesty's Stationery Office.

Woodward, J. (1965) *Industrial Organization: Theory and Practice*, Oxford: Oxford Univeristy Press.

Woodward, J. (ed.), (1970) *Industrial Organization: Behaviour and Control*, Oxford: Oxford University Press.

Wrigley, L. (1970) *Divisional Autonomy and Diversification*, Unpub. D.B.A. Thesis, Harvard Business School.

Yahoda, M. and Warren, N. (1966) *Attitudes*, Harmondsworth: Penguin.

Zald, I.M. (ed.), (1970) *Power in Organizations*, Nashville: Vanderbilt University Press.

Zauberman, A. (1975) *The Mathematical Revolution in Soviet Economics*, Oxford: Oxford University Press.

Indexes

There are two indexes—names and subjects. The name index includes authors mentioned in the text or in the notes but not in the bibliography. The subject index is selective to the extent that the reader's attention is not usually directed to a page which only contains a passing reference to a particular topic.

Both indexes follow a letter-by-letter arrangement. In the subject index there is some cross-referencing (by the use of *see also*) between groups of words which have special significance in the text. Autonomy, centralization and decentralization are obvious examples. Less obvious is a grouping like expertise, information, knowledge, and truth—four words with different meanings but each of which has a similar relationship to centralization.

Index of Names

Index of Subjects